THE ESSENTIAL
Southern Living®
COOKBOOK

CRISPY SWEET POTATO-GREEN
ONION CAKES, PAGE 253

THE ESSENTIAL
Southern Living®
COOKBOOK

OVER 450 OF OUR ALL-TIME FAVORITE RECIPES

PECAN-ESPRESSO
TOFFEE, PAGE 300

GRILLED STEAK WITH BLISTERED
BEANS AND PEPPERS, PAGE 82

CONTENTS

INTRODUCTION 6

APPETIZERS, SNACKS & DRINKS 8

BREAKFAST 38

MAIN DISHES 70

CLASSIC CASSEROLES 160

SANDWICHES, SALADS & SOUPS 186

SIDES 226

COOKIES, BARS & CANDY 286

DESSERTS 302

INDEX 354
METRIC EQUIVALENTS 367

UNIQUELY SOUTHERN

Simply put, there are some recipes every cook should have in their repertoire. For Southerners, it's essentials such as grits, fried chicken, biscuits and banana pudding. The foods we turn to again and again whatever the occasion.

The Essential Southern Living Cookbook is a collection of more than 450 of our favorite recipes. Our tried-and-true basics along with many new twists on old Southern favorites. They have been tested to perfection so they'll turn out just right every time. When time's short, stir up Snappy Cajun Shrimp (page 139—just 10 minutes start to finish— or toss together Dixie Chicken Salad with Grapes, Honey, Almonds and Broccoli (page 201). If a celebratory feast is in order, indulge in Prime Rib with Herbes de Provence Crust and Red Wine Sauce (page 73), paired with Caramelized Onion Mashed Potato Bake (page 232) and Green Bean Casserole with Fried Leeks (page 262).

Southern food is all about comfort, and when you find yourself in need of soothing, turn to Shepherd's Pie topped with Cheese-and-Carrot Mashed Potatoes (page 162) or Chicken-and-Biscuit Cobbler (page 172). And of course, if there's anything we love around here more than dessert, we can't think of it. Satisfy the famed Southern sweet tooth with classic Mississippi Mud (page 295) or celebrate a special occasion with Butter Toffee-Pecan Layer Cake (page 312).

From the legendary to the iconic to some unexpected delights, the recipes in *The Essential Southern Living Cookbook* will be ones you turn to again and again.

BLACKBERRY JAM CAKE,
PAGE 308

MUFFULETTA
DEVILED EGGS,
PAGE 14

APPETIZERS, SNACKS & DRINKS

BEST-EVER CRAB CAKES WITH GREEN TOMATO SLAW

ACTIVE 30 MIN. - TOTAL 45 MIN.
SERVES 6

CRAB CAKES

- 12 oz. fresh jumbo lump crabmeat, drained and picked over
- 12 oz. fresh lump crabmeat, drained and picked over
- 4½ Tbsp. salted butter, melted and cooled
- 4½ Tbsp. chopped scallions (from 4 scallions)
- 1½ Tbsp. finely chopped fresh flat-leaf parsley
- 1½ Tbsp. finely chopped fresh dill
- 1½ tsp. lemon zest plus 1½ Tbsp. fresh juice (from 1 lemon)
- 1½ tsp. kosher salt
- 1½ tsp. hot sauce (such as Tabasco)
- 3 large eggs, lightly beaten
- 1 large garlic clove, minced (about 2 tsp.)
- 2¼ cups panko (Japanese-style breadcrumbs), divided
- 4 Tbsp. canola oil

GREEN TOMATO SLAW

- 2 medium-size green tomatoes, thinly sliced and cut into matchsticks (about 2 cups)
- 1 celery stalk, thinly sliced (about ½ cup)
- 1 small sweet onion, thinly sliced (about 1 cup)
- 1 small red bell pepper, thinly sliced (about 1 cup)
- 2 Tbsp. chopped fresh flat-leaf parsley
- 2 Tbsp. olive oil
- 2 Tbsp. white wine vinegar
- 1 Tbsp. granulated sugar
- 1½ tsp. kosher salt
- ½ tsp. black pepper

1. Prepare the Crab Cakes: Place first 11 ingredients and 1¾ cups of the panko in a large bowl and gently combine.

2. Shape crabmeat mixture into 6 (3-inch) cakes. Sprinkle remaining ½ cup panko on a large plate; gently transfer cakes to plate, pressing both sides in panko. Cover and chill until slightly firm, about 15 minutes.

3. Preheat oven to 375°F. Heat 2 tablespoons canola oil in a large nonstick skillet over medium-high. Gently reshape 3 crab cakes, and place in hot oil. Cook until golden brown, 4 to 5 minutes on each side. Transfer to a wire rack set in a baking sheet. Repeat with remaining oil and cakes. Bake in preheated oven until heated through, about 10 minutes.

4. Prepare the Green Tomato Slaw: Toss together all slaw ingredients in a medium bowl. Serve over crab cakes.

BUTTERNUT-GOAT CHEESE-STUFFED MUSHROOMS

ACTIVE 45 MIN. - TOTAL 1 HOUR
SERVES 12

- 12 oz. butternut squash, cut into ¼-inch cubes (about 3 cups)
- 1 Tbsp. olive oil
- 1½ tsp. finely chopped fresh sage leaves
- 3 Tbsp. butter, divided
- ¼ cup dry white wine (such as Chardonnay)
- 3 (8-oz.) pkg. fresh mushrooms
- 1 (4-oz.) goat cheese log, cut in chunks
- ½ tsp. kosher salt
- ¼ tsp. freshly ground black pepper
- ¼ cup panko (Japanese-style breadcrumbs)
  Chopped fresh chives, for garnish

1. Preheat oven to 375°F. Cook squash in hot oil in a large skillet over high, stirring occasionally, 8 to 10 minutes or until browned. Add sage and 1 tablespoon butter, and cook, stirring constantly, 2 minutes. Add wine, and cook, stirring constantly, 3 minutes or until wine has evaporated. Transfer squash to a medium bowl, and cool about 10 minutes.

2. Meanwhile, rinse mushrooms, and pat dry. Remove and discard stems.

3. Stir goat cheese, salt, and black pepper into squash mixture just until combined.

4. Microwave remaining 2 tablespoons butter in a medium microwave-safe bowl at HIGH 30 seconds. Stir breadcrumbs into melted butter just until combined. Spoon desired amount of goat cheese mixture into each mushroom cap. Holding each filled mushroom over breadcrumb mixture, press about 1 tablespoon crumb mixture onto filling. Set a wire rack in a jelly-roll pan. Lightly coat rack with cooking spray. Place mushrooms on rack in a single layer. Bake in preheated oven for 15 to 20 minutes or until breadcrumbs are toasted and golden brown.

BEST-EVER CRAB CAKES
WITH GREEN TOMATO SLAW

GRILLED SALT-AND-PEPPER
CHICKEN WINGS

GRILLED SALT-AND-PEPPER CHICKEN WINGS

You can also broil wings instead of grilling. Broil on a rimmed foil-lined baking sheet 8 inches from heat for 20 minutes or until done, turning halfway through.

ACTIVE 10 MIN. - TOTAL 35 MIN., NOT INCLUDING DRIZZLE
SERVES 6 TO 8

- 2 lb. chicken wings
- 2 Tbsp. olive oil
- 1½ tsp. kosher salt
- ½ tsp. black pepper
  Desired Honey Drizzle (recipes follow)

Preheat grill to medium-high (350°F to 400°F). Toss together wings and oil in a large bowl. Sprinkle with salt and pepper; toss to coat. Grill, covered, 25 to 30 minutes or until skin is crisp and wings are done, turning occasionally. Toss with desired Honey Drizzle.

CIDER VINEGAR–BROWN BUTTER HONEY DRIZZLE

ACTIVE 10 MIN. - TOTAL 15 MIN.
MAKES ABOUT ¾ CUP

Cook ¼ cup **butter** in a saucepan over medium-high 5 minutes or until brown and fragrant. Transfer to a small bowl, and cool 5 minutes. Heat ½ cup **honey** and 1 Tbsp. **apple cider vinegar** in a saucepan over medium, stirring often, 2 minutes or until heated through. Whisk in brown butter.

HORSERADISH–HONEY MUSTARD DRIZZLE

ACTIVE 5 MIN. - TOTAL 5 MIN.
MAKES ABOUT ¾ CUP

Heat ½ cup **honey**, 3 Tbsp. **prepared horseradish**, and 2 Tbsp. **coarse-grain mustard** in a small saucepan over medium, stirring, 2 minutes or until heated through.

CRACKED PEPPER–ROSEMARY HONEY DRIZZLE

ACTIVE 5 MIN. - TOTAL 5 MIN.
MAKES ABOUT ½ CUP

Cook ½ cup **honey**, 2 Tbsp. **water**, 1 tsp. **cracked black pepper**, and 1 (3-inch) f**resh rosemary sprig** in a saucepan over medium, stirring often, 2 minutes or until heated through. Discard rosemary.

CHILI-LEMON HONEY DRIZZLE

ACTIVE 5 MIN. - TOTAL 5 MIN.
MAKES ABOUT 1 CUP

Heat ½ cup **honey**, ¼ cup bottled **chili sauce**, and 2 Tbsp. fresh **lemon juice** over medium, stirring often, 2 minutes or until heated through.

- -

CHICKEN WONTONS WITH HOISIN-PEANUT DIPPING SAUCE

ACTIVE 20 MIN. - TOTAL 20 MIN.
MAKES 3 DOZEN

- 1 cup diced cooked chicken
- 4 scallions, diced
- 1 cup finely shredded cabbage
- 2 Tbsp. diced fresh cilantro
- 2 tsp. brown sugar
- 1 Tbsp. hoisin sauce
- 1 tsp. sesame oil
- 36 wonton wrappers
  Peanut oil
  Peanut Dipping Sauce (recipe follows)

1. Stir together first 7 ingredients. Spoon 1 teaspoon mixture in center of each wonton wrapper. Moisten wonton edges with water. Bring corners together, pressing to seal.

2. Pour oil to a depth of 3 inches into a Dutch oven; heat to 375°F. Fry wontons in batches until golden, turning once. Drain on wire racks over paper towels. Serve with Peanut Dipping Sauce.

PEANUT DIPPING SAUCE

ACTIVE 5 MIN. - TOTAL 5 MIN.
MAKES ABOUT ¾ CUP

- ½ cup chicken broth
- 2 Tbsp. hoisin sauce
- 2 Tbsp. sesame oil
- 2 Tbsp. soy sauce
- 1 Tbsp. creamy peanut butter
- 1 tsp. cornstarch

Bring all ingredients to a boil in a small saucepan, whisking constantly; boil 1 minute.

MUFFULETTA DEVILED EGGS

(Photo, page 8)

ACTIVE 10 MIN. - TOTAL 25 MIN.
SERVES 24

- 12 large eggs
- ¼ cup mayonnaise
- 6 Tbsp. Olive Salad (recipe follows)
- 3 oz. salami, very thinly sliced

1. Place eggs in a single layer in a stainless-steel saucepan. (Do not use nonstick.) Add water to depth of 3 inches. Bring to a rolling boil. Cover, remove from heat, and let stand 15 minutes. Tap each egg on the counter until cracks form all over the shell. Peel under cold running water.

2. Slice eggs in half lengthwise; remove yolks and place in a bowl. Mash yolks with a fork. Stir in mayonnaise until smooth. Fold in Olive Salad. Spoon mixture into egg white halves.

3. Heat a small skillet over low 1 to 2 minutes or until hot. Add salami and cook, stirring often, 2 to 3 minutes or until lightly browned and crisp. Remove from skillet and drain on paper towels. Top eggs with salami. Serve immediately, or cover and chill up to 24 hours.

OLIVE SALAD

ACTIVE 5 MIN. - TOTAL 5 MIN.
MAKES 4 CUPS

- 1 (16-oz.) jar mixed pickled vegetables, undrained
- 1 (7-oz.) jar pimiento-Kalamata olives, drained
- 2 Tbsp. extra-virgin olive oil
- ½ tsp. drained capers
- ½ tsp. dried oregano
- ½ tsp. black pepper
- 1 garlic clove, minced
- ⅛ tsp. paprika
- ⅛ tsp. cayenne pepper

Pulse all ingredients in a food processor 5 times or until coarsely chopped. Use immediately or refrigerate up to 1 week.

QUESO-FILLED MINI PEPPERS

ACTIVE 25 MIN. - TOTAL 1 HOUR
SERVES 10

- 2 (16-oz.) pkg. mini sweet peppers
- 1 Tbsp. canola oil
- ¾ tsp. kosher salt
- 8 oz. pepper Jack cheese, shredded (about 2 cups)
- ½ cup evaporated milk
- 2 oz. cream cheese, softened
- ¼ cup chopped pickled jalapeños
- 2 Tbsp. unsalted butter
- ½ cup panko (Japanese-style breadcrumbs)
- ¼ tsp. black pepper
- 2 Tbsp. finely chopped fresh cilantro

1. Preheat broiler on HIGH with oven rack 5 inches from heat. Toss peppers with oil and ½ teaspoon of the salt; arrange in a single layer on a rimmed aluminum foil-lined baking sheet. Broil until tops are lightly charred, 3 to 5 minutes. Let cool to room temperature, 30 minutes. Reduce oven temperature to 425°F.

2. Flip over peppers so charred side is on bottom; cut and remove top third of each pepper (from stem end to tip). Discard cut-off part, or reserve for another use. Scoop out and discard membranes and seeds.

3. Whisk together pepper Jack cheese and milk in the top of a double boiler over simmering water over medium. Whisk until smooth, 5 minutes. Remove from heat; stir in cream cheese, jalapeños, and remaining ¼ teaspoon salt. Spoon a heaping teaspoon of cheese mixture into each pepper. Place on a baking sheet. Bake until tops are golden, 5 minutes.

4. Meanwhile, melt butter in a skillet over medium. Add panko and pepper; cook, stirring, until golden brown, 3 more minutes. Sprinkle peppers with panko mixture and cilantro.

Make Ahead: Place filled peppers in a baking dish; cover and chill 1 day. Bake, covered, at 425°F for 5 minutes; uncover and bake 3 more minutes. Top with panko mixture and cilantro.

QUESO-FILLED
MINI PEPPERS

SHEET PAN NACHOS WITH
CHORIZO AND REFRIED BEANS

SHEET PAN NACHOS WITH CHORIZO AND REFRIED BEANS

The remedy for fully loaded nachos that fall apart in your lap? Try a salsa-and-refried beans combo that helps toppings stick to the tortilla chips.

ACTIVE 20 MIN. - TOTAL 30 MIN.
SERVES 10

- 1 lb. fresh Mexican chorizo, casings removed
- ½ cup chopped yellow onion (from 1 small onion)
- 1 (15-oz.) can refried beans
- 1 (16-oz.) jar tomatillo salsa, divided
- 1 (12-oz.) pkg. tortilla chips
- 4 oz. Monterey Jack cheese, shredded (about 1 cup)
- 4 oz. sharp cheddar cheese, shredded (about 1 cup)
- 1 ripe avocado, chopped
- 1 jalapeño chile, thinly sliced
- ¾ cup sour cream
- ½ cup loosely packed fresh cilantro leaves
  Mexican hot sauce (such as Valentina, optional)

1. Preheat oven to 400°F. Cook chorizo and onion in a large nonstick skillet over medium, stirring often with a wooden spoon to crumble, until chorizo is well browned and onion is tender, about 8 minutes. Drain on a plate lined with paper towels.

2. Stir together refried beans and 1 cup of the tomatillo salsa in a small saucepan. Cook over medium-high, stirring often, until hot, about 3 minutes.

3. Line a large rimmed baking sheet with aluminum foil. Arrange chips in a single layer on foil. Top chips evenly with chorizo mixture, bean mixture, and cheeses.

4. Bake in preheated oven until cheeses melt and just begin to brown in places, about 8 minutes. Remove from oven and top with avocado, jalapeño, sour cream, cilantro, and remaining tomatillo salsa. Drizzle with hot sauce, if desired.

PEPPERONI PIZZA PINWHEELS

Serve these cheesy pinwheels as a salad accompaniment, or dip them into warm marinara sauce for a savory snack.

ACTIVE 10 MIN. - TOTAL 30 MIN.
MAKES 16 PINWHEELS

- 1 (11-oz.) can refrigerated French bread dough (such as Pillsbury)
- ¼ cup sun-dried tomato pesto (such as Classico)
- 18 slices turkey pepperoni
- 2 oz. part-skim mozzarella cheese, shredded (½ cup)

1. Preheat oven to 350°F. Unroll dough onto a work surface; lightly coat dough with cooking spray.

2. Spoon pesto onto dough, spreading to edges. Place pepperoni slices evenly over dough, and sprinkle with cheese. Starting at a long edge, roll up dough jelly-roll fashion; pinch seam to seal (do not seal ends of roll). Using a serrated knife, cut roll evenly into 16 slices. Place slices, cut sides down, on a baking sheet coated with cooking spray.

3. Bake in preheated oven until golden brown, about 20 minutes.

- -

SANTA FE CHICKEN QUESADILLAS

ACTIVE 10 MIN. - TOTAL 20 MIN.
MAKES 2 DOZEN

- 1¼ cups no-salt-added salsa, divided
- 1 cup chopped cooked chicken breast (skinned before cooking and cooked without salt)
- 2 Tbsp. chopped fresh cilantro
- 1 tsp. ground cumin
- 1 (4-oz.) can chopped green chiles, drained
- 6 (7-inch) flour tortillas
- 4 oz. reduced-fat sharp cheddar cheese, shredded (1 cup)

1. Combine ½ cup salsa, chicken, and the next 3 ingredients. Spoon mixture evenly onto half of each tortilla. Sprinkle with cheese.

2. Coat a nonstick skillet with cooking spray; heat over medium-high until hot. Add one tortilla; cook 1 minute. Fold unfilled tortilla half over filling; cook 30 seconds. Turn over; cook 30 seconds. Repeat with remaining tortillas. Cut each into 4 wedges. Top with remaining salsa.

COCKTAIL MEATBALLS

Cocktail meatballs hold a special place in the canon of Southern party appetizers. While we love the ones our mamas made with chili sauce and grape jelly, this recipe is the one we still pull out for company.

ACTIVE 40 MIN. · TOTAL 1 HOUR
MAKES 4 DOZEN

- 1½ lb. ground chuck
- ¼ cup seasoned breadcrumbs
- 2 tsp. prepared horseradish
- 2 garlic cloves, crushed
- ¾ cup tomato juice
- 2 tsp. kosher salt
- ¼ tsp. freshly ground black pepper
- 2 medium yellow onions, chopped (about 1½ cups), divided
- 2 Tbsp. butter
- 2 Tbsp. all-purpose flour
- 1½ cups beef broth
- ½ cup dry red wine
- 2 Tbsp. light brown sugar
- 2 Tbsp. ketchup
- 1 Tbsp. fresh lemon juice
- 3 gingersnaps, crumbled (about 3 Tbsp.)

1. Preheat oven to 450°F. Gently stir together ground chuck, next 6 ingredients, and ¾ cup chopped onions. Shape into 1-inch balls; place in a lightly greased (with cooking spray) 13- x 9-inch baking dish. Bake in preheated oven 20 minutes. Remove from oven, and drain off excess fat.

2. Heat butter in a large skillet over medium heat; add remaining onions, and cook, stirring occasionally, 4 to 6 minutes or until tender. Whisk in flour; cook, whisking constantly, 1 minute. Gradually whisk in beef broth; cook, whisking constantly, until smooth. Stir in wine and remaining 4 ingredients. Reduce heat to low; cook, stirring often, 15 minutes. Add meatballs; simmer, stirring occasionally, 5 minutes.

FIG FLATBREAD

ACTIVE 10 MIN. · TOTAL 30 MIN.
SERVES 4

- 1 Tbsp. olive oil
- 1 small red onion, sliced
- ½ tsp. kosher salt, divided
- ½ tsp. black pepper, divided
- 14 oz. store-bought fresh pizza dough
- 6 figs, thinly sliced crosswise, divided
- 8 oz. goat cheese, crumbled (about 2 cups)
- ¼ cup balsamic vinegar
- 1 cup loosely packed arugula

1. Preheat oven to 450°F. Heat oil in a saucepan over medium. Add red onion and ¼ teaspoon each of the salt and black pepper. Cook and stir until tender, about 2 minutes.

2. Roll pizza dough into a ¼-inch-thick, 17- x 11-inch rectangle. Place on a large baking sheet lined with parchment paper. Sprinkle with remaining ¼ teaspoon each salt and pepper. Top evenly with cooked onions, one-third of the fig slices, and cheese. Bake until crust is lightly browned and done, 15 to 20 minutes.

3. Meanwhile, heat balsamic vinegar in a small saucepan over medium-high until reduced by half, about 5 minutes. Top flatbread with remaining figs, arugula, and balsamic reduction.

FIG FLATBREAD

PARTY-PERFECT
MEATBALLS

PARTY-PERFECT MEATBALLS

To make ahead, prepare meatballs through Step 2, then freeze in zip-top plastic freezer bags up to 1 month. To reheat from frozen, pick up with Step 3 and warm the meatballs in the sauce over low. To serve, keep warm in a slow cooker, in a Dutch oven over low, or in a fondue pot.

ACTIVE 35 MIN. · TOTAL 50 MIN.

SERVES 20

- 1 cup pitted Kalamata olives
- ½ small red onion, coarsely chopped
- ¾ cup coarsely chopped fresh mint leaves
- ½ cup coarsely chopped fresh parsley
- 2 tsp. lemon zest
- ¾ cup panko (Japanese-style breadcrumbs)
- ½ cup ricotta cheese
- 2 large eggs
- 1½ tsp. kosher salt
- ½ tsp. freshly ground black pepper
- 1 lb. ground beef
- 1 lb. mild Italian sausage, casings removed
- 1 (6-oz.) can tomato paste
- 3 cups beef broth
- ⅓ cup hot pepper jelly

1. Preheat oven to 450°F. Pulse first 5 ingredients in a food processor 8 to 10 times or until chopped. Stir together panko, next 6 ingredients, and olive mixture in a large bowl until well combined. Shape mixture into 1-inch balls, and place 1 inch apart on jelly-roll pans lined with aluminum foil.

2. Bake in preheated oven 12 minutes. Cool 5 minutes.

3. Meanwhile, heat a large saucepan over medium 2 minutes. Add tomato paste to dry pan; cook, stirring occasionally, 3 minutes or until paste begins to brown and coat bottom of pan. Increase heat to high, and add beef broth, stirring to loosen bits of tomato paste from bottom of pan. Whisk until smooth. Whisk in hot pepper jelly until combined. Reduce heat to low. Add cooked meatballs. Serve warm.

Note: Sauce may be refrigerated in an airtight container up to 3 days.

BARBECUE DEVILED EGGS

Chopped barbecued pork is the filling's surprising ingredient in this old-fashioned Southern favorite. If you want to omit the chopped pork, add a drop of liquid smoke to provide barbecue-like flavor.

ACTIVE 15 MIN. · TOTAL 30 MIN.

SERVES 12

- 12 large eggs
- ¼ cup mayonnaise
- 1 Tbsp. Dijon mustard
- ¼ tsp. table salt
- ½ tsp. pepper
- ⅛ tsp. hot sauce
- ⅓ cup finely chopped barbecued pork (without sauce)
  Paprika, chopped dill pickle, for garnish

1. Place eggs in a single layer in a large saucepan; add water to a depth of 3 inches. Bring to a boil; cover, remove from heat, and let stand 15 minutes.

2. Drain and fill pan with cold water and ice. Tap each egg firmly on a counter until shell is cracked. Peel under cold running water.

3. Cut eggs in half lengthwise, and carefully remove yolks to a bowl. Mash yolks with mayonnaise. Stir in mustard and next 3 ingredients; blend well. Gently stir in pork.

4. Spoon yolk mixture into egg white halves. Chill until ready to serve. Garnish, if desired.

BALSAMIC MARINATED OLIVES

Marinate a variety of olives in vinegar, olive oil, and Italian seasoning for an easy make-ahead dish as part of an appetizer spread.

ACTIVE 5 MIN. - TOTAL 8 HOURS, 35 MIN., INCLUDING CHILLING AND STANDING
MAKES 6 CUPS

- 2 (8-oz.) jars ripe olives, drained
- 2 (7-oz.) jars Kalamata olives, drained
- 2 (7-oz.) jars pimiento-stuffed olives, drained
- ½ cup olive oil
- ½ cup balsamic vinegar
- 1 Tbsp. Italian seasoning

Combine all ingredients in a medium bowl; cover and chill at least 8 hours. Let stand 30 minutes at room temperature before serving. Serve with a slotted spoon.

- -

ONE-MINUTE SALSA

Got a minute and a blender? Then you have time to make this spunky, super-quick, four-ingredient salsa.

ACTIVE 1 MIN. - TOTAL 1 MIN.
MAKES 3 CUPS

- 1 (10-oz.) can diced tomatoes and green chiles, undrained
- 1 (14½-oz.) can no-salt-added stewed tomatoes, undrained
- 1 tsp. black pepper
- 1 garlic clove, minced
  Tortilla chips

Combine first 4 ingredients in a blender. Cover and blend for 30 seconds, stopping once to scrape down sides. Serve with tortilla chips.

CAST-IRON SALSA

Turn your skillet into a Mexican comal (aka griddle) by slowly charring onions, garlic, and peppers in a dry skillet. We like to use this traditional dry char technique because it coaxes sweet, earthy flavors from the vegetables and gives them just a hint of smokiness.

ACTIVE 20 MIN. - TOTAL 30 MIN.
MAKES 1½ CUPS

- 3 plum tomatoes, halved
- 3 garlic cloves, unpeeled
- 1 red or green jalapeño pepper, halved
- 1 medium white onion, cut into 16 wedges
- 1½ Tbsp. fresh lime juice
- ¾ tsp. kosher salt
- ⅓ cup chopped fresh cilantro leaves

1. Heat a 12-inch cast-iron skillet or griddle over medium for 5 minutes. Place tomatoes, cut-side down, in skillet, spacing evenly; add garlic and jalapeño pepper. Cook, turning occasionally, about 6 minutes or until slightly charred and softened. Transfer tomatoes and jalapeño pepper to a blender or food processor. Peel garlic, and place in blender. Add onion wedges to skillet; cook 5 to 6 minutes or until slightly charred and softened. Transfer onion to blender.

2. Process vegetables 30 to 40 seconds or to desired consistency. Add lime juice and salt to blender, and process until combined. Cool completely (about 10 minutes). Stir in cilantro. Serve at room temperature, or refrigerate in an airtight container up to 3 days.

Note: Use red jalapeño peppers for a redder salsa.

CAST-IRON
SALSA

CLASSIC PIMIENTO
CHEESE

TOMATO CROSTINI

ACTIVE 10 MIN. - TOTAL 10 MIN.
SERVES 4

- 1½ oz. goat cheese (¼ cup)
- 1½ oz. cream cheese, softened (¼ cup)
- 1 (6-inch) Italian bread shell
- 5 plum tomatoes, chopped
- 2 tsp. chopped fresh herbs (parsley, thyme, basil, or rosemary)

Stir together goat cheese and cream cheese in a small bowl; spread on bread shell. Cut into wedges; top with tomatoes and herbs.

- -

BLUE CHEESE CRISPS

ACTIVE 5 MIN. - TOTAL 15 MIN.
MAKES 32 CRISPS

- ½ cup butter or margarine, softened
- 1 (4-oz.) pkg. crumbled blue cheese, softened
- ½ cup finely chopped pecans or walnuts
- 1 French baguette, sliced
  Chopped fresh flat-leaf parsley, for garnish (optional)

1. Preheat oven to 350°F. Stir together softened butter and blue cheese until blended; stir in chopped nuts. Set aside.

2. Place baguette slices in a single layer on baking sheets. Bake in preheated oven for 3 to 5 minutes. Turn slices, then spread evenly with blue cheese mixture. Bake 5 minutes more. Garnish, if desired. Serve crisps immediately.

CLASSIC PIMIENTO CHEESE

ACTIVE 20 MIN. - TOTAL 8 HOURS, 50 MIN., INCLUDING CHILLING
MAKES 3½ CUPS

- ⅓ cup mayonnaise
- 3 Tbsp. cream cheese, at room temperature
- 2 tsp. Worcestershire sauce
- 2 tsp. fresh lemon juice or apple cider vinegar
- 1½ tsp. dried mustard
- 1½ tsp. hot sauce
- 1 tsp. granulated sugar
- ½ tsp. kosher salt
- ¼ tsp. freshly ground black pepper
- 2 Tbsp. finely grated onion
- 1 (12-oz.) jar diced pimiento
- 8 oz. extra-sharp white cheddar cheese, coarsely shredded (2 cups)
- 8 oz. sharp yellow cheddar cheese, coarsely shredded (2 cups)

Stir together first 9 ingredients in a medium bowl until smooth. Stir in onion. Fold in pimiento and cheeses. Cover and chill 8 to 12 hours. Let stand at room temperature 30 minutes, and stir well before serving.

Tip: For a smoother spread that can be piped onto celery sticks, pulse pimiento cheese in the food processor a few seconds. This recipe is also delicious spooned onto fried green tomatoes, smeared on a burger, or stirred into deviled eggs.

HOT SPINACH–ARTICHOKE DIP

ACTIVE 15 MIN. - TOTAL 45 MIN.
SERVES 8

- 3 oz. Parmesan cheese, grated (1 cup)
- 1 cup reduced-fat sour cream
- ½ cup mayonnaise
- 4 scallions, sliced
- 3 Tbsp. fresh lemon juice
- 1 garlic clove, pressed
- 5 oz. pepper Jack cheese, shredded (1¼ cups)
- 1 (10-oz.) pkg. frozen chopped spinach, thawed and well drained
- 1 (14-oz.) can artichoke hearts, drained and chopped
  Freshly cracked black pepper
  Crackers and assorted fresh vegetables

1. Preheat oven to 350°F. Stir together first 6 ingredients and 1 cup pepper Jack cheese. Fold in spinach and artichokes. Spoon into a lightly greased 1-quart baking dish. Sprinkle with remaining ¼ cup pepper Jack cheese.

2. Bake in preheated oven until center is hot and edges are bubbly, about 30 minutes. Sprinkle with freshly ground pepper to taste. Serve with crackers and vegetables.

Hot Spinach-Artichoke Dip with Crab:
Increase mayonnaise to 1 cup and Parmesan cheese to 1¼ cups. Prepare recipe as directed in Step 1, folding in 1 lb. **fresh jumbo lump crabmeat**, drained and picked, with spinach and artichokes. Spoon into a 2-qt. baking dish. Bake at 350°F until center is hot and edges are bubbly, about 40 minutes.

BACON–BLUE CHEESE DIP

This warm blue cheese dip is ideal for entertaining. Bake it in individual cups or a 1-quart dish.

ACTIVE 20 MIN. - TOTAL 35 MIN.
SERVES 12 TO 15

- 7 bacon slices, chopped
- 2 garlic cloves, minced
- 2 (8-oz.) pkg. cream cheese, softened
- ⅓ cup half-and-half
- 4 oz. crumbled blue cheese (⅔ cup)
- 2 Tbsp. chopped fresh chives
- 3 Tbsp. chopped walnuts, toasted
  Grape clusters
  Flatbread or assorted crackers

1. Preheat oven to 350°F. Cook chopped bacon in a skillet over medium-high 10 minutes or until crisp. Drain bacon, and set aside. Add minced garlic to skillet, and sauté 1 minute.

2. Beat cream cheese at medium speed with an electric mixer until smooth. Add half-and-half, beating until combined. Stir in bacon, garlic, blue cheese, and chives. Spoon mixture evenly into 4 (1-cup) individual baking dishes.

3. Bake in preheated oven until golden and bubbly, about 15 minutes. Sprinkle with chopped walnuts, and serve with grape clusters and flatbread or assorted crackers.

- -

PIZZA DIP

PREP 10 MIN. - TOTAL 10 MIN.
SERVES 6 TO 8

- 1 (8-oz.) pkg. cream cheese, softened
- ½ cup pizza sauce
- 2 oz. mozzarella cheese, shredded (½ cup)
- 2 Tbsp. grated Parmesan cheese
- 2 Tbsp. chopped red bell pepper
- 2 Tbsp. chopped green bell pepper
- 1 tsp. dried Italian seasoning
  Crackers
  Assorted fresh cut vegetables

Spread cream cheese in a microwave-safe 9-inch pie plate. Top with pizza sauce and next 5 ingredients. Microwave at HIGH 2 minutes or until thoroughly heated. Serve with crackers or assorted vegetables.

HOT SPINACH-
ARTICHOKE DIP

BEER-CHEESE
FONDUE

LAYERED NACHO DIP

This classic 1981 Southern Living *recipe has stood the test of time.*

ACTIVE 10 MIN. - TOTAL 10 MIN.
MAKES 8 CUPS

- 1 (16-oz.) can refried beans
- 2 tsp. taco seasoning mix
- 1 (6-oz.) container avocado dip
- 1 (8-oz.) container sour cream
- 1 (4.5-oz.) can chopped ripe olives, drained
- 2 large tomatoes, diced
- 1 small onion, diced
- 1 (4-oz.) can chopped green chiles
- 6 oz. Monterey Jack cheese, shredded (1½ cups)
  Corn or tortilla chips

1. Stir together beans and seasoning mix in a small bowl; spread into an 11- x 7-inch baking dish. Spread avocado dip and sour cream evenly over bean mixture. Sprinkle with olives and next 4 ingredients. Serve with chips.

- -

QUICK CREAMY VEGETABLE DIP

ACTIVE 10 MIN. - TOTAL 2 HOURS, 10 MIN.
MAKES ABOUT 1½ CUPS

- ½ cup mayonnaise
- ½ cup sour cream
- ¼ cup drained, chopped jarred roasted red bell peppers or 1 (2-oz.) jar diced pimiento, drained
- ¼ cup finely chopped onion
- ¼ cup finely chopped green bell pepper
- ½ tsp. table salt
- ⅛ tsp. garlic powder
- ⅛ tsp. black pepper
- ⅛ tsp. hot sauce
  Baby carrots, celery sticks, radish slices

Stir together first 9 ingredients in a medium bowl. Cover and chill at least 2 hours. Serve dip with baby carrots, celery sticks, and radish slices.

BEER-CHEESE FONDUE

ACTIVE 15 MIN. - TOTAL 15 MIN.
SERVES 8

- ¼ cup unsalted butter
- ⅓ cup all-purpose flour
- 1 (12-oz.) bottle lager beer
- ¼ cup heavy cream
- 6 oz. Gruyère cheese, shredded (about 1½ cups)
- 6 oz. mild cheddar cheese, shredded (about 1½ cups)
- ½ tsp. Worcestershire sauce
- ½ tsp. dry mustard
  Serving suggestions: cubed bread, sliced cooked bratwurst, steamed broccoli florets, roasted Brussels sprouts, roasted fingerling potatoes

Melt butter in a medium saucepan over medium-low. Gradually whisk in flour. Cook, whisking constantly, until lightly browned, about 1 minute. Gradually whisk in beer and heavy cream. Cook, whisking constantly, until sauce has thickened and begins to bubble, 3 to 4 minutes. Gradually add Gruyère and cheddar, whisking constantly, allowing each addition to melt and become incorporated before adding more. Whisk in Worcestershire sauce and dry mustard until smooth. Transfer mixture to a fondue pot; cover and keep warm. Serve immediately.

- -

SWEET 'N' SAVORY SNACK MIX

ACTIVE 10 MIN. - TOTAL 20 MIN.
MAKES 8 CUPS

- 3 cups crispy corn or rice cereal squares
- 1 cup small pretzels
- 1 (6-oz.) can roasted almonds
- 1 (8-oz.) jar salted peanuts
- ⅓ cup firmly packed light brown sugar
- 1½ Tbsp. Worcestershire sauce
- 1 cup bear-shape graham crackers
- ½ cup raisins

1. Preheat oven to 325°F. Combine first 4 ingredients in a large bowl. Stir together brown sugar and Worcestershire sauce until blended; pour over cereal mixture. Spray a 15- x 10-inch jelly-roll pan with cooking spray; spread cereal mixture in a single layer in pan, stirring to coat.

2. Bake in preheated oven 12 minutes, stirring every 5 minutes. Stir in graham crackers and raisins.

SPICED PECANS

Not only is this a sweet and crunchy snack, but you can sprinkle pecans over low-sugar ice cream for quick and easy desserts.

ACTIVE 10 MIN. - TOTAL 35 MIN.
SERVES 20

- ½ cup "measures-like-sugar" calorie-free sweetener
- 1½ tsp. ground cinnamon
- 1 tsp. ground nutmeg
- ¼ tsp. table salt
- 1 large egg white
- 4½ tsp. water
- 2½ cups pecan halves

1. Preheat oven to 300°F.

2. Combine first 4 ingredients in a medium bowl, stirring well.

3. Beat egg white and water with an electric mixer on medium speed until foamy. Gradually add sweetener mixture, 1 tablespoon at a time, beating until stiff peaks form; fold in pecan halves.

4. Pour pecan mixture onto a jelly-roll pan coated with cooking spray. Bake in the preheated oven for 25 minutes, stirring every 10 minutes.

5. Cool completely in pan. Store in an airtight container.

- - - - - - - - - - - - - - - - - - - -

ALOHA PUNCH

ACTIVE 5 MIN. - TOTAL 5 MIN.
MAKES 6 CUPS

- 2 cups pineapple juice
- 1 cup strawberry juice
- 1 cup guava juice
- 1 cup pear nectar
- 1 cup orange carbonated beverage
  Paper parasols, for garnish

Stir together first 5 ingredients in a large pitcher or bowl. Serve over crushed ice. Garnish, if desired.

BERRY-COLADA PUNCH

ACTIVE 5 MIN. - TOTAL 5 MIN.
MAKES 2½ QUARTS

- 1 (16-oz.) pkg. frozen strawberries, thawed
- 1 (15-oz.) can cream of coconut
- 3 cups pineapple juice, chilled
- 3 cups club soda, chilled
- 2 cups rum (optional)
  Crushed ice

Process strawberries and cream of coconut in a blender until smooth; pour into a pitcher or large bowl. Stir in pineapple juice, club soda, and, if desired, rum. Serve over crushed ice.

- - - - - - - - - - - - - - - - - - - -

CRANBERRY SANGRÍA PUNCH

This wintry, ruby-red spin on sangría is a staff favorite. The recipe comes with a warning: It goes down easy. Make it a day ahead, and add the Champagne right before serving.

ACTIVE 20 MIN. - TOTAL 40 MIN.
SERVES 10

- 2 cups frozen or fresh cranberries
- 1 cup granulated sugar
- 1 cup water
- 1 (750-ml) bottle sangría, chilled
- ¼ cup (2 oz.) Campari
- 1 large navel orange, thinly sliced
- 1 large Granny Smith apple, thinly sliced
- 1 (750-ml) bottle brut Champagne, chilled
  Ice

1. Combine cranberries, sugar, and water in a medium saucepan over medium-high; bring to a boil, stirring often until sugar dissolves and berries just begin to pop, 3 to 4 minutes. Remove from heat; cool 30 minutes.

2. Stir together sangría, Campari, and cooled cranberries with liquid in a large pitcher or small punch bowl. Add orange and apple slices. Just before serving, add Champagne.

3. Serve over ice with a few pieces of fruit in each glass.

CRANBERRY
SANGRÍA PUNCH

BIG-BATCH
ARNOLD PALMERS

BOURBON-PEACH ICED TEA

ACTIVE 20 MIN. · TOTAL 40 MIN.
SERVES 10

2	cups chopped fresh peaches (from 2 ripe peaches)
1½	cups granulated sugar
8	black tea bags
1	cup (8 oz.) bourbon
	Ice
	Peach slices, for garnish

Bring chopped peaches, sugar, and 1 cup water to a boil in a saucepan over medium-high. Reduce heat to low; simmer, stirring often, about 10 minutes. Cool slightly; process in a blender 30 seconds. Pour through a fine-mesh strainer into a 1-gallon container. Bring 3 cups water to a boil over high in a saucepan. Add tea bags,and boil 1 minute. Remove from heat. Cover; steep 10 minutes. Discard tea bags. Stir the tea, bourbon, and 6 cups cold water into peach mixture. Serve in highball glasses over ice, and garnish with peach slices.

BLACKBERRY LEMONADE

ACTIVE 10 MIN. · TOTAL 10 MIN.
MAKES 6 CUPS

1	(14-oz.) pkg. frozen blackberries
1	(16-oz.) jar maraschino cherries without stems
1¼	cups granulated sugar
¾	cup fresh lemon juice (about 5 lemons)
¼	cup fresh lime juice (about 1 large lime)
	Ice

Process the first 5 ingredients in a blender until smooth, stopping to scrape down sides. Pour fruit mixture through a wire-mesh strainer into a pitcher, discarding solids. Stir in 3 cups water. Serve over ice.

BIG-BATCH ARNOLD PALMERS

ACTIVE 10 MIN. · TOTAL 2 HOURS, 10 MIN.
MAKES ABOUT 13 CUPS

6	cups unsweetened iced tea
4	cups bottled lemonade
2¼	cups bourbon
⅔	cup simple syrup
3	lemons, thinly sliced
	Ice
	Mint sprigs, lemon slices, for garnish

Stir together iced tea, lemonade, bourbon, and simple syrup in a large bowl or pitcher. Add lemon slices to pitcher. Refrigerate until chilled, at least 2 hours or up to 24 hours. Serve over ice, and garnish with mint sprigs and lemon slices.

STRAWBERRY-MINT TEA

This family recipe is refreshing on its own or spiked with gin for a sparkling cocktail.

ACTIVE 15 MIN. · TOTAL 30 MIN.
SERVES 6

2	cups hulled and chopped fresh strawberries
4	cups granulated sugar
8	fresh peppermint sprigs
6	cups sparkling water, chilled
	Ice

1. Place strawberries and in a saucepan; muddle using a wooden spoon. Cook over low, stirring occasionally, until sugar is dissolved, 5 minutes.

2. Place a peppermint sprig in the palm of your hand; give it a good slap (to bring out volatile oils). Repeat with remaining peppermint sprigs. Stir sprigs into strawberry mixture; remove from heat. Cool to room temperature, 15 minutes.

3. Remove and discard mint. Pour mixture through a fine-mesh strainer into a half-gallon pitcher. Stir in 6 cups chilled sparkling water. Serve over ice.

CHERRY SPARKLER

ACTIVE 10 MIN. - TOTAL 8 HOURS, 10 MIN., INCLUDING FREEZING
MAKES 8 CUPS

- 2 (6-oz.) jars red maraschino cherries, drained
- 2 (6-oz.) jars green maraschino cherries, drained
- ½ gallon distilled water
- 1 (2-liter) bottle cherry-flavor, lemon-lime soft drink, chilled

Place 1 red or green cherry in each compartment of 4 ice-cube trays. Fill trays with distilled water; freeze for 8 hours. Serve soft drink over cherry-filled ice cubes.

- -

SOUTHERN SUNRISE

ACTIVE 10 MIN. - TOTAL 10 MIN.
SERVES 2

- 6 oz. fresh orange juice (from 2 oranges)
- 3 oz. tequila
  Ice
- 1 oz. grenadine, divided
  Maraschino cherries, Sparkling Orange Wheels (recipe follows), for garnish

Stir together the orange juice and tequila in a pitcher. Pour mixture into 2 ice-filled highball glasses. Slowly add ½ ounce grenadine to each glass. Do not stir. Top each with a cherry and a Sparkling Orange Wheel.

SPARKLING ORANGE WHEELS

ACTIVE 5 MIN. - TOTAL 35 MIN.
SERVES 2

- 1 small orange
- 1 Tbsp. light corn syrup
  Sparkling sugar

Cut orange into six ⅛-inch-thick rounds, and discard the seeds. Microwave corn syrup in a microwavable bowl on HIGH until warm, 5 seconds. Using a small brush, coat both sides and edges of rounds with corn syrup. Sprinkle with sugar. Place wheels on a wire rack to dry for 30 minutes; use within 2 hours.

FROSTED BELLINIS

ACTIVE 5 MIN. - TOTAL 5 MIN.
MAKES 6 CUPS

- 1 (750-ml. bottle champagne
- 2 (11.5-oz.) cans peach nectar
- ½ cup peach schnapps
  Crushed ice

Combine the first 3 ingredients in a large pitcher, stirring until well blended. Serve immediately over crushed ice.

- -

MANGO MARGARITA

For a margarita that's extra refreshing, add buttery mango slices, fresh orange juice, and freshly squeezed Key lime juice to the standard tequila and orange liqueur mix. For the best flavor and texture, chill the ingredients, especially to serve poolside on a hot day. Conventional mangoes are fine here, but use champagne mangoes for the sweetest results.

ACTIVE 10 MIN. - TOTAL 10 MIN.
MAKES 4 CUPS

- ¾ cup fresh orange juice
- 1 large mango, seeded and chopped
- ¼ cup Key lime juice
- ⅓ cup tequila
- ¼ cup Cointreau or other orange-flavor liqueur
- ¼ cup Simple Syrup (recipe follows)
  Ice

Combine first 6 ingredients in a blender, cover with lid, and process until smooth. Add ice to equal 4 cups; process until smooth.

SIMPLE SYRUP

ACTIVE 10 MIN. - TOTAL 1 HOUR, 10 MIN., INCLUDING COOLING
MAKES ¾ CUP

- ½ cup granulated sugar
- ½ cup water

Bring sugar and water to boil in a small saucepan over medium-low, stirring occasionally. Remove from heat, and cool to room temperature, about 1 hour

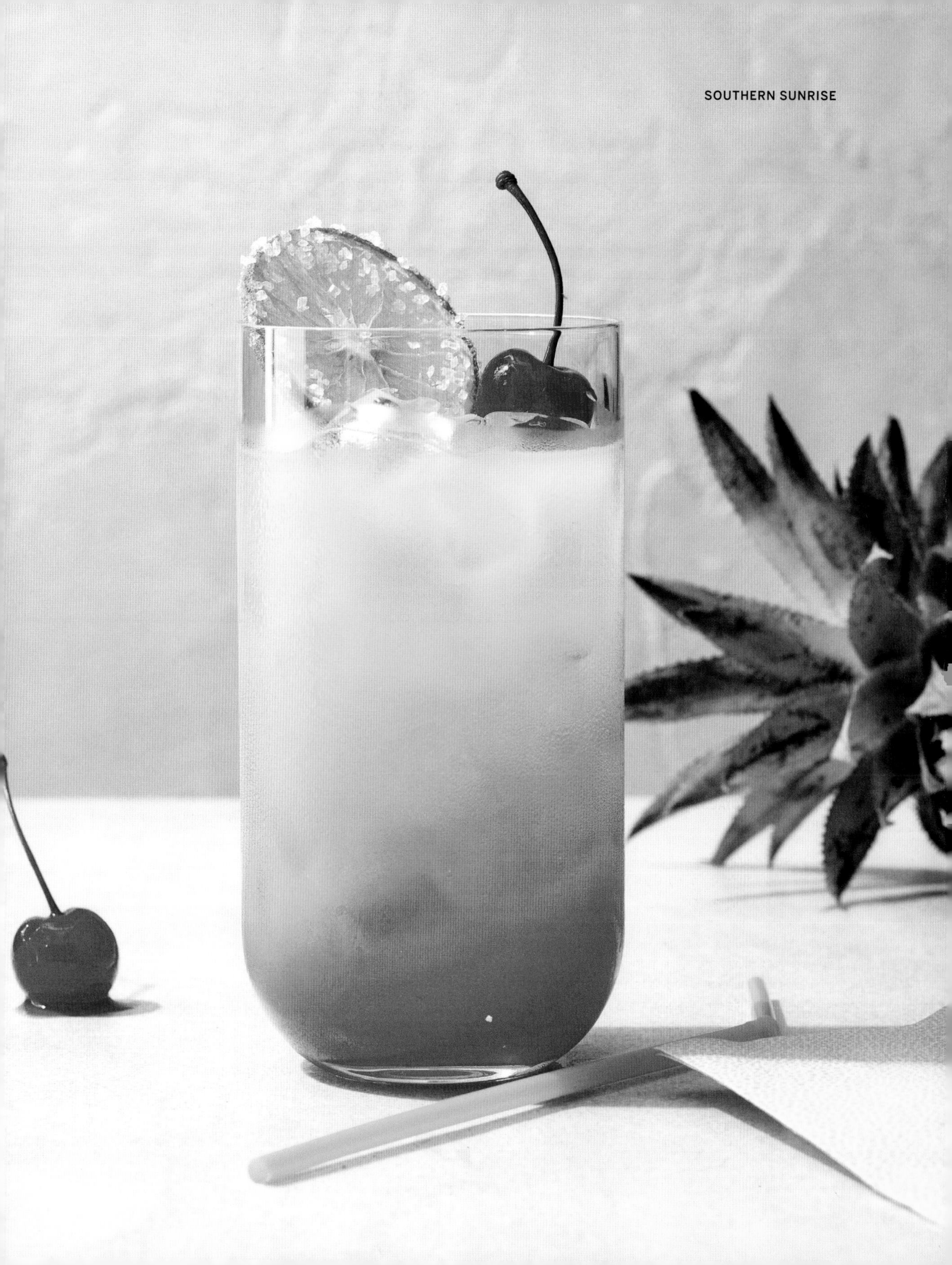
SOUTHERN SUNRISE

WATERMELON-
GINGER MOJITOS

WATERMELON-GINGER MOJITOS

ACTIVE 20 MIN. - TOTAL 1 HOUR, 35 MIN., INCLUDING CHILLING
SERVES 10

- ½ cup granulated sugar
- 5 large fresh mint sprigs, plus more for garnish
- 8 cups seedless watermelon cubes (from 1 [7½-lb.] seedless watermelon)
- 3 cups (24 oz.) light rum (such as Bacardí Superior), chilled
- 1 (12-oz.) bottle ginger beer, chilled
- ½ cup fresh lime juice (from 4 limes)
  Ice
  Small watermelon wedges, for garnish

1. Bring ½ cup water and sugar to a simmer in a small saucepan over high. Simmer, stirring often, until sugar dissolves, 1 to 2 minutes. Remove from heat; add mint, and stir until mint is submerged. Refrigerate until mixture is completely cool, 1 hour. Pour mint syrup through a fine-mesh strainer into a bowl; discard solids. Chill mint syrup until ready to use.

2. While syrup cools, place watermelon in a blender, and process until smooth, about 20 seconds. Pour through a fine-mesh strainer into a large measuring cup, pressing gently to squeeze out juice. Discard solids, and refrigerate 15 minutes. Strain a second time. (You should have about 4 cups watermelon juice.)

3. Stir together mint syrup, watermelon juice, rum, ginger beer, and lime juice in a large pitcher.

4. Pour evenly into 10 highball glasses filled with ice; garnish each with a mint sprig and small watermelon wedge cut to sit on rim of glass.

PRALINE COFFEE

ACTIVE 5 MIN. - TOTAL 5 MIN.
MAKES 5 CUPS

- 3 cups hot brewed coffee
- ⅔ to ¾ cup firmly packed light brown sugar
- ¾ cup half-and-half
- ¾ cup praline liqueur
  Sweetened whipped cream

Heat first 3 ingredients in a large saucepan over medium, stirring constantly, until thoroughly heated. (Do not boil.) Stir in liqueur. Serve coffee with sweetened whipped cream.

- -

SOUTHERN EGGNOG

Eggnog, a beloved holiday beverage, is a cherished Southern tradition—with or without the bourbon.

ACTIVE 10 MIN. - TOTAL 24 HOURS, 30 MIN., INCLUDING CHILLING
MAKES 5 CUPS

- 1 quart milk
- 4 large eggs
- 1 cup granulated sugar
- 2 tsp. vanilla extract
- ¼ tsp. table salt
- ⅔ cup bourbon

1. Heat milk in a heavy nonaluminum saucepan over medium, stirring often, 10 minutes or just until it begins to steam. (Do not boil.) Remove from heat.

2. Whisk together eggs and next 3 ingredients until blended. Gradually whisk 1 cup hot milk into egg mixture; whisk egg mixture into remaining hot milk.

3. Cook over medium heat, stirring constantly, 8 to 10 minutes or until a candy thermometer registers between 170°F and 180°F. (Do not boil.)

4. Remove from heat. Pour custard through a fine-mesh strainer into a bowl. Place heavy-duty plastic wrap directly on warm custard (to prevent a film from forming), and chill at least 24 hours or up to 3 days. (Eggnog will thicken as it cools.) Stir in bourbon just before serving.

PEACHES-AND-CREAM
PANCAKES, PAGE 42

BREAKFAST

EASY FRENCH TOAST CASSEROLE

Serve sliced fresh strawberries and a cold glass of milk alongside this sweet breakfast treat. Make sure your French bread has a soft crust so it's easy to cut.

ACTIVE 30 MIN. - TOTAL 9 HOURS, INCLUDING CHILLING
SERVES 6

- 2/3 cup firmly packed dark brown sugar
- 2 Tbsp. butter
- 2 Tbsp. dark corn syrup
- 2 large eggs
- 1 large egg white
- 1½ cups milk
- 1 tsp. vanilla extract
- ¼ tsp. table salt
- 6 (1-inch-thick) French bread baguette slices
- ¼ cup chopped toasted pecans
  Strawberry slices, powdered sugar, for garnish

1. Combine first 3 ingredients in a small heavy saucepan. Cook over medium until bubbly and sugar dissolves, stirring constantly. Pour sugar mixture into an 11- x 7-inch baking dish coated with cooking spray, spreading evenly over bottom of dish.

2. Whisk together eggs and egg white in a shallow dish or pie plate. Stir in milk, vanilla, and salt. Lightly press bread slices, 1 at a time, into egg mixture, coating both sides of bread. Arrange over sugar mixture. Pour any remaining egg mixture evenly over bread slices. Cover and chill 8 to 24 hours.

3. Preheat oven to 350°F. Bake casserole, uncovered, until lightly browned, about 30 minutes.

4. Sprinkle casserole with pecans and strawberries, and dust with powdered sugar.

ALMOND FRENCH TOAST

For the taste of extravagance with the ease of assembly, this breakfast recipe merits rave reviews.

ACTIVE 20 MIN. - TOTAL 50 MIN.
SERVES 3

- 6 (1-inch-thick) French bread slices
- 4 large eggs
- ½ cup milk
- 1 Tbsp. granulated sugar
- 1 tsp. almond extract
- ½ tsp. vanilla extract
- 2 Tbsp. almond liqueur (optional)
- 3 Tbsp. butter, melted
- ½ cup sliced almonds, toasted
  Powdered sugar
  Maple syrup, warmed

1. Arrange French bread slices in a 13- x 9-inch baking dish.

2. Whisk together eggs, next 4 ingredients, and, if desired, liqueur in a medium bowl; pour over bread. Let stand 5 minutes, turning once. Cover and chill 8 hours, if desired.

3. Preheat oven to 400°F. Pour melted butter into a 15- x 10-inch jelly-roll pan; add soaked bread slices.

4. Bake in preheated oven for 15 minutes; turn each slice, and bake 8 to 10 minutes more or until golden. Sprinkle with almonds and powdered sugar. Serve with maple syrup.

PRALINE-PECAN FRENCH TOAST

Traditional New Orleans-style French toast gets a nutty-spicy lift to brighten breakfast or brunch.

ACTIVE 20 MIN. - TOTAL 8 HOURS, 30 MIN., INCLUDING CHILLING
SERVES 8 TO 10

- 1 (16-oz.) French bread loaf, sliced
- 1 cup firmly packed light brown sugar
- 1/3 cup butter, melted
- 2 Tbsp. maple syrup
- 3/4 cup chopped pecans
- 4 large eggs, lightly beaten
- 1 cup 2% reduced-fat milk
- 2 Tbsp. granulated sugar
- 1 tsp. ground cinnamon
- 1 tsp. vanilla extract

1. Cut 10 (1-inch-thick) slices of bread. Reserve remaining bread for another use.

2. Stir together brown sugar, butter, and maple syrup. Pour into a lightly greased 13- x 9-inch baking dish. Sprinkle with chopped pecans.

3. Whisk together eggs and remaining ingredients. Arrange bread slices on pecans; pour egg mixture over bread. Cover and chill 8 hours or overnight.

4. Preheat oven to 350°F. Bake until golden brown, 35 to 37 minutes. Serve immediately.

PEACHES-AND-CREAM PANCAKES

(Photo, page 38)

These thin crêpe-like pancakes are gluten free, but you can swap out the gluten-free flour for an equal amount of all-purpose flour.

ACTIVE 20 MIN. - TOTAL 20 MIN.
SERVES 2

- 2 fresh peaches (about 2/3 lb.)
- 1/4 cup pure maple syrup
- 4 large eggs
- 1 Tbsp. granulated sugar
- 1/2 tsp. vanilla extract
- 1/2 cup gluten-free flour
- 1/2 cup cottage cheese
- 1 Tbsp. salted butter
  Sweetened whipped cream

1. Gently rub peaches under running water to remove fuzz. Thinly slice peaches, and cut them in half. Toss together peach slices and maple syrup in a medium bowl.

2. Whisk together eggs, sugar, and vanilla in a medium bowl until combined. Whisk in flour until smooth. Add cottage cheese and stir to combine.

3. Heat a 9-inch nonstick skillet over medium-high. Add 1/2 teaspoon of the butter to skillet. Spoon 1/3 cup of pancake batter into melted butter in skillet, swirling to distribute batter evenly in a thin layer. Cook until batter begins to firm up, about 1 minute. Flip pancake, and cook until firm, about 1 minute more. Transfer to a baking sheet, and keep warm in a 200°F oven. Repeat with remaining butter and batter.

4. To serve, layer 3 pancakes and top with peaches on each of 2 plates; top with whipped cream.

PRALINE-PECAN
FRENCH TOAST

BRUNCH POPOVER
PANCAKE

BRUNCH POPOVER PANCAKE

Scrambled eggs and bacon love to pair up with this pancake, full of fruity flavors. The batter rises or "pops over" the skillet when cooked then quickly deflates, providing a center for filling and a rustic-looking rim.

ACTIVE 15 MIN. - TOTAL 40 MIN.
SERVES 4

- 4 large eggs, lightly beaten
- 1 cup milk
- 1 cup all-purpose flour
- ¼ tsp. table salt
- ⅓ cup butter, melted
- 3 Tbsp. orange marmalade
- 3 Tbsp. butter
- 1 Tbsp. fresh lemon juice
- 1 (16-oz.) pkg. frozen sliced peaches, thawed and drained
- 1 cup frozen blueberries, thawed

1. Preheat oven to 425°F. Place a well-greased 12-inch cast-iron skillet in oven for 5 minutes.

2. Whisk together eggs and next 4 ingredients in large bowl.

3. Remove skillet from oven. Pour egg mixture into hot skillet.

4. Bake in preheated oven 20 to 25 minutes. (The pancake will resemble a giant popover that falls quickly after removing from oven.)

5. Combine marmalade, 3 tablespoons butter, and lemon juice in a saucepan; bring to a boil. Add peaches, and cook over medium heat, stirring constantly, 2 to 3 minutes. Spoon on baked pancake. Sprinkle with blueberries.

EASY BANANA PANCAKES

To make these pancakes without cookie cutters, pour batter by ¼ cupfuls onto hot griddle, and proceed as directed.

ACTIVE 10 MIN. - TOTAL 10 MIN.
MAKES 12 PANCAKES

- 1 cup all-purpose flour
- 1 Tbsp. baking powder
- 2 tsp. granulated sugar
- 1 tsp. table salt
- 1 cup plus 2 Tbsp. milk (use more for thinner batter)
- 1 large egg, lightly beaten
- 1 cup chopped banana
- 2 to 4 (4½- to 5-inch) heavy metal cookie cutters

1. Combine flour and next 3 ingredients in a bowl; whisk in milk and egg until mixture is blended. Stir in banana.

2. Lightly grease heavy metal cookie cutters, and place on hot (375°F), lightly greased griddle. Pour pancake batter (approximately 2 tablespoons) into each cutter. Using tongs, remove cutters after 1 minute (cutters will be hot); cook pancakes 2 minutes more. Turn pancakes over, and cook 2 to 3 minutes or until done.

BACON AND EGGS BREAD PUDDING

Put day-old bread to good use as the base of this rich and hearty breakfast bake. The recipe comes together in less than an hour and tastes as if you've been cooking all morning.

ACTIVE 10 MIN. - TOTAL 40 MIN.
SERVES 4 TO 6

 4 large eggs
 1 cup milk
 1 oz. Parmesan cheese, grated (⅓ cup)
 3 Tbsp. butter, melted
 1 tsp. table salt
 ½ tsp. freshly ground black pepper
 ⅓ cup sliced scallions (optional)
 5 hickory-smoked bacon slices, cooked and crumbled
 ½ (16-oz.) French bread loaf, cut into 1-inch cubes

1. Preheat oven to 350°F. Whisk together first 6 ingredients and, if desired, scallions. Add bacon and bread cubes; toss well to coat. Spoon bread mixture into a lightly greased 11- x 7-inch baking dish. Let stand at room temperature 10 minutes.

2. Bake in preheated oven, uncovered, until golden brown and set in center, about 30 minutes.

BAKED EGGS WITH SPINACH AND TOMATOES

Using prepared pasta sauce in this savory egg bake keeps total prep and cooking time less than an hour.

ACTIVE 20 MIN. - TOTAL 45 MIN.
SERVES 6

 6 Tbsp. low-fat garlic-and-herb spreadable cheese
 48 fresh spinach leaves, torn
 6 large eggs
 ¾ cup jarred pasta sauce
 6 Tbsp. half-and-half
 ¾ tsp. freshly ground black pepper
   Toast

1. Preheat oven to 350°F. Coat 6 (6- to 8-oz.) ramekins with cooking spray. Layer 1 tablespoon spreadable cheese, 8 torn spinach leaves, 1 egg, 2 tablespoons pasta sauce, 1 tablespoon half-and-half, and ⅛ teaspoon pepper in each ramekin.

2. Place ramekins on a baking sheet. Bake in preheated oven until cooked to desired firmness, 20 to 25 minutes. Let stand 5 minutes. Serve with toast.

BREAKFAST BURRITOS

ACTIVE 10 MIN. - TOTAL 15 MIN.
SERVES 4

 ½ lb. hot or mild ground pork sausage
 1 Tbsp. taco seasoning mix
 6 large eggs, lightly beaten
 ½ cup shredded Mexican four-cheese blend
 4 burrito-size flour tortillas
   Salsa

1. Cook sausage and taco seasoning in a large nonstick skillet, stirring often, until sausage is browned, about 5 minutes. Add eggs and cook, without stirring, until eggs begin to set on bottom. Draw a spatula across bottom of pan to form large curds. Continue to cook until eggs are thickened but still moist, about 5 minutes.

2. Sprinkle eggs evenly with cheese. Turn off heat, and cover. Let stand 5 minutes or until cheese is melted.

3. Spoon eggs evenly into 4 tortillas, roll up, and serve with salsa.

BACON AND EGGS
BREAD PUDDING

BREAKFAST ENCHILADAS

This Mexican-inspired morning meal can be made ahead without baking and refrigerated overnight. Let it come to room temperature for 30 minutes before placing it in the oven.

ACTIVE 20 MIN. - TOTAL 1 HOUR, INCLUDING CHEESE SAUCE

SERVES 8

- 1 (1-lb.) pkg. hot ground pork sausage
- 2 Tbsp. butter
- 4 scallions, thinly sliced
- 2 Tbsp. chopped fresh cilantro
- 14 large eggs, beaten
- ¾ tsp. table salt
- ½ tsp. freshly ground black pepper
  Cheese Sauce (recipe follows)
- 8 (8-inch) flour tortillas
- 1 cup (4 oz.) shredded Monterey Jack cheese with jalapeños
  Cilantro Pesto (recipe follows)
  Toppings: halved grape tomatoes, sliced scallions, fresh cilantro sprigs

1. Preheat oven to 350°F. Cook sausage in a large nonstick skillet over medium-high, stirring often, until sausage crumbles and is no longer pink, 6 to 8 minutes. Remove from pan; drain well.

2. Melt butter in a large nonstick skillet over medium. Add scallions and cilantro; cook 1 minute. Add eggs, salt, and pepper; cook, without stirring, until eggs begin to set on bottom. Draw spatula across bottom of pan to form large curds. Continue to cook until eggs are thickened but still moist; do not stir. Remove from heat and gently fold in 1½ cups Cheese Sauce and the sausage.

3. Spoon about ⅓ cup egg mixture along the center of each flour tortilla; roll up. Place, seam side down, in a lightly greased 13- x- 9-inch baking dish. Pour remaining Cheese Sauce evenly over tortillas; sprinkle evenly with Monterey Jack cheese. (At this point, the dish can be covered with foil and refrigerated up to 24 hours.) Bake in preheated oven until sauce is bubbly, about 30 minutes.

CHEESE SAUCE

ACTIVE 10 MIN. - TOTAL 10 MIN.

MAKES ABOUT 4 CUPS

- ⅓ cup butter
- ⅓ cup flour
- 3 cups milk
- 8 oz. cheddar cheese, shredded (2 cups)
- 1 (4.5-oz.) can chopped green chiles, undrained
- ¾ tsp. table salt

Melt butter in a heavy saucepan over medium-low heat; whisk in flour until smooth. Cook, whisking constantly, 1 minute. Gradually whisk in milk; cook over medium heat, whisking constantly, 5 minutes or until thickened. Remove from heat and whisk in remaining ingredients.

CILANTRO PESTO

ACTIVE 10 MIN. - TOTAL 20 MIN.

MAKES ABOUT ¾ CUPS

- ½ cup chopped pecans
- 1 tsp. cumin seeds
- 2 cups loosely packed fresh cilantro leaves
- ½ cup freshly grated Parmesan cheese
- ⅓ cup olive oil
- ¼ cup cold water
- 2 garlic cloves
- 1 Tbsp. lemon juice
- ½ tsp. table salt

Preheat oven to 350°F. Bake pecans in shallow pan 5 to 6 minutes or until toasted. Cool 10 minutes. Meanwhile, place a small skillet over medium-high; add cumin seeds, and toast 1 to 2 minutes. Cool 10 minutes. Process pecans, cumin seeds, cilantro, Parmesan cheese, oil, the water, garlic, lemon juice, and salt in a food processor until smooth.

CHEDDAR CHEESE GRITS CASSEROLE

Using a quick grits in this breakfast casserole cuts cooking time significantly, but if you prefer rustic coarse-ground grits, simply cook them according to package instructions, then proceed with recipe Step 2.

ACTIVE 10 MIN. - TOTAL 50 MIN.
SERVES 6

- 4 cups milk
- ¼ cup butter
- 1 cup uncooked quick-cooking grits
- 1 large egg, lightly beaten
- 8 oz. shredded sharp cheddar cheese (2 cups)
- 1 tsp. table salt
- ½ tsp. freshly ground black pepper
- ¾ oz. Parmesan cheese, grated (¼ cup)

1. Preheat oven to 350°F. Bring milk just to a boil in a large saucepan over medium-high; gradually whisk in butter and grits. Reduce heat, and simmer, whisking constantly, 5 to 7 minutes or until grits are done. Remove from heat.

2. Stir in egg and next 3 ingredients. Pour into a lightly greased 11- x 7-inch baking dish. Sprinkle with grated Parmesan cheese.

3. Bake, covered, in preheated oven until set, 35 to 40 minutes. Serve immediately.

COUNTRY BREAKFAST CASSEROLE

ACTIVE 10 MIN. - TOTAL 1 HOUR.
SERVES 6

- 1 lb. ground mild pork sausage
- 1 tsp. table salt
- 1 cup uncooked quick-cooking grits
- 6 oz. shredded Cheddar cheese (1½ cups), divided
- 4 large eggs, lightly beaten
- ¾ cup milk
- ¼ cup butter, melted
- ¼ tsp. black pepper

1. Preheat oven to 350°F. Brown sausage in a large skillet over medium, stirring until no longer pink; drain off any fat.

2. Bring 3½ cups water and the salt to a boil in a medium saucepan; stir in grits. Return to a boil; cover, reduce heat, and simmer 5 minutes, stirring occasionally. Remove from heat; add 1 cup cheese, stirring until cheese melts. Stir in sausage, eggs, and next 3 ingredients.

3. Pour mixture into a greased 11- x 7-inch baking dish; sprinkle with remaining ½ cup cheese.

4. Bake in preheated oven, uncovered, until set, about 45 minutes. Let stand 5 minutes before serving.

GOLDEN POTATO-AND-SMOKED SAUSAGE HASH

To make this hash even heartier, top each serving with a fried egg.

ACTIVE 35 MIN. - TOTAL 1 HOUR
SERVES 6

- 1 lb. baby golden potatoes, each cut into 8 pieces
- ¼ cup kosher salt
- 1 lb. smoked sausage, sliced
- 1 medium-size sweet onion, thinly sliced
- 2 Tbsp. red wine vinegar
- 3 cups arugula
- ¼ cup shaved Parmesan cheese

1. Place potatoes, salt, and water to cover in a medium saucepan. Bring to a boil over high; reduce heat to medium-low and simmer until tender when pierced, 10 minutes. Drain, then place in a single layer on a baking sheet. Cool completely, 15 minutes.

2. Meanwhile, cook the sausage in a large skillet over medium-high, stirring often, until browned, 10 minutes. Remove with a slotted spoon and drain on paper towels, reserving drippings in skillet.

3. Cook potatoes in hot drippings over medium, stirring occasionally, until potatoes are brown and crisp, 10 minutes. Add onions and cook, stirring occasionally, until tender, 10 minutes. Add red wine vinegar and cook 30 seconds.

4. Stir in sausage and arugula; cook, stirring until arugula is wilted, about 5 minutes. Top servings with Parmesan.

GOLDEN POTATO-AND-
SMOKED SAUSAGE HASH

INDIVIDUAL COUNTRY GRITS-AND-SAUSAGE CASSEROLES

INDIVIDUAL COUNTRY GRITS-AND-SAUSAGE CASSEROLES

What's better than one big dish of grits, sausage, and sharp cheddar cheese? Ten ramekins baked with breakfast goodness. The individual servings are ideal to serve guests or for ready-to-serve mid week meals.

ACTIVE 30 MIN. - TOTAL 9 HOURS, 30 MIN., INCLUDING CHILLING
SERVES 10

- 2 lb. mild ground sausage
- 1¼ cups uncooked quick-cooking grits
- 12 oz. sharp cheddar cheese, shredded (3 cups)
- 1 cup milk
- ½ tsp. garlic salt
- 4 large eggs, lightly beaten
  Paprika
  Chopped fresh chives, for garnish

1. Brown sausage in a large skillet, stirring often, 6 to 8 minutes or until sausage crumbles and is no longer pink. Drain well; pat dry.

2. Bring 4 cups water to a boil in a large saucepan; gradually stir in grits. Return to a boil; cover, reduce heat, and simmer, stirring occasionally, 5 minutes. Remove from heat; add cheese, milk, and garlic salt, stirring until cheese melts. Stir in sausage and eggs. Spoon mixture into 10 lightly greased 8-ounce ramekins; sprinkle each with paprika.

3. Cover ramekins with plastic wrap; chill for 8 to 24 hours.

4. Preheat oven to 350°F. Remove and discard plastic wrap. Let stand at room temperature 30 minutes. Bake until golden and mixture is set, 45 to 50 minutes.

Hot 'n' Spicy Grits-and-Sausage Casseroles:
Use hot pork sausage in place of mild pork sausage, and substitute shredded pepper Jack cheese in place of sharp cheddar cheese.

Country Grits-and-Sausage Casserole:
Prepare recipe as directed, using a lightly greased 13- x 9-inch baking dish in place of ramekins.

HAM AND CHEESE STRATA

The classic pairing of ham and cheese comes together in this easy breakfast strata.

ACTIVE 20 MIN. - TOTAL 3 HOURS, 30 MIN., INCLUDING CHILLING
SERVES 8

- 4 English muffins, split, toasted, and cubed
- 8 Canadian bacon slices, cut into 1-inch pieces
- 4 oz. sharp cheddar cheese, shredded (1 cup)
- 4 large eggs
- 8 large egg whites
- 3 cups milk
- 1 tsp. dry mustard
- 1 tsp. Worcestershire sauce
- ½ tsp. freshly ground black pepper
- ½ tsp. onion powder
- ¼ tsp. hot pepper sauce

1. Combine muffin cubes and Canadian bacon in a 13- x 9-inch baking dish coated with cooking spray; sprinkle with cheese.

2. Beat eggs and egg whites with an electric mixer on medium speed until blended. Add milk and remaining 5 ingredients, beating at low speed until blended. Pour egg mixture over muffin mixture. Cover and chill at least 2 hours to overnight.

3. Preheat oven to 350°F. Remove casserole from refrigerator and let stand while oven preheats. Uncover casserole; bake 45 to 50 minutes or until browned. Let stand 15 minutes before serving.

HAM 'N' SWISS OMELETS

ACTIVE 15 MIN. - TOTAL 20 MIN.
SERVES 2

- 2 oz. lean ham, chopped
- ¼ cup chopped scallions
- ¼ cup chopped peeled, seeded tomato
  Dash black pepper
- 2 large egg whites
- ¾ cup egg substitute
- ½ tsp. dried basil
- ½ tsp. hot sauce
- ⅛ tsp. black pepper
- 1 oz. reduced-fat Swiss cheese, shredded (¼ cup), divided

1. Coat a 6-inch nonstick skillet with cooking spray; place over medium heat. Add ham, scallions, tomato, and a dash of black pepper; cook 2 minutes. Remove ham mixture from pan; set aside and keep warm.

2. Beat egg whites with an electric mixer on high speed until stiff peaks form; set aside. Combine egg substitute, 2 tablespoons water, and next 3 ingredients in a medium bowl, stir well. Gently fold egg whites into egg substitute mixture.

3. Recoat pan with cooking spray, then place over medium heat. Pour half the egg white mixture into pan. Cover, reduce heat, and cook 5 minutes or until set (do not stir). Spoon half the ham mixture over omelet, and sprinkle with 2 tablespoons cheese; fold omelet in half. Slide omelet onto a serving plate; set aside and keep warm. Repeat procedure with remaining egg white mixture, ham mixture, and cheese.

SAUSAGE-HASH BROWN BREAKFAST CASSEROLE

Frozen hash browns keep this casserole quick and easy.

ACTIVE 25 MIN. - TOTAL 1 HR., 5 MIN.
SERVES 8

- 1 lb. mild ground pork sausage
- 1 lb. hot ground pork sausage
- 1 (30-oz.) pkg. frozen hash browns
- 1½ tsp. table salt, divided
- ½ tsp. freshly ground black pepper
- 1 cup shredded cheddar cheese
- 6 large eggs
- 2 cups milk
  Thinly sliced scallions, for garnish

1. Preheat oven to 350°F. Cook sausages in a large skillet over medium-high heat, stirring often, 6 to 8 minutes or until sausage crumbles and is no longer pink. Drain well.

2. Prepare hash browns according to package directions, using ½ teaspoon salt and the black pepper.

3. Stir together hash browns, sausage, and cheese. Pour into a lightly greased 13- x 9-inch baking dish.

4. Whisk together eggs, milk, and remaining 1 teaspoon salt. Pour evenly over potato mixture. Bake in preheated oven until throughly heated, 35 to 40 minutes.

- -

GOUDA GRITS

ACTIVE 10 MIN. - TOTAL 25 MIN.
SERVES 8

- 4 cups chicken broth
- 1 cup whipping cream
- 1 tsp. table salt
- 1½ tsp. freshly ground black pepper
- 2 cups uncooked quick-cooking grits
- 8 oz. gouda cheese, shredded (2 cups)
- ½ cup buttermilk
- ¼ cup butter
- 2 tsp. hot sauce

Bring first 4 ingredients and 4 cups water to a boil in a Dutch oven over high heat. Whisk in grits; reduce heat to medium-low. Simmer, stirring occasionally, until thickened, about 15 minutes. Remove from heat; stir in remaining ingredients.

SAUSAGE-HASH BROWN
BREAKFAST CASSEROLE

SUNNY SKILLET
BREAKFAST

SUNNY SKILLET BREAKFAST

Use this recipe as a blueprint for favorite veggies and breakfast meats. For a crisper top, transfer the skillet from the center oven rack to the top rack during the last few minutes of baking to brown the top slightly.

ACTIVE 15 MIN. - TOTAL 28 MIN.

SERVES 6

- 3 (8-oz.) baking potatoes*, peeled and shredded (about 3 cups firmly packed)
- 1 Tbsp. butter
- 2 Tbsp. vegetable oil
- 1 small red bell pepper, diced
- 1 medium onion, diced
- 1 garlic clove, minced
- ¾ tsp. table salt, divided
- 6 large eggs
- ¼ tsp. freshly ground black pepper
  Fresh flat-leaf parsley leaves, for garnish

1. Preheat oven to 350°F. Place shredded potatoes in a large bowl; add cold water to cover. Let stand 5 minutes; drain and pat dry.

2. Melt butter with oil in a 10-inch cast-iron skillet over medium. Add bell pepper and onion; cook over medium-high 3 to 5 minutes or until tender. Add garlic; cook 1 minute. Stir in shredded potatoes and ½ teaspoon salt; cook, stirring often, 10 minutes or until potatoes are golden and tender.

3. Remove from heat. Make 6 indentations in potato mixture, using back of a spoon. Break 1 egg into each indentation. Sprinkle eggs with pepper and remaining ¼ teaspoon salt.

4. Bake in preheated oven until eggs are set, 12 to 14 minutes. Garnish with parsley. Serve immediately.

Note: You may substitute 3 cups firmly packed frozen shredded potatoes for the fresh; omit soaking potatoes.

Veggie Confetti Frittata:
Prepare recipe as directed through Step 2, sautéing ½ (8-oz.) pkg. sliced **fresh mushrooms** with bell peppers and onion. Remove from heat; stir in ¼ cup sliced **ripe black olives**, drained, and ¼ cup thinly sliced **sun-dried tomatoes in oil**, drained. Whisk together eggs, black pepper, and remaining ¼ tsp. salt; whisk in ½ cup (2 oz.) shredded **Swiss cheese**. Pour egg mixture over potato mixture in skillet. Bake at 350°F until set, 9 to 10 minutes. Cut into wedges, and serve immediately.

KING RANCH BREAKFAST STRATA

Break out this bad boy for brunch, and let chicken, tortillas, and zesty pepper Jack cheese wow the crowd. For best results, assemble it the night before. In the morning, pour the remaining milk over the top, sprinkle with remaining cheese, and let it stand 45 minutes before baking.

ACTIVE 40 MIN. - TOTAL 10 HOURS, 45 MIN., INCLUDING CHILLING

SERVES 8

- ½ (16-oz.) French bread loaf, cubed (about 4 to 5 cups)
- 8 (6-inch) fajita-size corn tortillas, cut into strips
- 2 cups shredded cooked chicken
- 10 oz. pepper Jack cheese, shredded (2½ cups), divided
- 3 Tbsp. butter
- 1 (14.5-oz.) can diced tomatoes, drained
- ¾ cup chopped onion
- ½ cup chopped celery
- 1 (4-oz.) can diced green chiles, drained
- 2 garlic cloves, pressed
- 1 bell pepper, chopped
- 1 tsp. kosher salt
- ¾ tsp. ground cumin
- ½ tsp. dried oregano
- 10 large eggs
- 1 (10¾-oz.) can condensed cream of mushroom soup
- 2½ cups milk, divided

1. Toss together bread cubes and tortilla strips and place in a lightly greased 13- x 9-inch baking dish. Sprinkle with chicken and 2 cups cheese.

2. Melt butter in a medium saucepan over medium. Add tomatoes and next 8 ingredients; cook, stirring often, 5 to 8 minutes or until tender. Remove from heat and cool 10 minutes.

3. Whisk together eggs, soup, and 1½ cups milk in a large bowl. Pour over bread mixture. Sprinkle with cooled onion mixture. Cover with plastic wrap, and chill 8 to 24 hours.

4. Pour remaining 1 cup milk over strata; top with remaining ½ cup cheese. Let stand 45 minutes.

5. Preheat oven to 325°F. Bake strata until set, about 1 hour and 10 minutes. Serve immediately.

SAUSAGE, PEPPER, AND GRITS CASSEROLE

A breakfast take on shepherd's pie, this hearty dish has cheese grits as a crust to seal in the savory—and sausage-y—flavors.

ACTIVE 50 MIN. · TOTAL 1 HR., 25 MIN.
SERVES 6 TO 8

CHEESE GRITS CRUST
- 1 cup milk
- ½ cup uncooked quick-cooking grits
- 8 oz. sharp cheddar cheese, shredded (2 cups)
- 1 Tbsp. fresh thyme leaves
- ¾ tsp. kosher salt
- ½ tsp. freshly ground black pepper
- 2 large eggs, lightly beaten

SAUSAGE FILLING
- 1 (19-oz.) pkg. mild Italian sausage with casings
- 1 Tbsp. canola oil
- 2 large red bell peppers, sliced
- 1 medium-size red onion, sliced
- 3 garlic cloves, minced
- 1 (14.5-oz.) can diced tomatoes with garlic and onion, drained
- ¼ cup butter
- ¼ cup all-purpose flour
- 1½ cups chicken broth
- 1½ Tbsp. grape jelly
- 1 tsp. red wine vinegar
- ½ tsp. freshly ground black pepper
- ¼ tsp. kosher salt

1. Prepare Cheese Grits Crust: Bring milk and 1 cup water to a boil in a large saucepan over medium; add grits and cook, stirring often, 5 minutes or until thickened. Stir in cheese and next 3 ingredients; remove from heat.

2. Gradually stir about one-fourth of hot grits mixture into eggs; add egg mixture to remaining hot grits mixture, stirring until blended.

3. Prepare Sausage Filling: Preheat oven to 375°F. Cook sausage in hot oil in a Dutch oven over medium 7 to 8 minutes on each side or until browned. Remove sausage from Dutch oven, reserving 1 tablespoon drippings.

4. Cook bell pepper and onion in hot drippings over medium-high, stirring often, until tender, about 5 minutes. Add garlic and cook 2 minutes. Cut sausage into ½-inch slices. Stir together tomatoes, bell pepper mixture, and sausage in a large bowl.

5. Melt butter in Dutch oven over medium; whisk in flour and cook, whisking constantly, 4 to 5 minutes or until smooth and medium brown. Gradually whisk in broth. Bring to a boil, whisking constantly.

6. Reduce heat to medium-low; simmer, stirring occasionally, 5 minutes or until thickened. Stir in jelly and remaining ingredients. Stir into sausage mixture. Spoon into a lightly greased 11- x 7-inch baking dish. Gently spread Cheese Grits Crust over top.

7. Bake in preheated oven until lightly browned, 20 to 25 minutes. Let stand 10 minutes before serving.

- -

SMOKY BROWN SUGAR BACON

This bacon takes awhile to prepare, but it's more than worth it. Any remaining bacon after breakfast makes for primo sandwiches.

ACTIVE 10 MIN. · TOTAL 30 MIN.
MAKES 24 SLICES

- 3 cups firmly packed light brown sugar
- 24 slices applewood smoked bacon

1. Preheat oven to 425°F. Spread brown sugar onto a large plate; dredge the bacon in sugar, pressing to ensure plenty of sugar sticks to both sides of bacon. Line a rimmed baking sheet with foil, then set a large wire rack in baking sheet. Place bacon in a single layer on wire rack.

2. Bake in preheated oven, in batches if necessary, until bacon is crisp, 18 to 20 minutes. Remove bacon from rack to a serving platter or parchment paper to cool.

SAVORY HAM-AND-SWISS BREAKFAST PIE

Serve this savory breakfast pie with fresh sliced summer tomatoes or a simple salad.

ACTIVE 20 MIN. · TOTAL 1 HOUR, 40 MIN.
SERVES 8

- 1 cup whipping cream
- 2 garlic cloves, minced
- 2 Tbsp. butter
- 1 tsp. table salt
- ¼ tsp. freshly ground black pepper
- ⅔ cup uncooked quick-cooking grits
- 5 oz. Swiss cheese, shredded (1¼ cups), divided
- 8 large eggs, divided
- ½ lb. cooked ham, diced
- 4 scallions, chopped
- ½ cup milk
  Thinly sliced scallions, for garnish

1. Preheat oven to 350°F. Bring 1⅔ cups water and the first 5 ingredients to a boil in a medium saucepan; gradually whisk in grits. Cover, reduce heat, and simmer, whisking occasionally, 5 to 7 minutes. Add ½ cup cheese, stirring until cheese melts. Remove from heat and let stand 10 minutes. Lightly beat 2 eggs, then stir into grits mixture; pour into a lightly greased 10-inch deep pie plate.

2. Bake in preheated oven for 20 minutes; remove from oven. Increase oven temperature to 400°F.

3. Cook ham and scallions in a nonstick skillet over medium-high, stirring often, until scallions are tender, about 5 minutes. Layer ham mixture evenly over grits crust. Whisk together milk and remaining 6 eggs; pour over ham mixture. Sprinkle remaining ¾ cup cheese evenly over egg mixture.

4. Bake at 400°F for 35 minutes. Let stand 10 minutes, then cut into wedges.

"ANY-BERRY" MUFFINS WITH CORNMEAL STREUSEL

Raspberry, blueberry, blackberry—whip up these cornmeal muffins with any combination you have on hand. Small berries can be added to the batter whole. Chop larger ones to ensure fruit is evenly distributed throughout the muffins.

ACTIVE 15 MIN. · TOTAL 50 MIN.
MAKES 1 DOZEN

- 1½ tsp. baking powder
- ½ tsp. table salt
- 1⅔ cups all-purpose flour, divided
- ⅓ cup plus 2 Tbsp. plain yellow cornmeal, divided
- 1 cup granulated sugar, divided
- ½ cup unsalted butter, melted and divided
- ½ cup whole-milk buttermilk
- 1 large egg
- 1 large egg yolk
- 1½ tsp. vanilla extract
- 1⅓ cups fresh berries (such as strawberries, blueberries, raspberries, or blackberries)

1. Preheat oven to 425°F. Line a 12-cup muffin pan with 12 paper cupcake liners. Whisk together baking powder, salt, 1⅓ cups of the flour, and ⅓ cup of the cornmeal in a medium bowl; set aside.

2. Stir together ¼ cup of the sugar, 3 tablespoons of the melted butter, and remaining ⅓ cup flour and 2 tablespoons cornmeal in a separate bowl until crumbly; reserve for streusel topping.

3. Whisk together buttermilk, egg and yolk, vanilla, and remaining ¾ cup sugar in a medium bowl until well combined. Make a well in center of flour mixture. Slowly pour buttermilk mixture into flour mixture, stirring with a spatula just until combined (batter will be lumpy). Fold in berries and remaining 5 tablespoons melted butter.

4. Scoop batter into prepared muffin cups until each cup is three-fourths full (about 3 tablespoons each). Top each with about 1 tablespoon reserved streusel topping. Bake in preheated oven until a wooden pick inserted in centers comes out clean, about 18 minutes. Remove from oven; cool in pan 5 minutes. Cool muffins on a wire rack about 10 minutes.

CHOCOLATE-PEAR
MUFFINS

CHOCOLATE-PEAR MUFFINS

ACTIVE 20 MIN. - TOTAL 1 HOUR, 35 MIN.
MAKES 2 DOZEN

- 1 cup unsalted butter, softened
- 1 cup granulated sugar
- ½ cup packed light brown sugar
- 2 large eggs
- 1 tsp. vanilla extract
- 2¾ cups all-purpose flour
- ½ cup unsweetened cocoa
- 1½ Tbsp. baking powder
- ½ tsp. baking soda
- ½ tsp. kosher salt
- ¾ cup whole buttermilk
- 2 medium Anjou pears, peeled and chopped (about 2 cups)
- 1¼ cups semisweet chocolate chunks

1. Preheat oven to 350°F. Beat butter and sugars with an electric mixer on medium speed until light and fluffy, about 4 minutes. Add eggs, 1 at a time, beating on low just until combined after each addition. Add vanilla; beat just until smooth.

2. Whisk together flour, cocoa, baking powder, baking soda, and salt in a large bowl. Alternately add to butter mixture in thirds with buttermilk, beginning and ending with flour mixture, beating on low just until combined after each addition.

3. Fold in 1¾ cups chopped pears and 1 cup chocolate chunks. Divide batter among 2 (12-cup) muffin pans lined with paper baking cups. Sprinkle tops with remaining ¼ cup chocolate chunks and ¼ cup chopped pears.

4. Bake in preheated oven until a wooden pick inserted in center of muffins comes out with moist crumbs, 25 to 30 minutes. Cool in pans on wire racks 15 minutes. Remove muffins to wire racks to cool completely, about 30 minutes.

BLUEBERRY-STREUSEL MUFFINS

ACTIVE 15 MIN. - TOTAL 30 MIN.
MAKES 1 DOZEN

- ¼ cup slivered almonds
- ¼ cup firmly packed brown sugar
- 3 Tbsp. all-purpose flour, divided
- 2 Tbsp. butter or margarine
- ½ cup uncooked regular oats
- 2 cups all-purpose flour
- ½ cup granulated sugar
- 2 tsp. baking powder
- ¼ tsp. baking soda
- ¼ tsp. table salt
- 2 tsp. lemon zest
- ¾ cup buttermilk
- ¼ cup oil
- 1 large egg
- 1½ cups fresh or frozen blueberries

1. Preheat oven to 400°F. Pulse almonds 2 or 3 times in a blender or food processor until chopped. Add brown sugar and 1 tablespoon flour; process 5 seconds. Add butter; pulse 5 or 6 times, or until mixture is crumbly. Stir in oats; set aside.

2. Combine 2 cups flour and next 5 ingredients in a large bowl; make a well in center of flour mixture.

3. Whisk together buttermilk, oil, and egg; add to flour mixture, stirring just until moistened.

4. Toss blueberries with remaining 2 tablespoons flour; gently fold into batter. Spoon batter into greased muffin pans, filling two-thirds full; sprinkle batter with oat mixture.

5. Bake in preheated oven until golden brown, 15 to 20 minutes. Remove immediately from pans to cool on wire racks.

CRANBERRY-PECAN COFFEE CAKE

ACTIVE 25 MIN. - TOTAL 1 HOUR, 10 MIN., PLUS 1 HOUR, 15 MIN. COOLING

SERVES 12

- ¾ cup toasted chopped pecans
- ½ tsp. ground cinnamon
- 3¼ cups all-purpose flour, divided, plus more for pan
- 1¼ cups packed light brown sugar, divided
- 1 tsp. kosher salt, divided
- ⅓ cup unsalted butter, melted
  Vegetable shortening, for greasing pan
- 1 cup frozen cranberries
- 1 cup granulated sugar, divided
- ¾ cup unsalted butter, softened
- 2 large eggs
- 1 large egg yolk
- 2 tsp. vanilla extract
- 2 tsp. baking powder
- ¼ tsp. baking soda
- 1 (8-oz.) container sour cream

1. Stir together pecans, cinnamon, ¾ cup of the flour, ¾ cup of the brown sugar, and ½ teaspoon of the salt in a bowl. Stir in melted butter. Freeze until hardened, about 20 minutes.

2. Meanwhile, preheat oven to 350°F. Grease a 10-inch tube pan with shortening; dust pan with flour. Pulse cranberries and ¼ cup of the granulated sugar in a food processor until finely chopped, 6 to 8 times. Transfer to a bowl; chill until ready to use.

3. Beat softened butter, remaining ½ cup brown sugar, and remaining ¾ cup granulated sugar with a stand mixer fitted with a paddle attachment on medium-high speed until light and fluffy, 2 minutes. Add eggs and yolk, 1 at a time, beating well on low speed after each addition. Stir in vanilla.

4. Stir together baking powder, baking soda, remaining 2½ cups flour, and remaining ½ teaspoon salt in a bowl. Alternately add flour mixture to softened butter mixture with sour cream in 3 additions (beginning and ending with flour mixture), beating on low speed until just combined after each addition.

5. Stir ¾ cup of the batter into chilled cranberry mixture. Spoon half the remaining plain batter into prepared pan. Spoon cranberry-batter mixture over, smoothing into an even layer. Top with remaining plain batter. Crumble frozen pecan-cinnamon mixture into chunks. Sprinkle evenly over cake.

6. Bake in preheated oven until a wooden pick inserted in center comes out clean, 45 to 55 minutes, tenting with aluminum foil after 35 minutes, if needed, to prevent excessive browning. Cool in pan on a wire rack 15 minutes. Remove from pan. Cool completely on rack 1 hour.

- -

BLUEBERRY COFFEE CAKE

ACTIVE 20 MIN. - TOTAL 1 HOUR

SERVES 10

- 1 large egg
- ½ cup fat-free milk
- ½ cup plain fat-free yogurt
- 3 Tbsp. vegetable oil
- 2 cups all-purpose flour
- ½ cup granulated sugar
- 4 tsp. baking powder
- ½ tsp. table salt
- 1½ cups frozen blueberries
- 1 Tbsp. all-purpose flour
- 2 Tbsp. turbinado sugar
- 2 Tbsp. sliced almonds
- ¼ tsp. ground cinnamon

1. Preheat oven to 400°F. Whisk together first 4 ingredients in a large bowl.

2. Sift together 2 cups flour and next 3 ingredients in another bowl. Stir flour mixture into egg mixture just until dry ingredients are moistened.

3. Toss 1¼ cups blueberries in 1 tablespoon flour; fold into batter. Pour into a lightly greased 9-inch springform pan. Sprinkle with remaining ¼ cup blueberries.

4. Stir together turbinado sugar, sliced almonds, and cinnamon; sprinkle over batter.

5. Bake in preheated oven until a wooden pick inserted in center comes out clean, 25 to 30 minutes. Cool in pan on a wire rack 15 minutes; remove sides of pan.

BLUEBERRY
COFFEE CAKE

CINNAMON-
RAISIN ROLLS

CINNAMON-RAISIN ROLLS

These scrumptious breakfast rolls are made from a package of frozen biscuits. They're so easy to prepare, you don't even need a rolling pin.

ACTIVE 10 MIN. - TOTAL 1 HOUR, 35 MIN., INCLUDING STANDING
MAKES 12 ROLLS

- 1 (26.4-oz.) pkg. frozen biscuits
  All-purpose flour
- ¼ cup butter, softened
- ¾ cup firmly packed brown sugar
- 1 tsp. ground cinnamon
- 1 cup golden raisins or raisins
- ½ cup chopped pecans, toasted
- 1 cup powdered sugar
- 3 Tbsp. milk
- ½ tsp. vanilla extract

1. Arrange frozen biscuits, sides touching, in 3 rows of 4 biscuits on a lightly floured surface. Let stand 30 to 45 minutes or until biscuits are thawed but still cool to the touch.

2. Preheat oven to 375°F. Sprinkle thawed biscuits lightly with flour. Press biscuit edges together, and pat to form a 12- x 10-inch rectangle of dough; spread with softened butter. Stir together brown sugar and cinnamon; sprinkle over butter. Sprinkle raisins and pecans over brown sugar mixture.

3. Roll up dough, starting at one long end; cut into 12 (about 1-inch-thick) slices. Place rolls in a lightly greased 10-inch cast-iron skillet, 10-inch round pan, or 9-inch square pan.

4. Bake in preheated oven until center rolls are golden brown, 35 to 40 minutes. Cool slightly

5. Stir together powdered sugar, milk, and vanilla; drizzle over rolls.

Note: For individual rolls, prepare as directed, placing 1 slice in each of 12 lightly greased 3-inch muffin cups. Bake at 375°F for 20 to 25 minutes or until golden brown. Cool slightly, and remove from pan. Drizzle with glaze.

CARAMEL-PECAN ROLLS

ACTIVE 30 MIN. - TOTAL 2 HOURS, 30 MIN., INCLUDING RISING
MAKES 16 ROLLS

- 5 cups bread flour, divided
- ½ cup granulated sugar
- 1 tsp. table salt
- 2 pkg. active dry yeast
- 2 cups whole milk
- ¼ cup unsalted butter
- ½ cup cooked potato, mashed
- ¼ cup bread flour
- 1 Tbsp. unsalted butter, melted
- 2 cups firmly packed brown sugar, divided
- 1 tsp. ground cinnamon
- 1½ cups chopped pecans
- ¾ cup whipping cream

1. Combine 2 cups flour, ½ cup sugar, salt, and yeast; stir well. Combine milk, ¼ cup butter, and potato in a saucepan; heat until butter melts, stirring occasionally. Cool to 120°F to 130°F. Add liquid mixture to flour mixture; beat with an electric mixer on medium speed for 30 seconds. Beat an additional 2 minutes on medium speed. Add ¾ cup flour, beating 2 minutes on medium speed. Stir in enough of the remaining 2¼ cups flour to make a soft dough.

2. Sprinkle ¼ cup flour over work surface. Turn dough out; knead until smooth and elastic (about 8 minutes). Place in a greased bowl, turning to grease top. Cover and let rise in a warm place (85°F), free from drafts, 1 hour or until doubled in bulk.

3. Punch dough down; roll to a 24- x 6-inch rectangle. Brush with melted butter. Combine ½ cup brown sugar and the cinnamon; sprinkle over dough. Roll up, starting at long side. Pinch seam to seal (do not seal ends). Cut into 16 (1½-inch) slices.

4. Spoon remaining 1½ cups brown sugar into a greased 13- x 9-inch baking dish. Sprinkle pecans over sugar. Place slices on sugar. Pour whipping cream around rolls. Cover and let rise in a warm place, free from drafts, 30 minutes or until doubled in bulk.

5. Preheat oven to 375°F. Bake until golden, about 30 minutes. Let cool 2 minutes; remove from pan.

CINNAMON-PECAN ROLLS

Wake up the family with the aroma of sweet cinnamon rolls baked with buttery pecans then topped with frosting. Beginning bakers, take note: The easy dough rises in just 30 minutes.

ACTIVE 45 MIN. - TOTAL 1 HR., 20 MIN., INCLUDING RISING
MAKES 12 ROLLS

- 1 (16-oz.) pkg. hot roll mix
- ½ cup butter, softened
- 1 cup firmly packed light brown sugar
- 2 tsp. ground cinnamon
- 1 cup chopped toasted pecans
- 1 cup powdered sugar
- 2 Tbsp. milk
- 1 tsp. vanilla extract

1. Prepare hot roll dough according to package directions; let dough stand 5 minutes. Roll dough into a 15- x 10-inch rectangle; spread with softened butter. Stir together brown sugar and cinnamon; sprinkle over butter. Sprinkle pecans over brown sugar mixture. Roll up tightly, starting at one long end; cut into 12 slices. Place rolls, cut-sides down, in a lightly greased 12-inch cast-iron skillet or 13- x 9-inch pan. Cover loosely with plastic wrap and a cloth towel; let rise in a warm place (85°F), free from drafts, 30 minutes or until doubled in bulk.

2. Preheat oven to 375°F. Uncover rolls, and bake for 20 to 25 minutes or until center rolls are golden brown and done. Cool in pan on a wire rack 10 minutes. Stir together powdered sugar, milk, and vanilla; drizzle over rolls.

CARAMEL-NUT PULL-APART BREAD

ACTIVE 20 MIN. - TOTAL 50 MIN.
SERVES 12

- 1 cup plus 2 Tbsp. firmly packed brown sugar
- 1 cup chopped walnuts
- ¾ cup butter, melted
- 3 (10-oz.) cans refrigerated cinnamon-sugar biscuits

1. Preheat oven to 350°F. Combine brown sugar and walnuts in a small bowl. Stir in butter. Spoon half the sugar mixture in a greased tube pan.

2. Cut each biscuit in half (use kitchen scissors for quick cutting). Place half the biscuit halves on sugar mixture. Spoon remaining sugar mixture over biscuits in pan; top with remaining biscuits.

3. Bake in preheated oven until browned, 30 to 35 minutes. Immediately turn out onto a serving platter, spooning any sauce in pan over bread.

LEMON-POPPY SEED ZUCCHINI BREAD

Tender, fine-crumb texture and bright citrus flavor offer a refreshing change from traditionally spiced zucchini breads.

ACTIVE 20 MIN. - TOTAL 1 HOUR, 40 MIN.
MAKES 3 (5- X 3-INCH) LOAVES

- ½ cup butter, softened
- 1⅓ cups granulated sugar
- 3 large eggs
- 1½ cups all-purpose flour
- ½ tsp. table salt
- ⅛ tsp. baking soda
- ½ cup sour cream
- 1 cup shredded zucchini
- 1 Tbsp. lemon zest
- 2 tsp. poppy seeds

1. Preheat oven to 325°F. Beat butter with a heavy-duty stand mixer or electric mixer on medium speed until creamy. Gradually add sugar, beating until light and fluffy. Add eggs, 1 at a time, beating just until blended after each addition.

2. Stir together flour, salt, and baking soda. Alternately add to butter mixture with sour cream, beginning and ending with flour mixture. Beat on low speed just until blended after each addition. Stir in zucchini and remaining ingredients. Spoon batter into 3 greased and floured 5- x 3-inch disposable aluminum foil loaf pans (about 1⅓ cups batter per pan).

3. Bake in preheated oven until golden and a wooden pick inserted in center comes out clean, 40 to 45 minutes. Cool in pans on wire racks 10 minutes; remove from pans to wire racks, and cool completely, about 30 minutes.

CINNAMON-
PECAN ROLLS

BANANA BREAD

The best-tasting banana bread comes from using overripe bananas. Yogurt adds a nice tang to this recipe.

ACTIVE 15 MIN. - TOTAL 1 HOUR, 30 MIN., INCLUDING COOLING
MAKES 1 (9- X 5-INCH) LOAF

- 2 cups self-rising flour
- 1 cup granulated sugar
- ¼ cup toasted wheat germ
- ½ tsp. baking soda
- ½ cup butter, melted
- 3 very ripe bananas, mashed (1½ cups)
- 2 large eggs, lightly beaten
- ¼ cup strawberry yogurt or vanilla yogurt
- 1½ tsp. vanilla extract

1. Preheat oven to 350°F. Grease and flour a 9- x 5-inch loaf pan; set aside.

2. Combine first 4 ingredients in a large bowl; make a well in center of mixture. Stir together melted butter, and remaining ingredients. Add to dry ingredients; stir just until moistened. Pour batter into prepared pan.

3. Bake in preheated oven until a wooden pick inserted in center comes out clean, 1 hour and 5 minutes. Cover loosely with aluminum foil after 40 minutes if loaf begins to brown too quickly.

4. Cool in pan on wire rack 10 minutes; remove from pan, and cool completely on wire rack.

Note: For muffins, spoon batter into lightly greased or paper-lined muffin cups, filling each cup three-fourths full. Bake at 350°F for 19 to 21 minutes or until lightly browned. Remove from pans immediately. Let cool on wire racks.

Banana-Nut Bread: Add 1 cup chopped, toasted pecans to batter before baking.

Chocolate Chip-Banana Bread: Add 1 cup semisweet chocolate morsels to batter before baking.

GLUTEN-FREE BANANA BREAD

For best results, use a light-color pan. Or turn your dark pan into a shiny one by wrapping the outside of it with heavy-duty aluminum foil.

ACTIVE 15 MIN. - TOTAL 2 HOURS, 35 MIN., INCLUDING COOLING
MAKES 1 (9- X 5-INCH) LOAF

- 1 cup boiling water
- ½ cup chopped dates
- 4 large eggs
- 2 cups mashed, very ripe bananas (about 4)
- ¾ cup granulated sugar
- ½ cup unsweetened applesauce
- 1 tsp. vanilla extract
- 1½ cups brown rice flour
- ½ cup sorghum flour
- 1 tsp. baking soda
- ½ tsp. table salt
- ¼ tsp. ground nutmeg
- ⅓ cup butter, melted
- ½ cup chopped walnuts

1. Preheat oven to 350°F. Pour 1 cup boiling water over dates in a small bowl. Let stand 10 minutes. Drain and pat dry.

2. Lightly beat eggs with a whisk in a large bowl. Whisk in bananas and next 3 ingredients until blended.

3. Stir together brown rice flour and next 4 ingredients in a small bowl. Gently stir flour mixture into egg mixture just until blended. Gently stir in melted butter, walnuts, and dates. Spoon mixture into a lightly greased 9- x 5-inch loaf pan.

4. Bake in preheated oven until a wooden pick inserted in center comes out clean, 1 hour to 1 hour and 10 minutes. Cool in pan on a wire rack 10 minutes. Remove from pan to wire rack; cool completely (about 1 hour).

GLUTEN-FREE
BANANA BREAD

HERB-ROASTED
PORK LOIN, PAGE 93

MAIN DISHES

PRIME RIB WITH HERBES DE PROVENCE CRUST AND RED WINE SAUCE

PRIME RIB WITH HERBES DE PROVENCE CRUST AND RED WINE SAUCE

Garnish the sliced roast with a few sprigs of herbs (rosemary, lavender, thyme) inspired by the herbes de Provence used in the aromatic rub.

ACTIVE 30 MIN. · TOTAL 4 HOURS, 15 MIN., PLUS 12 HOURS CHILLING

SERVES 10

- 1 (8-lb.) 5-rib standing rib roast, chine bone removed
- 2 Tbsp. extra-virgin olive oil
- 3 Tbsp. herbes de Provence
- 4½ tsp. kosher salt, divided
- 2¼ tsp. black pepper, divided
- 2 Tbsp. butter
- ½ cup minced shallots (from 2 medium shallots)
- 1 cup (8 oz.) dry red wine
- 2 cups lower-sodium beef broth
- 2 Tbsp. Dijon mustard
  Fresh herb sprigs (such as rosemary, thyme, and lavender), for garnish

1. Rub rib roast evenly with oil. Stir together herbes de Provence, 4 teaspoons of the salt, and 2 teaspoons of the pepper in a small bowl. Spread mixture evenly over roast. Chill, uncovered, at least 12 hours or up to 24 hours.

2. Let roast stand at room temperature 1 hour. Meanwhile, preheat oven to 450°F with rack in lowest position.

3. Lightly coat a wire rack with cooking spray; set inside a roasting pan. Place roast, bone side down, on prepared rack. Roast in preheated oven on lowest oven rack 45 minutes. Reduce oven temperature to 350°F (do not remove roast from oven). Continue roasting until a thermometer inserted in thickest portion of roast registers 120°F to 130°F for medium-rare (about 1 hour, 30 minutes) or 130°F to 135°F for medium (about 1 hour, 45 minutes). Remove from oven; let rest 30 minutes. Transfer roast to a serving platter, and cover with aluminum foil to keep warm. Discard drippings from pan, reserving any browned bits in pan.

4. Place roasting pan on stove top over one burner. Add butter to pan; melt butter over medium-high, stirring occasionally and moving pan as needed to prevent hot spots. Add shallots; cook, stirring occasionally, until tender, 2 to 3 minutes. Stir in wine; cook, stirring occasionally, until liquid is mostly reduced, about 3 minutes. Stir in broth; cook, stirring constantly, until thickened, 3 to 4 minutes. Stir in mustard; cook, stirring constantly, until sauce thickens and reduces to 1½ cups, about 5 minutes. Stir in remaining ½ teaspoon salt and ¼ teaspoon pepper. Pour sauce into a serving bowl or gravy boat. Garnish roast with herb sprigs and serve with sauce.

- -

HERB-AND-POTATO-CHIP-CRUSTED BEEF TENDERLOIN

ACTIVE 40 MIN. · TOTAL 2 HOURS, 20 MIN.

SERVES 6 TO 8

- 1 (4- to 5-lb.) beef tenderloin, trimmed
- 3 tsp. kosher salt, divided
- ¾ cup panko (Japanese-style breadcrumbs)
- 3 garlic cloves, minced
- 2 tsp. coarsely ground black pepper, divided
- 3 Tbsp. olive oil, divided
- 1¼ cups crushed plain kettle-cooked potato chips
- ¼ cup finely chopped fresh parsley
- 1 Tbsp. finely chopped fresh thyme
- 1 bay leaf, crushed
- 1 egg white, lightly beaten
- 1 Tbsp. Dijon mustard
  Fresh sage, garnish (optional)

1. Preheat oven to 400°F. Sprinkle tenderloin with 2 teaspoons salt. Let stand 30 to 45 minutes.

2. Meanwhile, cook panko, garlic, 1 teaspoon black pepper, and remaining 1 teaspoon salt in 1 tablespoon hot oil in a skillet over medium, until deep golden brown, 2 to 3 minutes. Let cool completely (about 10 minutes). Stir in potato chips and next 4 ingredients.

3. Pat tenderloin dry with paper towels, then sprinkle with remaining 1 teaspoon pepper. Brown beef in remaining 2 tablespoons hot oil in a roasting pan over medium-high until browned on all sides (2 to 3 minutes per side). Transfer tenderloin to a wire rack in an aluminum foil-lined jelly-roll pan. Let stand 10 minutes.

4. Spread mustard over tenderloin. Press panko mixture onto top and sides.

5. Bake 40 to 45 minutes or until coating is crisp and a meat thermometer inserted into thickest portion registers 130°F (rare). Let stand 10 minutes. Garnish with sage, if desired.

Note: For medium-rare, cook tenderloin to 135°F; for medium, cook to 150°F.

BEEF BURGUNDY

ACTIVE 10 MIN. - TOTAL 10 HOURS, 10 MIN.
SERVES 8

- ¼ cup all-purpose flour
- ½ tsp. table salt
- ½ tsp. black pepper
- 1 tsp. minced garlic (about 2 cloves)
- 2 lb. lean, boneless round steak, cut into 1½-inch pieces
- ¾ cup dry red wine
- ¾ cup canned no-salt-added beef broth
- 1 Tbsp. tomato paste
- 1 Tbsp. chopped fresh thyme or 1 tsp. dried thyme
- 8 oz. baby carrots (about 40 small)
- 1 large onion, cut into eighths
- 1 bay leaf
- 1 (8-oz.) pkg. presliced fresh mushrooms
- ½ (12-oz.) pkg. yolk-free medium egg noodles

1. Combine first 4 ingredients in a large heavy-duty, zip-top plastic bag; add beef and seal bag. Shake to coat beef.

2. Coat a large nonstick skillet with cooking spray; place over medium-high until hot. Add beef and cook 10 minutes, or until browned on all sides, stirring often.

3. Transfer beef to a 4-quart electric slow cooker coated with cooking spray. Add wine and next 6 ingredients; toss well. Cover and cook 6 hours on HIGH setting or 8 to 10 hours on LOW setting, until meat is tender and sauce thickens. Add mushrooms 1 hour before cooking is completed. Remove and discard bay leaf. Stir thoroughly.

4. Ten minutes before sauce is done, cook noodles according to package directions, omitting salt and fat; drain. Place ½ cup noodles on each of 8 individual serving plates. Spoon beef mixture evenly over hot noodles.

COLA POT ROAST

Instead of broth, this roast cooks in cola, which adds a slightly sweet flavor note to the meat and vegetables. Grind additional fresh pepper over the roast before serving, if desired.

ACTIVE 30 MIN. - TOTAL 12 HOURS, 40 MIN., INCLUDING CHILLING
SERVES 6 TO 8

- 1 (12-oz.) can cola soft drink
- 1 medium onion, chopped
- 8 garlic cloves, minced
- 1 lemon, thinly sliced
- 1 cup soy sauce
- 3 Tbsp. vegetable oil, divided
- 1 (3- to 4-lb.) boneless chuck roast, trimmed
- 1 tsp. fresh coarsely ground pepper
- 8 large carrots (about 1½ lb.), cut into 1½-inch chunks
- 7 Yukon gold potatoes (about 2¼ lb.), cut into quarters
- 2 large onions, cut into eighths
- 2 Tbsp. cornstarch
- ½ cup cold water
  Fresh oregano or thyme sprigs, for garnish

1. Combine first 5 ingredients and 2 tablespoons oil in a large zip-top plastic freezer bag. Add roast, turning to coat. Seal and chill 8 to 24 hours. Remove roast from marinade; discard lemon slices, and reserve marinade. Sprinkle roast with pepper.

2. Preheat oven to 300°F. Brown roast 4 minutes on each side in remaining 1 tablespoon hot oil in a large skillet over medium-high. Remove roast from skillet, and transfer to a large roasting pan. Add reserved marinade to skillet, stirring to loosen particles from bottom. Bring to a boil. Remove from heat.

3. Arrange carrots, potatoes, and onions around roast in pan; pour hot marinade over roast and vegetables. Roast in preheated oven until meat and vegetables are tender, about 4 hours. Transfer roast and vegetables to a serving platter. Skim fat from juices in roasting pan.

4. Whisk together cornstarch and ½ cup cold water in a small bowl until smooth. Whisk cornstarch mixture into juices in pan; cook over medium-high 3 minutes or until thickened, whisking to loosen particles. Serve gravy with roast and vegetables. Garnish, if desired.

COLA POT ROAST

CAST-IRON
COWBOY STEAK

CAST-IRON COWBOY STEAK

This is the best way to cook a thick, juicy bone-in steak restaurant-style without smoking up the house. Use your grill to heat the cast-iron skillet; the skillet surface area promotes a more assertive flavor and better sear than grill grates, yielding a steak with the proper steakhouse crust.

ACTIVE 20 MIN. - TOTAL 1 HOUR, INCLUDING HEATING AND STANDING

SERVES 2 TO 4

Kosher salt and freshly ground black pepper
1 (1½- to 2-lb.) bone-in rib-eye or porterhouse steak (about 2 inches thick)
1 Tbsp. vegetable oil
3 Tbsp. butter
8 fresh herb sprigs (such as thyme, rosemary, and oregano)
3 garlic cloves, peeled and smashed

1. Preheat grill to high (400°F to 450°F). Heat a 12-inch cast-iron skillet with lid, grill lid closed, 15 minutes. Sprinkle salt and pepper generously over steak.

2. Add oil to skillet (oil should smoke.) Using tongs, place steak in skillet. Place skillet on the grill; grill lid open, until dark brown and crusty, about 10 minutes. Turn steak on fatty edge in skillet, holding upright with tongs, and cook 2 minutes. Place steak, uncooked side down, in skillet. Cook on grill, grill lid closed, 8 to 10 minutes or to desired doneness, 120°F to 125°F for medium-rare. (Temperature will rise as steak rests.)

3. Add butter, herbs, and garlic to one side of skillet; heat 2 to 3 minutes or until butter foams. Tilt skillet slightly, and spoon butter mixture over steak 20 times (being careful not to splatter).

4. Transfer steak, herbs, and garlic to a platter; let stand 5 to 10 minutes. Slice steak against the grain.

BEEF STROGANOFF

A universal homey entrée, this stroganoff turns out a big yield with plenty of gravy for sopping.

ACTIVE 15 MIN. - TOTAL 55 MIN.

SERVES 6 TO 8

1 cup all-purpose flour
1½ tsp. table salt
½ tsp. black pepper
2 lb. sirloin steak, cut into strips
½ cup butter, melted
2 Tbsp. butter
1 (8-oz.) pkg. sliced fresh mushrooms
1 small onion, chopped
2 garlic cloves, minced
½ cup dry sherry or dry white wine
3 cups beef broth
2 Tbsp. tomato paste
1 Tbsp. Dijon mustard
1 Tbsp. Worcestershire sauce
1 (16-oz.) container sour cream
Hot cooked egg noodles or mashed potatoes
Chopped fresh flat-leaf parsley

1. Combine first 3 ingredients in a large zip-top plastic freezer bag; add steak. Seal bag, and shake until meat is coated.

2. Brown meat in ½ cup melted butter in a large skillet over medium-high. Remove meat from pan; cover and keep warm. Add 2 tablespoons butter to hot pan; sauté mushrooms, onion, and garlic until browned and tender. Remove from pan; keep warm.

3. Add sherry or wine to pan; cook over high, stirring to loosen particles from bottom of pan. Add beef broth and next 3 ingredients, stirring until smooth. Return meat and sautéed mushroom mixture to pan; cook over medium until thickened, stirring frequently. Stir in sour cream; cook just until thoroughly heated. Serve over egg noodles or mashed potatoes; sprinkle with parsley.

GRILLED ASIAN FLANK STEAK

ACTIVE 10 MIN. - TOTAL 4 HOURS, 24 MIN., INCLUDING CHILLING
SERVES 4 TO 6

- ¼ cup lite soy sauce
- 3 Tbsp. lite teriyaki sauce
- 3 Tbsp. rice wine vinegar
- 1 Tbsp. Asian garlic-chili sauce
- 1 Tbsp. minced fresh ginger
- 2 scallions, chopped
- 1½ lb. beef flank steak

1. Combine the first 6 4 ingredients in a large heavy-duty zip-top bag or shallow dish. Add steak and turn to coat. Seal or cover, and chill 4 hours, turning occasionally.

2. Remove steak from marinade discard marinade.

3. Grill flank steak, grill lid closed, over medium-high (350°F to 400°F) 5 to 7 minutes on each side or to desired doneness. Let stand 10 minutes before slicing. Cut diagonally across the grain into thin strips.

- -

PAN-SEARED STEAKS WITH ROASTED RED PEPPER SAUCE

ACTIVE 5 MIN. - TOTAL 15 MIN.
SERVES 4

- 1 tsp. roasted garlic-pepper seasoning or ½ tsp. black pepper and ½ tsp. garlic powder
- ½ tsp. table salt, divided
- 4 (4-oz.) lean boneless beef tenderloin steaks (1 inch thick)
- 1 (7-oz.) jar roasted red peppers in water, drained

1. Combine garlic-pepper seasoning and ¼ teaspoon salt. Rub both sides of steaks with pepper mixture.

2. Place a large nonstick skillet coated with cooking spray over medium-high until hot. Add steaks; cook 2 to 3 minutes on each side or until done.

3. While steaks cook, place peppers and remaining ¼ teaspoon salt in container of electric blender. Cover and blend until smooth. Serve steaks with roasted red pepper sauce.

SKILLET STEAK AND WILTED KALE

Sprinkle this restaurant-style steak salad with crumbled blue cheese for even more flavor.

ACTIVE 20 MIN. - TOTAL 20 MIN.
SERVES 4

- 1 bunch kale, stems removed
- 2 (¾-inch-thick) beef strip steaks
- 1 tsp. kosher salt
- ½ tsp. ground black pepper
- 1 Tbsp. olive oil
- 2 Tbsp. butter
- 1 large sweet onion, such as Vidalia, thinly sliced
- 1 Tbsp. red wine vinegar
- 1 tsp. honey

1. Preheat oven to 425°F. Chop kale. Sprinkle steaks with salt and pepper. Cook steaks in hot oil in a large skillet over medium-high 3 minutes on each side. Place on a wire rack in a jelly-roll pan; bake 6 minutes.

2. Meanwhile, wipe skillet clean, then melt butter over medium-high. Add onion and cook, stirring often, until tender, about 5 minutes.

3. Remove steaks from oven; loosely cover with foil to keep warm. Add kale to onion mixture, and cook, stirring constantly, 5 minutes or until kale is wilted. Stir in vinegar and honey; season with salt and pepper. Serve with sliced steak.

SKILLET STEAK
AND WILTED KALE

TYLER'S COUNTRY-
FRIED STEAK WITH
UNCLE ELLIS'S
CORNMEAL GRAVY

TYLER'S COUNTRY-FRIED STEAK WITH UNCLE ELLIS'S CORNMEAL GRAVY

ACTIVE 15 MIN. - TOTAL 1 HOUR, INCLUDING GRAVY
SERVES 6

- 6 (6-oz.) top sirloin steaks, cubed
- 1 tsp. kosher salt
- ¼ tsp. black pepper
- 3 cups all-purpose flour
- 1½ cups finely crushed round buttery crackers
- 6 Tbsp. chopped fresh marjoram
- 3 large eggs
- 2 cups buttermilk
- Vegetable oil
- Uncle Ellis's Cornmeal Gravy (recipe follows)

1. Sprinkle cubed steaks with salt and pepper. Combine flour, crushed crackers, and marjoram in a shallow dish. Whisk eggs and buttermilk in a bowl.

2. Dip steaks in egg mixture; dredge in cracker mixture. Repeat procedure.

3. Pour oil to depth of 1½ inches in a large heavy skillet. Heat to 325°F. Fry steaks, in batches, 5 to 7 minutes on each side or until golden. Drain on a wire rack set in a jelly-roll pan. Serve with Uncle Ellis's Cornmeal Gravy.

UNCLE ELLIS'S CORNMEAL GRAVY

ACTIVE 20 MIN.- TOTAL 20 MIN.
MAKES ABOUT 1²/₃ CUPS

- ½ cup plain red or white cornmeal
- ½ tsp. table salt
- ½ tsp. black pepper
- 1 tsp. bacon drippings
- 1 cup buttermilk
- 1 cup hot water

Cook cornmeal in a heavy skillet over medium-high, stirring constantly, 4 to 5 minutes or until golden brown. Stir in salt, pepper, and bacon drippings. Stir together buttermilk and the hot water; gradually whisk into cornmeal mixture. Bring to a boil, whisking constantly. Reduce heat. Cook, whisking constantly, until thickened. Whisk in additional buttermilk for desired consistency.

GARLIC-HERB STEAKS

ACTIVE 5 MIN. - TOTAL 1 HOUR, 15 MIN., INCLUDING CHILLING
SERVES 4

- 4 (4-oz.) beef tenderloin steaks
- ¼ tsp. table salt
- ¼ tsp. freshly ground black pepper
- ¼ cup minced garlic
- 2 Tbsp. chopped fresh flat-leaf parsley
- 1 Tbsp. minced fresh rosemary

1. Sprinkle steaks with salt and pepper; coat with garlic, parsley, and rosemary. Chill 1 hour.

2. Preheat oven to 350°F. Cook steaks in an ovenproof nonstick skillet coated with cooking spray over medium-high for 4 minutes on each side.

3. Transfer skillet to oven. Bake in preheated oven to desired doneness, about 10 minutes for medium rare.

- -

PEPPERED FILET MIGNON WITH HORSERADISH CREAM

ACTIVE 5 MIN. - TOTAL 15 MIN.
SERVES 4

- ½ cup mayonnaise
- 2 Tbsp. half-and-half
- 2 Tbsp. prepared horseradish
- 2 Tbsp. black pepper
- ½ tsp. table salt
- 4 (4-oz.) beef tenderloin steaks, trimmed (about ½ inch thick)

1. Preheat broiler.

2. Combine first 3 ingredients in a small bowl; set aside.

3. Combine pepper and salt in a shallow dish. Dredge steaks in pepper mixture.

4. Place steaks on a broiler pan coated with cooking spray; broil 6 minutes. Turn steaks over. Broil 5 minutes or until desired doneness. Serve immediately with horseradish cream.

CHICKEN-FRIED STEAK

Authentic chicken-fried steak is crunchy outside, tender inside, and served with plenty of cream gravy made from pan drippings. Bring it on!

ACTIVE 20 MIN. - TOTAL 50 MIN.
SERVES 6

2¼ tsp. table salt, divided
1¾ tsp. black pepper, divided
6 (4-oz.) cube steaks
38 saltine crackers (1 sleeve), crushed
1¼ cups all-purpose flour, divided
½ tsp. baking powder
½ tsp. cayenne pepper
4¾ cups milk, divided
2 large eggs
3½ cups peanut oil
Mashed potatoes

1. Sprinkle ¼ teaspoon each salt and black pepper over steaks. Set aside.

2. Combine cracker crumbs, 1 cup flour, the baking powder, 1 teaspoon salt, ½ teaspoon black pepper, and cayenne pepper in a shallow dish.

3. Whisk together ¾ cup milk and eggs in another shallow dish. Dredge steaks in cracker crumb mixture; dip in milk mixture, and dredge in cracker mixture again.

4. Preheat oven to 225°F. Pour oil into a 12-inch skillet; heat to 360°F. (Do not use a nonstick skillet.) Fry steaks, in batches, 10 minutes. Turn and fry each batch 4 to 5 minutes more or until golden brown. Remove to a wire rack on a jelly-roll pan. Keep steaks warm in preheated oven. Carefully drain hot oil, reserving cooked bits and 1 tablespoon drippings in skillet.

5. Whisk together remaining ¼ cup flour, 1 teaspoon salt, 1 teaspoon black pepper, and 4 cups milk. Pour mixture into reserved drippings in skillet; cook over medium-high, whisking constantly, until thickened, 10 to 12 minutes. Serve gravy with steaks and mashed potatoes.

GRILLED STEAK WITH BLISTERED BEANS AND PEPPERS

ACTIVE 25 MIN. - TOTAL 40 MIN.
SERVES 4

4 (6-oz.) boneless beef strip steaks (1 inch thick), trimmed
3 large garlic cloves, minced (about 1 Tbsp.)
1½ tsp. kosher salt, divided
¾ tsp. black pepper, divided
2 Tbsp. canola oil, divided
3 Tbsp. salted butter
1½ Tbsp. chopped fresh flat-leaf parsley
2 tsp. chopped fresh thyme
6 oz. fresh green beans, trimmed and halved on an angle (1½ cups)
5 oz. sweet mini peppers, halved lengthwise (1½ cups)
¾ cup sliced red onion (from 1 onion)
2 Tbsp. fresh lemon juice (from 1 lemon)

1. Pat steaks dry with a paper towel. Rub garlic evenly over steaks; sprinkle with 1 teaspoon salt and ½ teaspoon black pepper. Let stand at room temperature 15 minutes.

2. Place a 12-inch cast-iron skillet on grill grates, and preheat grill to high (450°F to 500°F). Add 1 tablespoon oil to skillet; immediately add steaks to skillet. Cook until well browned, 4 to 5 minutes. Add butter to skillet, and flip steaks. Cook, tilting pan and constantly spooning butter mixture over steaks, until a thermometer inserted in thickest portion registers 125°F, 1 to 2 minutes. Remove from heat. Transfer to a cutting board, and let rest 10 minutes. Transfer skillet drippings to a small bowl; stir in parsley and thyme, and set aside. Slice steak; transfer to a serving platter.

3. Wipe skillet clean; return to grill over high. Add remaining 1 tablespoon oil to skillet. Add green beans and peppers; cook, stirring occasionally, until charred, about 4 minutes. Stir in onion and lemon juice. Cover and cook until vegetables are tender, about 2 minutes. Sprinkle with remaining ½ teaspoon salt and ¼ teaspoon black pepper. Arrange vegetables and steak on serving platter; spoon parsley-thyme mixture over vegetables and steak.

GRILLED STEAK WITH BLISTERED
BEANS AND PEPPERS

GONZALES MEAT LOAF

Cilantro, brown sugar, and a heavy shake of hot sauce season this meat loaf well. As expected, leftovers make a hearty sandwich.

ACTIVE 15 MIN. - TOTAL 1 HOUR, 35 MIN.
SERVES 6 TO 8

- 2 lb. ground sirloin
- 3 large eggs, lightly beaten
- 1 cup fine, dry breadcrumbs
- 4 garlic cloves, minced
- 1 medium red onion, chopped
- 2 plum tomatoes, seeded and chopped
- 6 oz. Monterey Jack cheese, shredded (1½ cups)
- ¼ to ½ cup firmly packed brown sugar
- ½ cup chopped fresh cilantro
- ¼ cup Worcestershire sauce
- 2 Tbsp. hot sauce
- 2 tsp. table salt
- 1 tsp. black pepper

1. Preheat oven to 350°F. Combine all ingredients. Shape into a free-form 9- x 5-inch loaf, and place on a lightly greased rack in a broiler pan.

2. Bake in preheated oven for 45 minutes. Increase oven temperature to 425°F. Bake until a thermometer inserted into center registers 160°F, 15 to 25 minutes more. Let meat loaf stand 5 minutes before serving.

SOUTHWESTERN MEAT LOAF

ACTIVE 20 MIN. - TOTAL 1 HOUR, 40 MIN.
SERVES 6

- ½ cup finely crushed whole-grain tortilla chips
- 1 tsp. ground cumin
- ½ tsp. garlic powder
- ¼ tsp. freshly ground black pepper
- 1 cup plus 1 Tbsp. bottled chipotle salsa, divided
- 1 tsp. kosher salt, divided
- 1¾ lb. ground beef
- 1½ cups (6 oz.) shredded sharp cheddar cheese
- 2 large eggs
- 2 Tbsp. ketchup
- 1 tsp. fresh lime juice

1. Preheat oven to 350°F. Stir together tortilla chips, ground cumin, garlic powder, black pepper, 1 cup chipotle salsa, and ¾ teaspoon kosher salt in a large bowl.

2. Gently stir in ground beef , cheese, and eggs. Line a broiler pan with aluminum foil; coat with cooking spray. Shape mixture into a 9- x 5-inch loaf, and place loaf on a lightly greased rack in broiler pan.

3. Bake in preheated oven for 50 minutes. Stir together ketchup, lime juice, and remaining 1 tablespoon salsa and ¼ teaspoon salt in a small bowl. Brush ketchup mixture over top of meat loaf; bake 15 to 20 minutes more or until a meat thermometer inserted into center registers 160°F. Let stand 5 minutes before serving.

ONE-SKILLET SPAGHETTI

ACTIVE 15 MIN. - TOTAL 1 HOUR, 15 MIN.
SERVES 6

- 1 lb. ground beef
- 1 large onion, chopped
- 2 garlic cloves, minced
- 1 (8-oz.) can tomato sauce
- 1 (6-oz.) can tomato paste
- 3 cups tomato juice
- 1 cup water
- 1 tsp. table salt
- 1 tsp. sugar
- 2 to 3 tsp. chili powder
- 1 tsp. dried oregano
  Dash of black pepper
- 1 (7-oz.) pkg. spaghetti, uncooked
  Grated Parmesan cheese
  Fresh Italian parsley sprigs, for garnish

1. Cook first 3 ingredients in a Dutch oven, stirring until beef crumbles and is no longer pink; drain well. Stir the tomato sauce and next 8 ingredients into beef mixture in pan; bring to a boil. Cover, reduce heat, and simmer, stirring often, 30 minutes.

2. Add pasta; cover and simmer, stirring often, 20 minutes or until pasta is tender. Serve with cheese; garnish, if desired.

- -

MEXICAN LASAGNA

ACTIVE 30 MIN. - TOTAL 1 HOUR, 10 MIN.
SERVES 8 TO 10

- 1 lb. ground beef
- 1 (16-oz.) can whole kernel corn, drained
- 1 (15-oz.) can tomato sauce
- 1 cup picante sauce
- 1 Tbsp. chili powder
- 1½ tsp. ground cumin
- 1 (24-oz.) container low-fat small-curd cottage cheese
- 2 large eggs
- ¼ cup grated Parmesan cheese
- 1 tsp. dried oregano
- ½ tsp. garlic salt
- 12 (5-inch) corn tortillas
- 1 cup (4 oz.) shredded cheddar cheese

1. Preheat oven to 375°F. Brown ground beef in a large skillet over medium heat, stirring until it crumbles and is no longer pink; drain. Stir in corn and next 4 ingredients; bring to a boil. Reduce heat, and simmer, stirring often, 5 minutes. Remove from heat, and set aside.

2. Stir together cottage cheese and next 4 ingredients.

3. Arrange 6 tortillas on bottom and 1½ inches up sides of a lightly greased 13- x 9-inch baking dish. Spoon half the meat mixture on tortillas; top with cottage cheese mixture. Arrange remaining tortillas on cheese mixture; top with remaining meat mixture.

4. Bake in preheated oven until thoroughly heated, about 30 minutes. Remove from oven, and sprinkle with cheddar cheese. Let stand 10 minutes before serving.

- -

EASY SKILLET TACOS

ACTIVE 10 MIN. - TOTAL 40 MIN.
SERVES 4 TO 6

- 1 lb. ground beef
- 1 small onion, chopped
- 1 tsp. olive oil
- 1 Tbsp. chili powder
- 1½ tsp. ground cumin
- 1 tsp. table salt
- 1 (15-oz.) can pinto beans, rinsed and drained
- 1 (8-oz.) can tomato sauce
- ½ cup salsa
- 6 oz. cheddar cheese, shredded (1½ cups)
- 1 Tbsp. chopped fresh cilantro
  Taco shells or flour tortillas, warmed
  Fresh salsa (or pico de gallo), avocado, sliced jalapeño peppers, for topping

1. Cook ground beef in a large skillet over medium-high, stirring until beef crumbles and is no longer pink. Drain well. Remove beef; wipe skillet with a paper towel.

2. Cook onion in hot oil in same skillet over medium-high until softened, about 5 minutes. Add chili powder, cumin, salt, and beef. Cook 5 to 7 minutes, stirring occasionally. Stir in beans, tomato sauce, ¾ cup water, and the salsa. Mash pinto beans in skillet with a fork, leaving some beans whole. Bring to a boil; reduce heat and simmer, uncovered, 8 to 10 minutes or until liquid is reduced.

3. Top evenly with cheese and cilantro. Cover, turn off heat, and let stand 5 minutes or until cheese melts. Serve with taco shells or tortillas and desired toppings.

EASY SKILLET
TACOS

SWISS BURGERS IN TOMATO GRAVY WITH ROASTED POTATOES

SWISS BURGERS IN TOMATO GRAVY WITH ROASTED POTATOES

Simmer ground sirloin patties in a rich tomato gravy to create luscious, fork-tender burgers. Serve with steamed green beans.

ACTIVE 25 MIN. - TOTAL 45 MIN.
SERVES 6

- 8 red potatoes, cut into 4 wedges each
- 2 Tbsp. olive oil
- 1½ tsp. kosher salt, divided
- 1½ lb. ground sirloin
- 1 large egg, lightly beaten
- ½ tsp. black pepper
- 1 medium white onion, sliced
- 2 (15-oz.) cans fire-roasted diced tomatoes
- 1 chicken bouillon cube
- 6 (1-oz.) Swiss cheese slices
  Chopped fresh basil (optional)

1. Preheat oven to 425°F. Toss together potatoes, oil, and ½ teaspoon salt in a bowl. Spread potatoes in a single layer in a rimmed baking pan, and bake 35 to 40 minutes or until golden and tender.

2. Meanwhile, stir together sirloin, egg, pepper, and remaining 1 teaspoon salt in a large bowl. Shape into 6 patties.

3. Cook patties in a large skillet over medium-high 4 to 5 minutes on each side or until browned. Remove patties, reserving drippings. Sauté onion in hot drippings 2 minutes. Add tomatoes, bouillon, and ½ cup water. Cook, stirring occasionally, 3 to 4 minutes or until bubbly.

4. Return patties to skillet; spoon tomato mixture over patties. Cover and cook 15 minutes; uncover and cook 5 minutes or until no longer pink in center. Place 1 cheese slice on each patty. Cover and cook 3 minutes. Sprinkle with basil, if desired. Serve with potatoes.

EASY SLOPPY JOES

ACTIVE 20 MIN. - TOTAL 20 MIN.
SERVES 8

- 1½ lb. ground round
- 1 cup chopped onion
- ½ cup chopped green bell pepper
- 1 cup ketchup
- 1 (8-oz.) can no-salt-added tomato sauce
- 1½ Tbsp. low-sodium Worcestershire sauce
- 1½ Tbsp. lemon juice
- 1½ Tbsp. prepared mustard
- 2 teaspoons chili powder
- ¼ tsp. garlic powder
- ¼ tsp. black pepper
- 8 hamburger buns

1. Cook meat, onion, and green bell pepper in a large nonstick skillet over medium-high until meat is browned, stirring until it crumbles. Drain, if necessary.

2. Add ketchup and next 7 ingredients; stir well. Cook, uncovered, over medium 10 minutes or until thoroughly heated and slightly thickened, stirring frequently.

3. Spoon sloppy joes evenly onto bottom halves of buns. Top with remaining bun halves.

FIESTA BURGERS

ACTIVE 15 MIN. - TOTAL 50 MIN., INCLUDING CHILLING
SERVES 8

- 1⅓ cups chopped seeded tomato
- ¼ cup finely chopped onion
- ¼ cup taco sauce
- 1 (4.5-oz.) can chopped green chiles, drained
- 2 lb. ground round
- 2 Tbsp. Worcestershire sauce
- ½ tsp. ground cumin
- ¼ tsp. onion powder
- ¼ tsp. garlic powder
- 8 green leaf lettuce leaves
- 8 hamburger buns, split and toasted

1. Combine first 4 ingredients; cover and chill 30 minutes.

2. Preheat broiler.

3. Combine meat and next 4 ingredients; divide mixture into 8 equal portions, shaping each into a 4-inch patty. Broil 4 minutes on each side or until no longer pink in center.

4. Place a lettuce leaf on bottom half of each bun; top each with a patty. Top evenly with tomato mixture and cover with bun tops.

- -

TERIYAKI BURGERS

ACTIVE 10 MIN. - TOTAL 20 MIN.
SERVES 4

- 1 lb. ground round
- ¼ cup low-sodium soy sauce
- ¼ cup chopped scallions
- 1 tsp. grated peeled fresh ginger
- ¼ tsp. black pepper
- 1 garlic clove, minced

1. Combine all ingredients in a bowl. Divide beef mixture into 4 equal portions, shaping each into a ½-inch-thick patty.

2. Preheat grill to medium-high (350°F to 400°F). Place patties on grill rack; grill 4 minutes on each side or until no longer pink in center.

THE PERFECT BURGERS

A simple, rustic burger right off the grill is the favorite dish of many.

ACTIVE 10 MIN. - TOTAL 50 MIN., INCLUDING STANDING
SERVES 6

- 1½ lb. ground beef (75/25)
- 1½ tsp. kosher salt
- 1½ tsp. coarsely ground black pepper
- 6 (1-oz.) cheddar cheese slices
- 6 hamburger buns
  Lettuce leaves, red onion slices, tomato slices, for topping

1. Preheat grill to medium-high (350°F to 400°F). Gently combine beef, salt, and pepper. Shape into 6 (4-inch) 1-inch-thick patties. Using thumb and forefinger, lightly press center of patties, creating an indentation. Let stand at room temperature 30 minutes.

2. Grill, with grill lid closed, 6 to 7 minutes on each side or until no longer pink in center. Top each burger with 1 cheese slice, and grill, covered, with lid closed, 1 to 2 minutes or until cheese is melted. Remove from grill and let stand 5 minutes. Serve on hamburger buns with desired toppings.

THE PERFECT
BURGERS

HERB-ROASTED
PORK LOIN

SLOW-COOKER BBQ PORK

This super-simple recipe delivers big flavor to reduce the fat but not the flavor in this juicy cut of pork. Prepare it a day ahead, cool, then refrigerate several hours. Remove and discard any solidified fat before reheating.

ACTIVE 10 MIN. - TOTAL 6 HOURS, 10 MIN.
SERVES 6

- 1 (3- to 4-lb.) shoulder pork roast
- 1 (18-oz.) bottle barbecue sauce
- 1 (12-oz.) can cola soft drink

1. Place pork roast in a 6-quart slow cooker; pour barbecue sauce and cola over roast.

2. Cover, and cook on HIGH 6 to 7 hours or until meat is tender and shreds easily. Serve on buns with slaw or over hot toasted cornbread.

Note: If you don't have a slow cooker, preheat oven to 350°F. Place roast in a lightly greased Dutch oven; stir together barbecue sauce and cola, and pour over roast. Before placing lid on Dutch oven, cover roast with a double layer of aluminum foil. Bake in preheated oven, tightly covered, until tender, about 3½ hours.

MOLASSES-GRILLED PORK TENDERLOIN

ACTIVE 10 MIN. - TOTAL 8 HOURS, 25 MIN., INCLUDING CHILLING
SERVES 8

- ¼ cup molasses
- 2 Tbsp. coarse-grain Dijon mustard
- 1 Tbsp. apple cider vinegar
- 4 (¾-pound) pork tenderloins, trimmed

1. Combine first 3 ingredients; brush mixture on tenderloins. Cover and chill 8 hours.

2. Preheat grill to medium (350°F to 400°F). Cook tenderloins, grill lid closed, until a thermometer inserted into thickest portion registers 145°F, about 15 minutes, turning once.

HERB-ROASTED PORK LOIN

Seasoning and chilling the meat uncovered will help form a crust, ensuring a beautiful golden-brown color during cooking.

ACTIVE 25 MIN. - TOTAL 9 HOURS, 45 MIN., INCLUDING CHILLING AND STANDING
SERVES 6 TO 8

- 2 Tbsp. chopped fresh thyme
- 2 Tbsp. chopped fresh rosemary
- 2 Tbsp. kosher salt
- 1 Tbsp. loosely packed lemon zest
- 1 Tbsp. light brown sugar
- 3 garlic cloves, pressed
- 2 tsp. freshly ground black pepper
- 1 tsp. finely crushed coriander seeds
- 1 tsp. dry mustard
- ¼ tsp. crushed red pepper
- 1 (2½- to 3-lb.) boneless pork loin
- 3 Tbsp. olive oil

1. Combine first 10 ingredients in a small bowl. Rub over pork. Chill, uncovered, 8 to 12 hours.

2. Let pork stand at room temperature 30 minutes.

3. Preheat oven to 400°F. Cook pork in hot oil in a large skillet over medium-high 2 minutes on each side or until browned. Lightly grease a wire rack with cooking spray. Place pork on rack in a roasting pan.

4. Bake in preheated oven until a thermometer inserted into thickest portion registers 145°F, 40 to 50 minutes. Remove from oven; let stand 15 minutes before serving.

STUFFED PORK CHOPS

This hearty dish is a delicious way to mix up your usual pork chop recipe, and it's sure to please your family.

ACTIVE 20 MIN. - TOTAL 50 MIN.
SERVES 6

- 6 bacon slices
- 2 Granny Smith apples, peeled and diced
- 2 shallots, finely chopped
- 1 Tbsp. chopped fresh ginger
- 1 Tbsp. chopped fresh sage
- 1 cup cubed fontina cheese
- 6 (1½-inch-thick) center-cut pork loin chops
- 1 tsp. table salt
- 1¼ tsp. black pepper
- 2 Tbsp. olive oil

1. Preheat oven to 425°F. Cook bacon in a large skillet until crisp; remove bacon, and drain on paper towels, reserving 2 tablespoons drippings in skillet. Crumble bacon, and set aside.

2. Sauté apples, shallots, and ginger in hot drippings 5 minutes or until tender. Remove from heat; stir in sage.

3. Stir together apple mixture, bacon, and cheese in a bowl.

4. Cut a horizontal slit through thickest portion of each pork chop, cutting to, but not through, other side to form a pocket. Sprinkle both sides and pocket of each pork chop with salt and pepper. Spoon apple mixture evenly into pockets, and secure with wooden picks.

5. Cook pork chops, in 2 batches, in hot olive oil in a large skillet over medium-high 1 to 2 minutes on each side or until golden. Place pork chops in a lightly greased roasting pan or large shallow baking dish.

6. Bake in preheated oven until a thermometer inserted into thickest portion registers 145°F, 25 to 30 minutes.

PORK CHOPS, CABBAGE, AND APPLES

This delightful combination is hearty autumn or winter home-cooking at its most comforting.

ACTIVE 20 MIN. - TOTAL 1 HOUR, 10 MIN.
SERVES 6

- 3 tsp. paprika, divided
- 2 tsp. chopped fresh thyme or 1 tsp. dried thyme, divided
- 2 tsp. kosher salt, divided
- 1½ tsp. freshly ground black pepper, divided
- 2 tsp. chopped fresh sage or 1 tsp. dried sage, divided
- 6 (½-inch-thick) bone-in pork loin chops
- 2 bacon slices
- 1 head cabbage (about 2 lb.), coarsely chopped
- 2 medium onions, thinly sliced
- 1 large Granny Smith apple, peeled and sliced
- 1 Tbsp. tomato paste
- 1 (12-oz.) bottle lager beer or ¾ cup apple cider
  Fresh thyme sprigs, for garnish

1. Combine 2 teaspoons paprika, 1 teaspoon fresh or ½ teaspoon dried thyme, 1 teaspoon salt, 1 teaspoon pepper, and 1 teaspoon fresh or ½ teaspoon dried sage; rub over pork chops.

2. Cook bacon in a large deep skillet over medium-high 6 to 8 minutes or until crisp. Remove bacon, and drain on paper towels, reserving drippings in skillet. Crumble bacon.

3. Cook pork in hot drippings 3 minutes on each side or until browned and done; remove pork from skillet, and keep warm.

4. Add cabbage, onions, and apple to skillet. Cover and reduce heat to medium; cook, stirring occasionally, 15 minutes or until cabbage begins to wilt. Add tomato paste, beer, bacon, remaining 1 teaspoon paprika, 1 teaspoon fresh or ½ teaspoon dried thyme, 1 teaspoon salt, ½ teaspoon pepper, and 1 teaspoon fresh or ½ teaspoon dried sage, stirring to loosen particles from bottom of skillet. Cover and cook 15 minutes or until cabbage is tender and liquid is slightly thickened. Add pork, and cook, uncovered, 5 minutes or until thoroughly heated. Garnish, if desired.

PORK CHOPS, CABBAGE,
AND APPLES

PORK CHOPS WITH
ROASTED APPLES AND
BRUSSELS SPROUTS

PORK CHOPS WITH ROASTED APPLES AND BRUSSELS SPROUTS

ACTIVE 15 MIN. · TOTAL 40 MIN.
SERVES 4

- 1 tsp. paprika
- 1 tsp. chili powder
- 1 tsp. garlic salt
- ⅛ tsp. cayenne pepper
- ⅛ tsp. ground cinnamon
- 3 Tbsp. light brown sugar, divided
- 2 tsp. finely chopped fresh rosemary, divided
- 1 tsp. kosher salt, divided
- ½ tsp. freshly ground black pepper, divided
- 4 (1-inch-thick) bone-in, center-cut pork chops
- 3 Tbsp. plus 2 tsp. olive oil, divided
- 3 Tbsp. apple cider vinegar
- 1 Gala apple, cut into ½-inch wedges
- 1 lb. Brussels sprouts, trimmed and cut in half

1. Preheat oven to 425°F. Stir together first 5 ingredients, 1 tablespoon brown sugar, 1 teaspoon rosemary, ½ teaspoon salt, and ¼ teaspoon black pepper in a small bowl. Rub each pork chop with ½ teaspoon olive oil; rub both sides with brown sugar mixture.

2. Whisk together apple cider vinegar and remaining 2 tablespoons brown sugar, 1 teaspoon rosemary, ½ teaspoon salt, and ¼ teaspoon black pepper in a small bowl; slowly whisk in remaining 3 tablespoons olive oil until blended. Place apples, Brussels sprouts, and ¼ cup vinegar mixture in a large bowl; toss to coat.

3. Place pork chops in center of a lightly greased (with cooking spray) heavy-duty aluminum foil-lined sheet pan; place apple mixture around pork chops.

4. Bake in preheated oven 12 minutes; turn pork chops over, and bake 10 to 14 minutes more or until a thermometer inserted in thickest portion registers 140°F. Transfer pork chops to a serving platter, and cover with foil to keep warm. Stir apple mixture in sheet pan, and spread in an even layer.

5. Increase oven temperature to broil. Broil apple mixture 3 to 4 minutes or until browned and slightly charred. Transfer apple mixture to a medium bowl. Toss together apple mixture and remaining vinegar mixture. Season with additional kosher salt, and serve with pork chops.

PORK CHOPS AND GRAVY

ACTIVE 15 MIN. · TOTAL 2 HOURS, 15 MIN.
SERVES 6

- ½ cup all-purpose flour
- 1½ tsp. dry mustard
- ½ tsp. table salt
- ½ tsp. garlic powder
- 6 (1-inch-thick) lean pork chops
- 1 (10¾-oz.) can condensed chicken broth, undiluted
- 2 Tbsp. vegetable oil
  Hot rice or mashed potatoes, for serving

1. Combine first 4 ingredients in a shallow dish; dredge chops in flour mixture, and set aside.

2. Combine remaining flour mixture and chicken broth in a 3½-quart slow cooker.

3. Pour oil into a large skillet; place over medium-high until hot. Cook chops in hot oil just until browned on both sides; place in slow cooker.

4. Cook, covered, on HIGH until tender, 2 to 2½ hours. Serve with hot rice or mashed potatoes.

SPICY-SWEET RIBS AND BEANS

For tender, flavorful ribs, cook them in a slow cooker on low for 6 hours. Serve this Spicy-Sweet Ribs and Beans dinner recipe with cornbread and a simple green salad with creamy Italian or ranch dressing.

ACTIVE 20 MIN. · TOTAL 7 HOURS, 20 MIN.
SERVES 8

- 4 lb. country-style pork ribs, trimmed
- 1 tsp. garlic powder
- ½ tsp. table salt
- ½ tsp. black pepper
- 1 (10.5-oz.) jar red pepper jelly
- 1 (18-oz.) bottle hickory-flavor barbecue sauce
- 1 medium onion, chopped
- 2 (16-oz.) cans pinto beans, drained and rinsed

1. Cut ribs apart; sprinkle evenly with garlic powder, salt, and pepper. Place ribs in a single layer in a broiler pan lined with th aluminum foil.

2. Broil 5½ inches from heat 9 to 10 minutes on each side or until browned.

3. Whisk together jelly and barbecue sauce in a small bowl until blended.

4. Combine ribs, sauce mixture, and onion in a 5-quart slow cooker. Cover and cook on LOW 6 hours. Add beans, cover, and cook 1 hour more. Remove ribs and drain bean mixture, reserving sauce. Skim fat from sauce. Transfer bean mixture to a serving platter; top with ribs. Serve with sauce.

HONEY-AND-SOY-LACQUERED RIBS

Bake these sweet and spicy ribs up to 2 days ahead. Then simply reheat and broil before serving.

ACTIVE 30 MIN. · TOTAL 2 HOURS, 35 MIN.
SERVES 6 TO 8

- 2 (2- to 2½-lb.) slabs St. Louis-style pork ribs
- 1 Tbsp. kosher salt
- 2 tsp. freshly ground black pepper
- ½ cup honey
- 2 Tbsp. soy sauce
- 2 Tbsp. Asian chili-garlic sauce
- 1 Tbsp. fresh lime juice
- 1 Tbsp. butter
- 1 tsp. dry mustard
- 1 tsp. ground ginger

1. Preheat oven to 325°F. Rinse slabs and pat dry. Remove thin membrane from back of slabs by slicing into it and pulling it off. (This will make the ribs more tender.) Sprinkle salt and black pepper over slabs; wrap each slab tightly in aluminum foil. Place slabs on a jelly-roll pan.

2. Bake until tender and meat pulls away from bone, 2 to 2½ hours.

3. Bring honey and remaining ingredients to a boil in a saucepan over high, stirring occasionally. Reduce heat to medium-low; simmer 5 minutes or until reduced by half. Transfer to a bowl.

4. Remove slabs from oven. Increase oven temperature to broil on HIGH. Carefully remove slabs from foil; place on a foil-lined baking sheet. Brush each slab with 3 Tbsp. honey mixture.

5. Broil 5 minutes or until browned and sticky. Brush with remaining honey mixture.

HONEY-AND-SOY-
LACQUERED RIBS

HAM-AND-DIJON
BISCUITS WITH
CARAMELIZED ONION
BUTTER

HAM-AND-DIJON BISCUITS WITH CARAMELIZED ONION BUTTER

These Southern ham biscuits qualify as wedding reception worthy, but they're equally at home on a holiday sideboard. Use the Holiday Ham (recipe right), or any baked ham or thinly sliced ham from the deli.

ACTIVE 15 MIN. - TOTAL 30 MIN.
MAKES 4 DOZEN

- 9 cups all-purpose baking mix
- 2 cups milk
- ½ cup Dijon mustard
- ¼ cup honey
  Caramelized Onion Butter (recipe follows)
- 2 pounds ham, thinly sliced

1. Preheat oven to 450°F. Make a well in center of baking mix in a large bowl.

2. Whisk together milk, mustard, and honey. Add milk mixture to baking mix, stirring just until moistened.

3. Turn out soft dough onto a floured surface; knead 3 or 4 times.

4. Roll half the dough at a time to ½-inch thickness. Cut with a 2-inch round cutter, and place on lightly greased baking sheets. Reroll and cut remaining dough and cut scraps.

5. Bake in preheated oven until lightly browned, about 8 minutes. Split warm biscuits. Spread with Caramelized Onion Butter and fill with ham. Cover biscuits loosely with aluminum foil.

6. Reduce oven temperature to 350°F. Bake just until thoroughly heated, 5 to 7 minutes.

Note: To make ahead, place assembled biscuits in an airtight container and chill up to 8 hours or freeze up to 3 weeks. Thaw frozen biscuits in refrigerator. To reheat, place biscuits on baking sheets and cover loosely with aluminum foil. Bake at 350°F for 10 to 12 minutes or until thoroughly heated.

CARAMELIZED ONION BUTTER

ACTIVE 5 MIN. - TOTAL 25 MIN.
MAKES 2½ CUPS

- 1¾ cups butter, softened and divided
- 2 large sweet onions, finely chopped
- ¼ cup firmly packed brown sugar
- 1 Tbsp. balsamic vinegar

Melt ¼ cup butter over medium-high in a large skillet. Add onions and brown sugar, and cook, stirring often, 15 to 20 minutes or until a deep caramel color. Remove from heat; cool slightly. Stir in remaining 1½ cups butter and vinegar. Use in Ham-and-Dijon Biscuits recipe, or cover and chill. Return to room temperature before serving.

- -

HOLIDAY HAM

Baked ham is convenient to have on hand during holidays. Use it to make Ham-and-Dijon Biscuits (recipe left), or serve it for breakfast along with hot biscuits, cheese grits, and fresh fruit.

ACTIVE 25 MIN. - TOTAL 2 HOURS, 25 MIN.
SERVES 12

- 1 (8- to 10-lb.) fully cooked, bone-in ham
- 1 (0.62-oz.) jar whole cloves
- 1 (16-oz.) pkg. dark brown sugar
- 1 cup spicy brown mustard
- 1 cup apple cider
- ½ cup bourbon
- 1 cup hot brewed coffee (optional)
  Fresh rosemary, fresh sage, orange wedges, for garnish (optional)

1. Preheat oven to 350°F. Remove skin from ham, and trim fat to ¼-inch thickness. Make shallow diamond-pattern cuts in fat. Insert cloves into ham in a decorative pattern; place ham in a lightly greased roasting pan or 13- x 9-inch pan.

2. Stir together brown sugar and next 3 ingredients. Pour mixture over ham. Bake in preheated oven on lower oven rack until a meat thermometer inserted into thickest portion registers 140°F, basting with pan juices every 20 minutes, for 2 to 2½ hours. (Tent ham with aluminum foil after 1½ hours to prevent excessive browning, if necessary.) Remove ham to a serving platter, and let cool.

3. Meanwhile, if desired, stir coffee into drippings to loosen browned particles in pan. Pour drippings into a saucepan, and cook 5 to 8 minutes or until slightly thickened. Serve sauce with ham. Garnish ham platter, if desired. Separately cover and store ham and sauce in refrigerator up to 5 days.

COUNTRY HAM WITH RED-EYE GRAVY

For true red-eye gravy, Southerners use caffeinated coffee for its pick-me-up quality.

ACTIVE 10 MIN. - TOTAL 40 MIN.
SERVES 6

- 2 cups hot strong brewed coffee
- ¼ cup firmly packed brown sugar
- 2 (12-oz.) slices boneless country ham

1. Stir together coffee and sugar; let mixture cool.

2. Cook ham in a large cast-iron skillet over medium 5 to 7 minutes on each side or until browned. Remove ham and keep warm, reserving drippings in skillet.

3. Add coffee mixture to skillet, stirring to loosen particles from bottom; bring to a boil. Boil, stirring occasionally, until reduced by half (about 15 minutes). Serve with ham.

BRATWURST WITH PEPPERS AND ONIONS

ACTIVE 15 MIN. - TOTAL 1 HOUR
SERVES 6

- 2 large red bell peppers, cut into strips
- 1 large yellow bell pepper, cut into strips
- 2 large sweet onions, cut into strips
- 1 Tbsp. olive oil
- 1 tsp. kosher salt
- ¼ tsp. freshly ground black pepper
- 6 fresh bratwurst sausages (about 1½ lb.)
- 6 hoagie rolls, lightly toasted and split

1. Preheat oven to 375°F. Toss together first 6 ingredients in a large bowl. Spread mixture in an even layer in a lightly greased (with cooking spray) heavy-duty sheet pan lined with aluminum foil.

2. Pierce each sausage 6 times with a wooden pick. Place sausages 3 to 4 inches apart on pepper mixture.

3. Bake in preheated oven for 40 minutes; increase oven temperature to broil. Broil 6 to 8 minutes or until browned, turning sausages halfway through.

4. Place 1 sausage in each roll and top with peppers and onions.

ITALIAN SAUSAGE AND PEPPERS SKILLET

ACTIVE 10 MIN. - TOTAL 30 MIN.
SERVES 4

- 1 lb. Italian turkey sausage links, cut in half crosswise (about 4)
- 1 medium green bell pepper, cut into strips
- 1 medium red bell pepper strips, cut into strips
- 4 garlic cloves, minced
- ¾ cup tomato-basil pasta sauce

1. Heat a large nonstick skillet coated with cooking spray over medium. Add sausage; cook 5 minutes, turning occasionally. Add pepper strips and garlic; cook 5 minutes, stirring often.

2. Stir in pasta sauce; cover, reduce heat, and simmer 8 to 10 minutes or until sausage is done. Uncover and simmer 3 minutes or until sauce thickens and peppers are tender.

ZITI WITH SAUSAGE AND BROCCOLI

ACTIVE 10 MIN. - TOTAL 45 MIN.
SERVES 4

- Table salt and black pepper
- 8 oz. hot Italian sausage, casings removed
- 2 Tbsp. unsalted butter
- 2 Tbsp. all-purpose flour
- 2 cups milk
- 8 oz. ziti pasta
- 1½ lb. broccoli (about 1 large head), stems removed, florets cut into 1-inch pieces
- 3 oz. Parmesan cheese, grated (½ cup)

1. Bring a large pot of salted water to a boil over high. Preheat oven to 350°F. Lightly grease an 11- x- 7-inch baking dish. In a large skillet over medium-high, cook sausage, stirring often, until no longer pink, about 3 minutes. Stir in butter. Sprinkle flour on top; stir. Slowly pour in milk and cook, stirring constantly, until smooth and thickened, 3 to 4 minutes. Season with salt and pepper.

2. Add ziti to boiling water; cook until tender, about 5 minutes, then add broccoli and cook for 3 minutes. Drain ziti and broccoli; transfer to baking dish. Stir in sausage. Sprinkle Parmesan on top. Bake in preheated oven until golden brown and bubbly, about 35 minutes.

BRATWURST WITH
PEPPERS AND ONIONS

CLASSIC
HOPPIN' JOHN

CLASSIC HOPPIN' JOHN

Thick-cut bacon adds the right amount of smokiness; a ham hock can overpower the dish. Carolina Gold, an heirloom long-grain rice, has sweet, mild flavor and toothsome texture.

ACTIVE 25 MIN. · TOTAL 1 HOUR, 30 MIN.
SERVES 6

- 6 thick-cut bacon slices, chopped
- 4 celery stalks, sliced (about 1½ cups)
- 1 medium-size yellow onion, chopped (about 1½ cups)
- 1 small green bell pepper, finely chopped (about 1 cup)
- 3 garlic cloves, chopped (about 1 Tbsp.)
- 1 tsp. chopped fresh thyme
- ½ tsp. black pepper
- ¼ tsp. cayenne pepper
- 1½ tsp. kosher salt
- 8 cups lower-sodium chicken broth
- 4 cups fresh or frozen black-eyed peas
- 2 Tbsp. olive oil
- 1½ cups uncooked Carolina Gold rice
  Fresh scallions, sliced

1. Cook bacon in a Dutch oven over medium-high, stirring occasionally, until starting to crisp, about 10 minutes. Add celery, onion, bell pepper, garlic, thyme, black pepper, cayenne, and 1 teaspoon of the salt. Cook, stirring occasionally, until onion is tender, about 8 minutes. Add broth and black-eyed peas, and bring to a boil over medium-high. Reduce heat to medium-low; simmer until peas are tender, about 40 minutes. Drain pea mixture, reserving cooking liquid. Return pea mixture and 1 cup of the cooking liquid to Dutch oven. Cover to keep warm; set aside.

2. Heat oil in a medium saucepan over medium-high. Add rice and cook, stirring often, until fragrant and lightly toasted, 3 to 4 minutes. Stir in 3 cups of the reserved cooking liquid and remaining ½ teaspoon salt. Bring to a boil, then reduce heat to medium-low; cover and cook until rice is tender, 15 to 18 minutes. Fluff rice with a fork; gently stir into pea mixture in Dutch oven. Stir in remaining cooking liquid, ¼ cup at a time, until desired consistency is reached. Sprinkle servings with sliced fresh scallions.

CLASSIC DOUBLE ROAST CHICKENS

ACTIVE 20 MIN. · TOTAL 2 HOURS
MAKES 2 CHICKENS

- 4 tsp. kosher salt
- 2 tsp. freshly ground black pepper
- 2 (4- to 5-lb.) whole chickens
- 2 lemons, halved
- 2 fresh rosemary sprigs
- 1 Tbsp. olive oil

1. Preheat oven to 375°F. Stir together salt and pepper. If applicable, remove necks and giblets from chickens, and reserve for another use. Pat chickens dry.

2. Sprinkle ½ teaspoon salt mixture in cavity of each chicken. Place 2 lemon halves and 1 rosemary sprig in cavity of each chicken. Rub 1½ teaspoons olive oil into skin of each chicken. Sprinkle with remaining salt mixture; rub into skin. Tuck chicken wings under, if desired. Lightly grease a wire rack set in a 17- x 12-inch rimmed baking pan with cooking spray. Place chickens, breast sides up and facing in opposite directions (for even browning), on wire rack.

3. Roast in preheated oven until a thermometer inserted in thigh registers 170°F, about 1¼ hours. Cover and let stand 10 minutes before slicing.

TOP-SHELF
CHICKEN
UNDER A BRICK

TOP-SHELF CHICKEN UNDER A BRICK

The "top-shelf" in this recipe speaks to the crispy skin, superior flavor, and juiciness of the bird. It also refers to a novel new technique: cooking potatoes in the heavy cast-iron skillet that's used as a weight on the chicken. The weight presses the chicken flat against the grill grates, cutting the cooking time in half. Plus, you'll be cooking your side dish at the same time.

ACTIVE 45 MIN. - TOTAL 1 HOUR, 50 MIN.
SERVES 4

- 1 lb. small red or Yukon gold potatoes, halved
- 3 tsp. kosher salt, divided
- 1 (3- to 4-lb.) whole chicken
- 2 Tbsp. olive oil, divided
- ½ tsp. freshly ground black pepper
- 12 fresh herb sprigs (such as thyme, rosemary, sage, or tarragon)
- 2 lemons, halved

1. Bring potatoes, salt, and water to cover to a boil in a large saucepan over high. Reduce heat to medium, and simmer 5 to 7 minutes or until potatoes are just tender. Drain.

2. Heat 1 one side of grill to medium (300°F to 350°F); leave other side unlit. Remove and discard giblets and neck from chicken. Place chicken, breast down, on a cutting board. Using kitchen shears, cut along both sides of backbone, separating backbone from chicken; discard backbone. Open chicken as you would a book. Turn chicken, breast up, and press firmly against breastbone with the heel of your hand until bone cracks. Tuck wing tips under. Rub with 1 tablespoon oil. Sprinkle chicken with pepper and remaining 2 teaspoons salt.

3. Heat a 12-inch cast-iron skillet on lit side of grill 10 minutes. Add remaining 1 tablespoon oil to hot skillet; place potatoes, cut-sides down, in skillet. Transfer skillet to unlit side of grill.

4. Place chicken, breast down, on lit side of grill; top with herbs. Place cast-iron skillet with potatoes on chicken to flatten. Grill with grill lid closed, until chicken is browned, 10 to 15 minutes. Remove skillet. Transfer chicken to unlit side of grill. Place cast-iron skillet on chicken. Grill, with lid covered, 45 minutes or until a meat thermometer inserted in thickest portion of breast registers 165°F. Remove chicken from grill and let stand 5 minutes. (For crisper skin, place chicken on lit side of grill. Grill with lid closed until crisp, about 5 minutes.)

5. Meanwhile, place lemons, cut-sides down, on lit side of grill. Grill with grill lid closed, until charred and softened about 5 minutes. Serve chicken with potatoes and charred lemon.

- -

LEMON-GARLIC ROAST CHICKEN WITH SAUTÉED GREEN BEANS

After roasting the chicken, sauté the green beans in the rich pan juices.

ACTIVE 10 MIN. - TOTAL 1 HOUR, 35 MIN.
SERVES 4

- 3 Tbsp. chopped fresh flat-leaf parsley
- 2 Tbsp. butter, softened
- 2 Tbsp. olive oil
- 2 tsp. lemon zest
- 2 garlic cloves, minced
- 1 tsp. table salt
- ½ tsp. black pepper
- 1 (4-lb.) whole chicken
- 1 (12-oz.) bag fresh green beans or 1 (16-oz.) pkg. frozen whole green beans
  Table salt and black pepper, to taste
  Lemon wedges, fresh parsley sprigs, for garnish

1. Preheat oven to 450°F. Stir together first 7 ingredients. Starting at neck cavity, loosen skin from chicken breast and drumsticks by inserting fingers and gently pushing between skin and meat. (Do not completely detach skin.) Rub half the butter mixture under skin.

2. Tie ends of legs together with string; tuck wing tips under. Spread remaining half of butter mixture on chicken. Place chicken, breast-side up, on a lightly greased rack in a lightly greased shallow roasting pan.

3. Bake in preheated oven for 30 minutes. Reduce oven temperature to 350°F. Bake until a meat thermometer inserted into thigh registers 170°F, about 40 minutes. Cover chicken loosely with aluminum foil to prevent excessive browning, if necessary. Remove chicken to a serving platter, reserving drippings in pan. Cover chicken with foil, and let stand 10 minutes before slicing.

5. Bring pan juices to a boil in a large skillet; add green beans, and cook 5 to 7 minutes or to desired tenderness. Season with salt and pepper to taste. Serve beans on platter with chicken. Garnish, if desired.

MAMA'S FRIED CHICKEN

ACTIVE 30 MIN. - TOTAL 3 HOURS, INCLUDING CHILLING
SERVES 4 TO 6

- 1 (3- to 4-lb.) whole chicken, cut into pieces
- 1 tsp. table salt
- 1 tsp. black pepper
- 2 cups buttermilk
  Self-rising flour
  Vegetable oil

1. Sprinkle chicken with salt and black pepper. Place chicken in a shallow dish or zip-top plastic freezer bag, and add buttermilk. Cover or seal, and chill at least 2 hours.

2. Remove chicken from buttermilk, discarding buttermilk. Dredge chicken in flour.

3. Pour oil to a depth of 1½ inches in a deep skillet or Dutch oven; heat to 360°F. Add chicken, a few pieces at a time; cover and cook 6 minutes. Uncover chicken, and cook 9 minutes. Turn chicken; cover and cook 6 minutes. Uncover and cook until a meat thermometer inserted into thigh registers 170°F, 5 to 9 minutes, turning chicken the last 3 minutes for even browning, if necessary. Drain on paper towels. Sprinkle lightly with salt while chicken is hot, if desired.

- -

LIGHTER PAN-FRIED CHICKEN WITH GREEN BEANS AND TOMATOES

ACTIVE 25 MIN. - TOTAL 8 HOURS, 45 MIN., INCLUDING CHILLING
SERVES 8

- 2 cups whole buttermilk
- 2 large eggs, beaten
- 3 garlic cloves, smashed
- 4¾ tsp. kosher salt, divided
- 2½ tsp. black pepper, divided
- 2 lb. bone-in, skinless chicken thighs
- 2 lb. boneless, skinless chicken breasts, cut in half
- 2 cups canola oil
- 3 cups all-purpose flour
- 2 Tbsp. cornstarch

- 1 lb. trimmed fresh green beans
- 1 large shallot, thinly sliced (about ½ cup)
- 1 pt. cherry tomatoes
- 2 tsp. fresh lemon juice (from 1 lemon)

1. Whisk together buttermilk, eggs, garlic cloves, 2 teaspoons of the salt, and 1 teaspoon of the pepper in a large bowl. Place chicken in a large zip-top plastic freezer bag; pour buttermilk mixture over chicken. Seal bag, removing as much air as possible. (Or combine in a large bowl, and cover with a tight-fitting lid.) Chill 8 to 24 hours.

2. Preheat oven to 425°F. Pour oil into a large cast-iron skillet, and heat over medium-high.

3. Drain chicken well; discard buttermilk mixture. Whisk together flour, cornstarch, 2 teaspoons of the salt, and 1 teaspoon of the pepper in a large bowl. Working with 1 piece at a time, dredge chicken in flour mixture until well coated. Place coated chicken pieces on a large piece of aluminum foil. Let stand to allow coating to dry out, about 15 minutes.

4. Fry chicken, in batches of 4 pieces at a time, in hot oil until golden, about 3 minutes per side. Transfer browned chicken to a wire rack set in a large rimmed baking sheet. Bake in preheated oven until chicken is deep golden brown and cooked through, about 10 minutes.

5. Meanwhile, let skillet rest off heat about 5 minutes while chicken bakes. Carefully pour all the frying oil into a metal bowl; allow flour to settle to bottom of bowl. Wipe skillet clean.

6. Add 2 tablespoons of the frying oil to skillet; place skillet over medium-high. Add green beans and shallot; cook, without stirring, until beginning to brown, about 4 minutes. Stir in tomatoes and cook, without stirring, until beans and shallot are charred and tomatoes begin to burst, about 2 minutes. Stir in remaining ¾ teaspoon salt and ½ teaspoon pepper. Transfer vegetables to a serving platter, and toss with lemon juice. Serve vegetables immediately with fried chicken.

MAMA'S
FRIED CHICKEN

LEMON-ROSEMARY-
GARLIC CHICKEN
AND POTATOES

PECAN CHICKEN

ACTIVE 10 MIN. · TOTAL 35 MIN.

SERVES 4

- 1½ cups finely chopped pecans, toasted
- 2 Tbsp. chopped fresh flat-leaf parsley
- 1½ tsp. table salt
- 2 egg whites
- 4 boneless, skinless chicken breasts

1. Preheat oven to 400°F. Combine first 3 ingredients in a bowl.

2. Beat egg whites with a fork just until foamy. Dip both sides of chicken in egg; dredge in pecan mixture. Arrange chicken breasts on a lightly greased baking sheet lined with aluminum foil.

3. Bake in preheated oven until a thermometer inserted into breast registers 165°F, 20 to 25 minutes.

- -

LEMON-ROSEMARY-GARLIC CHICKEN AND POTATOES

Nicknamed "Anytime Chicken," this winner of a chicken dinner is our new favorite roasting-pan meal for weeknights or easy entertaining with friends.

ACTIVE 20 MIN. · TOTAL 1 HOUR, 5 MIN.

SERVES 6

- ⅓ cup olive oil
- ¼ cup fresh lemon juice
- 1 (3.5-oz.) jar capers, drained
- 2 lemons, sliced
- 10 garlic cloves, smashed
- 3 Tbsp. fresh rosemary leaves
- 2 tsp. kosher salt
- 1 tsp. freshly ground black pepper
- 3 Tbsp. olive oil
- 6 chicken legs (about 1½ lb.)
- 4 bone-in, skin-on chicken thighs (about 2½ lb.)
- 2 lb. small red potatoes
  Crusty French bread

1. Preheat oven to 450°F. Stir together first 8 ingredients in a medium bowl.

2. Place a roasting pan on stove top over two burners. Add 3 tablespoons olive oil, and heat pan over medium-high. Sprinkle chicken with desired amount of salt and pepper. Place chicken, skin down, in pan. Add potatoes. Cook 9 to 10 minutes or until chicken is browned. Turn chicken, and pour lemon mixture over chicken.

3. Bake until a thermometer inserted into thigh registers 170°F, 45 to 50 minutes. Serve chicken with sauce and French bread.

- -

CHICKEN PARMESAN

Whip up homemade Chicken Parmesan for an Italian-inspired meal that's perfect for busy weeknights.

ACTIVE 10 MIN. · TOTAL 35 MIN.

SERVES 2

- 1 cup Italian-seasoned breadcrumbs
- 2 Tbsp. all-purpose flour
- ½ tsp. cayenne pepper
- 2 boneless, skinless chicken breasts
- 2 egg whites, lightly beaten
- 1 Tbsp. olive oil
- 1½ cups jarred marinara sauce
- 1 cup shredded mozzarella cheese
- ¼ cup freshly grated Parmesan cheese

1. Combine breadcrumbs, flour, and cayenne pepper in a small bowl; set aside.

2. Place chicken between two sheets of heavy-duty plastic wrap. Flatten breasts to ¼-inch thickness, using a meat mallet or rolling pin.

3. Dip 1 chicken breast in egg whites, then coat with breadcrumb mixture. Dip again in egg mixture, and coat again in breadcrumb mixture. Repeat for second chicken breast.

5. Cook chicken in hot oil over medium 2 to 3 minutes on each side or until done.

6. Place chicken breasts in a single layer in a lightly greased 8-inch square baking dish. Top evenly with marinara sauce and cheeses.

7. Bake in preheated oven until a thermometer inserted into breast registers 165°F, about 20 minutes.

CHICKEN PICCATA

This quick and easy version of an Italian classic, chicken piccata, is ready in about 30 minutes. Boil the water for the noodles first, then let the noodles cook while you prepare the chicken.

ACTIVE 20 MIN. - TOTAL 30 MIN.
SERVES 4

  1 lb. chicken breasts
  ½ tsp. table salt
  ½ tsp. black pepper
  ½ cup Italian-seasoned breadcrumbs
  2 Tbsp. olive oil
  ¼ cup chicken broth
  3 Tbsp. lemon juice
  2 Tbsp. butter
  2 Tbsp. chopped fresh flat-leaf parsley
  1 (12-oz.) pkg. cooked noodles

1. Cut each chicken breast in half horizontally. Place chicken between two sheets of heavy-duty plastic wrap; flatten to ¼-inch thickness, using a rolling pin or flat side of a meat mallet.

2. Sprinkle chicken evenly with salt and pepper; lightly dredge in breadcrumbs.

3. Cook half the chicken in 1 tablespoon hot oil in a large nonstick skillet over medium-high 2 minutes on each side or until golden brown and a thermometer inserted into breast registers 165°F. Remove chicken to a serving platter and cover with aluminum foil. Repeat with remaining chicken and 1 tablespoon olive oil.

4. Add broth and lemon juice to skillet; cook, stirring to loosen particles from bottom of skillet, until sauce is slightly thickened. Remove from heat; add butter and parsley, stirring until butter melts. Pour sauce over chicken and serve over warm noodles.

CITRUS-BRAISED CHICKEN THIGHS

Braising gives the chicken tender, tasty results and a pan sauce to boot.

ACTIVE 55 MIN. - TOTAL 1 HOUR, 30 MIN.
SERVES 4 TO 6

     Kosher salt
     Black pepper
  8 bone-in, skin-on chicken thighs, trimmed
  2 Tbsp. olive oil
  2 carrots, sliced
  1 yellow onion, sliced
  3 garlic cloves, minced
  1 cup fresh orange juice
  2 Tbsp. fresh lemon juice
  ½ tsp. ground cumin
  ½ cup green olives, pitted
  1 Tbsp. chopped fresh flat-leaf parsley

1. Sprinkle salt and pepper on chicken. Cook 4 chicken thighs in 1 tablespoon hot oil in a large Dutch oven over medium-high 6 minutes on each side. Remove chicken; wipe Dutch oven clean. Repeat with remaining 1 tablespoon oil and remaining chicken thighs. Reserve 1 tablespoon drippings in Dutch oven.

2. Reduce heat to medium; add carrots and cook, stirring occasionally, 2 minutes. Add onion and cook, stirring occasionally, 5 to 7 minutes or until tender. Add garlic and cook, stirring occasionally, 1 minute. Stir in orange juice, lemon juice, and cumin. Increase heat to high and bring to a boil.

3. Add chicken and olives. Reduce heat to medium-low; cover and simmer until a thermometer inserted into thigh registers 170°F, 35 to 40 minutes. Just before serving, stir in parsley and add salt and pepper to taste.

CITRUS-BRAISED
CHICKEN THIGHS

GREEK CHICKEN WITH
ROASTED POTATOES

CRISPY OVEN-FRIED CHICKEN CUTLETS WITH ROASTED BROCCOLI

If your family's favorite side dish is broccoli drenched in cheese sauce, try this spicy spin with tangy Parmesan Cream Sauce.

ACTIVE 15 MIN. · TOTAL 35 MIN.
SERVES 4

- ½ cup salted butter, melted
- 2 Tbsp. Dijon mustard
- 1½ tsp. kosher salt, divided
- 1 tsp. black pepper, divided
- ⅔ cup panko (Japanese-style breadcrumbs)
- ½ cup crushed cornflakes cereal
- 2 oz. Parmesan cheese, grated (about ½ cup)
- 4 chicken breast cutlets (about 1¼ lb.)
- 3½ Tbsp. olive oil
- 3 garlic cloves, minced
- 1 tsp. crushed red pepper
- 1 lb. fresh broccoli florets (about 8 cups)
  Parmesan Cream Sauce (recipe follows)

1. Preheat oven to 400°F. Stir together butter, mustard, and ½ teaspoon each of the salt and black pepper in a shallow bowl. Stir together panko, cornflakes, and Parmesan in a second shallow bowl. Dip chicken in butter mixture; dredge in panko mixture, pressing to adhere. Place on a baking sheet lined with aluminum foil. Bake in preheated oven until chicken is browned and done, about 17 minutes.

2. Meanwhile, stir together oil, garlic, crushed red pepper, and remaining 1 teaspoon salt and ½ teaspoon black pepper in a large bowl. Add broccoli and toss to coat. Transfer to a rimmed baking sheet, and roast at 400°F until broccoli is browned and tender, about 17 minutes. Serve chicken and broccoli with Parmesan Cream Sauce.

PARMESAN CREAM SAUCE

ACTIVE 15 MIN. · TOTAL 15 MIN.
MAKES 1 CUP

- 2 Tbsp. salted butter
- 1 Tbsp. all-purpose flour
- 1 cup whole milk
- 1 oz. Parmesan cheese, grated (¼ cup)
- 1 tsp. fresh lemon juice
- ¼ tsp. kosher salt
- ¼ tsp. black pepper

Melt butter in a 3-quart saucepan over medium-high. Whisk in flour; cook, whisking constantly, 1 minute. Gradually whisk in milk. Bring to a boil and cook, whisking constantly, until thickened, 1 to 2 minutes. Whisk in Parmesan cheese, lemon juice, salt, and pepper. Serve immediately.

- -

GREEK CHICKEN WITH ROASTED POTATOES

ACTIVE 15 MIN. · TOTAL 1 HOUR
SERVES 4

- 2 tsp. onion powder
- 2 tsp. kosher salt
- 2 tsp. dried thyme
- 1 tsp. black pepper
- ¼ tsp. ground cinnamon
- ¼ tsp. ground nutmeg
- ¼ cup chopped fresh flat-leaf parsley, divided
- 3 tsp. chopped fresh oregano leaves, divided
- ¼ cup extra-virgin olive oil
- 4 (12-oz.) bone-in, skin-on chicken breasts, trimmed
- 8 thin lemon slices
- 1½ lb. Yukon Gold potatoes (about 1½-inch diameter), halved lengthwise
- ½ cup chopped tomato
- ½ cup Kalamata olives, coarsely chopped
- 2 oz. feta cheese, crumbled (about ¼ cup)

1. Preheat oven to 400°F with rack about 8 inches from heat. Combine onion powder, salt, thyme, pepper, cinnamon, nutmeg, 2 tablespoons of the parsley, and 2 teaspoons of the oregano in a mini food processor; pulse several times until well blended. Add oil; pulse until combined.

2. Place chicken and lemons on a rimmed baking sheet; rub chicken evenly with ¼ cup of the herb mixture. Toss potatoes with remaining 3 tablespoons herb mixture. Arrange potatoes around chicken and lemon slices. Roast in preheated oven until a thermometer inserted in thickest portion of chicken registers 155°F and potatoes are tender, about 30 minutes.

3. Increase oven temperature to broil. Broil until chicken skin is browned and crisp, about 5 minutes. Remove from oven and let stand 5 to 10 minutes. Sprinkle with tomato, olives, feta, and remaining 2 tablespoons parsley and 1 teaspoon oregano.

GRILLED CHICKEN KEBABS WITH ARUGULA PESTO

Put your grill to work with flavorful kebabs of chicken, sweet onion, and zucchini with a zippy arugula pesto. Serve with plenty of crusty bread to mop up the pesto.

ACTIVE 30 MIN. - TOTAL 30 MIN.
SERVES 4

- 2 cups packed baby arugula leaves
- 1 cup loosely packed basil leaves
- ¼ cup pine nuts, toasted
- 2 small garlic cloves, coarsely chopped
- 1 Tbsp. fresh lemon juice
- 1 tsp. kosher salt
- ½ tsp. black pepper
- 5 Tbsp. extra-virgin olive oil, divided
- 1 small zucchini, cut into ¼-inch-thick slices, then cut into half-moons (about 1½ cups)
- 1 small yellow squash, cut into ¼-inch-thick slices, then cut into half-moons (about 1½ cups)
- 1 small Vidalia or other sweet onion, cut into 8 wedges and separated into pieces (about 1 cup)
- 1 tsp. sherry vinegar
- 1¼ lb. chicken breast tenders, cut crosswise into thirds

1. Place arugula, basil, pine nuts, garlic, lemon juice, salt, pepper, and 4 tablespoons of the oil in the bowl of a mini food processor; pulse until smooth, about 10 times, scraping sides of bowl occasionally.

2. Place zucchini, squash, and onion in a medium bowl; toss with vinegar, 2 tablespoons of the pesto, and remaining 1 tablespoon oil. Place chicken pieces in a separate bowl, then toss with 2 tablespoons of pesto.

3. Preheat grill to medium-high (about 450°F). Alternately thread chicken and vegetables onto each of 8 (6-inch) bamboo skewers. Place kebabs on oiled grates; grill, uncovered, until chicken is cooked through and vegetables are tender and lightly charred, about 4 minutes per side. Serve chicken-and-vegetable kebabs with remaining pesto.

GRILLED CHICKEN TACOS

ACTIVE 30 MIN. - TOTAL 45 MIN., PLUS 3 HOURS CHILLING
SERVES 8

- 2 to 3 lb. boneless, skin-on chicken thighs
- 3 cups fresh orange juice
- ½ cup fresh lime juice
- 4 garlic cloves
- 1 Tbsp. kosher salt
- 3 Tbsp. minced fresh cilantro
- 1 (7-oz.) container achiote paste
- 1 fresh pineapple, peeled, cored, and cut into ½-inch-thick slices
- 1 cup firmly packed fresh cilantro leaves
- 1 (1½-lb.) jicama, peeled and diced (about 2 cups)
- 8 (6-inch) corn or flour tortillas
  Lime wedges
  Salsa

1. Place chicken thighs in a large zip-top plastic freezer bag. Process next 6 ingredients in a blender until smooth. Pour over chicken; seal bag, and turn to coat. Chill 3 hours.

2. Preheat grill to medium (350°F to 450°F). Place pineapple slices on oiled grates; grill, uncovered, until slightly charred, 2 to 3 minutes per side. Chill 30 minutes.

3. Meanwhile, remove chicken from marinade; discard marinade. Place chicken on oiled grates and grill, covered, until a thermometer inserted in thickest portion registers 165°F, 6 to 7 minutes per side. Remove from grill; cover with foil while pineapple chills.

4. Dice grilled pineapple; toss with cilantro leaves and jicama.

5. Slice chicken and divide among warmed tortillas. Top tacos with pineapple mixture. Serve with lime wedges and salsa.

GRILLED CHICKEN
KEBABS WITH
ARUGULA PESTO

CHICKEN AND
SNOW PEA
STIR-FRY

CHICKEN LASAGNA WITH ROASTED RED BELL PEPPER SAUCE

A hot pan of lasagna is eagerly welcomed on a cold winter's night, especially when paired with a robust red wine.

ACTIVE 20 MIN. - TOTAL 1 HOUR, 30 MIN.
SERVES 6 TO 8

- 4 cups finely chopped cooked chicken
- 2 (8-oz.) containers chive-and-onion cream cheese
- 1 (10-oz.) pkg. frozen chopped spinach, thawed and well drained
- 1 tsp. seasoned pepper
- 3/4 tsp. garlic salt
   Roasted Red Bell Pepper Sauce (recipe follows)
- 9 no-boil lasagna noodles
- 2 cups (8 oz.) shredded Italian three-cheese blend

1. Preheat oven to 350°F. Stir together first 5 ingredients.

2. Layer a lightly greased 11- x 7-inch baking dish with one-third of Roasted Red Bell Pepper Sauce, 3 noodles, one-third of chicken mixture, and one-third of cheese. Repeat layers twice. Place baking dish on a baking sheet.

3. Bake, covered, in preheated oven until thoroughly heated, 50 to 55 minutes. Uncover and bake 15 minutes more.

ROASTED RED BELL PEPPER SAUCE

Also serve sauce over your favorite noodles.

TOTAL 5 MIN.
MAKES 3 1/2 CUPS

- 1 (12-oz.) jar roasted red bell peppers, drained
- 1 (16-oz.) jar creamy Alfredo sauce
- 1 (3-oz.) pkg. shredded Parmesan cheese
- 1/2 tsp. crushed red pepper

Process all ingredients in a food processor until smooth, stopping to scrape down sides.

CHEESY CHICKEN PENNE

ACTIVE 10 MIN. - TOTAL 20 MIN.
SERVES 4 TO 6

- 8 oz. uncooked penne pasta
- 1 (16-oz.) loaf pasteurized prepared cheese product, cubed
- 1 (8-oz.) container sour cream
- 1/2 cup milk
- 2 1/2 cups chopped cooked chicken

1. Cook pasta in salted water according to package directions; drain.

2. Heat cubed cheese, sour cream, and milk over medium-low heat, stirring constantly, 5 minutes or until cheese melts. Stir in pasta and chicken, and cook through.

- -

CHICKEN AND SNOW PEA STIR-FRY

ACTIVE 15 MIN. - TOTAL 25 MIN.
SERVES 2

- 3/4 cup chicken broth
- 1/4 cup soy sauce
- 2 Tbsp. cornstarch
- 1 Tbsp. peanut or vegetable oil
- 2 boneless, skinless chicken breast halves, cut into 1/4-inch strips
- 1 1/2 cups sliced celery
- 1/4 lb. fresh snow pea pods
- 4 large mushrooms, sliced
- 3 scallions, sliced
- 1/2 cup slivered almonds, toasted
   Hot cooked rice

1. Combine first 3 ingredients in a small bowl; set aside.

2. Pour oil into a preheated nonstick wok or large skillet, coating sides; heat at medium-high 1 minute. Add chicken; cook, stirring constantly, 4 minutes or until chicken is almost done.

3. Add celery and next 3 ingredients; cook, stirring constantly, 3 minutes or until chicken is done. Stir in toasted almonds.

4. Stir in broth mixture; cook, stirring constantly, until mixture thickens and boils. Boil 1 minute, stirring constantly. Serve stir-fry over rice.

LEMON CHICKEN STIR-FRY

ACTIVE 20 MIN. - TOTAL 30 MIN.
SERVES 4

- 1 red bell pepper (about ½ lb.)
- ¼ lb. pea pods
- 2 cups precooked dried white rice
- 1 lb. boneless, skinless chicken breasts
- 3 cups chicken broth
- 1 Tbsp. minced fresh serrano or jalapeño chiles
- 1 Tbsp. lemon zest
- 1 Tbsp. cornstarch
- 2 Tbsp. lemon juice
- ¼ cup chopped scallions (including tops)

1. Stem and seed bell pepper, then cut into ¼-inch-wide strips.

2. Remove and discard stem ends and strings from pea pods. Rinse pods and cut in half crosswise.

3. Put rice in a wide 3- to 4-quart bowl.

4. Rinse chicken breasts and cut into 1-inch chunks.

5. In a 10- to 12-inch nonstick frying pan over high, bring 2 cups broth to a boil. Pour over rice, cover, and let stand until liquid is absorbed and rice is tender to bite, about 7 minutes. Fluff with a fork.

6. Meanwhile, return pan to heat. Add chicken and stir until surface is no longer pink, 1 to 2 minutes. Add bell pepper, pea pods, chiles, and lemon zest. Stir just until chicken is no longer pink in center of thickest part (cut to test), about 5 minutes.

7. Blend cornstarch and remaining broth until smooth. Stir into pan and continue stirring until mixture boils, about 1 minute. Add lemon juice.

8. Pour chicken over rice. Sprinkle with scallions.

CHICKEN CAPRESE PASTA

ACTIVE 15 MIN. - TOTAL 20 MIN.
SERVES 4

- 1 (9-oz.) pkg. fresh linguine
- 2 Tbsp. kosher salt
- 2 Tbsp. olive oil
- 2 pt. cherry tomatoes
- 1 shallot, thinly sliced
- 2 garlic cloves, minced
- 4 cups shredded rotisserie chicken
  Fresh Herb Pesto (recipe follows)
- ¼ cup small fresh basil leaves
- 4 oz. fresh mozzarella cheese, torn into ½-inch pieces

1. Cook pasta according to package directions in a large Dutch oven, adding salt once water comes to a boil. Drain pasta, reserving 1½ cups cooking water.

2. Wipe Dutch oven clean, and add olive oil. Heat oil over medium-high. Add tomatoes to hot oil and cook, stirring often, until slightly softened, about 2 minutes. Add shallot, and cook, stirring often, until softened, about 2 minutes. Stir in garlic; cook, stirring constantly, 1 minute.

3. Add chicken, pasta, Fresh Herb Pesto, and ½ cup of reserved cooking water to tomato mixture, stirring to combine. Gradually stir in remaining cooking water, ¼ cup at a time, until desired consistency is reached.

4. Transfer to a serving platter, and sprinkle with basil and mozzarella. Serve immediately.

FRESH HERB PESTO

ACTIVE 10 MIN. - TOTAL 10 MIN.
MAKES ¾ CUP

- 4½ oz. Parmesan cheese, finely shredded (1½ cups)
- 1½ cups loosely packed fresh flat-leaf parsley
- 1½ cups loosely packed fresh basil
- ¾ cup fresh chives cut in ½-inch pieces
- ⅓ cup olive oil
- 2 Tbsp. fresh lemon juice
- 1¼ tsp. kosher salt

Process Parmesan cheese, parsley, basil, chives, oil, lemon juice, and salt in a food processor until well combined, 1 to 2 minutes. Use immediately or cover and chill up to 1 day.

CHICKEN
CAPRESE PASTA

CREAMY CHICKEN AND
BACON WITH HERBED
PUFF PASTRY

CREAMY CHICKEN AND BACON WITH HERBED PUFF PASTRY

With rich cheese sauce, crispy bacon, and buttery puff pastry topper, our latest take on chicken pot pie is even more sophisticated than the original.

ACTIVE 45 MIN. - TOTAL 1 HOUR
SERVES 4

- 4 boneless, skinless chicken breasts (about 1½ lb.)
- 3 cups chicken stock
- 1 tsp. kosher salt, divided
- 1 frozen puff pastry sheet, thawed (½ of 17.3-oz. pkg.)
- 1 large egg, lightly beaten
- 12 parsley leaves
- ¼ tsp. black pepper
- 2 (6-oz.) pkg. steam-in-bag fresh English peas or 3 cups frozen English peas
- 4 bacon slices
- 3 Tbsp. salted butter
- 1 cup chopped Vidalia or other sweet onion (from 1 medium onion)
- ½ cup (¼-inch) diagonally sliced celery (from 1 large stalk)
- ¼ cup all-purpose flour
- ½ cup heavy cream
- 2 oz. fontina cheese, shredded (about ½ cup)

1. Preheat oven to 400°F. Place chicken, stock, and ½ teaspoon salt in a large saucepan; bring to a boil over high. Reduce heat to medium-low; cover and cook until chicken is cooked through, about 15 minutes. Remove from heat and let stand about 20 minutes. Remove chicken from stock, reserving 2½ cups of the stock. Coarsely shred chicken.

2. Meanwhile, place puff pastry sheet on a baking sheet lined with parchment paper. Cut pastry sheet into 4 squares; separate squares. Brush squares lightly with egg; top each square with 3 parsley leaves, pressing gently to adhere. Sprinkle with pepper. Bake on oven rack in lower third of preheated oven until dough is puffed and golden brown, 12 to 14 minutes.

3. Cook peas according to package directions; keep warm.

4. Cook bacon in a large skillet over medium-high until crisp, about 6 minutes. Remove bacon to a paper-towel-lined plate, reserving drippings in skillet; crumble bacon. Add butter to hot drippings in skillet; cook over medium until butter melts, about 1 minute. Add onion and celery; cook, stirring often, until onion is tender and celery is tender-crisp, about 8 minutes. Add flour and cook, stirring constantly, about 1 minute. Stir in cream and reserved 2½ cups stock; bring to a simmer, stirring often. Stir in peas, cheese, chicken, bacon, and remaining ½ teaspoon salt; reduce heat to medium-low. Cook until thickened and thoroughly heated, about 10 minutes.

5. Divide chicken mixture among 4 shallow bowls. Top each with a puff pastry square. Serve immediately.

- -

EASY CHICKEN POT PIE

In this easy chicken pot pie, chicken and vegetables are combined with a creamy sauce from condensed soup, then topped with a golden biscuit crust.

ACTIVE 10 MIN. - TOTAL 40 MIN.
SERVES 4

- 1 (10¾-oz.) can condensed cream of chicken soup
- 1 (9-oz.) pkg. frozen mixed vegetables, thawed
- 1 cup cubed cooked chicken or turkey
- ½ cup milk
- 1 egg
- 1 cup all-purpose baking mix

1. Preheat the oven to 400°F. Stir together soup, vegetables, and chicken in a 9-inch pie plate. Stir the milk, egg, and baking mix in a small bowl. Spread batter over chicken mixture.

2. Bake in preheated oven until topping is golden brown, about 30 minutes.

CHICKEN POT PIE

The rich, flaky browned crust beckons to dig into this comfort meal.

ACTIVE 20 MIN. - TOTAL 1 HOUR, 15 MIN.
SERVES 6

- ½ cup butter
- ½ cup all-purpose flour
- 1½ cups chicken broth
- 1½ cups half-and-half
- ¾ tsp. table salt
- ½ tsp. freshly ground black pepper
- 2 Tbsp. butter
- 1 (8-oz.) pkg. sliced fresh mushrooms
  Table salt and black pepper, to taste
- 1 small onion, chopped
- 1 cup frozen green peas
- 3½ cups chopped cooked chicken
- 2 hard-cooked eggs, chopped
- 1 (15-oz.) pkg. refrigerated piecrusts
- 1 Tbsp. whipping cream
- 1 large egg, lightly beaten

1. Melt ½ cup butter in a heavy saucepan over low; whisk in flour, whisking until smooth. Cook, whisking constantly, 1 minute. Gradually add chicken broth and half-and-half; cook over medium, stirring constantly, until thickened and bubbly. Stir in ¾ teaspoon salt and ½ teaspoon pepper; set white sauce aside.

2. Melt 1 tablespoon butter in a large skillet over medium-high; add mushrooms, season lightly with salt and pepper, and cook until nicely browned, about 10 minutes. Don't overstir. Add mushrooms to white sauce. Add remaining 1 tablespoon butter to skillet. Add onion; sauté until tender. Stir in peas. Add vegetable mixture, chicken, and chopped eggs to white sauce.

3. Preheat oven to 375°F. Fit 1 piecrust into a 9-inch deep-dish pie plate according to package directions. Spoon filling into crust; top with remaining piecrust. Trim off excess pastry. Fold under and flute edges. Cut slits in top. Combine cream and egg; brush egg wash over pastry.

4. Bake in preheated oven until browned and bubbly, 30 to 40 minutes.

Note: To make individual pot pies, spoon filling into 6 lightly greased 1-cup baking dishes. Cut out 6 circles of piecrust dough slightly larger than diameter of baking dishes. Top each dish with a round of dough; fold under and flute edges. Cut slits in tops. Brush with egg wash. Bake at 375° for 30 to 35 minutes or until browned and bubbly.

COUSCOUS PILAF WITH ROASTED CARROTS, CHICKEN, AND FETA

Flavored with golden raisins, toasted almonds, and an ingeniously simple lemon-brown butter sauce, this fluffy couscous is delicious on its own, but roasted carrots and chicken turn it into a memorable one-bowl meal.

ACTIVE 20 MIN. - TOTAL 1 HOUR, 5 MIN.
SERVES 4

- 4 large carrots, peeled and diagonally sliced ¼ inch thick (about 12 oz.)
- 1 Tbsp. olive oil
- ¼ tsp. black pepper
- 1 tsp. kosher salt, divided
- ½ cup butter
- 2 tsp. lemon zest, plus ¼ cup fresh juice (from 1 large lemon), divided
- 1 cup uncooked couscous
- ½ cup golden raisins
- ⅓ cup chopped fresh flat-leaf parsley, plus more for garnish
- ¼ cup toasted sliced almonds
- 2 cups shredded rotisserie chicken, warmed (about 12 oz., from 1 chicken)
- 2 oz. feta cheese, crumbled (about ½ cup)

1. Preheat oven to 450°F. Combine carrots, oil, pepper, and ½ teaspoon of the salt on a large rimmed baking sheet. Toss to coat; spread in an even layer. Roast in preheated oven until tender, 16 to 18 minutes, stirring once. Remove from oven.

2. While carrots roast, melt butter in a small saucepan over medium-high. Cook until milk solids turn golden brown and have a nutty fragrance, swirling pan occasionally as mixture bubbles, about 5 minutes. Transfer to a bowl; let stand 1 minute. Stir in lemon juice; set aside.

3. Bring 1½ cups water and remaining ½ teaspoon salt to a boil in a medium saucepan over high. Stir in couscous. Cover and remove from heat; let stand 5 minutes. Fluff with a fork; stir in raisins, parsley, almonds, and 5 tablespoons of the browned butter mixture.

4. Combine carrots, chicken, and 2 tablespoons of the browned butter mixture in a bowl; toss to coat. Divide couscous pilaf evenly among 4 bowls; top with chicken mixture. Sprinkle with cheese; drizzle with remaining 1 tablespoon browned butter mixture. Top with lemon zest and parsley.

COUSCOUS PILAF WITH
ROASTED CARROTS,
CHICKEN, AND FETA

CREOLE DEEP-FRIED TURKEY

ACTIVE 20 MIN. - TOTAL 2 HOURS, 10 MIN.
SERVES 8

Peanut oil (about 3 gal.)
1 (12- to 14-lb.) whole fresh turkey*
4 Tbsp. Creole seasoning, divided
Figs, fig leaves, apples, fresh cranberries, for garnish (optional)

1. Pour oil, 10 to 12 inches from top, into a deep propane turkey fryer; heat to 350°F over a medium-low flame according to manufacturer's instructions (about 45 minutes).

2. Meanwhile, remove giblets and neck from turkey, and rinse turkey with cold water. Drain cavity well; pat dry. Loosen and lift skin from turkey with fingers, without totally detaching skin; spread 1 tablespoon Creole seasoning under skin. Carefully replace skin. Sprinkle 1 tablespoon Creole seasoning inside cavity; rub into cavity. Sprinkle outside of turkey with remaining 2 tablespoons Creole seasoning, and rub into skin. Let turkey stand at room temperature 30 minutes.

3. Place turkey on fryer rod. Carefully lower turkey into hot oil with rod attachment.

4. Fry 35 to 45 minutes or until a meat thermometer inserted in thickest portion of thigh registers 165°F (about 3 minutes per pound, plus an additional 5 minutes. Keep oil temperature between 300°F and 325°F). Remove turkey from oil; drain and let stand 30 minutes before slicing. Garnish, if desired.

*Note: Frozen whole turkey, thawed, may be substituted.

ROAST TURKEY AND GRAVY

ACTIVE 14 MIN. - TOTAL 3 HOURS., 10 MIN.
SERVES 12 TO 14

1 (12- to 14-lb.) turkey
1 Tbsp. table salt
2 tsp. black pepper
½ cup butter, softened
1 Golden Delicious apple, quartered
1 large yellow onion, quartered
2 large carrots, cut into 3-inch pieces
3 celery ribs with leaves, cut into 3-inch pieces
4 cups hot water
⅓ cup all-purpose flour

1. Preheat oven to 425°F. Remove giblets and neck from turkey; rinse and reserve for another use.

2. Rinse turkey with cold water, and pat dry. Sprinkle cavity with ½ tablespoon salt and 1 teaspoon pepper. Rub skin of turkey with butter, and sprinkle with remaining ½ tablespoon salt and 1 teaspoon pepper.

3. Place apple, onion, carrots, and celery in turkey cavity. Lift wingtips up and over back, and tuck under bird. Place turkey, breast-side up, on a lightly greased rack in a roasting pan.

4. Roast in preheated oven on lower oven rack 20 minutes. Reduce oven temperature to 325°F. Add hot water to pan, and roast 2 to 2½ hours or until a meat thermometer inserted in turkey thigh registers 170°F, shielding turkey with foil after 1 hour and basting with pan juices every 20 minutes. Let stand 15 minutes. Transfer to a serving platter; reserve 2½ cups drippings.

5. Whisk together drippings and ⅓ cup flour in a medium saucepan. Cook over medium, whisking constantly, 5 to 7 minutes or until thick and bubbly. Season gravy to taste. Serve with roasted turkey.

ROAST TURKEY
AND GRAVY

MINI TURKEY POT PIES WITH DRESSING TOPS

For this recipe, you'll need eight 3½-inch cast-iron skillets.

ACTIVE 1 HOUR · TOTAL 3 HOURS, 15 MIN.
SERVES 8

CRUST
- 3¾ cups all-purpose flour, plus more for work surface
- 1½ tsp. sea salt
- 1½ cups cold unsalted butter, cut into cubes
- 1 cup cold whole buttermilk

FILLING
- 6 Tbsp. unsalted butter, divided
- ½ cup all-purpose flour
- 2 cups chicken stock
- 1¾ cups whole milk
- 1½ tsp. sea salt
- ¾ tsp. freshly cracked black pepper
- 1 medium-size yellow onion, finely chopped
- 2 garlic cloves, minced
- 1½ cups thinly sliced peeled carrots
- 1½ cups sliced fresh green beans
- 1 cup frozen green peas, thawed
- 1 Tbsp. chopped fresh thyme leaves
- 1 Tbsp. chopped fresh sage leaves
- 2 lb. cooked turkey breast, chopped (about 4 heaping cups)

TOPPING
- ½ cup unsalted butter
- 2 (6-oz.) pkg. stuffing mix

1. Prepare the Crust: Whisk together flour and salt in a medium bowl. Add cold cubed butter, and use your fingers to quickly work butter into flour mixture. (Some butter pieces will be the size of oat flakes, and some will be the size of peas.) Create a well in flour mixture, and pour in cold buttermilk. Use a fork to bring dough together, moistening all flour bits. Turn dough mixture onto a lightly floured work surface. Dough will be moist and shaggy. Divide dough in 2 pieces, and gently knead each piece into a disk. Wrap each disk in plastic wrap, and chill 1 hour.

2. Meanwhile, prepare the Filling: Melt 4 tablespoons of the butter in a large saucepan over medium. Whisk in flour, and cook, whisking constantly, about 1 minute. (Mixture will be very thick.) Reduce heat to low; gradually add chicken stock, whisking constantly until no flour bits remain. Whisk in milk. Increase heat to medium-low; cook, whisking often, until mixture is consistency of thick pudding, about 20 minutes. Remove from heat, and whisk in salt and pepper.

3. Melt remaining 2 tablespoons butter in a large skillet over medium. Add onion; cook, stirring constantly, until translucent, about 3 minutes. Add garlic; cook, stirring constantly, 1 minute. Add carrots and green beans; cook, stirring occasionally, 5 minutes. (Vegetables will not be cooked through.) Stir in peas, thyme, and sage; cook 1 minute. Remove from heat, and stir in turkey. Stir turkey-vegetable mixture into stock mixture in saucepan; cool slightly, about 5 minutes.

4. Prepare the Topping: Bring 3 cups water and the butter to a boil in a large saucepan over medium, stirring occasionally to melt butter. Add stuffing mix, and gently stir to combine. Cover and remove from heat. Let stand 10 minutes.

5. Remove 1 pie dough disk from refrigerator. Unwrap and roll dough into a ¼-inch-thick round on a lightly floured surface. Cut an 8-inch circle from a piece of parchment paper. Use parchment round as a guide to cut 8-inch rounds from piecrust using a sharp knife. Fit 1 piecrust round in bottom and up sides of each skillet. Repeat with remaining dough disk, rerolling scraps as needed, until all 8 skillets are lined.

6. Place racks in lower and upper thirds of oven. Preheat oven to 375°F. Spoon about 1½ cups filling into each crust; cover with about ¾ cup topping. Bake in preheated oven until crust is golden brown and filling is lightly bubbling, 45 to 50 minutes, rotating skillets halfway through baking. Remove from oven, and let stand 20 minutes before serving.

BAKED PENNE WITH TURKEY

ACTIVE 18 MIN. - TOTAL 1 HOUR, 10 MIN.
SERVES 10

- 12 oz. uncooked penne
- 1 Tbsp. olive oil
- 2 (8-oz.) pkg. sliced mushrooms
- 2 Tbsp. dry sherry
- 1 cup chopped onion
- 2 tsp. minced garlic
- 5 Tbsp. all-purpose flour
- 3 cups organic vegetable broth
- 1 cup milk
- 1 Tbsp. fresh thyme leaves
- ¾ tsp. table salt
- ½ tsp. freshly ground black pepper
- ¼ cup unsalted butter
- 4 cups chopped cooked turkey breast
- 1 cup frozen petite green peas, thawed
- 4 oz. grated fresh Parmesan cheese (about 1 cup), divided
- Thyme leaves, for garnish (optional)

1. Preheat oven to 350°F.

2. Cook pasta according to package directions, omitting salt and fat. Drain and return to pan. Cover and keep warm.

3. Heat a large nonstick skillet over medium-high. Add oil; swirl to coat. Add mushrooms; cook 8 minutes or until browned and tender, stirring occasionally. Stir in sherry, scraping pan to loosen browned bits. Cook 1 minute or until liquid evaporates. Remove mushrooms from pan. Add onion and garlic to pan; sauté over medium 4 minutes. Add 1 tablespoon water; cook 1 minute or until tender, stirring constantly.

4. Place flour in a large saucepan; gradually add vegetable broth and next 4 ingredients, stirring with a whisk until blended. Place over medium heat; cook until thick (about 5 minutes), stirring constantly. Add butter, stirring until melted. Add sauce, mushrooms, onion mixture, turkey, peas, and ½ cup cheese to pasta, stirring until cheese melts. Pour mixture into a 13- x 9-inch glass or ceramic baking dish coated with cooking spray. Sprinkle with remaining ½ cup cheese.

5. Bake in preheated oven, uncovered, until bubbly and thoroughly heated, about 25 minutes. Let stand 5 minutes. Garnish with thyme, if desired.

RANCH TURKEY BURGERS

A mix of reduced-fat sour cream, mayonnaise, and buttermilk keeps the patties moist, while a few spice-rack staples add the ranch flavor everyone loves.

ACTIVE 15 MIN. - TOTAL 20 MIN.
SERVES 4

- 1¼ lb. ground turkey
- ½ tsp. garlic powder
- ½ tsp. onion powder
- ½ tsp. dried dill
- ¼ cup reduced-fat sour cream, divided
- ¼ cup mayonnaise, divided
- 3 Tbsp. reduced-fat buttermilk, divided
- ¾ tsp. kosher salt, divided
- ¾ tsp. black pepper, divided
- 1 Tbsp. olive oil
- 1 tsp. apple cider vinegar
- 4 hamburger buns, toasted
- Romaine lettuce heart leaves, thin tomato slices, and red onion slices for topping

1. Combine turkey, garlic powder, onion powder, dill, and 1 tablespoon each of sour cream, mayonnaise, and buttermilk in a medium bowl. Divide turkey mixture into 4 (5-ounce) portions; shape into 1-inch-thick patties. Sprinkle patties with ½ teaspoon each of the salt and pepper.

2. Heat oil in a large nonstick skillet over medium-high. Add burgers to skillet; cover and cook until bottoms are browned, about 4 minutes. Turn burgers; cover and cook until browned and a meat thermometer inserted in thickest portion registers 165°F, about 3 minutes.

3. Stir together apple cider vinegar and remaining 3 tablespoons each of sour cream and mayonnaise, 2 tablespoons buttermilk, and ¼ teaspoon each of salt and pepper in a small bowl. Spread about 1 tablespoon of the mixture on each bun half. Place 1 patty on each bottom half of bun; top each with lettuce, tomato, red onion slices, and bun top.

RANCH TURKEY
BURGERS

TURKEY AND SPINACH MEATBALL SANDWICHES

Make these meatballs extra tender with sautéed spinach. Mild fresh spinach can be slipped into just about any recipe. Simply wilt it in a pan with a little water or oil until it cooks down. Let the spinach cool; then wring out any excess moisture. Add it to pastas, top a pizza, or stir it into scrambled eggs. Also, layer sliced leaves on hearty sandwiches for extra color and nutrients.

ACTIVE 40 MIN. - TOTAL 40 MIN.
SERVES 4

1	(8-oz.) pkg. fresh baby spinach, divided
1	Tbsp. extra-virgin olive oil
1½	tsp. minced garlic
½	tsp. kosher salt, divided
½	tsp. black pepper, divided
½	lb. ground turkey (with dark meat)
½	lb. spicy Italian turkey sausage, casings removed
½	cup fine dry breadcrumbs
⅓	cup minced onion
1½	oz. Parmesan cheese, grated (about ⅓ cup)
2	large eggs, lightly beaten
1½	cups jarred marinara sauce
4	oz. provolone cheese, shredded (about 2 cups)
4	French hoagie rolls

1. Thinly slice 1 cup of the spinach; set aside. Heat oil in a Dutch oven over medium. Add garlic; cook until lightly browned and fragrant, about 1 minute. Stir in remaining spinach; cook, stirring constantly, about 2 minutes. Add ¼ teaspoon each of the salt and pepper; cook, stirring often, 2 minutes. Drain well, and finely chop spinach mixture.

2. Stir together ground turkey, next 5 ingredients, chopped spinach mixture, and remaining ¼ teaspoon each salt and pepper in a large bowl until well blended. Gently shape turkey mixture into 20 (1-inch) balls.

3. Bring marinara sauce and ¼ cup water to a boil in a large skillet over medium, stirring occasionally. Reduce heat to medium-low, and maintain at a simmer. Add meatballs, and cook until meatballs are cooked through, 6 to 8 minutes. Reduce heat to low; cover and cook for 10 minutes.

4. Remove from heat; sprinkle with provolone cheese. Let stand, covered, until cheese melts, 1 to 2 minutes. Divide meatballs and sauce among hoagie rolls. Top evenly with reserved sliced spinach. Serve immediately.

HONEY-SOY-GLAZED SALMON WITH VEGGIES AND ORANGES

Here's the delicious proof that you can serve a complete no-mess fish dinner in fewer than 30 minutes. For better, richer flavor, apply layers of glaze several times throughout the cooking process.

ACTIVE 25 MIN. - TOTAL 25 MIN.
SERVES 4

4	Tbsp. honey
1	Tbsp. soy sauce
1	Tbsp. Dijon mustard
1	tsp. seasoned rice wine vinegar
¼	tsp. crushed red pepper
1	lb. fresh asparagus
8	oz. fresh green beans, trimmed
1	small orange, cut into ¼- to ½-inch slices
1	Tbsp. olive oil
1	tsp. kosher salt
¼	tsp. freshly ground black pepper
4	(5- to 6-oz.) fresh salmon fillets
	Toasted sesame seeds, for garnish

1. Preheat broiler with oven rack 6 inches from heat. Whisk together honey and next 4 ingredients in a small bowl.

2. Snap off and discard tough ends of asparagus. Place asparagus, green beans, and next 4 ingredients in a large bowl, and toss to coat.

3. Place salmon in center of a sheet pan lined with aluminum foil. Brush salmon with about 2 tablespoons honey mixture. Spread asparagus mixture around salmon.

4. Broil 4 minutes; remove from oven and brush salmon with about 2 tablespoons honey mixture. Return to oven, and broil 4 minutes more. Remove from oven and brush salmon with remaining honey mixture. Return to oven and broil 2 minutes more. Serve immediately.

132

HONEY-SOY-GLAZED SALMON WITH
VEGGIES AND ORANGES

FRIED DELACATA CATFISH

ACTIVE 35 MIN. - TOTAL 40 MIN.
SERVES 6

>   Peanut oil
> 6   (4-oz.) Delacata catfish fillets
> 1   cup whole milk or buttermilk
> ¾   cup fine yellow cornmeal
> ½   cup all-purpose flour
> 1   tsp. garlic powder
> 1   tsp. black pepper
> 1   tsp. dried thyme
> 1   tsp. paprika
> ½   tsp. cayenne pepper
> ¼   tsp. celery seeds
> 2   tsp. kosher salt, divided
>   Lemon wedges, for serving
>   Black-Eyed Pea Ranchero Sauce, for serving
>   (recipe follows)

1. Preheat oven to 200°F. Pour peanut oil into a large, heavy frying pan to ½ inch up sides. (Cast iron is best.) Heat over medium-high until oil reaches 350°F. (A good test is to flick a little of the dry breading into the oil. If it sizzles at once, it's ready to cook.)

2. While oil is heating, soak catfish in milk 5 minutes. Set a wire rack a large rimmed baking sheet, and place in preheated oven.

3. Combine the next 7 ingredients, and 1 teaspoon of the salt in a shallow dish for dredging. (Or substitute your favorite seasoning.)

4. Once the oil is hot, remove catfish fillets from milk, and dredge them in flour mixture, shaking off excess. Working in two batches, carefully place fillets in hot oil; fry until golden brown and cooked through, about 4 minutes per side. Sprinkle remaining salt (about ½ teaspoon per batch) on fish when it comes out of the pan.

5. Transfer cooked catfish to wire rack in baking sheet in preheated oven. Serve catfish with lemon wedges and Black-Eyed Pea Ranchero Sauce.

BLACK-EYED PEA RANCHERO SAUCE

ACTIVE 20 MIN. - TOTAL 25 MIN.
SERVES 10

> 1   Tbsp. olive oil
> 1   (15.5-oz.) can black-eyed peas, drained and rinsed
> 1   cup chopped white onion (from 1 onion)
> ½   cup chopped, seeded jalapeño chiles (from 3 large chiles)
> 1   garlic clove, minced
> 1   (15-oz.) can whole peeled plum tomatoes
> 1½ tsp. kosher salt
> ½   tsp. black pepper
> ½   tsp. ground cumin
> ½   tsp. paprika

Heat oil in a medium saucepan over medium-high. Add peas, onion, and jalapeño; cook, stirring constantly, until softened, about 5 minutes. Add garlic and cook, stirring constantly until soft, about 1 minute. Carefully add tomatoes, breaking up tomatoes using the back of a wooden spoon. Stir in salt, pepper, cumin, and paprika. Reduce heat to medium-low; simmer, stirring occasionally, until tomato liquid is partially thickened, about 10 minutes. Remove from heat, and cool slightly, about 5 minutes.

CRISPY PAN-FRIED CATFISH

ACTIVE 10 MIN. - TOTAL 20 MIN.
SERVES 4

- 1 egg white, lightly beaten
- ¼ cup yellow cornmeal
- 2 Tbsp. grated Parmesan cheese
- 1 Tbsp. chopped fresh thyme
- ¼ tsp. black pepper
- 4 (4-oz.) catfish fillets
- 3 Tbsp. all-purpose flour
  Chopped fresh thyme (optional)
  Lemon wedges (optional)

1. Combine egg white and 1 tablespoon water; stir well and set aside. Combine cornmeal and next 3 ingredients; set aside. Dredge fillets in flour; dip in egg white mixture, and dredge in cornmeal mixture.

2. Coat a large nonstick skillet with cooking spray; place over medium-high until hot. Add fillets; cook 3 minutes on each side or until fish flakes easily with a fork. If desired, sprinkle with chopped fresh thyme and serve with lemon wedges.

- -

GRILLED TUNA STEAKS WITH HORSERADISH SAUCE

ACTIVE 10 MIN. - TOTAL 1 HOUR, 25 MIN., INCLUDING MARINATING
SERVES 4

- ¼ cup Worcestershire sauce
- 2 Tbsp. low-sodium soy sauce
- 1 Tbsp. olive oil
- 1 tsp. dried oregano
- ½ tsp. freshly ground black pepper
- 2 garlic cloves, minced
- 4 (6-oz.) tuna steaks (about 1 inch thick)
- ½ cup reduced-fat sour cream
- 1½ tsp. prepared horseradish
- ½ tsp. table salt
- ½ tsp. Dijon mustard
- ¼ tsp. Worcestershire sauce

1. Combine first 6 ingredients in a large zip-top plastic bag. Add fish to bag; seal and marinate in refrigerator 1 hour, turning once.

2. Combine sour cream and remaining ingredients in a small bowl; set aside.

3. Preheat grill to medium (350°F to 400°F).

4. Remove fish from marinade; transfer marinade to a small saucepan. Bring marinade to boiling over medium; boil for 5 minutes. Place fish on grill rack coated with cooking spray. Grill, with lid closed, 6 minutes on each side or just until fish flakes with a fork but is pink in the center, basting frequently with marinade. Serve with horseradish sauce.

- -

SHRIMP-AND-BLACK BEAN STIR-FRY

This tropical pairing of sweet and savory will wake up tired taste buds at the dinner table.

ACTIVE 30 MIN. - TOTAL 30 MIN.
SERVES 4

- ½ medium red onion, sliced
- 1 medium red bell pepper, sliced
- 3 Tbsp. olive oil, divided
- 1 cup fresh corn kernels (about 2 ears)
- 1 lb. large peeled, deveined raw shrimp
- 3 garlic cloves, sliced
- 1 cup chopped fresh mango or pineapple
- 1 (15-oz.) can black beans, drained and rinsed
- ½ cup teriyaki baste-and-glaze sauce
- ¼ cup pineapple juice
  Hot cooked rice
  Fresh cilantro leaves, for garnish

1. Stir-fry onion and bell pepper in 1 tablespoon hot oil in a large cast-iron skillet over medium-high 2 to 3 minutes or until lightly browned. Transfer onion mixture to a plate, using a slotted spoon; keep warm.

2. Add corn and 1 tablespoon oil to skillet; stir-fry 2 to 3 minutes. Transfer corn to plate with onion mixture, using a slotted spoon.

3. Pat shrimp dry. Add shrimp, garlic, and remaining 1 tablespoon oil to skillet; stir-fry 2 to 3 minutes or just until shrimp begin to turn pink.

4. Add mango and black beans; stir-fry 2 to 3 minutes or until thoroughly heated. Add teriyaki sauce and pineapple juice; cook 1 to 2 minutes or until bubbling. Stir in corn and onion mixture. Serve over hot cooked rice and sprinkle with cilantro.

SHRIMP-AND-BLACK
BEAN STIR-FRY

JAMBALAYA
KEBABS

JAMBALAYA KEBABS

ACTIVE 20 MIN. - TOTAL 20 MIN.
SERVES 4

- 8 oz. large peeled, deveined raw shrimp (about 16)
- 6 oz. smoked sausage, cut into 1/2-inch rounds (about 1 cup)
- 1 small sweet onion, cut into 1-inch pieces (about 1 cup)
- 1 small red bell pepper, cut into 1-inch pieces (about 3/4 cup)
- 16 cherry tomatoes (about 1/2 pint)
- 3 Tbsp. olive oil
- 2 tsp. Cajun seasoning
- 1 tsp. chopped fresh thyme
- 1/2 tsp. chopped fresh oregano
- 2 Tbsp. chopped fresh flat-leaf parsley

1. Preheat grill to high (450°F to 500°F), or heat a grill pan over high. Combine first 9 ingredients in a large bowl; toss to coat. Thread mixture onto 8 (10-inch) skewers, alternating ingredients.

2. Place kebabs on oiled grill grates. Grill, uncovered, until vegetables and sausage are lightly charred and shrimp is cooked through, about 2 minutes per side. Transfer kebabs to a serving plate, and sprinkle with parsley.

- -

SNAPPY CAJUN SHRIMP

Serve this spicy Cajun shrimp recipe with an easy side dish, such as cheese grits. Simply stir grated cheese into any variety of cooked grits.

ACTIVE 10 MIN. - TOTAL 10 MIN.
SERVES 4

- 1 1/2 lb. large peeled, deveined raw shrimp
- 1 tsp. paprika
- 3/4 tsp. dried thyme
- 3/4 tsp. dried oregano
- 1/4 tsp. garlic powder
- 1/4 tsp. table salt
- 1/4 tsp. black pepper
- 1/4 tsp. cayenne pepper
- 1 Tbsp. vegetable oil

Combine first 8 ingredients in a large zip-top plastic bag; seal bag and shake to coat. Heat oil in a large nonstick skillet over medium-high until hot. Add shrimp; cook, stirring frequently, just until shrimp begin to turn pink, about 4 minutes.

- -

SHRIMP KEBABS

For authentic Italian presentation, thread the shrimp on sturdy rosemary sprigs before grilling. In place of fresh rosemary sprigs, thread shrimp onto wooden skewers (soak skewers in water for 30 minutes first).

ACTIVE 10 MIN. - TOTAL 30 MIN.
SERVES 6

- 1 tsp. chopped fresh thyme
- 1 tsp. chopped fresh oregano
- 1/2 tsp. chopped fresh rosemary
- 1/2 tsp. lemon zest
- 1/2 tsp. olive oil
- 1/4 tsp. table salt
- 1/4 tsp. freshly ground black pepper
- 1 garlic clove, minced
  Dash cayenne pepper
- 18 large peeled, deveined raw shrimp
- 6 (6-inch) rosemary sprigs

1. Preheat grill to medium (350°F to 400°F).

2. Combine first 10 ingredients in a zip-top plastic bag; seal and shake well. Marinate in refrigerator for 15 minutes, turning occasionally.

3. Thread 3 shrimp on each rosemary sprig. Place prepared sprigs on grill rack coated with cooking spray. Grill 2 minutes on each side, or until shrimp just begin to turn pink.

LEMON-GARLIC BUTTER SHRIMP AND BROCCOLI

ACTIVE 20 MIN. - TOTAL 40 MIN.
SERVES 4

- 6 Tbsp. unsalted butter
- 4 garlic cloves, finely chopped (1 Tbsp.)
- 1 Tbsp. fresh lemon juice (from 1 lemon)
- ½ tsp. black pepper
- ½ tsp. crushed red pepper
- 1½ tsp. kosher salt, divided
- 1 (6-oz.) box long-grain and wild rice mix
- 2¼ cups lower-sodium chicken broth
- 3 cups broccoli florets (from 1 head)
- 3 Tbsp. olive oil
- 1 medium lemon, thinly sliced
- 12 oz. large peeled, deveined raw shrimp

1. Preheat oven to 450°F. Combine butter, garlic, lemon juice, black pepper, crushed red pepper, and 1 teaspoon of the salt in a small microwavable bowl. Microwave on HIGH until melted, about 45 seconds; set aside.

2. Cook rice according to package directions, substituting the broth for water. Fluff with a fork; stir in 1 tablespoon of the butter mixture. Cover to keep warm.

3. Meanwhile, toss together broccoli, oil, lemon slices, and remaining ½ teaspoon salt on a rimmed baking sheet; spread in a single layer. Roast in preheated oven until broccoli is crisp-tender, about 13 minutes.

4. Arrange shrimp on baking sheet with broccoli. Drizzle with remaining butter mixture. Roast at 450°F until shrimp are pink, about 5 minutes. Serve with rice.

PASTA PRIMAVERA WITH SHRIMP

ACTIVE 20 MIN. - TOTAL 30 MIN.
SERVES 4

- 2 Tbsp. olive oil
- 1 lb. medium peeled, deveined raw shrimp
- ¾ tsp. kosher salt
- 1 large red bell pepper, chopped (about 1¼ cups)
- 5 oz. snap peas, diagonally halved crosswise (about 1¼ cups)
- ¼ cup chopped shallot (about 1 medium shallot)
- 10 oz. uncooked gemelli pasta
- 4 cups unsalted chicken stock
- 4 oz. baby spinach (about 4 cups)
- 1½ cups chopped Broccolini (about 4 oz.)
- 2 Tbsp. white wine vinegar
- ½ oz. Pecorino Romano cheese, shredded (about 2 Tbsp.)
- ½ tsp. crushed red pepper

1. Heat 1 tablespoon of the oil in a Dutch oven over medium-high. Sprinkle shrimp with ¼ teaspoon of the salt. Add shrimp to Dutch oven; cook until cooked through, 3 to 4 minutes, stirring once. Remove shrimp; set aside. Pour off any remaining drippings from Dutch oven. Add remaining 1 tablespoon oil. Add bell pepper, snap peas, and shallot; cook, stirring often, until vegetables are tender, about 4 minutes. Add bell pepper mixture to shrimp; cover to keep warm.

2. Add pasta, stock, and remaining ½ teaspoon salt to Dutch oven; bring to a boil over medium-high. Boil pasta, stirring occasionally, until pasta is almost tender and stock is almost absorbed, about 9 minutes. Add spinach and Broccolini; cook until spinach is wilted, 1 to 2 minutes. Stir in shrimp mixture and vinegar. Remove from heat. Divide evenly among 4 bowls; top with cheese and crushed red pepper.

PASTA PRIMAVERA
WITH SHRIMP

GRILLED CLAMBAKE
FOIL PACKETS WITH
HERB BUTTER

GRILLED CLAMBAKE FOIL PACKETS WITH HERB BUTTER

Mesh bags are often used at clambakes, but we prefer foil packets for this recipe. The foil pouches concentrate the flavors of this summery seafood meal and its buttery seasoned sauce.

ACTIVE 20 MIN. - TOTAL 40 MIN.
SERVES 6

1½ cups (12 oz.) unsalted butter, softened
¼ cup finely chopped shallot (about 1 shallot)
2 Tbsp. chopped fresh flat-leaf parsley
1 Tbsp. chopped fresh dill
1½ tsp. lemon zest (from 1 lemon)
3 Tbsp. Old Bay seasoning, divided
12 small red potatoes (about 2 lb.), cut into ½-inch wedges
3 ears corn, husks removed, each ear cut into 4 pieces
24 unpeeled medium raw shrimp (about ⅔ lb.)
24 littleneck clams in shells, scrubbed (about 1 lb., 3 oz.)
1 lb. smoked sausage, cut diagonally into 1-inch-thick slices
3 lemons, cut into quarters
6 thyme sprigs
  Grilled French bread

1. Stir together butter, shallot, parsley, dill, lemon zest, and 1 tablespoon of the Old Bay seasoning in a medium bowl until well blended.

2. Combine potatoes and ¼ cup water in a medium-size microwavable bowl; cover with plastic wrap. Microwave on HIGH until tender and a knife can be inserted easily in center of potatoes, about 5 minutes. Drain and let stand 5 minutes.

3. Preheat a grill to medium (400°F to 450°F). Cut 12 (12-inch) squares of heavy-duty aluminum foil. Place 6 squares of foil on a work surface. Divide potato wedges and corn evenly among foil. Top each with 4 shrimp and 4 clams. Top evenly with sausage slices and lemon wedges. Dollop each with about ¼ cup butter mixture. Top each with 1 thyme sprig, and sprinkle each with 1 teaspoon Old Bay. Top each mound with a foil square, then crimp all sides together to seal tightly.

4. Grill packets, covered, until shrimp are done and clams open, 8 to 10 minutes, rotating packets on grill halfway through cooking time. Discard any clams that do not open. Serve with grilled French bread.

GRILLED OYSTERS

Unlike a traditional Low-country oyster roast (which requires cooking oysters under a layer of wet burlap on a large metal slab, usually with the help of several people), this simplified version is easy to pull off.

ACTIVE 40 MIN. - TOTAL 2 HOURS, 40 MIN.
SERVES 16

8 dozen oysters in the shell, scrubbed and dried

1. Place firewood and/or natural lump charcoal in base of grill, and ignite fuel. Once fire has burned down, and coals are glowing orange and white and have reached medium-high (400°F to 450°F), place 3 to 4 dozen oysters, cupped sides down, on grill grate. Grill, covered, until oysters just begin to open at the wide end, 8 to 10 minutes. Discard any that do not open.

2. Use tongs to carefully transfer hot oysters to a serving platter, retaining as much liquid as possible. Let stand until cool enough to handle with a towel, 10 minutes. Using an oyster or paring knife, pry open oysters, discard top shells, and place the half shells on the platter. Serve immediately. Repeat with remaining oysters.

HOT PEPPER VINEGAR

ACTIVE 5 MIN. - TOTAL 15 MIN., PLUS 8 HOURS CHILLING
MAKES ABOUT 2 CUPS

Place 6 halved, stemmed, and seeded **jalapeños** in a medium bowl or jar. Whisk together 2 cups **apple cider vinegar** and 2 Tbsp. **kosher salt** in a small saucepan over medium. Bring to a boil. Remove from heat; immediately pour vinegar mixture over chiles. Let cool completely. Store, covered, in refrigerator at least 8 hours or overnight. (For best flavor, make several days in advance.) When ready to serve with oysters, thinly slice a few of the chiles, and place slices in a serving bowl. Add some of the vinegar, and stir in 1 Tbsp. chopped **fresh cilantro** before serving with oysters.

MEYER LEMON-GINGER MIGNONETTE

ACTIVE 10 MIN. - TOTAL 10 MIN., PLUS 30 MIN. STANDING
MAKES ABOUT 2 CUPS

Combine ½ cup **champagne vinegar**, 1½ Tbsp. fresh Meyer lemon zest and 6 Tbsp. juice (from 1 **Meyer lemon**), 1 minced **shallot** (about 6 Tbsp.), 2 Tbsp. peeled and minced **fresh ginger** (from a 1-inch piece), 1 tsp. **black pepper**, and ½ tsp. fine **sea salt** in a bowl. Stir well; let stand 30 minutes before serving with oysters.

FIELD PEA CAKES WITH TOMATO-GINGER JAM

ACTIVE 30 MIN. - TOTAL 45 MIN.
SERVES 6

- 3 cups shelled fresh or thawed frozen field peas (1 lb.), rinsed
- 2 tsp. kosher salt, divided
- 2 Tbsp. peanut oil or canola oil, plus more for frying
- ½ cup finely chopped yellow onion (from 1 small onion)
- ½ cup finely chopped red bell pepper (from 1 small bell pepper)
- 1 tsp. curry powder or garam masala
- 2 cups panko breadcrumbs, divided
- ½ cup all-purpose flour
- 2 large eggs
  Tomato-Ginger Jam (recipe follows)
  Sliced scallions for topping

1. Stir together peas and 1 teaspoon of the salt in a medium saucepan. Add water to cover by 1 inch. Bring to a boil over high, skimming foam that rises to the top. Reduce heat to medium; partially cover, and simmer until tender, 15 to 25 minutes. Drain and set aside.

2. Heat oil in a large skillet over medium-high. Stir in onion and bell pepper; cook, stirring occasionally, until tender, about 5 minutes. Stir in curry powder; cook, stirring constantly, 1 minute. Transfer mixture to a food processor. Add 2 cups of cooked peas and remaining 1 teaspoon salt. Pulse until mixture forms a coarse paste, 5 to 6 times. Transfer mixture to a medium bowl. Fold in ½ cup of the panko and remaining 1 cup cooked peas. Form into 12 (3-inch) cakes.

3. Place flour in a shallow bowl. Lightly beat eggs in a separate shallow bowl. Place remaining 1½ cups panko in a third shallow bowl. Working with 1 cake at a time, coat with flour, dip in eggs, and then coat with panko, pressing gently to adhere.

4. Pour oil into a large skillet to a depth of ¼ inch; heat over medium-high. Working in batches, add cakes to hot oil; cook until browned and crisp, about 2 minutes per side, flipping once. Drain on paper towels. (Skim and discard panko bits between batches to prevent burning.) Serve warm with Tomato-Ginger Jam; top with scallions.

TOMATO-GINGER JAM

ACTIVE 20 MIN. - TOTAL 40 MIN.
MAKES ABOUT 1¼ CUPS

- 1 cup canned crushed tomatoes in puree
- ¼ cup packed light brown sugar
- 2 Tbsp. sherry vinegar
- 2 Tbsp. very finely chopped fresh ginger (from 1-inch piece ginger)
- ½ tsp. kosher salt
- ½ tsp. curry powder or garam masala
- ½ tsp. yellow mustard seeds
- ¼ tsp. ground cinnamon
- ¼ tsp. cayenne pepper

Stir together all ingredients in a saucepan. Bring to simmer over medium-high, stirring to dissolve sugar. Reduce heat to low; simmer, stirring occasionally, until slightly thickened, about 15 minutes. Cool 20 minutes. Transfer to an airtight container; cover and chill up to 2 weeks. Serve slightly chilled.

SKILLET VEGETABLE
PIE WITH GOAT CHEESE

SKILLET VEGETABLE PIE WITH GOAT CHEESE

Crisp, buttery phyllo makes a beautiful crust for this veggie-filled skillet pie—no dough-making required.

ACTIVE 30 MIN. - TOTAL 2 HOURS
SERVES 6

>   5 Tbsp. olive oil, divided
>   1 small yellow onion, chopped
>   2 cups cubed butternut squash
>   1 lb. Broccolini, chopped
>   4 oz. fresh cremini mushrooms, chopped
>   (1¾ cups)
>   2 small garlic cloves, chopped
> 1¼ oz. Parmesan cheese, shredded (about ½ cup)
>   1 large egg, beaten
>   1 tsp. kosher salt
>   ½ tsp. black pepper
>   ½ tsp. crushed red pepper
>   6 Tbsp. unsalted butter, melted
>   12 (14- x 9-inch) sheets frozen phyllo dough,
>   thawed
>   2 oz. goat cheese, crumbled (about ½ cup)

1. Preheat oven to 350°F. Heat 2 tablespoons of the oil in a 9-inch cast-iron skillet over medium. Add onion and cook, stirring often, until softened, about 6 minutes. Add squash; cover and cook, stirring occasionally, until almost tender, about 8 minutes. Transfer mixture to a medium bowl. Add remaining 3 tablespoons oil to skillet over medium-high. Add Broccolini, mushrooms, and garlic. (Skillet will be very full; vegetables will cook down.) Cook, stirring occasionally, until almost tender, about 8 minutes. Transfer to bowl with squash mixture. Wipe skillet clean. Let vegetable mixture cool 30 minutes. Add Parmesan, egg, salt, black pepper, and crushed red pepper to squash mixture; stir to combine.

2. Brush skillet lightly with butter. Fit 1 phyllo sheet into skillet, allowing edges to hang over sides. (Cover remaining sheets with a damp paper towel to prevent them from drying out.) Quickly brush sheet lightly with butter, and turn skillet 45 degrees. Continuing to work quickly, top with a second sheet; brush lightly with butter. Repeat with remaining sheets and butter, reserving 1 tablespoon of the butter.

3. Spoon vegetable mixture evenly over phyllo layers in skillet. Sprinkle goat cheese over top. Fold edges of phyllo sheets up and over, toward center, overlapping slightly, leaving center exposed. Brush top of phyllo with remaining 1 tablespoon butter. Bake in preheated oven until crust is golden brown, about 40 minutes. Transfer skillet to a wire rack. Cool 15 minutes before serving.

FETTUCCINE PRIMAVERA

The mix of vegetables and herbs, the creaminess of evaporated milk, and the combination of cheeses make this Fettuccine Primavera dish a family favorite. Taste a bit of Italy at home!

ACTIVE 20 MIN. - TOTAL 30 MIN.
SERVES 4

>   1 (9-oz.) pkg. refrigerated fettuccine, prepared
>   according to package directions, kept hot
>   1 cup broccoli florets
>   ½ cup sliced carrots
>   ½ cup red bell pepper strips
>   3 Tbsp. butter or margarine
>   2 Tbsp. all-purpose flour
>   1 cup evaporated milk
>   ½ cup chicken broth
> 1½ oz. Parmesan cheese, shredded (½ cup)
>   2 oz. provolone cheese, shredded (½ cup)
>   ¼ tsp. cayenne pepper
>   Freshly ground black pepper, to taste

1. Heat ¾ cup water in a medium saucepan to boiling. Add broccoli, carrots, and bell pepper. Reduce heat to low; cook 5 to 7 minutes. Drain; set aside.

2. Melt butter in same saucepan over medium; stir in flour. Gradually add evaporated milk and chicken broth. Cook, stirring constantly, until mixture comes to a boil and thickens. Stir in Parmesan cheese, provolone cheese, cayenne pepper, and black pepper until cheese is melted. Toss with pasta. Add vegetables; stir to coat. Serve immediately.

Note: May substitute 1 pound frozen vegetables, cooked according to package directions, for fresh vegetables.

MACARONI AND CHEESE

This over-the-top macaroni and cheese recipe has four cheeses plus chopped spinach and a Parmesan-breadcrumb topping.

ACTIVE 15 MIN. - TOTAL 40 MIN.
SERVES 8

     2   Tbsp. butter or margarine
     2   garlic cloves, pressed
 1½   cups milk
     3   oz. Parmesan cheese, shredded (1 cup), divided
     1   (8-oz.) pkg. cream cheese, softened
     1   (8-oz.) pkg. mascarpone cheese
     4   oz. Gorgonzola cheese
     1   tsp. table salt
     1   tsp. ground white pepper
  ¼   tsp. ground nutmeg
     1   (10-oz.) pkg. frozen chopped spinach, thawed and drained (optional)
   16   oz. penne, cooked
     1   cup soft breadcrumbs

1. Preheat oven to 400°F. Melt butter in a Dutch oven over medium; add garlic and cook until tender. Add milk and cook, stirring often, until thoroughly heated. Gradually stir in ½ cup Parmesan cheese and next 6 ingredients until smooth. Stir in spinach, if desired. Add pasta, tossing to coat; spoon into a lightly greased 13- x 9-inch baking dish.

2. Bake in preheated oven 7 minutes. Remove from oven; sprinkle with remaining ½ cup Parmesan cheese and breadcrumbs. Reduce oven temperature to 350°F and bake until bubbly, about 20 minutes.

- -

THREE-CHEESE PASTA BAKE

This rich, cheesy bake is ideal as a meatless main, and it pairs perfectly with grilled chicken or steak.

ACTIVE 20 MIN. - TOTAL 50 MIN.
SERVES 8 TO 10

     1   (16-oz.) pkg. ziti, penne, or rigatoni
     2   (10-oz.) containers refrigerated Alfredo sauce
     1   (8-oz.) container sour cream
     1   (15-oz.) container ricotta cheese
     2   large eggs, lightly beaten

     1   oz. Parmesan cheese, grated (¼ cup)
  ¼   cup chopped fresh flat-leaf parsley, plus more for garnishing
     9   oz. shredded mozzarella cheese (1½ cups)

1. Preheat oven to 350°F. Cook pasta according to package directions; drain and return to pot.

2. Stir together Alfredo sauce and sour cream; toss with pasta until evenly coated. Spoon half the pasta mixture into a lightly greased 13- x 9-inch baking dish.

3. Stir together ricotta cheese and next 3 ingredients; spread evenly over pasta mixture in baking dish. Spoon remaining pasta mixture over ricotta cheese layer; sprinkle evenly with mozzarella cheese.

4. Bake in preheated oven until bubbly, about 30 minutes. Garnish with additional parsley.

- -

SPINACH-RAVIOLI BAKE

Pasta meets pesto in this simple ravioli bake filled with greens galore.

ACTIVE 15 MIN. - TOTAL 50 MIN.
SERVES 6 TO 8

     1   (6-oz.) pkg. fresh baby spinach
  ⅓   cup refrigerated pesto sauce
     1   (15-oz.) jar Alfredo sauce
  ¼   cup vegetable broth
     1   (25-oz.) pkg. frozen cheese-filled ravioli (do not thaw)
     4   oz. shredded Italian six-cheese blend (1 cup)

1. Preheat oven to 375°F. Chop spinach and toss with pesto in a medium bowl.

2. Combine Alfredo sauce and vegetable broth. Spoon one-third of Alfredo sauce mixture (about ½ cup) into a lightly greased 2.2-quart or 11- x 7-inch baking dish. Top with half the spinach mixture. Arrange half the ravioli in a single layer over spinach mixture. Repeat layers. Top with remaining Alfredo sauce.

3. Bake in preheated oven 30 minutes. Sprinkle with shredded cheese. Bake until bubbly, about 5 minutes.

SPINACH-RAVIOLI
BAKE

EGGPLANT PARMESAN
LASAGNA

EGGPLANT PARMESAN LASAGNA

Bitterness be gone! Slice eggplant, sprinkle with salt, and place it on layers of paper towels for 10 minutes to rid it of excess moisture and bitterness.

ACTIVE 1 HOUR, 10 MIN. · TOTAL 2 HOURS, 35 MIN.
SERVES 8 TO 10

- 2 (26-oz.) jars tomato, garlic, and onion pasta sauce
- ¼ cup chopped fresh basil
- ½ tsp. crushed red pepper
- ½ cup whipping cream
- 1 cup grated Parmesan cheese
- 1 large eggplant (about 1½ lb.)
- ½ tsp. table salt
- ¼ tsp. freshly ground black pepper
- 3 large eggs, lightly beaten
- 1 cup all-purpose flour
- 6 Tbsp. olive oil
- 6 lasagna noodles, cooked and drained
- 1 (15-oz.) container low-fat ricotta cheese
- 8 oz. mozzarella cheese, shredded (2 cups)
  Fresh basil leaves, for garnish

1. Preheat oven to 350°F. Cook first 3 ingredients in a 3½-quart saucepan over medium-low heat 30 minutes. Remove from heat; stir in cream and Parmesan cheese. Set aside.

2. Peel eggplant, then cut crosswise into ¼-inch-thick slices. Sprinkle slices evenly with salt and black pepper. Stir together eggs and 3 tablespoons water. Dredge eggplant in flour; dip into egg mixture, and dredge again in flour, shaking off excess.

3. Cook eggplant, in batches, in 1½ tablespoons hot oil in a large nonstick skillet over medium-high heat 4 minutes on each side or until golden brown and slightly softened. Drain on paper towels. Repeat with remaining oil and eggplant, wiping skillet clean after each batch, if necessary.

4. Layer 3 lasagna noodles lengthwise in a lightly greased 13- x 9-inch baking dish. Top with one-third tomato sauce mixture and half the eggplant. Dollop half the ricotta cheese on eggplant; top with half the mozzarella. Repeat layers with remaining noodles, one-third sauce mixture, remaining eggplant, and remaining ricotta. Top with remaining one-third sauce mixture and mozzarella cheese.

5. Bake in preheated oven until bubbly and golden brown, 35 to 40 minutes. Let stand 20 minutes before serving.

FRESH VEGETABLE LASAGNA

Veggie lasagna is ideal for utilizing everything from zucchini and mushrooms to red and yellow bell peppers.

ACTIVE 30 MIN. · TOTAL 3 HOURS, 15 MIN., INCLUDING SAUCE
SERVES 8

- 4 medium zucchini, halved lengthwise and thinly sliced
- 1 (8-oz.) pkg. sliced fresh mushrooms
- 2 garlic cloves, minced
- 1 medium red bell pepper, chopped
- 1 medium yellow bell pepper, chopped
- 1 yellow onion, chopped
- ½ tsp. table salt
- 1½ cups ricotta cheese
- 1 large egg
- 8 oz. part-skim mozzarella cheese, shredded (2 cups), divided
- ½ cup freshly grated Parmesan cheese, divided
- 2 (24-oz.) jars marinara sauce
- 1 (8-oz.) pkg. no-boil lasagna noodles
  Fresh basil leaves, for garnish

1. Preheat oven to 450°F. Place zucchini, mushrooms, and garlic in a jelly-roll pan coated with cooking spray. Bake for 12 to 14 minutes or until vegetables are crisp-tender, stirring halfway through. Repeat procedure with bell peppers and onion. Reduce oven temperature to 350°F. Toss together vegetables and salt in a bowl.

2. Stir together ricotta, egg, 1½ cups shredded mozzarella cheese, and ¼ cup grated Parmesan cheese.

3. Spread 1 cup marinara in a 13- x 9-inch baking dish coated with cooking spray. Top with 3 noodles, 1 cup sauce, one-third of ricotta mixture, and one-third of vegetable mixture; repeat layers twice, beginning with 3 noodles. Top with remaining noodles and 1 cup sauce. Sprinkle with remaining ½ cup shredded mozzarella and ¼ cup grated Parmesan.

4. Bake at 350°F, covered, 45 minutes. Uncover and bake until cheese is melted and golden, 10 to 15 minutes. Let stand 10 minutes.

EGGPLANT PIZZAS

To substitute fresh herbs on this pizza loaded with eggplant and veggies, use three times more than dried.

ACTIVE 30 MIN. - TOTAL 50 MIN.
MAKES 6 SERVINGS

- 1 large eggplant, peeled and coarsely chopped
- 1 medium tomato, coarsely chopped
- 1 red bell pepper, coarsely chopped
- 1 onion, coarsely chopped
- 1 small zucchini, coarsely chopped
- 3 Tbsp. olive oil, divided
- 1 (16-oz.) pkg. prebaked Italian pizza crust
- 8 oz. mozzarella cheese, shredded (2 cups)
- ½ tsp. dried basil
- ½ tsp. dried oregano
- ½ tsp. dried thyme
- ¼ tsp. garlic powder
- ½ tsp. table salt
- ¼ tsp. freshly ground black pepper

1. Preheat oven to 425°F. Sauté the first 5 ingredients in 1 tablespoon oil in a large skillet over medium-high until tender, about 10 minutes.

2. Layer pizza crust evenly with cheese and vegetables; sprinkle with basil and next 5 ingredients. Drizzle with remaining 2 tablespoons oil.

3. Bake in the preheated oven until golden, about 10 minutes.

PORTOBELLO 'N' SHIITAKE MUSHROOM POT PIES

For the best flavor, choose plump shiitakes with edges that curl under, and avoid those with broken caps.

ACTIVE 30 MIN. - TOTAL 1 HOUR
SERVES 4

- 1 (12-oz.) French bread baguette
- 3 Tbsp. butter
- 1 large sweet onion, sliced
- ¼ lb. shiitake mushrooms, sliced
- ½ lb. portobello mushrooms, sliced
- 2 garlic cloves, pressed
- 1 (14.5-oz.) can vegetable broth
- ¼ cup dry red wine or vegetable broth
- 2 Tbsp. all-purpose flour
- ¼ tsp. freshly ground black pepper
- ¼ cup shredded Italian cheese blend
- 2 Tbsp. chopped fresh flat-leaf parsley
  Fried sage leaves, for garnish (optional)

1. Preheat oven to 400°F. Cut baguette into 4 (1-inch) slices and 8 (¼-inch) slices, and place slices on a baking sheet. Reserve remaining baguette for another use.

2. Bake in preheated oven until toasted, about 5 minutes. Remove bread slices from oven; reduce oven temperature to 350°F.

3. Melt butter in a large skillet over medium heat; add onion, and cook, stirring often, 20 minutes or until caramel colored. Add mushrooms and garlic; cook, stirring constantly, 3 minutes. Stir in broth and wine; bring to a boil. Reduce heat and simmer, stirring occasionally, 20 minutes or until slightly thickened.

4. Stir together ½ cup water and the flour until smooth. Stir flour mixture and pepper into mushroom mixture; cook, stirring constantly, 1 minute.

5. Place 1-inch baguette slices in bottoms of 4 (8-oz.) ramekins or ovenproof glass bowls. Spoon mushroom mixture evenly over bread in ramekins. Top each with 2 (¼-inch) baguette slices. Sprinkle with cheese.

6. Bake at 350°F until cheese is melted, about 5 minutes. Top with fried sage leaves, if desired.

PORTOBELLO 'N'
SHIITAKE MUSHROOM
POT PIES

SPRING
ONION PIE

SPRING ONION PIE

Onions, the workhorse of so many dishes, step into the spotlight in this easy recipe. The accompanying Gruyère cheese adds a sweet, slightly salty flavor without overshadowing the onion.

ACTIVE 20 MIN. - TOTAL 45 MIN.
SERVES 6

- 10 thin spring onions
- 4 large eggs, lightly beaten
- 1 cup milk
- ¾ cup all-purpose flour
- 1 tsp. kosher salt
- ½ tsp. baking powder
- ¼ tsp. freshly ground black pepper
- 2 Tbsp. butter
- 5 oz. Gruyère cheese, cubed

1. Preheat oven to 400°F. Heat a 10-inch cast-iron skillet in oven. Trim and discard roots from onions. Chop half of onions.

2. Whisk together eggs and milk. Sift together flour and next 3 ingredients. Gradually add flour mixture to egg mixture, whisking rapidly 20 to 30 seconds or just until blended and smooth. (There should be no lumps.) Stir in chopped onions. Let stand 5 minutes.

3. Carefully remove hot skillet from oven. Add butter, and let stand until butter is melted. Place skillet over medium-high. Pour batter into skillet. Arrange cheese and remaining whole onions on batter. Cook 30 seconds to 1 minute, or until edges begin to set. Transfer skillet to top oven rack.

4. Bake in preheated oven until golden brown and puffy, 22 to 25 minutes. (Outside edges should be crispy, and inside texture should resemble a custard popover. Pie will deflate quickly.) Serve immediately.

ENCHILADA CASSEROLE

ACTIVE 20 MIN. - TOTAL 5 HOURS, 20 MIN.
SERVES 6

- 3 Tbsp. diced green chiles, divided
- ½ cup salsa
- ¼ cup chopped scallions
- ¼ cup chopped fresh cilantro
- 1 (15-oz.) can black beans, rinsed and drained
- 1 (11-oz.) can corn with red and green peppers, drained
- 1 (10-oz.) can enchilada sauce
- ½ cup egg substitute or 2 large eggs
- 1 (8 ½-oz.) pkg. corn muffin mix
- 2 Tbsp. chopped bottled roasted red bell peppers
- 6 oz. reduced-fat Mexican-blend or cheddar cheese, shredded (1½ cups)
- 6 Tbsp. low-fat sour cream
- 1½ tsp. thinly sliced fresh cilantro

1. Place 2 tablespoons green chiles and next 6 ingredients in a 3½-quart slow cooker; stir well. Cover with lid; cook on LOW setting 4 hours.

2. Combine remaining 1 tablespoon green chiles, egg substitute, muffin mix, and roasted bell peppers in a bowl. Spoon batter evenly over bean mixture in slow cooker. Cover and cook 1 hour or until corn bread is done.

3. Sprinkle cheese over corn bread. Cover and cook 5 minutes or until cheese melts. Top each serving with sour cream; sprinkle with cilantro.

SPANISH-STYLE LENTILS AND RICE

Lentils are small, but these mighty legumes are packed with protein and incredibly filling.

ACTIVE 20 MIN. - TOTAL 40 MIN.
SERVES 6

- 1 cup uncooked long-grain white rice
- 1 cup dried lentils
- 1 tsp. table salt
- 1 medium onion, diced
- 1 green bell pepper, diced
- ½ tsp. ground cumin
- ½ tsp. chili powder
- ¼ tsp. garlic powder
- 1 (10-oz.) can diced tomatoes with green chiles
- 4 oz. sharp cheddar cheese, shredded (1 cup)

1. Preheat oven to 350°F. Bring 3½ cups water and first 3 ingredients to a boil in a medium saucepan over high; reduce heat, cover, and simmer 20 to 25 minutes or until lentils are tender.

2. Cook onion and bell pepper in a large skillet over medium-high, stirring often, until tender, about 5 minutes. Add cumin, chili powder, and garlic powder; cook, stirring constantly, 2 minutes.

3. Stir onion mixture and tomatoes into rice mixture, and spoon into a lightly greased 13- x 9-inch baking dish.

4. Bake in preheated oven 15 minutes; top with shredded cheddar cheese, and bake 5 minutes more.

- -

BLACK BEAN 'N' SPINACH ENCHILADAS

These vegetarian enchiladas get a big flavor boost—and a little heat—from super simple Spinach Madeleine.

ACTIVE 25 MIN. - TOTAL 1 HOUR, 10 MIN., INCLUDING SPINACH MADELEINE
SERVES 8

- 2 (15-oz.) cans black beans, rinsed and drained
- 2 Tbsp. fresh lime juice
- 1 tsp. Creole seasoning
- 1 tsp. chili powder
- ½ tsp. ground cumin
- ½ tsp. garlic powder
- ½ tsp. onion powder

- ½ recipe Spinach Madeleine (2 cups) (recipe follows)
- 1 (8-oz.) container sour cream
- 8 (8-inch) flour tortillas
- 1 (12-oz.) block Monterey Jack cheese, shredded
  Fresh flat-leaf, for garnish

1. Preheat oven to 350°F. Combine first 7 ingredients in a medium bowl.

2. Stir together Spinach Madeleine and sour cream until blended.

3. Spoon about ½ cup black bean mixture along center of each tortilla. Top each with ⅓ cup Spinach Madeleine mixture, then sprinkle with 3 Tbsp. cheese. Roll up and place, seam-sides down, in 2 lightly greased 11- x 7-inch baking dishes. Sprinkle remaining cheese evenly over tops.

4. Bake, covered, in preheated oven for 25 minutes. Uncover and bake until cheese is melted, 5 to 10 minutes more.

SPINACH MADELEINE

ACTIVE 25 MIN. - TOTAL 1 HOUR
MAKES 4 CUPS

- 2 (10-oz.) pkg. frozen chopped spinach
- ¼ cup butter
- ½ tsp. minced fresh garlic
- 2 Tbsp. all-purpose flour
- 1 cup milk
- 1 (8-oz.) loaf pasteurized prepared cheese product, cubed
- 1 tsp. hot sauce
- ½ tsp. Creole seasoning

1. Cook spinach according to package directions; drain.

2. Meanwhile, melt butter in a medium saucepan over medium; add garlic, and sauté 1 minute. Whisk in flour until smooth; cook, whisking constantly, 1 minute. Gradually whisk in milk; cook, whisking constantly, 2 minutes or until mixture is thickened and bubbly.

3. Add cheese, hot sauce, and Creole seasoning; whisk until cheese is melted. Stir in spinach, and cook until thoroughly heated.

BLACK BEAN 'N' SPINACH ENCHILADAS

BLACK BEAN CAKES AND
AVOCADO-CORN SALSA

BLACK BEAN CAKES AND AVOCADO-CORN SALSA

ACTIVE 15 MIN. - TOTAL 40 MIN., INCLUDING SALSA
SERVES 6

- ¾ cup diced red onion
- 4 Tbsp. canola oil, divided
- 2 garlic cloves, minced
  Avocado-Corn Salsa (recipe follows)
- 1 Tbsp. taco seasoning mix
- 2 (15-oz.) cans black beans, drained and rinsed
- ½ cup panko (Japanese breadcrumbs)
- 1 large egg, lightly beaten
- ⅓ cup chopped fresh cilantro
- 6 oz. pepper Jack cheese, shredded (1½ cups), divided
- 6 tostada shells
- 2 oz. cheddar cheese, shredded (½ cup)

1. Preheat oven to 400°F. Sauté onion in 1 tablespoon hot oil in a small skillet over medium-high 4 minutes or until tender. Stir in garlic. Remove from heat.

2. Prepare Avocado-Corn Salsa; chill until ready to serve.

3. Mash together taco seasoning and 2 cups black beans in a large bowl with a fork. Stir in panko, egg, cilantro, onion mixture, 1 cup pepper Jack, and remaining black beans until blended. Shape into 6 patties.

4. Cook patties in remaining 3 tablespoons hot oil in a large nonstick skillet over medium 4 to 5 minutes on each side or until golden brown.

5. Place tostadas on a 15- x 10-inch rimmed baking pan; top with cheddar and remaining pepper Jack. Bake until cheese is melted. Top with black bean cakes and salsa.

AVOCADO-CORN SALSA

ACTIVE 10 MIN. - TOTAL 10 MIN.
SERVES 6

- 1 Tbsp. lime juice
- 2 Tbsp. canola oil
- 1 tsp. Dijon mustard
- ¼ tsp. crushed red pepper
- 1 cup fresh corn kernels
- 1 cup halved grape tomatoes
- 1 small avocado, diced
- ⅓ cup diced red onion
- 2 Tbsp. chopped fresh basil
- 2 Tbsp. chopped fresh cilantro
  Table salt and black pepper, to taste

Whisk together lime juice, oil, mustard, and crushed red pepper in a large bowl. Stir in corn, tomatoes, avocado, onion, basil, and cilantro. Season with salt and black pepper to taste Serve with Black Bean Cakes.

BEAN-AND-CHEESE CHIMICHANGAS

Chimichangas may be frozen in heavy-duty zip-top plastic bags up to 3 months.

ACTIVE 10 MIN. - TOTAL 30 MIN.
SERVES 2 OR 4

- 1 (16-oz.) can refried beans
- 1 cup (4 oz.) shredded Monterey Jack cheese
- ⅓ cup medium salsa
- 1 Tbsp. taco seasoning mix
- ½ (5-oz.) pkg. yellow rice mix, cooked (optional)
- 5 (10-inch) flour tortillas
- 2 cups vegetable oil
  Shredded lettuce
  Salsa, guacamole, sour cream, for topping (optional)

1. Stir together first 4 ingredients in a large bowl. Stir in rice, if desired. Place ⅓ cup mixture just below center of each tortilla. Fold opposite sides of tortillas over filling, forming rectangles; secure with picks.

2. Pour oil into a large skillet; heat to 325°F. Fry in batches, 4 to 5 minutes on each side or until lightly browned. Drain on paper towels. Remove picks; arrange on lettuce. Serve with toppings, if desired.

LOADED CHICKEN-
BACON POT PIE,
PAGE 176

CLASSIC CASSEROLES

SHEPHERD'S PIE

The cheese-and-carrot mashed potato topping gives this traditional beefy pie a tasty twist. The carrots add a touch of sweetness to the creamy potatoes, the perfect topping for this savory pie.

ACTIVE 40 MIN. - TOTAL 1 HOUR, 20 MIN., INCLUDING MASHED POTATOES

SERVES 8

- 1½ lb. ground round
- 1 cup chopped onion
- ½ (8-oz.) pkg. fresh mushrooms, sliced
- 1 garlic clove, minced
- 1 cup frozen peas, thawed
- 4 tsp. beef bouillon granules
- ½ tsp. table salt
- ½ tsp. dried thyme
- ¼ tsp. freshly ground black pepper
- 1 Tbsp. all-purpose flour
- 1 (14.5-oz.) can stewed tomatoes
- 1 bay leaf
- 2 Tbsp. red wine vinegar
  Cheese-and-Carrot Mashed Potatoes
  (recipe follows)

1. Preheat oven to 400°F. Brown beef in a large nonstick skillet over medium-high, stirring often, 10 minutes or until meat crumbles and is no longer pink. Remove ground beef from skillet using a slotted spoon; reserve 2 tablespoons drippings in skillet. Reduce heat to medium.

2. Cook onion, mushrooms, and garlic in hot drippings over medium 10 to 11 minutes or until tender. Stir in ground beef, peas, and next 4 ingredients. Sprinkle flour over meat mixture. Increase heat to medium-high; cook, stirring constantly, 1 minute. Stir in tomatoes, bay leaf, and vinegar, breaking up large tomato pieces with a spoon. Reduce heat to medium; cook, stirring often, 3 minutes or until slightly thickened. Remove bay leaf. Transfer mixture to a lightly greased 3-quart baking dish or pan. Spoon Cheese-and-Carrot Mashed Potatoes evenly over meat mixture, smoothing with back of spoon.

3. Bake in preheated oven until thoroughly heated, about 15 minutes. Let stand 5 minutes.

CHEESE-AND-CARROT MASHED POTATOES

ACTIVE 20 MIN. - TOTAL 30 MIN.

SERVES 8

- 1 (1-lb.) pkg. baby carrots
- 1 Tbsp. butter
- 1 (22-oz.) pkg. frozen mashed potatoes
- 2½ cups milk
- 4 oz. cheddar cheese, shredded (1 cup)
- 1 Tbsp. fresh thyme leaves
- 1 tsp. table salt
- ¼ tsp. freshly ground black pepper

1. Place carrots and ¼ cup water in a large microwave-safe bowl. Cover tightly with plastic wrap; fold back a small edge to allow steam to escape. Microwave on HIGH 8 to 10 minutes or until carrots are tender. Drain.

2. Stir in butter. Coarsely mash carrots with a potato masher.

3. Prepare potatoes according to package directions, using the 2½ cups milk. Stir in cheese, next 3 ingredients, and mashed carrots until well blended.

SHEPHERD'S PIE

SPEEDY SHEPHERD'S PIE

This down-home casserole has a fast prep and the comfort-food appeal of a one-dish dinner.

ACTIVE 15 MIN. · TOTAL 45 MIN.
SERVES 4

- 1 lb. ground beef
- ¾ cup chopped onion
- 1½ tsp. olive oil
- 2 Tbsp. all-purpose flour
- 2 tsp. beef bouillon granules
- 1 tsp. Worcestershire sauce
- ¼ tsp. table salt
- ¼ tsp. black pepper
- 2 cups frozen mixed vegetables, thawed and patted dry
- 4 cups unbaked Walnut Mashed Potatoes (recipe follows)
- ¼ cup freshly grated Parmesan cheese
  Paprika

1. Cook ground beef in a large skillet, stirring until it crumbles and is no longer pink; drain well, and set aside. Wipe skillet clean.

2. Cook onion in hot oil in skillet over medium-high, stirring frequently, until tender. Add flour, stirring well; stir in 1⅓ cups water. Cook, stirring constantly, over medium-low, until thickened. Add bouillon and next 3 ingredients, stirring well. Add beef and thawed vegetables; stir well.

3. Spoon beef mixture into a lightly greased 2-quart casserole dish. Spread Walnut Mashed Potatoes over beef mixture; sprinkle with Parmesan cheese. Lightly sprinkle with paprika.

4. Bake, uncovered, in preheated oven until bubbly, about 30 minutes.

WALNUT MASHED POTATOES

ACTIVE 25 MIN. · TOTAL 1 HOUR
MAKES 14½ CUPS

- 6 lb. baking potatoes, peeled and cut into 1-inch pieces
- ¾ cup butter, cut into pieces
- 1½ cups half-and-half
- 2 tsp. table salt
- ½ tsp. black pepper
- 4 scallions, chopped
- 1½ Tbsp. olive oil
- 1¼ cups chopped walnuts, toasted

1. Cook potatoes in boiling water to cover until tender, about 30 minutes; drain. Return potatoes to pan. Add butter and mash with a potato masher until light and fluffy. Add half-and-half, salt, and black pepper. Mash to desired consistency.

2. Cook scallions in hot oil in a medium skillet over medium, stirring frequently, until crisp-tender, 5 minutes. Add scallions and walnuts to mashed potatoes, stir until blended.

- -

MEATBALL PASTA BAKE

The distinctive pairing of orange juice and fennel adds bright, fresh flavors to this meaty meal.

ACTIVE 30 MIN. · TOTAL 1 HOUR, 10 MIN.
SERVES 8 TO 10

- 1 (16-oz.) pkg. uncooked penne
- 1 small sweet onion, chopped
- 1 medium-size fennel bulb, thinly sliced (optional)
- 2 Tbsp. olive oil
- 3 garlic cloves, minced
- 1 tsp. fennel seeds
- 2 (24-oz.) jars marinara sauce
- 2 (14-oz.) pkg. frozen beef meatballs, thawed
- 1 cup fresh orange juice
- ¾ cup chicken broth
- 1 tsp. firmly packed orange zest
- 1 medium-size red bell pepper, chopped
- ½ tsp. kosher salt
- 1 cup torn fresh basil
- 1½ (8-oz.) pkg. fresh mozzarella cheese slices
  Torn fresh basil leaves, for garnish

1. Preheat oven to 350°F. Cook pasta according to package directions; drain.

2. Cook onion and fennel, if desired, in hot oil in a Dutch oven over medium until tender, 8 to 10 minutes. Add garlic and fennel seeds; cook 1 minute. Stir in marinara sauce and next 6 ingredients; increase heat to medium-high, and bring to a boil. Reduce heat to medium-low; cover and simmer 10 minutes. Remove from heat and stir in 1 cup basil and the cooked pasta, and salt to taste.

3. Transfer to a lightly greased 13- x 9-inch baking dish. Place dish on an aluminum foil-lined baking sheet. Top with cheese. Bake in preheated oven until bubbly, about 25 minutes. Garnish with additional basil.

HOMESTYLE GROUND BEEF CASSEROLE

Hamburger casserole is convenient for any weeknight and is a universal family favorite. Green beans and corn would round out the plate nicely.

ACTIVE 10 MIN. - TOTAL 1 HOUR, 20 MIN.

SERVES 6

- 1 lb. ground round
- 1 (14½-oz.) can diced tomatoes with basil, garlic, and oregano, undrained
- 1 (10-oz.) can diced tomatoes and green chiles, undrained
- 1 (6-oz.) can tomato paste
- 1 tsp. table salt
- ½ tsp. dried Italian seasoning
- ¼ tsp. black pepper
- 3 cups uncooked medium egg noodles
- 5 scallions, chopped
- 1 (8-oz.) container sour cream
- 1 (3-oz.) pkg. cream cheese, softened
- 4 oz. sharp cheddar cheese, shredded (1 cup)
- 3 oz. Parmesan cheese, shredded (1 cup)
- 4 oz. mozzarella cheese, shredded (1 cup)

1. Cook ground round in a large skillet over medium 8 minutes, stirring until it crumbles and is no longer pink. Stir in both cans diced tomatoes and next 4 ingredients. Bring to a boil; reduce heat, and simmer, uncovered, 5 minutes. Remove from heat; set aside.

2. Preheat oven to 350°F. Cook egg noodles in boiling salted water according to package directions; drain. Stir together hot cooked noodles, chopped scallions, sour cream, and cream cheese until blended.

3. Spoon egg noodles into a lightly greased 13- x 9-inch baking dish. Top with beef mixture; sprinkle with shredded cheeses in the order listed.

4. Bake, covered, in preheated oven 35 minutes. Uncover and bake 5 minutes more. Let stand 10 to 15 minutes before serving.

Note: Freeze assembled, unbaked casserole up to 1 month, if desired. Thaw in refrigerator overnight. Bake as directed.

TACO CASSEROLE

Certainly tacos qualify as timeless comfort food. This dish has of all the familiar elements, then a nacho chip topping. Serve it with salad and you've got a meal.

ACTIVE 10 MIN. - TOTAL 45 MIN.

SERVES 6

- 1 lb. ground chuck
- ½ cup chopped onion
- 1 (1.25-oz.) pkg. taco seasoning mix
- 1 (16-oz.) can chili beans, undrained
- 1 (8-oz.) can tomato sauce
- 8 oz. Colby cheese, shredded (2 cups)
- 5 cups coarsely crushed nacho cheese-flavor tortilla chips or other flavor tortilla chips (about 9 oz.)

1. Preheat oven to 350°F. Cook ground chuck with onion in a large skillet over medium, stirring often, until beef crumbles and onion is tender; drain any fat. Stir in taco seasoning, beans, and tomato sauce.

2. Layer half each of beef mixture, shredded cheese, and tortilla chips in a lightly greased 13- x 9-inch baking dish. Repeat procedure with remaining beef mixture, shredded cheese, and tortilla chips.

3. Bake, uncovered, in preheated oven until casserole is thoroughly heated, 25 minutes.

BAKED
LINGUINE
WITH MEAT
SAUCE

BAKED LINGUINE WITH MEAT SAUCE

Get a jump on tomorrow's dinner by with this linguine. Simply prepare the recipe as directed through Step 3, cover, and refrigerate. The next day continue with Step 4, adding 10 to 15 minutes baking time to thoroughly heat.

ACTIVE 30 MIN. - TOTAL 55 MIN.
SERVES 8

- 2 lb. lean ground beef
- 2 garlic cloves, minced
- 1 (28-oz.) can crushed tomatoes
- 1 (8-oz.) can tomato sauce
- 1 (6-oz.) can tomato paste
- 2 tsp. granulated sugar
- 1 tsp. table salt
- 8 oz. uncooked linguine
- 1 (16-oz.) container sour cream
- 1 (8-oz.) pkg. cream cheese, softened
- 1 bunch scallions, chopped
- 8 oz. sharp cheddar cheese, shredded (2 cups)
  Sliced scallions, for garnish

1. Preheat oven to 350°F. Brown ground beef and garlic in a Dutch oven over medium-high, stirring often, until meat crumbles and is no longer pink. Stir in tomatoes and next 4 ingredients; simmer 30 minutes. Set aside.

2. Cook pasta according to package directions; drain. Place in a lightly greased 13- x 9-inch baking dish.

3. Stir together sour cream, cream cheese, and scallions. Spread over pasta. Top with meat sauce.

4. Bake, uncovered, until thoroughly heated, 20 to 25 minutes. Sprinkle with cheddar cheese, and bake 5 minutes more or until cheese is melted. Let stand 5 minutes. Garnish with scallions.

BEEF LOMBARDI

There's nothing fancy about this simple mix of ground beef, chopped tomatoes, noodles, and cheese, and that's why you'll love it. It's easy to make ahead and can be frozen up to one month.

ACTIVE 50 MIN. - TOTAL 1 HOUR, 30 MIN.
SERVES 6

- 1 lb. lean ground beef
- 1 (14½-oz.) can chopped tomatoes
- 1 (10-oz.) can diced tomatoes and green chiles
- 2 tsp. granulated sugar
- 2 tsp. table salt
- ¼ tsp. freshly ground black pepper
- 1 (6-oz.) can tomato paste
- 1 bay leaf
- 1 (6-oz.) pkg. medium egg noodles
- 6 scallions, chopped (about ½ cup)
- 1 cup sour cream
- 4 oz. sharp cheddar cheese, shredded (1 cup)
- 3 oz. Parmesan cheese, shredded (1 cup)
- 4 oz. mozzarella cheese, shredded (1 cup)

1. Preheat oven to 350°F. Brown ground beef in a large skillet over medium 5 to 6 minutes, stirring until it crumbles and is no longer pink; drain.

2. Stir in chopped tomatoes and next 4 ingredients; cook 5 minutes. Add tomato paste and bay leaf; simmer 30 minutes. Remove bay leaf.

3. Cook egg noodles according to package directions; drain.

4. Stir together cooked egg noodles, chopped scallions, and sour cream until blended.

5. Place noodle mixture in bottom of a lightly greased 13- x 9-inch baking dish. Top with beef mixture; sprinkle with cheeses.

6. Bake, covered with aluminum foil, in preheated oven 35 minutes. Uncover, and bake 5 minutes more.

Note: To freeze, prepare recipe as directed through Step 5. Wrap casserole tightly with aluminum foil, then freeze up to 1 month. To reheat, thaw in refrigerator overnight. Bake as directed in Step 6.

PIZZA CASSEROLE DELUXE

Fresh mozzarella is responsible for the off-the-charts creaminess.

ACTIVE 40 MIN. - TOTAL 1 HOUR, 15 MIN.

SERVES 10

- 1 (1-lb.) pkg. ground mild Italian sausage
- 2 garlic cloves, minced
- 1 Tbsp. olive oil
- 1 (26-oz.) jar marinara sauce
- 1 tsp. kosher salt, divided
- ½ medium red onion, chopped
- ½ medium red bell pepper, chopped
- ½ medium green bell pepper, chopped
- ½ (8-oz.) pkg. sliced baby portobello mushrooms
- 1 cup sliced black olives
- ½ cup pepperoni slices, chopped
- 1 (16-oz.) pkg. rigatoni pasta
- 3 Tbsp. butter
- 3 Tbsp. all-purpose flour
- 3 cups half-and-half
- 8 oz. fresh mozzarella, shredded (2 cups)
- 1½ oz. Parmesan cheese, grated (½ cup)
- ½ tsp. freshly ground black pepper
- 1 (8-oz.) pkg. shredded mozzarella cheese
- 8 to 10 pepperoni slices

1. Preheat oven to 350°F. Cook sausage and garlic in hot oil in a large skillet over medium-high 5 to 7 minutes or until sausage crumbles and is no longer pink. Remove with a slotted spoon, reserving drippings in skillet. Drain sausage mixture on paper towels, then transfer to a medium bowl. Stir marinara sauce and ½ teaspoon salt into sausage mixture.

2. Cook onion and next 3 ingredients in hot drippings 5 minutes or until tender; stir in olives and chopped pepperoni. Set aside, reserving ¼ cup onion mixture.

3. Cook pasta according to package directions in a large Dutch oven.

4. Melt butter in a heavy saucepan over low; whisk in flour until smooth. Cook, whisking constantly, 1 minute. Gradually whisk in half-and-half; cook over medium, whisking constantly, 7 to 10 minutes or until sauce is thickened and bubbly. Stir in fresh mozzarella cheese, Parmesan cheese, black pepper, and remaining ½ teaspoon salt. Pour sauce over pasta in Dutch oven, stirring to coat. Stir in all but the reserved onion mixture.

5. Transfer pasta mixture to a lightly greased 13- x 9-inch baking dish. Top with sausage mixture, mozzarella cheese, reserved ¼ cup onion mixture, and the 8 to 10 pepperoni slices.

6. Bake in preheated oven until cheese is melted and lightly browned, 30 minutes. Let stand 5 minutes before serving.

- -

SAUCY SAUSAGE MANICOTTI

Having a dinner party? Make individual manicotti casseroles for a special presentation. Simply spoon ¼ cup sauce into seven lightly greased shallow 8-ounce baking dishes. Top with two filled manicotti noodles, cover with sauce and mozzarella cheese, and bake.

ACTIVE 30 MIN. - TOTAL 1 HOUR, 20 MIN.

SERVES 7

- 1 (8-oz.) pkg. manicotti
- 1 (16-oz.) pkg. Italian sausage, casings removed
- 1 large onion, chopped
- 9 garlic cloves, minced, divided
- 1 (26-oz.) jar tomato pasta sauce
- 1 (8-oz.) container chive-and-onion cream cheese
- 24 oz. mozzarella cheese, shredded (6 cups), divided
- 2 oz. Parmesan cheese, freshly grated (¾ cup)
- 1 (15-oz.) container ricotta cheese
- ¾ tsp. freshly ground black pepper

1. Preheat oven to 350°F. Cook pasta according to package directions; drain.

2. Meanwhile, cook sausage, onion, and half the garlic in a large Dutch oven over medium-high 6 minutes, stirring until sausage crumbles and is no longer pink. Stir in pasta sauce; bring to a boil. Remove from heat.

3. Combine cream cheese, 4 cups mozzarella, next 3 ingredients, and remaining garlic in a large bowl; stir until blended.

4. Spoon 1 cup sausage mixture into a lightly greased 13- x 9-inch baking dish. Cut a slit the length of each cooked manicotti noodle. Spoon cheese mixture evenly into noodles; gently press cut sides together. Arrange stuffed pasta on sauce in dish, seam sides down. Spoon remaining sauce over stuffed pasta. Sprinkle with remaining 2 cups mozzarella.

5. Bake, covered, in preheated oven until bubbly, about 50 minutes.

SAUCY SAUSAGE
MANICOTTI

HAM-AND-VEGETABLE
COBBLER

HAM-AND-VEGETABLE COBBLER

Believe it or not, this delicious cobbler has frozen veggies and premade piecrusts. The secret to what makes it so yummy is a basic homemade roux.

ACTIVE 30 MIN. - TOTAL 50 MIN.
SERVES 6

- ¼ cup butter
- ¼ cup all-purpose flour
- 3½ cups milk
- ½ tsp. dried thyme
- 1 tsp. chicken bouillon granules
- 2 cups diced cooked ham
- 1 (10-oz.) pkg. frozen sweet peas and mushrooms
- 1 cup frozen crinkle-cut carrots
- 1 (14.1-oz.) pkg. refrigerated piecrusts

1. Preheat oven to 450°F. Melt butter in a large saucepan over medium. Gradually whisk in flour; cook, whisking constantly, 1 minute. Add milk and next 2 ingredients; cook, stirring constantly, 6 to 8 minutes or until thickened and bubbly. Stir in ham and next 2 ingredients; cook 4 to 5 minutes or until mixture is thoroughly heated. Spoon into a lightly greased 11- x 7-inch baking dish.

2. Unroll each piecrust on a lightly floured surface. Cut piecrusts into 1¼-inch-wide strips. Arrange strips in a lattice design over ham mixture.

3. Bake in preheated oven until crust is browned and filling is bubbly, about 40 minutes.

CLASSIC CHICKEN TETRAZZINI

Tetrazzini is a classic, and this tried-and-true chicken and pasta recipe will become a family favorite. You'll love it for its simplicity.

ACTIVE 20 MIN. - TOTAL 55 MIN.
SERVES 8 TO 10

- 1½ (8-oz.) pkg. vermicelli
- ½ cup butter
- ½ cup all-purpose flour
- 4 cups milk
- ½ cup dry white wine
- 2 Tbsp. chicken bouillon granules
- 1 tsp. seasoned pepper
- 6 oz. freshly grated Parmesan cheese, freshly grated (2 cups), divided
- 4 cups diced cooked chicken
- 1 (6-oz.) jar sliced mushrooms, drained
- ¾ cup slivered almonds

1. Preheat oven to 350°F. Cook pasta according to package directions; drain.

2. Meanwhile, melt butter in a Dutch oven over low; whisk in flour until smooth. Cook 1 minute, whisking constantly. Gradually whisk in milk and wine; cook over medium, whisking constantly, 8 to 10 minutes or until mixture is thickened and bubbly. Whisk in bouillon granules, seasoned pepper, and 1 cup Parmesan cheese.

3. Remove from heat; stir in diced cooked chicken, sliced mushrooms, and hot cooked pasta.

4. Spoon mixture into a lightly greased 13- x 9-inch baking dish; sprinkle with slivered almonds and remaining 1 cup Parmesan cheese.

5. Bake in preheated oven until bubbly, about 35 minutes.

CHICKEN-AND-BISCUIT COBBLER

ACTIVE 1 HOUR, 15 MIN. - TOTAL 1 HOUR, 45 MIN.
SERVES 8

- 3 Tbsp. butter
- 1 cup sliced carrots
- 1 medium onion, chopped
- 2 (8-oz.) pkg. fresh mushrooms, quartered
- 2 garlic cloves, minced
- ½ cup dry white wine
- ⅓ cup all-purpose flour
- 3 cups reduced-sodium chicken broth
- ¾ cup whipping cream
- 1 Tbsp. white wine vinegar
- 3 Tbsp. sliced fresh chives
- 3 Tbsp. chopped fresh flat-leaf parsley
- 2 tsp. chopped fresh rosemary
- 2 tsp. chopped fresh thyme leaves
- 8 cups shredded cooked chicken
  Kosher salt
  Freshly ground black pepper
- 2½ cups self-rising flour
- ½ tsp. granulated sugar
- 1¼ cups chilled buttermilk
- ½ cup butter, melted
- ½ cup chopped cooked bacon (about 5 thick bacon slices)
  Chopped fresh chives and flat-leaf parsley, for garnish

1. Preheat oven to 400°F. Melt 3 tablespoons butter in a Dutch oven over medium-high. Add carrots and onion; cook 5 minutes. Add mushrooms; cook 5 minutes or until tender. Stir in garlic; cook 2 minutes. Add wine; cook 2 minutes. Sprinkle with ⅓ cup flour; cook, stirring constantly, 3 minutes. Slowly add broth, stirring constantly. Bring mixture to a boil, stirring constantly, 2 minutes or until thickened. Stir in cream and next 5 ingredients. Stir in chicken, and season to taste with salt and pepper. Cover and remove from heat.

2. Whisk together 2½ cups self-rising flour and the sugar in a medium bowl. Stir together buttermilk and ½ cup melted butter in a small bowl. Stir buttermilk mixture and bacon into flour mixture until dough pulls away from sides of bowl.

3. Return chicken mixture to medium-high; cook, stirring constantly, 2 minutes or until bubbly and hot. Spoon mixture into a buttered 3-quart glass baking dish. Drop biscuit dough by level ¼ cupfuls, ½ inch apart, onto chicken mixture.

4. Bake in preheated oven until browned and bubbly, 30 to 35 minutes.

- -

CHICKEN TETRAZZINI

Tetrazzini is a house-favorite cheese-and-chicken entrée. This version serves plenty of people.

ACTIVE 20 MIN. - TOTAL 55 MIN.
SERVES 12

- 1 (16-oz.) pkg. vermicelli
- ½ cup chicken broth
- 4 cups chopped cooked chicken
- 1 (10¾-oz.) can cream of mushroom soup
- 1 (10¾-oz.) can cream of chicken soup
- 1 (10¾-oz.) can cream of celery soup
- 1 (8-oz.) container sour cream
- 1 (6-oz.) jar sliced mushrooms, drained
- 2 oz. Parmesan cheese, shredded (½ cup)
- 1 tsp. black pepper
- ½ tsp. table salt
- 8 oz. cheddar cheese, shredded (2 cups)

1. Cook vermicelli according to package directions; drain. Return to pot and toss with chicken broth.

2. Preheat oven to 350°F. Stir together chopped cooked chicken and next 8 ingredients in a large bowl; add vermicelli, and toss well. Spoon chicken mixture into two lightly greased 11- x 7-inch baking dishes. Sprinkle with cheddar cheese.

3. Bake, covered, in preheated oven 30 minutes; uncover and bake until cheese is bubbly, 5 minutes more.

Note: Freeze unbaked casserole up to 1 month, if desired. Thaw casserole overnight in refrigerator. Let stand 30 minutes at room temperature, and bake as directed.

CHICKEN-
AND-BISCUIT
COBBLER

SKILLET CHICKEN
POT PIE

DOUBLE-CRUST CHICKEN POT PIE

ACTIVE 30 MIN. · TOTAL 1 HOUR, 40 MIN.
SERVES 6 TO 8

- ½ cup butter
- 2 medium leeks, sliced
- ½ cup all-purpose flour
- 1 (14.5-oz.) can chicken broth
- 3 cups chopped cooked chicken
- 1½ cups frozen cubed hash browns with onions and peppers
- 1 cup matchstick carrots
- ⅓ cup chopped fresh flat-leaf parsley
- ½ tsp. table salt
- ½ tsp. freshly ground black pepper
- 1 (17.3-oz.) pkg. frozen puff pastry sheets, thawed
- 1 large egg

1. Position a rack in the lower half of oven. Preheat oven to 375°F. Melt butter in a large skillet over medium; add leeks, and cook 3 minutes. Sprinkle with flour; cook, stirring constantly, 3 minutes. Whisk in chicken broth; bring to a boil, whisking constantly. Remove from heat; stir in chicken and next 5 ingredients.

2. Roll each pastry sheet into a 12- x 10-inch rectangle on a lightly floured surface. Fit 1 sheet into a 9-inch deep-dish pie plate; spoon chicken mixture into pastry. Place remaining pastry sheet over filling perpendicular to bottom sheet; fold edges under, and press with tines of a fork, sealing to bottom pastry. Whisk together egg and 1 tablespoon water; brush on pie pastry.

3. Bake in preheated oven on lower rack until browned, 55 to 60 minutes. Let stand 15 minutes.

SKILLET CHICKEN POT PIE

Packaged piecrusts and frozen hash browns shorten prep time for this hearty chicken pot pie—it's in the oven and to the table in just an hour!

ACTIVE 30 MIN. · TOTAL 1 HOUR, 30 MIN.
SERVES 6 TO 8

CHICKEN PIE FILLING
- ⅓ cup butter
- ⅓ cup all-purpose flour
- 1½ cups chicken broth
- 1½ cups milk
- 1½ tsp. Creole seasoning
- 2 Tbsp. butter
- 1 large sweet onion, diced
- 1 (8-oz.) pkg. sliced fresh mushrooms
- 4 cups shredded cooked chicken
- 2 cups frozen cubed hash browns
- 1 cup matchstick carrots
- 1 cup frozen small sweet peas
- ⅓ cup chopped fresh flat-leaf parsley

PASTRY CRUST
- 1 (14.1-oz.) pkg. refrigerated piecrusts
- 1 large egg white

1. Prepare Chicken Pie Filling: Preheat oven to 350°F. Melt ⅓ cup butter in a large saucepan over medium. Add all-purpose flour; cook, whisking constantly, 1 minute. Gradually add chicken broth and milk, and cook, whisking constantly, 6 to 7 minutes or until thickened and bubbly. Remove from heat, and stir in Creole seasoning.

2. Melt 2 tablespoons butter in a large Dutch oven over medium-high; add onion and mushrooms, and cook until tender, about 10 minutes. Stir in chicken, the next 4 ingredients, and the sauce.

3. Prepare Pastry Crust: Place 1 piecrust in a lightly greased 10-inch cast-iron skillet. Spoon filling into piecrust, then top with remaining piecrust.

4. Whisk egg white until foamy; brush top of piecrust with egg white. Cut 4 or 5 slits in top of pie for steam to escape.

5. Bake in preheated oven until golden brown and bubbly, about 1 hour.

LOADED CHICKEN-BACON POT PIE

(Photo, page 160)

ACTIVE 40 MIN. · TOTAL 1 HOUR, 35 MIN.
SERVES 6

- 5 thick bacon slices, diced (about 1 cup)
- 1 medium-size sweet onion, chopped
- 2 garlic cloves, chopped
- 1 cup chopped carrots
- 1 (8-oz.) pkg. fresh mushrooms, halved
- ½ cup dry white wine
- ⅓ cup all-purpose flour
- 3 cups reduced-sodium or organic chicken broth
- ¾ cup whipping cream
- 1½ Tbsp. dry mustard
- 2 tsp. fresh thyme leaves
- 1 tsp. kosher salt
- ⅛ tsp. cayenne pepper
- 4 cups shredded deli-roasted chicken
- 1 cup small frozen sweet peas
- ½ (17.3-oz.) pkg. frozen puff pastry sheets (1 sheet), thawed and cut into strips
- 1 large egg, lightly beaten
  Fresh thyme, for garnish

1. Position a rack in the lower half of oven. Preheat oven to 400°F. Cook bacon in a Dutch oven over medium until crisp, 8 to 10 minutes. Drain on paper towels, reserving 3 tablespoons drippings in skillet.

2. Add onion to hot drippings; cook 3 minutes. Add garlic and next 2 ingredients; cook until carrots are crisp-tender, 4 to 5 minutes. Remove from heat and add wine. Return to heat; cook 2 minutes. Sprinkle with flour; cook, stirring constantly, 3 minutes. Whisk in broth; bring to a boil, whisking constantly, 2 to 3 minutes or until thickened. Stir in cream and next 4 ingredients.

3. Remove from heat; stir in chicken, peas, and bacon. Spoon mixture into a lightly greased 11- x 7-inch baking dish. Place pastry over hot filling, pressing edges to seal and trimming off excess. (Use scraps to cover any exposed filling, if necessary.) Whisk together egg and 1 tablespoon water. Brush over pastry.

4. Bake in preheated oven on lower rack until browned and bubbly, 35 to 40 minutes. Let stand 15 minutes before serving. Garnish with additional thyme.

PASTA-CHICKEN-BROCCOLI BAKE

Cheesy tortellini, red bell pepper, and broccoli give this kid- and mom-friendly bake loads of flavor, while the chopped pecan topping adds crunch to every bite.

ACTIVE 30 MIN. · TOTAL 1 HOUR, 15 MIN.
SERVES 6 TO 8

- ½ cup butter
- ½ cup chopped sweet onion
- ½ cup chopped red bell pepper
- 2 garlic cloves, minced
- ¼ cup all-purpose flour
- 3 cups chicken broth
- 1½ cups half-and-half
- ½ cup dry white wine
- 3 oz. Parmesan cheese, freshly shredded (1 cup)
- ¼ tsp. table salt
- ¼ tsp. cayenne pepper
- 1 (20-oz.) pkg. refrigerated cheese-and-spinach tortellini
- 4 cups chopped fresh broccoli
- 4 cups chopped cooked chicken
- ½ cup grated Parmesan cheese
- 15 round buttery crackers, crushed
- ½ cup chopped pecans
- 3 Tbsp. butter, melted

1. Preheat oven to 350°F. Melt ½ cup butter in a Dutch oven over medium-high; add onion and next 2 ingredients. Cook until tender, 5 to 6 minutes.

2. Add flour, stirring until smooth. Cook, stirring constantly, 1 minute. Whisk in broth, half-and-half, and wine. Reduce heat to medium; cook, stirring constantly, 6 to 8 minutes or until thickened and bubbly.

3. Remove from heat; add 1 cup shredded cheese and next 2 ingredients, stirring until cheese melts. Stir in pasta and next 2 ingredients. Spoon into a lightly greased 13- x 9-inch baking dish.

4. Stir together ½ cup grated Parmesan and remaining 3 ingredients. Sprinkle over casserole. Bake in preheated oven until bubbly, 40 to 45 minutes.

PASTA·CHICKEN·
BROCCOLI BAKE

CHICKEN AND DRESSING

Thanksgiving cravings happen all year—not just at the end of November. Satisfy them with this all-in-one casserole filled with rotisserie chicken.

ACTIVE 30 MIN. - TOTAL 2 HOURS, 25 MIN., INCLUDING CORNBREAD

SERVES 8 TO 10

- 2 Tbsp. butter
- ½ cup diced white onion
- ½ cup diced celery
- 2 garlic cloves, minced
- 4 cups crumbled Family Cornbread (recipe follows)
- 3 cups chicken broth
- 6 white bread slices, torn into 1-inch pieces
- 4 Tbsp. unsalted butter, melted
- 2 large eggs
- 1 Tbsp. dried sage
- 1 tsp. table salt
- ½ tsp. freshly ground black pepper
- 4 cups shredded roasted or rotisserie chicken

1. Preheat oven to 375°F. Melt 2 tablespoons butter in a large skillet over medium. Add onion and next 2 ingredients. Cook, stirring frequently, 10 minutes or until softened and beginning to brown. Transfer to a large bowl. Add crumbled cornbread and next 7 ingredients. Let stand 15 minutes.

2. Spoon about one-third cornbread mixture into a lightly greased 13- x 9-inch baking dish. Arrange chicken over cornbread mixture. Top with remaining cornbread mixture. Bake in preheated oven until golden brown and set, 45 minutes.

FAMILY CORNBREAD

ACTIVE 10 MIN. - TOTAL 55 MIN.

SERVES 8 TO 10

- 3 Tbsp. bacon drippings
- 1 large egg
- 1 cup milk
- 1 cup self-rising white cornmeal mix
- ½ cup self-rising soft-wheat flour

1. Preheat oven to 500°F. Place bacon drippings in a 10-inch cast-iron skillet; heat in oven 4 minutes. Meanwhile, whisk together egg and milk in a small bowl. Whisk together cornmeal mix and flour in a medium bowl; gently whisk in egg mixture.

2. Remove skillet from oven; carefully pour half the hot drippings into batter. (Drippings will sizzle.) Whisk to combine. Pour batter into skillet.

3. Bake in preheated oven until golden brown and cornbread pulls away from sides of skillet, about 15 minutes. Cool 30 minutes.

- -

QUICK-AND-EASY KING RANCH CHICKEN CASSEROLE

ACTIVE 30 MIN. - TOTAL 1 HOUR, 50 MIN.

SERVES 8 TO 10

- 2 Tbsp. butter
- 1 medium onion, chopped
- 1 medium green bell pepper, chopped
- 1 garlic clove, pressed
- ¾ cup chicken broth
- 1 (10¾-oz.) can cream of mushroom soup
- 1 (10¾-oz.) can cream of chicken soup
- 2 (10-oz.) cans diced tomatoes and green chiles, drained
- 1 tsp. dried oregano
- 1 tsp. ground cumin
- 1 tsp. Mexican-style or other chili powder
- 3 lb. shredded roasted or rotisserie chicken
- 12 oz. sharp cheddar cheese, shredded (3 cups)
- 3 cups coarsely crumbled lime-flavor white corn tortilla chips

1. Preheat oven to 350°F. Melt butter in a large skillet over medium-high. Add onion; cook 5 minutes or until tender. Add bell pepper and garlic; cook 3 to 4 minutes. Stir in chicken broth, cream of mushroom soup, and next 5 ingredients. Cook, stirring occasionally, 8 minutes.

2. Layer half the shredded chicken in a lightly greased 13- x 9-inch baking dish. Top with half the soup mixture and 1 cup cheddar cheese. Cover with half the crumbled tortilla chips. Repeat layers. Top with remaining 1 cup cheese.

3. Bake in preheated oven until bubbly, about 55 minutes. Let stand 10 minutes before serving.

CRUNCHY CHICKEN CASSEROLE

Kids will love this chicken casserole topped with crushed potato chips—yes, potato chips! The salty chips add flavor and crisp crunch to every bite.

ACTIVE 20 MIN. - TOTAL 40 MIN.
SERVES 8

- 2 Tbsp. butter
- 1 medium onion, chopped
- 1 (8.8-oz.) pouch ready-to-serve long grain rice
- 3 cups chopped cooked chicken
- 1½ cups frozen petite peas
- 6 oz. sharp cheddar cheese, shredded (1½ cups)
- 1 cup mayonnaise
- 1 (10¾-oz.) can cream of chicken soup
- 1 (8-oz.) can sliced water chestnuts, drained
- 1 (4-oz.) jar sliced pimientos, drained
- 3 cups coarsely crushed ridged potato chips

1. Preheat oven to 350°F. Melt butter in a skillet over medium. Add onion and cook, stirring frequently, until tender, about 5 minutes.

2. Cook rice in a microwave according to package directions. Combine cooked onion, rice, chicken, and next 6 ingredients in a large bowl; toss gently. Spoon mixture into a lightly greased 13- x 9-inch baking dish. Top with potato chips.

3. Bake, uncovered, in preheated oven until bubbly, 20 to 25 minutes.

To make ahead: Prepare and spoon casserole into baking dish, omitting crushed chips. Cover and refrigerate up to 24 hours. Uncover and let stand 30 minutes. Add crushed chips, just before baking as directed.

POPPY SEED-CHICKEN CASSEROLE

This timeless casserole might be what put poppy seeds on the map. We gave this version a healthy spin with whole wheat crackers.

ACTIVE 12 MIN. - TOTAL 50 MIN.
SERVES 6

- 3 to 4 cups chopped cooked chicken or turkey
- 1 (10¾-oz.) can cream of chicken and mushroom soup
- 1 (16-oz.) container sour cream or light sour cream
- 6 oz. sharp cheddar cheese, shredded (1½ cups)
- 3 Tbsp. poppy seeds
- 1 sleeve whole wheat round buttery crackers, crushed
- ¼ cup butter, melted

1. Preheat oven to 350°F. Combine first 5 ingredients in a large bowl; stir well. Spoon into a lightly greased 11- x 7-inch baking dish. Top with crushed crackers. Drizzle with melted butter.

2. Bake, uncovered, in preheated oven until bubbly, 25 to 30 minutes. Let stand 10 minutes before serving.

CHICKEN AND WILD
RICE WITH PECANS

CHICKEN AND WILD RICE WITH PECANS

Here is the casserole for using up leftover chicken. Roast a whole chicken on a Sunday, then make this casserole later in the week for a quick and easy dinner.

ACTIVE 45 MIN. - TOTAL 1 HOUR, 5 MIN.
SERVES 6

- 1 cup uncooked long-grain and wild rice mix
- 1 leek, sliced
- 2 Tbsp. unsalted butter
- 1 (16-oz.) pkg. fresh mushrooms, stemmed and quartered
- ½ cup dry white wine
- 4 cups shredded roasted or rotisserie chicken
- 1 cup sour cream
- 1 tsp. table salt
- ½ tsp. freshly ground black pepper
- 2 oz. white cheddar cheese, shredded (½ cup)
- ½ cup coarsely chopped pecans
  Chopped chives, for garnish

1. Cook rice blend according to package directions. Reserve remaining rice for another use.

2. Meanwhile, remove and discard root ends and dark green tops of leek. Cut in half lengthwise, and rinse thoroughly under cold running water to remove grit and sand. Thinly slice leek.

3. Preheat oven to 350°F. Melt butter in a large skillet over medium-low. Add leek, and cook 6 to 7 minutes or until lightly browned. Add mushrooms, and cook, stirring often, 15 minutes. Add wine, and bring to a simmer; cook 3 minutes.

4. Transfer rice to a large bowl. Add leek mixture to rice; stir until blended. Add chicken and next 3 ingredients; stir until blended. Transfer to a lightly greased 11- x 7-inch baking dish. Top with cheese.

5. Bake in preheated oven 10 minutes. Top with pecans; bake until pecans are toasted and mixture is bubbly, about 10 minutes more. Garnish with chives.

CHICKEN-MUSHROOM-SAGE CASSEROLE

Protein-filled almonds top this hearty, herby meal. Allow this casserole to rest a few minutes after baking to let the rice absorb the creamy goodness.

ACTIVE 1 HOUR - TOTAL 1 HOUR, 40 MIN.
SERVES 6

- ½ cup butter, divided
- 6 boneless, skinless chicken breasts
- 3 shallots, chopped
- 2 garlic cloves, minced
- 1 lb. assorted fresh mushrooms, coarsely chopped
- ¼ cup sherry
- 3 Tbsp. all-purpose flour
- 2 (14-oz.) cans chicken broth
- 1 (6-oz.) pkg. long-grain and wild rice mix
- 1½ oz. Parmesan cheese, grated (½ cup)
- 2 Tbsp. chopped fresh flat-leaf parsley
- 1 Tbsp. chopped fresh sage
- ½ tsp. table salt
- ½ tsp. freshly ground black pepper
- ½ cup toasted sliced almonds
  Fresh sage leaves, for garnish

1. Preheat oven to 375°F. Melt 1 tablespoon of the butter in a large skillet over medium-high; add half the chicken. Cook 3 minutes or until browned; turn and cook 1 minute. Transfer to a plate. (Chicken will not be cooked thoroughly.) Repeat with 1 tablespoon butter and remaining chicken. Wipe skillet clean. Melt 2 tablespoons butter in skillet over medium-high. Add shallots, and cook 3 minutes or until translucent. Add garlic and cook 30 seconds. Add mushrooms; cook, stirring often, 4 to 5 minutes or until tender. Stir in sherry and cook, stirring often, 1 minute.

2. Melt remaining ¼ cup butter in a 3-quart saucepan over medium-high. Whisk in flour; cook, whisking constantly, 1 minute. Gradually whisk in broth. Bring to a boil, whisking constantly, and cook 1 to 2 minutes or until slightly thickened. Remove from heat and add rice (reserve flavor packet for another use), next 5 ingredients, and shallot mixture. Spoon into a lightly greased 13- x 9-inch baking dish. Top with chicken.

3. Bake in preheated oven until a thermometer inserted in breast registers 165°F, about 30 minutes. Let stand 10 minutes. Sprinkle with almonds, and garnish with sage leaves.

TURKEY POT PIE WITH CRANBERRY-PECAN CRUSTS

Fall flavors are reinvented under this fruity, nut-filled crust. Different shapes and sizes of cookie cutters create a beautiful casserole to remember.

ACTIVE 20 MIN. - TOTAL 1 HOUR, 15 MIN.; INCLUDING CRUSTS
SERVES 10 TO 12

- 3 Tbsp. butter, divided
- 2 large sweet onions, diced
- ½ cup all-purpose flour
- 1 tsp. table salt
- 1 tsp. freshly ground black pepper
- 3 lb. turkey tenderloins, cut into 1½-inch cubes
- 2 Tbsp. vegetable oil
- 1½ cups chicken broth
- 1 cup milk
- 1 (9-oz.) pkg. fresh spinach, torn
  Cranberry-Pecan Crusts (recipe follows)

1. Preheat oven to 350°F. Melt 1 tablespoon butter in a large skillet over medium-high; add onions, and cook 15 minutes or until caramel-color. Place onions in a bowl.

2. Combine flour, salt, and pepper; dredge turkey tenderloin cubes in flour mixture.

3. Melt remaining 2 tablespoons butter with oil in skillet over medium-high; add turkey tenderloin cubes, and brown on all sides. Gradually stir in chicken broth and milk. Bring to a boil; cook, stirring constantly, 1 minute or until thickened. Stir in onions. Add spinach, stirring just until wilted. Pour turkey mixture into a lightly greased 13- x 9-inch baking dish.

4. Bake, covered, in preheated oven 30 minutes. Remove from oven and arrange Cranberry-Pecan Crusts on pot pie before serving. Serve with any remaining crusts on the side.

CRANBERRY-PECAN CRUSTS

ACTIVE 15 MIN. - TOTAL 25 MIN.
MAKES 3 TO 4 DOZEN

- 1 (14.1-oz.) pkg. refrigerated piecrusts
- ½ cup finely chopped pecans, toasted
- ½ cup finely chopped sweetened dried cranberries

1. Preheat oven to 425°F. Unroll 1 piecrust on a lightly floured surface; sprinkle with pecans and cranberries; top with remaining piecrust. Roll into a 14-inch circle, sealing together piecrusts. Cut into desired shapes with a 2- to 3-inch cutter. Place pastry shapes on a lightly greased baking sheet.

2. Bake in preheated oven until golden, 8 to 10 minutes.

- -

FABULOUS TUNA-NOODLE CASSEROLE

ACTIVE 20 MIN. - TOTAL 1 HOUR, 15 MIN.
SERVES 6 TO 8

- ¼ cup butter
- 1 large red bell pepper, chopped
- 1 cup chopped onion
- 1 (8-oz.) pkg. sliced fresh mushrooms
- ⅓ cup all-purpose flour
- 3 cups milk
- 12 oz. cheddar cheese, shredded (3 cups)
- ¾ tsp. table salt
- ½ tsp. black pepper
- 1 (12-oz.) can solid white tuna in spring water, drained and flaked
- 1 (6-oz.) can solid white tuna in spring water, drained and flaked
- 1 (12-oz.) pkg. egg noodles, cooked
- ¼ cup chopped fresh flat-leaf parsley
- 1½ cups homemade breadcrumbs
- ⅓ cup butter, melted

1. Preheat oven to 375°F. Melt ¼ cup butter in a large skillet over medium-high. Add bell pepper, onion, and mushrooms; cook 5 minutes or until tender. Remove from skillet.

2. Whisk together flour and milk until smooth; add to skillet. Cook over medium, stirring constantly, 10 minutes or until thickened. Remove from heat; add cheese, salt, and black pepper, stirring until cheese is melted.

3. Stir in tuna, noodles, and parsley; stir in cooked vegetables. Spoon into a lightly greased 13- x 9-inch baking dish.

4. Bake, covered, in preheated oven 25 minutes. Stir together breadcrumbs and ⅓ cup melted butter; sprinkle over casserole. Bake, uncovered, 15 minutes or until golden.

TURKEY POT PIE WITH
CRANBERRY-PECAN
CRUSTS

NEW TUNA
CASSEROLE

NEW TUNA CASSEROLE

Mom's old standby tuna casserole goes gourmet with the simple addition of mushrooms, fresh herbs, and haricot verts.

ACTIVE 35 MIN. - TOTAL 1 HOUR, 30 MIN.

SERVES 8

- 1 (16-oz.) pkg. uncooked ziti pasta
- 2 medium leeks, sliced
- 1 (8-oz.) pkg. haricots verts (French green beans), cut into 1-inch pieces
- 6 Tbsp. butter, divided
- 2 (4-oz.) pkg. fresh gourmet mushroom blend
- ¼ cup all-purpose flour
- 3 cups heavy cream
- 1 cup vegetable broth
- 8 oz. sharp white cheddar cheese, shredded (2 cups)
- 6 Tbsp. grated Parmesan cheese, divided
- ¾ tsp. kosher salt
- ½ tsp. freshly ground black pepper
- 1 (12-oz.) can solid white tuna in spring water, drained
- 2 Tbsp. chopped fresh chives
- 1 Tbsp. chopped fresh tarragon or flat-leaf parsley
- ¼ cup crushed potato chips
- ¼ cup panko (Japanese breadcrumbs)
- 2 Tbsp. butter, melted
  Sliced fresh chives, for garnish

1. Preheat oven to 350°F. Cook pasta according to package directions.

2. Remove and discard root ends and dark green tops of leeks. Cut in half lengthwise; rinse thoroughly under cold running water to remove grit and sand. Thinly slice leeks.

3. Meanwhile, cook green beans in boiling salted water to cover 30 seconds to 1 minute or until crisp-tender; drain. Plunge into ice water to stop the cooking process; drain.

4. Melt 2 tablespoons butter in a large skillet over medium-high. Add leeks, and cook 2 minutes; add mushrooms, and cook 5 minutes or until lightly browned. Transfer leek mixture to a small bowl. Wipe skillet clean.

5. Melt remaining 4 tablespoons butter in skillet over medium; whisk in flour and cook, whisking constantly, 2 minutes. Gradually whisk in cream and broth. Bring mixture to a boil, stirring often. Reduce heat to medium-low; gradually whisk in cheddar cheese and 4 tablespoons Parmesan cheese until smooth. Stir in salt and black pepper.

6. Stir cream mixture into pasta. Stir in tuna, next 2 ingredients, green beans, and leek mixture; transfer to a lightly greased 13- x 9-inch baking dish.

7. Stir together potato chips, next 2 ingredients, and remaining 2 tablespoons Parmesan cheese in a small bowl; sprinkle over pasta mixture.

8. Bake in preheated oven until bubbly, 35 to 40 minutes. Let stand 5 minutes before serving. Garnish with additional chives.

SPICY PUMPKIN SOUP
WITH AVOCADO CREAM,
PAGE 223

SANDWICHES, SALADS & SOUPS

PORK TENDERLOIN SLIDERS

ACTIVE 25 MIN. - TOTAL 55 MIN., NOT INCLUDING SAUCES
MAKES 20 SLIDERS

- 2 pork tenderloins (about 2½ lb.), trimmed
- 3 Tbsp. olive oil, divided
- 2 tsp. kosher salt
- 1 tsp. freshly ground black pepper
- ¼ cup firmly packed dark brown sugar
- 2 Tbsp. Dijon mustard
- 3 Tbsp. fresh thyme leaves
- 2 Tbsp. chopped fresh rosemary
- 20 slider buns or dinner rolls, split
  Italian-Style Salsa Verde, Blackberry-Honey Mustard Sauce, or Bacon-and-Sweet Onion Jam (recipes follow)

1. Preheat oven to 400°F. Rub pork tenderloins with 1 tablespoon oil, and sprinkle with salt and pepper. Stir together sugar and next 3 ingredients; rub over pork.

2. Cook pork in remaining 2 tablespoons hot oil in a skillet over medium-high 5 minutes, browning on all sides. Place tenderloins on a wire rack in a jelly-roll pan.

3. Bake in preheated oven 20 minutes or until a thermometer inserted in thickest portion registers 155°F. Remove from oven, and let stand 10 minutes. Slice and serve on slider buns with sauces.

ITALIAN-STYLE SALSA VERDE

ACTIVE 30 MIN. - TOTAL 1 HOUR, 5 MIN.
MAKES ABOUT 1 CUP

- 1 small jalapeño pepper
- 2 medium banana peppers
- ½ cup extra-virgin olive oil
- ⅓ cup finely chopped fresh flat-leaf parsley
- 4½ tsp. chopped fresh chives
- 1 Tbsp. minced fresh oregano
- 2 garlic cloves, minced
- 1 tsp. kosher salt

1. Preheat broiler with oven rack 6 inches from heat. Broil jalapeño 3 to 4 minutes on each side or until blackened. Place in a small bowl, cover with plastic wrap, and let stand 10 minutes. Broil banana peppers 1 to 2 minutes on each side or just until blistered and slightly softened. Cool completely, and chop. Peel and finely chop jalapeño, discarding seeds.

2. Stir together oil, next 5 ingredients, and chopped peppers in a small bowl. Cover and let stand 30 minutes.

BLACKBERRY-HONEY MUSTARD SAUCE

ACTIVE 20 MIN. - TOTAL 1 HOUR, 20 MIN.
MAKES ABOUT 1¼ CUPS

- ⅓ cup granulated sugar
- 1 (6-oz.) container fresh blackberries
- ¼ cup honey
- 1 Tbsp. dry mustard
- 3 Tbsp. Dijon mustard
- 2 Tbsp. fresh lemon juice
- 1 tsp. kosher salt
- ⅓ cup extra-virgin olive oil

1. Bring sugar and blueberries to a boil in a small saucepan over medium-high, stirring occasionally and mashing berries with the back of a wooden spoon. Reduce heat to medium; simmer, stirring often and mashing berries until slightly thickened, 2 to 3 minutes. Remove from heat, and pour through a fine wire-mesh strainer into a blender, pressing with spoon to release juices; discard solids.

2. Add honey and next 4 ingredients to blender; process on low 20 seconds. Increase blender speed to high, and process 30 seconds. With blender running, add oil in a slow stream, processing until smooth. Chill 1 to 12 hours.

BACON-AND-SWEET ONION JAM

ACTIVE 35 MIN. - TOTAL 1 HOUR, 15 MIN.
MAKES 1½ CUPS

- 4 uncooked thick applewood-smoked bacon slices, chopped
- 1 Tbsp. butter
- 2 medium sweet onions, chopped
- 4 large shallots, chopped
- ½ cup balsamic vinegar
- 3 Tbsp. light brown sugar
- 2½ tsp. kosher salt
- 2 Tbsp. chopped fresh chives
- 2 tsp. chopped fresh thyme

1. Cook bacon in a medium skillet over medium-low, stirring occasionally, until crisp, 8 to 10 minutes. Remove bacon, and drain on paper towels, reserving drippings.

2. Add butter to drippings; stir until melted. Increase heat to medium; add onions, and cook until tender, 10 to 12 minutes. Add shallots, vinegar, sugar, and salt; cook, stirring constantly, until sugar is dissolved. Reduce heat to low; cook, stirring occasionally, 20 to 25 minutes or until onions are very tender and brown. Remove from heat; stir in chives, thyme, and bacon. Cool completely.

PORK TENDERLOIN
SLIDERS

COUNTRY HAM-AND-
PEACH PANINI

GOLDEN-BAKED MINI REUBENS

ACTIVE 20 MIN. - TOTAL 30 MIN.

MAKE: 20 SANDWICHES

- ½ cup Thousand Island dressing
- 1 (16-oz.) loaf party rye bread
- 1 (6-oz.) pkg. Swiss cheese slices, halved
- 12 oz. thinly sliced corned beef
- 1 (16-oz.) can shredded sauerkraut, well drained

1. Preheat oven to 375°F. Spread dressing evenly on one side of each bread slice; top half the slices evenly with half the cheese, the corned beef, sauerkraut, and remaining cheese. Top with remaining bread slices.

2. Coat a baking sheet with cooking spray; arrange sandwiches on baking sheet. Coat bottom of a second baking sheet with cooking spray; place, coated side down, on sandwiches.

3. Bake in preheated oven until bread is golden and cheese melts, 8 to 10 minutes.

Note: To make ahead, place unbaked sandwiches on baking sheets and freeze until firm; place sandwiches in heavy-duty zip-top plastic bags, and freeze. Bake as directed at 375°F for 15 minutes.

- -

COBB CLUBS

ACTIVE 15 MIN. - TOTAL 15 MIN.

SERVES 4

- 4 hoagie rolls, split and lightly toasted
- 1 cup blue cheese dressing
- ¾ lb. thinly sliced cooked turkey
- 4 (1-oz.) sharp cheddar cheese slices
- 1 large avocado, thinly sliced
- 8 crisp-cooked bacon slices
- 4 plum tomatoes, sliced
- 3 cups shredded leaf lettuce
- ¼ cup olive oil vinaigrette

1. Spread cut sides of each hoagie roll with dressing.

2. Layer bottom halves of rolls evenly with turkey and next 5 ingredients; drizzle with vinaigrette. Cover with top halves of rolls.

COUNTRY HAM-AND-PEACH PANINI

These panini are best with very thinly sliced ham, not thick ham steaks. Ask your deli to slice the ham thinly, or look for a packet of center- and end-cut slices, which tend to be small.

ACTIVE 20 MIN. - TOTAL 20 MIN.

SERVES 4

- 8 ciabatta* bread slices
- 4 tsp. coarse-grain Dijon mustard
  Freshly ground black pepper
- 4 (1-oz.) fontina cheese slices
- 4 oz. thinly sliced country ham, prosciutto, or Serrano ham
- 2 medium peaches (about ¾ lb.), unpeeled and sliced
- 4 tsp. honey (optional)
- 1 Tbsp. extra-virgin olive oil

1. Spread each of 4 bread slices with 1 teaspoon mustard, and sprinkle with desired amount of pepper. Layer with cheese, ham, peaches, and, if desired, honey. Top with remaining bread slices; press together gently. Brush sandwiches with olive oil.

2. Cook sandwiches, in batches, in a preheated nonstick grill pan over medium 3 to 4 minutes on each side. (Or use a preheated panini press; cook 3 to 4 minutes, until golden and cheese is melted.) Serve immediately.

*Note: Any firm white bread may be substituted.

GRILLED BACON, CHEESE, AND TOMATO SANDWICHES

ACTIVE 15 MIN. - TOTAL 28 MIN.
SERVES 4

- 8 (½-inch-thick) French bread slices
- ¼ cup butter or margarine, softened
- 8 (1-oz.) Jarlsberg or Swiss cheese slices
- 3 plum tomatoes, thinly sliced
- ½ tsp. dried basil
- 12 cooked bacon slices

1. Spread one side of bread slices with butter; turn 4 slices buttered-side down, and top each with a cheese slice. Layer evenly with tomato, basil, bacon, and remaining cheese slices; top with remaining bread slices, buttered side up.

2. Heat a large skillet over medium; cook sandwiches, two at a time, until golden, turning once.

- -

BLTS WITH A TWIST

How do you improve on the classic sandwich? Grill it. Cook the bacon outside (no smoky kitchen!), char the tomatoes, and toast the bread. Use thick-cut bacon because it won't crumble in the sandwich.

ACTIVE 25 MIN. - TOTAL 25 MIN.
SERVES 4

- 8 thick-cut hickory-smoked bacon slices
- 8 (5-grain) bread slices (about 1 inch thick)
- 3 small (5- to 6-oz.) tomatoes, cut into ½-inch slices
- 5 Tbsp. plus 1 tsp. mayonnaise
- 8 butterhead lettuce leaves (from 1 head)
- ½ tsp. kosher salt
- ½ tsp. black pepper

1. Preheat grill to medium-high (400°F to 450°F). Place a 12-inch cast-iron skillet or grill pan on grill grates. Working in two batches, add bacon to skillet. Cook, turning occasionally, until crisp, 7 to 8 minutes per batch. Transfer bacon to a plate lined with paper towels; let cool 2 minutes. Break each bacon slice in half. Remove skillet from grill; reserve 4 tablespoons drippings.

2. Brush reserved drippings evenly onto one side of bread slices. Place bread, greased sides down, on unoiled grates. Grill, uncovered, until lightly toasted, 2 to

3 minutes. Transfer bread to a plate; cover with aluminum foil to keep warm.

3. Place tomato slices on oiled grates. Grill, uncovered, until warmed and faint grill marks appear, about 30 seconds per side. Remove from grill.

4. Spread mayonnaise evenly onto the ungrilled sides of bread slices. Top 4 bread slices evenly (mayonnaise sides up) with bacon pieces, tomato slices, and lettuce. Sprinkle evenly with salt and pepper. Top with remaining 4 bread slices, mayonnaise sides down.

- -

CHICKEN-AND-BLACK BEAN CHIMICHANGAS

Upgrade burritos by crisping them in a skillet.

ACTIVE 20 MIN. - TOTAL 20 MIN.
SERVES 4

- 1 lb. shredded deli-roasted chicken
- 1 (15-oz.) can black beans, drained and rinsed
- 1 (4-oz.) can mild chopped green chiles
- ¼ cup salsa verde
- ½ tsp. kosher salt
- ¼ tsp. freshly ground black pepper
- ¼ cup chopped fresh cilantro
- 4 (10-inch) flour tortillas
- 4 oz. Monterey Jack cheese, shredded (1 cup)
- ⅓ cup canola oil
  Guacamole, sour cream, chopped tomatoes, for topping

1. Stir together first 7 ingredients in a large bowl. Divide chicken mixture among tortillas, placing mixture just below center of each tortilla. Sprinkle with cheese. Fold sides of tortilla over filling, and roll up.

2. Fry chimichangas, in two batches, in hot oil in a large skillet over medium-high until browned and crispy, 3 to 4 minutes on each side. Drain on paper towels. Serve with desired toppings.

CHICKEN-AND-BLACK
BEAN CHIMICHANGAS

TURKEY, BRIE, AND
APPLE PANINI WITH
BACON MARMALADE

TURKEY, BRIE, AND APPLE PANINI WITH BACON MARMALADE

ACTIVE 20 MIN. - TOTAL 1 HOUR, 15 MIN., INCLUDING MARMALADE
SERVES 4

- 1 (7-oz.) Brie round
- 8 Italian bread slices
- 1 medium Gala apple, sliced
- 1 cup loosely packed arugula
- 8 oz. thinly sliced smoked turkey
- 4 Tbsp. Bacon Marmalade (recipe follows)
  Melted butter

1. Trim and discard rind from Brie round. Cut Brie into ¼-inch slices. Layer 4 bread slices with Brie, apple slices, arugula, and turkey. Top each with one bread slice spread with 1 tablespoon Bacon Marmalade. Brush sandwiches with melted butter.

2. Cook sandwiches, in batches, in a preheated panini press until golden brown and cheese is melted, 3 to 4 minutes. Serve immediately.

BACON MARMALADE

Try this on toast with a triple-cream cheese or tossed with iceberg lettuce and blue cheese.

ACTIVE 25 MIN. - TOTAL 55 MIN.
MAKES 1¼ CUPS

- ½ (16-oz.) pkg. thick hickory-smoked bacon slices, diced
- 1 cup sorghum syrup
- 1½ cups cider vinegar
- ½ cup chicken broth
- 1 bay leaf
  Kosher salt and black pepper, to taste

Cook bacon in a skillet over medium-high, stirring often, just until dark golden brown, about 4 minutes. Drain bacon on paper towels. Wipe skillet clean; return bacon to skillet. Add sorghum; cook, stirring constantly, 1 minute. Add vinegar; cook, stirring often, until liquid is reduced by half, about 8 minutes. Add broth and bay leaf; cook until slightly thickened, about 5 minutes. Remove bay leaf. Add salt and black pepper to taste. Cool 30 minutes.

OPEN-FACED PHILLY SANDWICHES

This recipe is filling on its own, or add a salad or home fries for a side dish.

ACTIVE 20 MIN. - TOTAL 45 MIN.
SERVES 2

- 2 (8-inch) submarine rolls, unsliced
- ½ lb. boneless top round steak
- 2 Tbsp. Italian dressing
- ¼ tsp. dried crushed red pepper
- 2 Tbsp. butter
- 1 large onion, thinly sliced
- 1½ cups sliced fresh mushrooms
- 1 green bell pepper, cut into thin strips
- 1 garlic clove, minced
- 2 (¾-oz.) slices provolone cheese

1. Make a 1½- to 2-inch-deep vertical cut around outside edge of each roll, leaving a ½-inch border. Remove tops of rolls, and discard. Hollow out about 1½ inches of each bread roll, forming a boat. Set boats aside.

2. Cut steak diagonally across grain into ⅛-inch-thick strips; place in a small shallow bowl. Add dressing and crushed red pepper, tossing to coat; set aside.

3. Melt butter in a nonstick skillet over medium-high; add onion and mushrooms, and cook until onion slices are golden brown, 15 minutes. Add bell pepper, and cook until tender, 8 to 10 minutes. Add garlic, and cook 1 minute. Remove mixture from skillet, and set aside.

4. Stir-fry steak mixture in skillet over medium-high until steak strips are no longer pink, 2 to 3 minutes.

5. Fill bread boats evenly with layers of steak mixture and onion mixture; top with cheese.

6. Broil 5½ inches from heat until cheese is lightly browned, about 3 minutes.

195

WHITE CALZONES WITH MARINARA SAUCE

Ricotta often contains stabilizers, which can give it a gummy texture when baked. Choose one that's made with as few ingredients as possible—ideally milk, whey, vinegar, and salt.

ACTIVE 20 MIN. · TOTAL 55 MIN.
SERVES 4

- 1 lb. fresh prepared pizza dough (at room temperature)
- 6 oz. low-moisture part-skim mozzarella cheese, shredded (about 1½ cups)
- ¾ cup ricotta cheese
- 1 large egg yolk
- ½ tsp. lemon zest
- 2 garlic cloves, minced
- ½ tsp. kosher salt
- ¼ tsp. black pepper
- 1 large whole egg
- 1 oz. Parmesan cheese, grated (about ¼ cup)
- 1 tsp. dried Italian seasoning
- 1 cup jarred marinara sauce, warmed

1. Preheat oven to 450°F. Divide pizza dough into four equal pieces; form into small balls. Wrap each dough ball with plastic wrap; let rest 20 minutes.

2. While dough balls rest, stir together mozzarella cheese, ricotta cheese, egg yolk, lemon zest, garlic, salt, and black pepper in a medium bowl with a fork until well incorporated.

3. Unwrap and roll on a lightly floured surface into four flat disks, about 7 inches wide. Place disks on a baking sheet lined with parchment paper.

4. Divide cheese mixture among dough disks, adding mixture to one side of the disk, leaving a ½-inch border. Lightly beat whole egg in a small bowl. Brush edge of dough with half the egg; fold into half-moons, and crimp edges with fork. Brush tops of calzones with remaining egg; sprinkle with Parmesan cheese and Italian seasoning.

5. Bake in preheated oven until golden brown, 16 to 18 minutes. Serve with warm marinara sauce.

CHICKEN CAESAR SALAD SANDWICHES

Sandwich rolls, spread with the garlic-mayonnaise and toasted, are a good stand-in for the mini baguettes. The chicken salad tastes even better when prepped a day ahead, giving the flavors time to meld.

ACTIVE 20 MIN. · TOTAL 20 MIN.
SERVES 4

- 3 cups shredded rotisserie chicken
- 2 oil-packed anchovy fillets, finely chopped
- 1 garlic clove, minced
- 1 Tbsp. fresh lemon juice
- 1 Tbsp. red wine vinegar
- 1 tsp. Dijon mustard
- ½ tsp. Worcestershire sauce
- ¼ tsp. kosher salt
- ⅛ tsp. black pepper
- ⅓ cup extra-virgin olive oil
- ½ oz. Parmesan cheese, grated (⅓ cup)
- 3 Tbsp. mayonnaise
- ¼ tsp. garlic powder
- 4 mini baguettes or 1 French bread baguette cut into 4 portions, split
- 4 romaine lettuce leaves

1. Place chicken in a medium bowl. Process anchovy fillets and next 7 ingredients in a blender until smooth. Gradually add olive oil, and process until smooth; stir in Parmesan cheese. Pour dressing over chicken, then toss to coat.

2. Stir together mayonnaise and garlic powder in a small bowl. Brush cut sides of bread evenly with mayonnaise mixture. Heat a large skillet over medium-high. Cook bread, cut-side down, in hot skillet, until toasted and golden brown, about 2 minutes. Divide chicken mixture and lettuce leaves evenly among bottoms of toasted bread; cover with bread tops.

WHITE CALZONES WITH
MARINARA SAUCE

SOUTHWESTERN CHICKEN SALAD

ACTIVE 20 MIN. · TOTAL 20 MIN.
SERVES 6

- ¾ cup mayonnaise
- ¼ cup chopped fresh cilantro
- 3 Tbsp. fresh lime juice
- 2 tsp. chili powder
- 1 tsp. minced garlic
- ½ tsp. ground cumin
- 4 cups chopped grilled chicken
- ¾ cup diced poblano pepper
  Table salt, to taste
- 6 6- to 8-inch tortillas, warmed
  Diced mango, diced avocado, diced tomatoes, shredded Monterey Jack cheese, for topping

Whisk together first 6 ingredients in a large bowl. Stir in chicken and poblano pepper, and season with salt. Serve in warm tortillas with desired toppings.

- -

EGG SALAD SANDWICHES

Serve this egg salad to make finger sandwiches on thin white bread; or smear it on crostini, and top with fresh herbs.

ACTIVE 15 MIN. · TOTAL 15 MIN.
SERVES 3

- 6 large hard-cooked eggs
- 2 Tbsp. finely chopped celery
- 2 Tbsp. sweet pickle relish
- 3 Tbsp. mayonnaise
- 1 Tbsp. grated onion
- ¾ tsp. dried salad seasoning
- ½ tsp. Dijon mustard
- ¼ tsp. table salt
- ¼ tsp. granulated sugar
- ¼ tsp. freshly ground black pepper
- ½ cup sliced pimiento-stuffed green olives
- 6 bread slices

Mash 3 hard-cooked eggs in a large bowl using a fork or pastry blender. Chop remaining 3 eggs. Add chopped eggs, celery, and next 8 ingredients to mashed eggs; stir until blended. Gently stir in olives. Cover and chill, if desired. Divide egg salad among 3 bread slices; top with remaining bread slices.

DOUBLE-DECKER EGG SALAD SANDWICHES

Substitute fresh arugula for the spinach if you prefer its spicy bite. For a checkerboard effect, use both white and wheat breads.

ACTIVE 25 MIN. · TOTAL 25 MIN.
SERVES 6

- ⅔ cup mayonnaise, divided
- 4 large hard-cooked eggs, chopped
- 1 celery stalk, diced
- 4 bacon slices, cooked and crumbled
- ¼ cup chopped fresh chives
- 1 Tbsp. minced sweet onion
- ¼ tsp. seasoned salt
- ½ tsp. freshly ground black pepper
- 12 very thin white or wheat sandwich bread slices, lightly toasted
- 1 cup firmly packed fresh spinach

1. Stir together ⅓ cup mayonnaise and next 7 ingredients.

2. Spread remaining ⅓ cup mayonnaise evenly on one side of each bread slice. Spread 4 bread slices, mayonnaise-side up, evenly with half of the egg salad. Top with half the spinach and 4 bread slices.

3. Repeat with remaining egg salad, spinach, and bread slices.

Sweet-Pickle Egg Salad Club: Omit bacon and chives. Add 2 tablespoons instant potato flakes and 1 tablespoon sweet pickle relish. Proceed with recipe as directed.

Shrimp-Egg Salad Club: Omit bacon. Add ⅔ cup finely chopped boiled shrimp, ½ teaspoon lemon zest, and ¼ teaspoon cayenne pepper. Proceed with recipe as directed.

CUCUMBER SANDWICHES

Make these elegant sandwiches for the next afternoon luncheon or tea.

ACTIVE 15 MIN. - TOTAL 15 MIN.
MAKES 20 ROUNDS

- 1 (8-oz.) pkg. cream cheese, softened
- ⅓ cup mayonnaise
- 1 medium cucumber, peeled, seeded, and finely chopped
- ¼ tsp. garlic salt
- ½ tsp. chopped fresh dillweed
- 20 sandwich bread slices
- 20 thin wheat bread slices

1. Process cream cheese and mayonnaise in a blender or food processor until smooth, stopping once to scrape down sides.

2. Combine cream cheese mixture, cucumber, garlic salt, and dillweed in a medium bowl.

3. Spread cucumber mixture evenly onto white bread slices; top with wheat bread. Using a 2- to 3-inch round cutter, cut out sandwiches, discarding crusts. Store cucumber sandwiches in an airtight container up to 1 hour before serving.

SMOKY PIMIENTO CHEESE FINGER SANDWICHES

These pimiento cheese sandwiches are a quick and easy appetizers for any gathering.

ACTIVE 10 MIN. - TOTAL 15 MIN.
SERVES 7

- 1 (3-oz.) pkg. cream cheese, softened
- ½ cup mayonnaise
- 1 tsp. paprika
- ¼ tsp. table salt
- 8 oz. smoked cheddar cheese, shredded (2 cups)
- 8 oz. smoked gouda cheese, shredded (2 cups)
- ½ (8.5-oz.) jar sun-dried tomatoes in oil, drained and chopped
- 14 bread slices (sourdough and dark wheat)

1. Stir together cream cheese and next 3 ingredients in a large bowl until blended. Stir in shredded cheeses and sun-dried tomatoes until combined.

2. Spread cheese mixture on half the bread slices (about ⅓ cup on each); top with remaining bread slices.

FRENCH ONION SANDWICHES

Shave thin slices from an onion with a very sharp chef's knife or cut the onion in half and push slowly through the slicing blade of a food processor.

ACTIVE 15 MIN. - TOTAL 15 MIN.
SERVES 4

- 8 (1-oz.) slices French bread
- 2 tsp. butter or margarine
- 1 large onion, very thinly sliced
- 1½ Tbsp. brown sugar
- 4 oz. Swiss cheese, shredded (1 cup)

1. Preheat oven to 375°F. Arrange bread slices on a baking sheet. Bake until lightly toasted, about 8 minutes. Remove from oven, and leave bread slices on baking sheet.

3. While bread toasts, coat a large heavy saucepan with cooking spray; add butter, and place over high until butter melts. Add onion, and cook, stirring constantly, 3 minutes or until onion is tender. Add brown sugar; cook 5 minutes or until onion is tender and browned, stirring often.

4. Preheat broiler.

5. Spoon onion mixture evenly on bread slices; top with cheese. Broil 5½ inches from heat 2 minutes. Serve immediately.

DIXIE CHICKEN SALAD WITH GRAPES, HONEY, ALMONDS, AND BROCCOLI

DIXIE CHICKEN SALAD WITH GRAPES, HONEY, ALMONDS, AND BROCCOLI

ACTIVE 20 MIN. · TOTAL 20 MIN.
SERVES 4 TO 6

  2 large eggs, lightly beaten
  6 (4-oz.) chicken cutlets, ¼ to ½ inch thick
1½ cups seasoned breadcrumbs
 ½ cup apple cider vinegar
  2 Tbsp. honey
  1 Tbsp. Dijon mustard
 ½ tsp. kosher salt
 ¼ tsp. freshly ground black pepper
 ½ cup olive oil
  1 (5-oz.) pkg. spring lettuce mix
  3 cups broccoli florets
 ½ cup halved seedless red grapes
 ½ cup halved seedless green grapes
 ½ cup sliced honey-roasted almonds

1. Preheat oven to 425°F. Whisk together eggs and 3 tablespoons water in a small bowl. Dip chicken in egg mixture, and dredge in breadcrumbs, pressing firmly to adhere. Place on a baking sheet lined with aluminum foil. Bake until a thermometer inserted in center reads 165°F, about 15 minutes.

2. Meanwhile, whisk together vinegar and next 5 ingredients. Toss together lettuce, broccoli, red grapes, and green grapes; season with salt and pepper. Top with chicken and sliced almonds; serve with vinaigrette.

PICNIC IN A GLASS

This Southern spin on Middle Eastern fattoush salad can be assembled in the morning for the flavors to meld and pita chips to soften.

ACTIVE 30 MIN. · TOTAL 3 HOURS, INCLUDING DRESSING
SERVES 6 TO 8

  1 (19-oz.) can chickpeas, drained and rinsed
  2 Tbsp. chopped fresh flat-leaf parsley
  2 Tbsp. chopped fresh mint
  2 Tbsp. fresh lemon juice
  5 Tbsp. olive oil, divided
  1 (2½- to 3-lb.) rotisserie chicken, skinned, boned, and shredded
 ¾ cup chopped radishes
 ¼ cup finely chopped red onion
  1 pt. grape tomatoes, halved
1½ cups chopped English cucumbers
   Yogurt Dressing (recipe follows)
  3 cups coarsely crushed pita chips
   Lemon wedges, for serving

1. Stir together first 4 ingredients and 2 tablespoons olive oil; stir in shredded chicken. Add table salt and black pepper to taste; let stand 15 minutes.

2. Meanwhile, stir together radishes, onion, and 1 tablespoon olive oil. Stir together tomatoes and 1 tablespoon olive oil. Stir together cucumbers and remaining 1 tablespoon olive oil. Season each mixture with salt and pepper.

3. Layer chickpea mixture, radish mixture, ¾ cup Yogurt Dressing, tomato mixture, pita chips, and cucumber mixture in a 4-quart bowl; top with remaining Yogurt Dressing. Cover and chill 2 to 4 hours. Serve with lemon wedges and additional pita chips.

YOGURT DRESSING

ACTIVE 10 MIN. · TOTAL 10 MIN.
MAKES ABOUT 2 CUPS

Stir together 1 cup **Greek yogurt**; 4 ounces **feta cheese**, finely crumbled; 2 tablespoons chopped **fresh dill**; ⅓ cup **buttermilk**; 2 teaspoons **lemon zest**; 2 tablespoons fresh **lemon juice**; and 1 **garlic clove**, minced. Add **salt** and **black pepper** to taste. Let dressing stand 15 minutes.

KALE AND SWEET POTATO SALAD WITH CHICKEN

ACTIVE 30 MIN. - TOTAL 30 MIN.
SERVES 4

- 2 Tbsp. fresh lemon juice
- 1 tsp. Dijon mustard
- ½ tsp. honey
- 1 tsp. kosher salt, divided
- 6 Tbsp. olive oil, divided
- 1½ cups cubed sweet potatoes
- 1 tsp. finely chopped fresh rosemary, divided
- ½ tsp. black pepper, divided
- 4 (5-oz.) boneless, skin-on chicken breasts
- 1 tsp. salted butter
- 1 tsp. light brown sugar
- ¼ cup chopped pecans, toasted
- 8 oz. kale leaves, thinly sliced

1. Whisk together lemon juice, mustard, honey, and ½ teaspoon of the salt until combined. While whisking, slowly drizzle in 4 tablespoons of the oil to emulsify. Set dressing aside.

2. Preheat oven to 425°F. Toss together sweet potatoes, 1 tablespoon of the oil, ½ teaspoon of the rosemary, and ¼ teaspoon each of the salt and pepper. Spread in a single layer on one end of a large rimmed baking sheet.

3. Rub chicken with remaining 1 tablespoon oil; place chicken at opposite end of baking sheet, skin side up. Sprinkle with remaining ½ teaspoon rosemary, ¼ teaspoon salt, and ¼ teaspoon pepper.

4. Roast in preheated oven until sweet potatoes are tender (stirring potatoes once halfway through) and chicken is golden brown and a thermometer inserted in thickest portion registers 165°F, about 20 minutes. Let sweet potatoes and chicken cool.

5. Meanwhile, melt butter in a small skillet over medium. Add sugar and cook, stirring constantly, until dissolved, about 1 minute. Add pecans and cook, stirring, until sugar mixture no longer sticks to the pan and instead coats the pecans. Remove from heat. Spread pecans in a single layer on parchment paper; cool completely, 10 minutes.

6. Cut chicken into ½-inch slices. Combine kale and sweet potatoes in a large bowl. Drizzle with half the dressing; toss gently to coat. Divide vegetables among four plates; top with sliced chicken and candied pecans. Drizzle with remaining dressing.

CHICKEN-QUINOA SALAD WITH GREEN GODDESS DRESSING

Adding cooked quinoa is an easy and healthy way to make a simple salad more filling.

ACTIVE 10 MIN - TOTAL 30 MIN.
SERVES 4

- ⅔ cup mayonnaise
- 1 Tbsp. chopped fresh chives
- 1 tsp. white wine vinegar
- ½ tsp. anchovy paste
- 1 tsp. lemon zest plus 1 Tbsp. fresh lemon juice
- ¼ tsp. black pepper
- ½ cup loosely packed fresh flat-leaf parsley, divided
- ⅓ cup loosely packed fresh tarragon, divided
- ¾ tsp. kosher salt, divided
- ½ cup uncooked quinoa
- 5 cups torn butter lettuce
- 3 cups shredded rotisserie chicken
- ½ cup thinly sliced English cucumber
- ½ cup thinly sliced radishes

1. Process mayonnaise, chives, vinegar, anchovy paste, lemon zest, lemon juice, black pepper, ¼ cup of the fresh parsley, 1 tablespoon of the fresh tarragon, and ¼ teaspoon of the salt in a food processor until smooth, about 1 to 2 minutes. Set aside.

2. Bring ¾ cup water, the quinoa, and remaining ½ teaspoon salt to a boil in a medium saucepan over medium-high. Stir and cover. Reduce heat to low; cook until quinoa is tender and liquid is absorbed, about 15 minutes. Remove from heat; let stand 5 minutes. Remove lid and fluff quinoa with a fork.

3. Toss together butter lettuce and remaining ¼ cup each fresh parsley and fresh tarragon. Toss greens lightly with about ¼ cup dressing. Transfer to a serving platter. Sprinkle cooked quinoa on greens; top with chicken. Arrange cucumber and radish slices on salad. Drizzle salad with an additional ¼ cup dressing, and serve remaining dressing on the side, if desired.

CHICKEN-QUINOA SALAD WITH GREEN GODDESS DRESSING

SOUTHWESTERN
CHOPPED CHICKEN
SALAD

SOUTHWESTERN CHOPPED CHICKEN SALAD

Every bite of this salad is a delightful mix of flavors and textures, while the homemade baked tortilla chips on top steal the show. They're light, crunchy, and spiced with cumin; you'll never crave a traditional crouton again.

ACTIVE 45 MIN. - TOTAL 1 HOUR, 30 MIN.
SERVES 4

- 2 (10-inch) flour tortillas
- 1 tsp. ground cumin
- ⅓ cup plus 1 Tbsp. olive oil, divided
- 1 tsp. kosher salt, divided
- 2 tsp. lime zest plus ½ cup fresh lime juice
- 1 shallot, minced
- 1 Tbsp. apple cider vinegar
- 1 tsp. Dijon mustard
- 1 tsp. honey
- ¼ tsp. black pepper
- 4 cups chopped cooked chicken
- 2 cups chopped ripe avocado
- 2 romaine lettuce hearts, chopped
- ½ cup thinly sliced radishes
- ½ cup Pickled Red Onions (recipe follows)

1. Preheat oven to 425°F. Stack tortillas; cut in half, and cut crosswise into ½-inch strips. Place the tortilla strips on a rimmed baking sheet. Toss with cumin, 1 tablespoon of the olive oil, and ¼ teaspoon of the salt. Spread strips in a single layer; bake in preheated oven until golden brown and crisp, 10 to 12 minutes, turning halfway through baking. Cool strips to room temperature.

2. Meanwhile, whisk together lime zest, lime juice, shallot, apple cider vinegar, Dijon mustard, honey, pepper, and remaining ⅓ cup oil and ¾ teaspoon salt until well combined.

3. Toss together chicken, avocado, romaine, radishes, and Pickled Red Onions in a large bowl. Add about ½ cup vinaigrette; toss to coat. Place 2 cups salad on each of 4 plates; top each with baked tortilla strips. Serve with remaining vinaigrette.

PICKLED RED ONIONS

ACTIVE 5 MIN. - TOTAL 1 HOUR, 5 MIN.
MAKES 2 CUPS

- 1 cup hot water
- ½ cup red wine vinegar
- 1 Tbsp. granulated sugar
- 1½ tsp. kosher salt
- 1 red onion, thinly sliced

Stir together first 4 ingredients until sugar is completely dissolved. Place sliced onion in a medium bowl. Pour vinegar mixture over onion; let stand 1 hour. Store in an airtight container in refrigerator up to 1 month.

- -

SUMMER TORTELLINI SALAD

Toss tortellini with chicken and an array of herbs for a palate-pleasing summer salad.

ACTIVE 10 MIN. - TOTAL 45 MIN.
SERVES 4

- 1 (19-oz.) pkg. frozen cheese tortellini
- 2 cups chopped cooked chicken
- ¼ cup sliced green olives
- ¼ cup sliced black olives
- ¼ cup diced red bell pepper
- 2 Tbsp. chopped sweet onion
- 2 Tbsp. chopped fresh flat-leaf parsley
- 2 Tbsp. mayonnaise
- 1 Tbsp. red wine vinegar
- 1 tsp. herbes de Provence or dried Italian seasoning
- ¼ cup canola oil
  Table salt, to taste
  Fresh parsley sprigs, for garnish

1. Cook tortellini according to package directions; drain. Plunge into ice water to stop the cooking process; drain and place in a large bowl. Stir in chicken and next 5 ingredients.

2. Whisk together mayonnaise, red wine vinegar, and herbes de Provence. Add oil in a slow, steady stream, whisking constantly until smooth. Pour over tortellini mixture, tossing to coat. Stir in salt to taste. Cover and chill at least 25 minutes. Garnish with parsley, if desired.

ROASTED VEGETABLE ORZO SALAD

ACTIVE 15 MIN. - TOTAL 1 HOUR, 15 MIN.
SERVES 6

- 2 red, yellow, and/or green bell peppers
- 7 Tbsp. olive oil, divided
- 1 medium red onion, sliced
- 3 zucchini, chopped
  Table salt and black pepper
- 1 lb. orzo
- 3 Tbsp. fresh lemon juice
- 2 Tbsp. minced fresh flat-leaf parsley
- 1 Tbsp. minced fresh mint
- 1 Tbsp. minced chives
- 1 cup sliced green olives
- 4 oz. goat cheese

1. Preheat broiler. Quarter peppers lengthwise; remove cores. Rub with 1 teaspoon olive oil; place on baking sheet, cut side down. Broil until blistered, about 5 minutes. Let cool and remove skins. Cut into strips.

2. Preheat oven to 400°F. In a roasting pan, toss onion and zucchini with 2 tablespoons olive oil, and season with salt and black pepper. Roast, stirring often, until tender, 45 minutes.

3. Bring a pot of salted water to a boil. Cook orzo until al dente, about 11 minutes. Drain, rinse, and drain again. Pour into a bowl.

4. Whisk lemon juice, herbs, and remaining olive oil; season with salt and black pepper. Pour over orzo and toss. Add olives and vegetables. Crumble and add cheese before serving.

BEEF STEW WITH BUTTERY GARLIC BREAD

ACTIVE 40 MIN. - TOTAL 2 HOURS, 15 MIN.
SERVES 6

- 2 Tbsp. canola oil
- 2 lb. boneless beef chuck roast, cut into ¾-inch pieces
- 2 tsp. kosher salt, divided
- 1 tsp. black pepper, divided
- 12 oz. cremini mushrooms, quartered
- 2 medium carrots, chopped
- 1½ cups frozen pearl onions, thawed
- ¼ cup all-purpose flour
- 2 tsp. chopped garlic
- ¾ cup brown ale beer
- 3 cups unsalted beef stock
- 6 baguette bread slices
- 1 large garlic clove, halved lengthwise
- ¼ cup salted butter

1. Heat oil in a large cast-iron Dutch oven over medium-high. Add beef, and sprinkle with 1 teaspoon of the salt and ½ teaspoon of the pepper. Cook, stirring occasionally, until browned on all sides, about 6 minutes.

2. Add mushrooms, carrots, and onions; cook over medium-high, stirring often, until vegetables begin to soften, about 5 minutes. Add flour and garlic; cook, stirring constantly, 1 minute. Add beer, and simmer until reduced by about half, about 2 minutes. Add stock and remaining 1 teaspoon salt and ½ teaspoon pepper; bring to a boil. Reduce heat to medium-low; cover and simmer until beef is very tender, about 1½ hours.

3. Rub both sides of bread slices with cut sides of garlic clove. Melt 2 tablespoons of the butter in a large cast-iron skillet over medium-high. Once butter begins to foam, add 3 bread slices, turning immediately to ensure both sides are coated with melted butter. Cook until bottom is golden, about 1 minute. Turn bread slice, and cook until bottom is golden, about 1 minute. Repeat with remaining 2 tablespoons butter and 3 bread slices. Serve garlic bread alongside stew.

BEEF STEW WITH
BUTTERY GARLIC BREAD

CHUNKY BEEF CHILI

This hearty beef chili features boneless chuck roast and a medley of traditional chili seasonings. Served with cornbread, it's a complete meal.

ACTIVE 25 MIN. · TOTAL 2 HOURS, 10 MIN.
SERVES 6

- 4 lb. boneless chuck roast, cut into ½-inch pieces
- 2 Tbsp. chili powder
- 2 (6-oz.) cans tomato paste
- 1 (32-oz.) container beef broth
- 2 (8-oz.) cans tomato sauce
- 2 tsp. garlic powder
- 1 tsp. table salt
- 1 tsp. ground oregano
- 1 tsp. ground cumin
- 1 tsp. paprika
- 1 tsp. onion powder
- ½ tsp. black pepper
- ¼ tsp. cayenne pepper
  Cornbread (optional)
  Crushed tortilla chips, sour cream, shredded cheese, chopped onion, for topping

1. Brown meat, in batches, in a Dutch oven over medium-high. Use a slotted spoon to remove meat, reserving drippings in Dutch oven. Add chili powder to Dutch oven. Cook, stirring constantly, 1 minute. Stir in tomato paste; cook, stirring frequently, 2 minutes.

2. Return beef to Dutch oven. Stir in beef broth and next 9 ingredients; bring to a boil. Reduce heat to low. Simmer, uncovered, stirring occasionally, until beef is tender, about 1½ hours. Serve with cornbread, if desired, and desired toppings.

SEAFOOD GUMBO

This recipe serves a party crowd and freezes well if you happen to have leftovers.

ACTIVE 45 MIN. · TOTAL 3 HOURS
SERVES 18

- 2 lemons, sliced
- 1 (3-oz.) pkg. crab boil
- 1 tsp. table salt
- 2 lb. unpeeled medium raw shrimp
- 1 lb. bacon
- 1 cup all-purpose flour
- 2 onions, finely chopped
- 2 green bell peppers, finely chopped
- 4 garlic cloves, minced
- 1 lb. cooked ham, cubed
- 2 lb. fresh crabmeat, drained and flaked
- 3 lb. fresh okra, sliced
- 1 (28-oz.) can whole tomatoes, undrained and chopped
- ½ cup Worcestershire sauce
- 2 tsp. table salt
- 1 tsp. black pepper
  Hot cooked rice

1. Bring 1 gallon water, lemons, crab boil, and 1 teaspoon salt to a boil in a large Dutch oven. Add shrimp, and cook 3 to 5 minutes or until shrimp turn pink. Discard lemons and crab boil. Remove shrimp, reserving water. Peel shrimp. Chill.

2. Cook bacon in a large skillet until crisp; remove bacon, reserving drippings in skillet. Crumble bacon, and set aside.

3. Add flour to drippings in skillet; cook over medium heat, stirring constantly, until roux is caramel-color (about 5 minutes). Stir in onions, bell peppers, and garlic; cook over low heat 10 minutes or until vegetables are tender.

4. Add roux, ham, and next 6 ingredients to reserved water in Dutch oven. Bring to a boil; reduce heat, and simmer 1 hour and 50 minutes. Stir in chilled shrimp; cook 5 to 10 minutes. Serve gumbo over rice. Sprinkle with bacon.

SEAFOOD GUMBO

CHICKEN AND SAUSAGE JAMBALAYA

On the busiest weeknight, this hearty one-pot meal will transport you to New Orleans. Like it spicy? Serve with hot sauce on the side.

ACTIVE 25 MIN. - TOTAL 50 MIN.
SERVES 8

- 1 Tbsp. canola oil
- 2 lb. boneless, skinless chicken thighs, cut into 1½-inch cubes
- 1 lb. smoked sausage, cut into 1-inch pieces
- 1 large white onion, chopped
- 1 large green bell pepper, chopped (about 1½ cups)
- 1 cup chopped celery
- 3 garlic cloves, minced
- 2 bay leaves
- 1 Tbsp. Creole seasoning
- 1 tsp. dried thyme
- 1 tsp. dried oregano
- 2 cups uncooked converted rice
- 3 cups chicken broth
- 2 (14.5-oz.) cans diced fire-roasted tomatoes
  Sliced scallions (optional)

1. Heat oil in a Dutch oven over medium-high. Add chicken and sausage; cook, stirring constantly, until browned on all sides, 8 to 10 minutes. Remove with a slotted spoon to paper towels; blot with paper towels.

2. Add onion, bell pepper, celery, garlic, bay leaves, Creole seasoning, thyme, and oregano to hot drippings; cook over medium-high until vegetables are tender, 5 to 7 minutes. Stir in rice and cook until fragrant, about 3 minutes. Stir in chicken broth, tomatoes, chicken, and sausage. Bring to a boil over high. Cover and reduce heat to medium; simmer, stirring occasionally, until rice is tender, about 20 minutes. Garnish with sliced scallions, if desired.

CHICKEN-ANDOUILLE GUMBO WITH ROASTED POTATOES

ACTIVE 45 MIN. - TOTAL 3 HOURS, 10 MIN., INCLUDING POTATOES
MAKES 10 CUPS

- 1 lb. andouille sausage, cut into ¼-inch-thick slices
- ½ cup peanut oil
- ¾ cup all-purpose flour
- 1 large onion, coarsely chopped
- 1 red bell pepper, coarsely chopped
- 1 cup thinly sliced celery
- 2 garlic cloves, minced
- 2 tsp. Cajun seasoning
- ⅛ tsp. cayenne pepper
- 1 (48-oz.) pkg. chicken broth
- 2 lb. boneless, skinless chicken breasts
  Roasted Potatoes (recipe follows)
  Chopped fresh flat-leaf parsley, cooked and crumbled bacon, hot sauce, for topping

1. Cook sausage in a large skillet over medium, stirring often, until browned, 7 minutes. Remove and drain sausage; pat dry with paper towels.

2. Heat oil in a stainless-steel pot over medium; gradually whisk in flour, and cook, whisking constantly, 18 to 20 minutes or until flour is caramel-color. Reduce heat to low, and cook, whisking constantly, until mixture is milk chocolate-color and texture is smooth, about 2 minutes.

3. Increase heat to medium. Stir in onion and the next 5 ingredients. Cook, stirring constantly, 3 minutes. Gradually stir in chicken broth; add chicken and sausage. Increase heat to medium-high, and bring to a boil. Reduce heat to low. Simmer, stirring occasionally, until a thermometer inserted in chicken reads 165°F, about 1 hour and 30 minutes. Shred chicken into large pieces using two forks. Place Roasted Potatoes in serving bowls. Spoon gumbo over potatoes. Serve with desired toppings.

ROASTED POTATOES

ACTIVE 10 MIN. - TOTAL 50 MIN.
SERVES 6 TO 8

- 3 lb. baby red potatoes, quartered
- 1 Tbsp. peanut oil
- 1 tsp. kosher salt

Preheat oven to 450°F. Stir together all ingredients in a large bowl. Place potatoes in a single layer in a lightly greased 15- x 10-inch rimmed baking pan. Bake 40 to 45 minutes or until tender and browned, stirring twice.

LOUISIANA GUMBO

Prepare all the ingredients ahead for the gumbo. Watch carefully as the flour browns; if it burns, the aroma will tell. If there is a possibility the roux is burned, start over—one can never remove a burned taste from a dish.

ACTIVE 40 MIN. - TOTAL 40 MIN.
SERVES 8 TO 10

- ½ cup peanut oil
- ½ cup all-purpose flour
- 1 cup chopped sweet onion
- 1 cup chopped green bell pepper
- 1 cup chopped celery
- 2 tsp. Creole seasoning
- 2 tsp. minced garlic
- 3 (14-oz.) cans low-sodium chicken broth
- 4 cups shredded cooked chicken
- ½ lb. andouille sausage, cut into ¼-inch-thick slices
- 1½ cups frozen black-eyed peas, thawed
- 1 lb. peeled, jumbo raw shrimp

1. Heat oil in a large Dutch oven over medium-high; gradually whisk in flour and cook, whisking constantly, 5 to 7 minutes or until flour is chocolate-color. (Do not burn mixture.)

2. Reduce heat to medium. Stir in onion and next 4 ingredients, and cook, stirring constantly, 3 minutes. Gradually stir in chicken broth; add chicken and next 2 ingredients. Increase heat to medium-high, and bring to a boil. Reduce heat to low, and simmer, stirring occasionally, 20 minutes. Add shrimp, and cook 5 minutes or just until shrimp turn pink.

WHITE LIGHTNING CHICKEN CHILI

Don't drain the chopped green chiles or navy beans; the liquids add extra flavor to the chili. Serve chili with cornbread.

ACTIVE 30 MIN. - TOTAL 30 MIN., NOT INCLUDING SALSA
SERVES 8

- 1 large sweet onion, diced
- 2 garlic cloves, minced
- 2 Tbsp. olive oil
- 4 cups shredded cooked chicken
- 2 (14-oz.) cans chicken broth
- 2 (4.5-oz.) cans chopped green chiles
- 1 (1.25-oz.) pkg. white chicken chili seasoning mix
- 3 (16-oz.) cans navy beans
  Avocado-Mango Salsa (recipe follows), sour cream, shredded Monterey Jack cheese, fresh cilantro leaves, for topping

Cook onion and garlic in hot oil in a large Dutch oven over medium-high, stirring often, until onion is tender, about 5 minutes. Stir in chicken, next 3 ingredients, and 2 cans navy beans. Coarsely mash remaining can navy beans, and stir into chicken mixture. Bring to a boil, stirring often. Cover, reduce heat to medium-low, and simmer, stirring occasionally, 10 minutes. Serve with desired toppings.

AVOCADO-MANGO SALSA

ACTIVE 10 MIN. - TOTAL 10 MIN.
MAKES ABOUT 2 CUPS

- 1 large avocado, cubed
- 1 cup diced fresh mango
- ⅓ cup diced red onion
- 2 Tbsp. chopped fresh cilantro
- 2 Tbsp. fresh lime juice

Stir together all ingredients in a medium bowl.

LOUISIANA
GUMBO

SOUTHERN ITALIAN
CHICKEN SOUP

SOUTHERN ITALIAN CHICKEN SOUP

ACTIVE 45 MIN. - TOTAL 50 MIN.
SERVES 8

- 1 large onion, diced
- 1 celery rib, thinly sliced
- 2 carrots, chopped
- 1 garlic clove, minced
- 3 Tbsp. olive oil, divided
- 6 cups chicken broth
- 1 (14.5-oz.) can diced tomatoes
- 1 tsp. dried Italian seasoning
- ¼ tsp. dried crushed red pepper
- 4 (6- to 8-oz.) boneless, skinless chicken breasts
- ½ tsp. table salt
- ½ tsp. black pepper
- 2 cups sliced fresh okra
- 1 (15.5-oz.) can black-eyed peas, drained and rinsed
- 1 (9-oz.) pkg. refrigerated cheese-filled tortellini
  Freshly grated Parmesan cheese

1. Cook the first 4 ingredients in 2 tablespoons hot oil in a large Dutch oven over medium-high, stirring often, until tender, 3 to 5 minutes. Stir in broth and next 3 ingredients; bring to a boil, stirring occasionally. Reduce heat to medium, and simmer, stirring occasionally, 10 minutes.

2. Meanwhile, sprinkle chicken with salt and black pepper. Cook in remaining 1 tablespoon hot oil in a large nonstick skillet over medium-high 5 minutes on each side or until lightly browned. Cool slightly (about 5 minutes); cut into 1-inch pieces.

3. Add okra, black-eyed peas, and chicken to Dutch oven. Simmer, stirring occasionally, 10 minutes or until okra is tender. Add tortellini; cook, stirring occasionally, until tortellini is done, about 3 minutes. Serve with Parmesan cheese.

SMOKED CHICKEN TORTILLA SOUP

Everyone in Texas has a particular version of tortilla soup. This rendition has smoked chicken to add extra depth of flavor. New Mexico chile powder is a single-chile powder made from grinding dried New Mexico chiles and should not be confused with chili powder, which is a seasoning blend.

ACTIVE 25 MIN. - TOTAL 1 HOUR, 20 MIN.
SERVES 8 TO 10

- 1 large onion, diced
- 1 large jalapeño pepper, seeded and chopped
- 3 Tbsp. olive oil
- 3 garlic cloves, chopped
- 8 cups chicken broth
- 1 (15.25-oz.) can whole kernel corn, drained*
- 1 (15-oz.) can black beans, drained
- 1 (14.5-oz.) can fire-roasted diced tomatoes
- 1 (14.5-oz.) can diced tomatoes with chiles
- 3 Tbsp. ground cumin
- 1½ Tbsp. New Mexico chile powder
- 1½ tsp. table salt
- 1 tsp. Worcestershire sauce
- 5 cups shredded rotisserie chicken (from 2 rotisserie chickens)
  Tortilla strips, fresh cilantro, avocado slices, lime slices, crumbled queso fresco, for topping

1. Cook onion and jalapeño pepper in hot oil in a Dutch oven over medium-high, stirring often, 5 to 6 minutes. Add garlic, and cook 1 to 2 minutes.

2. Stir in broth and next 8 ingredients. Bring to a boil; reduce heat, and simmer 40 minutes.

3. Remove from heat, and stir in chicken. Let stand 10 minutes before serving. Serve with desired toppings.

*Note: Three to four ears fresh corn may be substituted for canned corn. Remove the husks, and cut kernels from the cobs.

CHICKEN AND GNOCCHI

ACTIVE 40 MIN. - TOTAL 1 HOUR
SERVES 4 TO 6

GNOCCHI

- 1 cup soft, fresh breadcrumbs
- ½ cup chicken broth
- 1 oz. Parmesan cheese, freshly grated
- 2 large egg yolks, lightly beaten
- 1½ Tbsp. chopped fresh flat-leaf parsley
- 1 tsp. chopped fresh thyme
- ¼ tsp. kosher salt
- ⅛ tsp. freshly ground black pepper
- ½ cup all-purpose flour

CHICKEN

- 2 fresh thyme sprigs
- 1 fresh sage sprig (optional)
- 4 Tbsp. butter
- 2 carrots, thinly sliced
- 1 celery stalk, finely chopped
- 2 garlic cloves, minced
- ½ cup dry white wine
- ¼ cup all-purpose flour
- 4 cups chicken broth
  Parmesan cheese rind (optional)
- 4 cups shredded cooked chicken

1. Prepare Gnocchi: Stir together first 8 ingredients in a large bowl until smooth. Very gently fold in flour just until blended. (Dough should be sticky, not loose. If not, stir in additional flour, 1 tablespoon at a time, until a sticky dough forms.)

2. Spoon dough into a zip-top plastic freezer bag. Snip 1 corner of bag to make a ½-inch hole. Squeeze 10 to 12 (1-inch) dough pieces into a pot of simmering salted water; cook 2 to 3 minutes or until gnocchi float. Lightly grease a pan with cooking spray. Transfer gnocchi to pan, using a slotted spoon. Cover with plastic wrap. Repeat with remaining dough.

3. Prepare Chicken: Tie together thyme and, if desired, sage with kitchen string. Melt butter in a Dutch oven over medium. Add carrots, celery, and herb bundle; cook 5 minutes or until carrots are tender. Add garlic; cook 1 minute. Stir in wine; cook 2 minutes or until reduced by half. Sprinkle with flour; cook, stirring constantly, 1 minute. Gradually whisk in broth. Add cheese rind, if desired.

4. Bring to a boil over medium-high. Reduce heat to medium-low; simmer, partially covered, 20 minutes or until slightly thickened. Discard herb bundle and rind. Stir in chicken and gnocchi; cook 5 minutes or until hot.

- -

CHICKEN NOODLE SOUP

Chicken soup still reigns as the ultimate food for the soul. This recipe is chock-full of good stuff. Use fresh vegetables if you prefer.

ACTIVE 25 MIN. - TOTAL 1 HOUR, 40 MIN.
SERVES 8

- 6 bone-in chicken breasts
- 1 celery stalk with leaves
- 1¼ tsp. table salt
- ¼ tsp. black pepper
- 1 (16-oz.) pkg. frozen mixed vegetables
- 1 small onion, chopped
- ¼ cup chopped fresh flat-leaf parsley or 1 Tbsp. dried parsley flakes ,
- 2 (3-oz.) pkg. chicken-flavor ramen soup mix
  Table salt and black pepper, to taste

1. Bring 3 quarts water and first 4 ingredients to a boil in a large Dutch oven. Cover, reduce heat, and simmer 30 to 40 minutes or until chicken is tender. Remove chicken, reserving broth in Dutch oven. Skin, bone, and shred chicken.

2. Add mixed vegetables, onion, and parsley to reserved broth. Cover and cook over medium 20 minutes. Add ramen noodles with seasoning packet, and cook, stirring occasionally, 5 minutes. Stir in chicken; cook 10 minutes. Season to taste with salt and pepper.

CHICKEN AND
GNOCCHI

TEX-MEX CHICKEN
CHILI WITH LIME

TEX-MEX CHICKEN CHILI WITH LIME

ACTIVE 30 MIN. - TOTAL 45 MIN.
SERVES 8

- 1 Tbsp. butter
- 2 Tbsp. olive oil
- 1 large white onion, diced
- 1 medium red onion, diced
- 1 poblano or bell pepper, seeded and diced
- 1 red or green jalapeño pepper, seeded and diced
- 1 large sweet potato, peeled and chopped
- 2 tsp. ground cumin
- 2 tsp. chipotle powder
- 2 tsp. kosher salt
- 3 garlic cloves, minced
- 2 (16-oz.) cans navy beans, drained
- 1 (12-oz.) bottle white ale
- 4 cups shredded rotisserie chicken
- 4 cups chicken broth
  Lime Cream (recipe follows)
  Fresh cilantro, scallions, lime wedges,
    for topping
  Green Chile Cheese Toast (recipe follows)

1. Melt butter with oil in a Dutch oven over medium. Add white onion and next 7 ingredients; cook until translucent, stirring often, about 8 minutes. Add garlic, and cook 30 seconds.

2. Stir in beans and ale, and cook 5 minutes or until liquid is reduced by half. Add chicken and broth; bring to a boil over high heat. Reduce heat to medium-low and simmer 30 minutes until thickened. Serve with desired toppings and Green Chile Cheese Toast.

LIME CREAM

ACTIVE 5 MIN. - TOTAL 5 MIN.
MAKES 1 CUP

Combine 1 cup **sour cream** and zest and juice of 1 **lime** in a small bowl. Season with salt to taste.

GREEN CHILE CHEESE TOAST

ACTIVE 10 MIN. - TOTAL 15 MIN.
MAKES 1 CUP

Stir together 1 cup (4 oz.) each shredded **pepper Jack cheese** and **white cheddar cheese**, ¾ cup **mayonnaise**, ½ cup freshly **grated Parmesan cheese**, 1 (4.5-oz.) can diced green chiles, and 1 Tbsp. **Ranch dressing mix**. Spread on toasted **French bread slices**. Broil 5 inches from heat until bubbly.

BRUNSWICK STEW

Brunswick stew is a classic Southern dish featuring meat, chopped bell pepper, lima beans, and corn in a tomato base. Developed in 19th-century Virginia, this stew originally included squirrel meat (we opt here for chicken). This version has flour to give the stew body and garlic bread on the side. Garnish with fresh thyme sprigs.

ACTIVE 20 MIN. - TOTAL 1 HOUR
SERVES 6 SERVINGS

- 1 cup chopped red bell pepper
- ¾ cup chopped yellow onion
- ½ cup chopped celery
- 1 Tbsp. peanut oil
- 1 Tbsp. all-purpose flour
- 1 lb. skinless, boneless chicken thighs, cut into ½-inch pieces
- 2 cups fat-free, less-sodium chicken broth
- 2 Tbsp. no-salt-added tomato paste
- 1 tsp. dried thyme
- ½ tsp. table salt
- ½ tsp. hot pepper sauce
- 1 (10-oz.) pkg. frozen whole-kernel corn, thawed
- 1 (10-oz.) pkg. frozen baby lima beans, thawed
- 6 (1-oz.) slices Italian bread, toasted
- 2 garlic cloves, halved

1. Coat a large Dutch oven with cooking spray, then heat over medium-high. Add bell pepper, onion, and celery to pan, and cook until softened, stirring occasionally, about 5 minutes. Add oil to pan. Combine flour and chicken in a medium bowl, tossing to coat. Add chicken to pan; cook 2 minutes or until lightly browned. Gradually stir in broth; bring to a boil. Cook 1 minute or until slightly thick, stirring constantly. Add tomato paste and next 5 ingredients (to pan. Cover, reduce heat, and simmer 30 minutes.

2. Rub toasted bread slices with cut sides of garlic; discard garlic. Serve bread with stew.

SPICY VEGETABLE SOUP

ACTIVE 10 MIN. - TOTAL 6 HOURS
SERVES 8

- 1 (16-oz.) pkg. frozen whole kernel corn, thawed
- 1 (10-oz.) pkg. frozen sliced okra, thawed
- 1 (10-oz.) pkg. frozen baby lima beans
- 1 medium onion, diced
- 2 garlic cloves, minced
- 3 (5½-oz.) cans no-salt-added vegetable juice
- 2 (14½-oz.) cans Cajun-style stewed tomatoes
- 1 cup water
- 3 Tbsp. vegetable broth concentrate
- 1 tsp. hot sauce
- 1 tsp. low-sodium Worcestershire sauce

1. Combine all ingredients in a 5-quart slow cooker.

2. Cover and cook on HIGH 5 to 6 hours.

- -

BLACK BEAN SOUP

ACTIVE 5 MIN. - TOTAL 6 HOURS
SERVES 6 TO 8

- 2 (15-oz.) cans black beans, drained and rinsed
- 2 (4½-oz.) cans chopped green chiles
- 1 (14½-oz.) can Mexican stewed tomatoes, undrained
- 1 (14½-oz.) can diced tomatoes, undrained
- 1 (11-oz.) can whole kernel corn, drained
- 4 scallions, sliced
- 2 to 3 Tbsp. chili powder
- 1 tsp. ground cumin
- ½ tsp. dried minced garlic

1. Combine all ingredients in a 5-quart slow cooker.

2. Cover and cook on HIGH 5 to 6 hours.

BEER-CHEESE SOUP

ACTIVE 15 MIN. - TOTAL 15 MIN.
SERVES 4 TO 6

- 2½ cups milk
- 1 (12-oz.) bottle beer, divided
- 2 (5-oz.) jars process cheese spread
- 1 (10½-oz.) can condensed chicken broth
- ½ tsp. Worcestershire sauce
- 2 dashes hot sauce
- 3 Tbsp. cornstarch

1. Combine milk and ¾ cup beer in a Dutch oven. Cook over medium, stirring constantly, 2 to 3 minutes or until thoroughly heated.

2. Add cheese spread and next 3 ingredients. Cook over low, stirring constantly, until thoroughly heated.

3. Combine cornstarch and remaining beer; add to cheese mixture. Simmer, stirring constantly, 10 minutes or until thickened (do not boil).

BUTTERNUT SQUASH SOUP

ACTIVE 25 MIN. - TOTAL 1 HOUR, 15 MIN.
SERVES 8

- 6 bacon slices
- 1 large onion, chopped
- 2 carrots, chopped
- 2 celery stalks, chopped
- 1 Granny Smith apple, peeled and finely chopped
- 2 garlic cloves, chopped
- 4 (12-oz.) pkg. frozen butternut squash, thawed
- 1 (32-oz.) container low-sodium, fat-free chicken broth
- 2 to 3 Tbsp. fresh lime juice
- 1½ Tbsp. honey
- 2 tsp. table salt
- 1 tsp. ground black pepper
- ⅛ tsp. ground allspice
- ⅛ tsp. ground nutmeg
- ⅛ tsp. cayenne pepper
- ¼ cup whipping cream
  Sour cream, fresh thyme sprigs, for garnish

1. Cook bacon slices in a Dutch oven until crisp. Remove bacon and drain on paper towels, reserving 2 tablespoons drippings in Dutch oven. Coarsely crumble bacon, and set aside.

2. Cook onion and carrots in hot bacon drippings in Dutch oven over medium-high, stirring occasionally, until onion is tender, 5 minutes. Add celery and apple; cook, stirring often, 5 minutes. Add garlic; cook 30 seconds. Add butternut squash and chicken broth. Bring to a boil; reduce heat, and simmer 20 minutes or until carrots are tender.

3. Process squash mixture, in batches, in a blender or food processor until smooth.

4. Return to Dutch oven. Add lime juice and next 7 ingredients. Simmer 10 to 15 minutes or until thickened. Garnish, if desired. Top each serving with bacon.

ROASTED GARLIC-POTATO SOUP

Roasted garlic instant potatoes add bold flavor to this easy 5-ingredient soup.

ACTIVE 10 MIN. - TOTAL 15 MIN.
SERVES 4

- 2 cups milk
- ½ (7.6-oz.) pkg. roasted garlic instant mashed potatoes
- 4 oz. shredded reduced-fat sharp cheddar cheese (1 cup), divided
- ¼ tsp. freshly ground black pepper

Combine milk and 1½ cups water in a large saucepan; bring to a boil over medium-high. Remove from heat; add potatoes, and stir with a whisk until well blended. Add ¾ cup cheese, stirring until cheese melts. Spoon into 4 bowls; sprinkle with remaining ¼ cup cheese and black pepper.

SPICY PUMPKIN SOUP
WITH AVOCADO CREAM

SPICY PUMPKIN SOUP WITH AVOCADO CREAM

ACTIVE 55 MIN. - TOTAL 55 MIN.
SERVES 6 TO 8

     1 cup diced yellow onion
     3 Tbsp. olive oil, divided
  1½ tsp. kosher salt, divided
     2 garlic cloves, chopped
     1 Tbsp. ground cumin
     1 (29-oz.) can pumpkin
     6 to 6½ cups reduced-sodium chicken broth
     1 canned chipotle pepper in adobo sauce
     1 Tbsp. adobo sauce from can
     1 medium avocado, peeled and diced
     ½ cup whole buttermilk
     2 Tbsp. fresh lime juice
     2 Tbsp. extra-virgin olive oil
     8 oz. smoked sausage, sliced
     1 cup black beans, drained and rinsed
     ½ tsp. smoked paprika

1. Place onion, 2 tablespoons olive oil, and 1 teaspoon salt in a Dutch oven over medium; cover and cook 5 to 6 minutes or until translucent. Stir in garlic and cumin; cook 2 minutes. Whisk in pumpkin and 6 cups broth; add chipotle pepper and 1 tablespoon adobo sauce. Increase heat to medium-high; simmer, stirring occasionally, about 12 minutes.

2. Process soup, in batches, in a food processor or blender 1 minute. Add up to ½ cup broth, 2 tablespoons at a time, to reach desired consistency.

3. Process avocado, next 3 ingredients, and remaining ½ teaspoon salt in a blender until smooth. Add up to ¼ cup water, 1 tablespoon at a time, to reach desired consistency.

4. Cook smoked sausage in remaining 1 tablespoon olive oil in a large skillet over medium, stirring occasionally, 3 minutes. Stir in black beans and paprika; cook 1 minute. Ladle soup into serving bowls; top with sausage mixture and avocado cream.

SPICY STEAK AND BLACK BEAN CHILI

ACTIVE 20 MIN. - TOTAL 8 HOURS, 20 MIN.
SERVES 8

     2 lb. boneless top sirloin steak, cubed*
     2 Tbsp. vegetable oil
     3 (15.5-oz.) cans black beans
     2 (14.5-oz.) cans diced tomatoes
     2 (4.5-oz.) cans chopped green chiles
     1 large sweet onion, diced
     1 green bell pepper, diced
     4 garlic cloves, minced
     1 (12-oz.) can beer
     1 (3.625-oz.) chili seasoning kit
        Shredded cheddar cheese, diced tomatoes and avocado, sour cream, sliced scallions, chopped fresh cilantro, for topping

1. Cook steak in hot oil in a large skillet over medium-high, stirring often, until browned, 4 to 5 minutes.

2. Place steak in a lightly greased 6-quart slow cooker; stir in black beans and next 6 ingredients. Stir in packets from chili kit, omitting masa and red pepper packets. Cover and cook on LOW 8 hours. Serve with desired toppings.

*Note: You may substitute 2 lb. ground round for the steak. Omit the oil, and brown ground round in a large skillet over medium-high, stirring often, 8 minutes or until meat crumbles and is no longer pink; drain. Proceed with recipe as directed.

TOMATO-AND-RED PEPPER SOUP

Red peppers adds tangy zest to this classic crowd-pleaser.

ACTIVE 15 MIN. - TOTAL 15 MIN.
SERVES 4 TO 6

- 1 (28-oz.) can whole tomatoes
- 1 (12-oz.) jar roasted red peppers, drained
- ¼ cup half-and-half
- 1½ tsp. kosher salt
- 1 tsp. granulated sugar
- ½ tsp. freshly ground black pepper
- 2 garlic cloves

Process all ingredients and ¼ cup water in a food processor until smooth, stopping to scrape down sides as needed. Transfer mixture to a medium saucepan; cook over medium-high, stirring often, 8 minutes or until hot. Serve immediately.

- -

SPICY TORTILLA SOUP

Don't let this long list of ingredients stop you—most of these items are in your pantry or fridge.

ACTIVE 20 MIN. - TOTAL 40 MIN.
SERVES 4

- 2 (14½-oz.) cans chicken broth
- 1 (14½-oz.) can Cajun-style stewed tomatoes
- 3 Tbsp. fresh lemon juice
- 3 garlic cloves, minced
- 2 tsp. chili powder
- ½ tsp. ground cumin
- ¼ tsp. cayenne pepper
- 1½ cups chopped cooked chicken
- 1 cup frozen corn kernels
- 1 (15-oz.) can black beans, rinsed and drained
- 2 Tbsp. half-and-half
- 1 scallion, thinly sliced
  Tortilla chips
- 4 oz. shredded Mexican four-cheese blend (1 cup) (optional)
  Sliced scallions (optional)

Bring first 7 ingredients to a boil. Reduce heat; add chicken and next 4 ingredients, and simmer 20 minutes. Serve with tortilla chips and, if desired, cheese and additional scallions.

SHRIMP-AND-NEW POTATO CHOWDER

Add shrimp a few minutes before serving so they cook briefly without getting overcooked. Cut onions and potatoes into similar-size pieces to ensure they cook uniformly.

ACTIVE 25 MIN. - TOTAL 50 MIN.
SERVES 6

- 2 Tbsp. butter
- 3 bunches scallions, sliced
- 1½ lb. new potatoes, diced
- 2 cups reduced-sodium chicken broth
- 1½ cups heavy cream
- ½ cup dry white wine
- 1 tsp. kosher salt
- ¼ tsp. black pepper
- ½ lb. medium peeled, deveined raw shrimp
- 2 tsp. hot sauce

1. Melt butter in a medium Dutch oven over medium. Add scallions; cook, stirring often, 1 minute.

2. Add potatoes and next 5 ingredients. Increase heat to high. Bring to a boil. Reduce heat to medium-low; cook, stirring occasionally, 25 minutes or until potatoes are tender.

3. Stir in shrimp and hot sauce; cook 3 minutes.

SHRIMP-AND-NEW
POTATO CHOWDER

PAN-FRIED OKRA
WITH CORNMEAL,
PAGE 261

SIDES

HOMEMADE APPLESAUCE

For the best taste and texture, use a variety of apples—such as Granny Smith, Golden Delicious, and Gala—when making applesauce and apple pie. Stir in a little chopped rosemary, and serve this applesauce as a side dish with pork chops or hash browns.

ACTIVE 20 MIN. · TOTAL 20 MIN.
MAKES ABOUT 6 CUPS

- 12 large apples, peeled and coarsely chopped
- 1 cup granulated sugar
- ½ lemon, sliced

Cook all ingredients in a Dutch oven over medium, stirring often, until apples are tender and juices are thickened, about 20 minutes. Remove and discard lemon slices. Serve applesauce warm, or let cool and store in an airtight container in the refrigerator up to 1 week.

Spiced Applesauce: Substitute ½ cup firmly packed brown sugar and ½ cup granulated sugar for 1 cup sugar. Omit lemon slices, and add 1 teaspoon ground cinnamon and ¼ teaspoon ground cloves; prepare as directed.

- -

FRENCH FRIES

These russet strips are twice-fried for extra-crispy results.

ACTIVE 30 MIN. · TOTAL 1 HOUR
SERVES 12

- 4 lb. russet or Idaho potatoes, peeled
  Vegetable oil
  Table salt, to taste

1. Cut potatoes into ¼-inch strips.

2. Pour vegetable oil to a depth of 4 inches in a Dutch oven; heat oil to 325°F. Fry potato strips, in batches, until lightly golden but not brown, 4 to 5 minutes per batch. Drain on paper towels.

3. Heat oil to 375°F. Fry strips, in small batches, until golden brown and crisp, 1 to 2 minutes per batch. Drain on clean paper towels. Sprinkle strips with salt, and serve immediately.

Salt-and-Pepper Fries: Prepare French Fries as directed. Grind some fresh pepper over hot fries after you sprinkle them with salt.

FENNEL-APPLE SLAW

This vibrant seasonal salad is an ideal way to showcase super crisp, tart, or sweet varieties of apples. Colorful peels contribute color and texture. Celery is a good substitute when fennel isn't available.

ACTIVE 20 MIN. · TOTAL 20 MIN.
SERVES 4 TO 6

- 1 cup thinly sliced celery
- 1 cup coarsely chopped fresh flat-leaf parsley
- 1 large shallot, thinly sliced
- ¼ cup extra-virgin olive oil
- 1 tsp. kosher salt
- ½ tsp. freshly ground black pepper
- 1 large fennel bulb
- 1 large crisp, sweet apple, thinly sliced
- 2 Tbsp. apple cider vinegar
- 1 tsp. granulated sugar

1. Toss together first 6 ingredients in a medium bowl. Slice fennel bulb thinly, reserving fronds. Finely chop fennel fronds to equal 1½ tablespoons and sprinkle over salad. Add fennel slices to salad.

2. Toss together apple slices, vinegar, and sugar in a small bowl. Add apple mixture to slaw; toss to combine.

FENNEL-APPLE
SLAW

CHIPOTLE SCALLOPED
POTATOES

HASH BROWN CASSEROLE

This down-home side dish boasts a buttery cornflake crust.

ACTIVE 20 MIN. - TOTAL 1 HOUR, 20 MIN.
SERVES 12

- ¾ cup chopped onion
- ½ tsp. paprika
- ½ tsp. freshly ground black pepper
- 1 (32-oz.) pkg. frozen Southern-style hash brown potatoes (diced)
- 2 Tbsp. butter, melted
- 1 (10¾-oz.) can condensed cream of chicken soup, undiluted
- 1 (8-oz.) pkg. pasteurized prepared cheese product, cubed
- 1 (8-oz.) carton sour cream
- 2½ cups cornflakes cereal, coarsely crushed
- 2 Tbsp. butter, melted

1. Preheat oven to 350°F. Combine first 5 ingredients in a large bowl; toss well.

2. Combine soup and cheese in a medium microwave-safe bowl. Microwave on HIGH 6 minutes or until cheese melts, stirring every 2 minutes. Stir in sour cream. Pour cheese mixture over potato mixture, and stir well. Spread into a lightly greased 13- x 9-inch baking dish.

3. Combine cornflakes and 2 tablespoons melted butter; sprinkle over potato mixture.

4. Bake in preheated oven, uncovered, 1 hour.

CHIPOTLE SCALLOPED POTATOES

Chipotle peppers are actually dried smoked jalapeños. They're often canned in adobo sauce—a thick red paste of ground chiles, herbs, and vinegar—and can pack quite a punch of heat. If you prefer less spice, skip the chopped pepper and include only the adobo sauce.

ACTIVE 30 MIN. - TOTAL 1 HOUR, 50 MIN.
SERVES 8 TO 10

- ½ cup half-and-half
- 2 garlic cloves, chopped
- 1 canned chipotle pepper in adobo sauce
- 1½ tsp. kosher salt
- ½ tsp. freshly ground black pepper
- ⅛ tsp. ground nutmeg
- 2½ cups whipping cream
- 3 lb. russet potatoes, peeled and cut into ⅛-inch slices
- 4 oz. sharp white cheddar cheese, shredded (1 cup)
- 4 cooked bacon slices, crumbled
  Chopped fresh chives, for garnish

1. Preheat oven to 400°F. Process first 6 ingredients in a blender or food processor until smooth. Transfer mixture to a medium bowl, and stir in whipping cream.

2. Lightly grease a 13- x 9-inch baking dish with cooking spray. Spread one-fourth of the potatoes in a single layer in prepared dish; top with one-fourth of the cream mixture. Repeat layers three times with remaining potatoes and cream mixture.

3. Bake, covered, 50 minutes. Uncover and sprinkle with cheese and bacon. Bake 20 minutes or until lightly browned and bubbly. Let stand 10 minutes. Garnish with chives, if desired.

BUTTERMILK MASHED POTATOES

ACTIVE 15 MIN. · TOTAL 40 MIN.
SERVES 6

- 3 lb. russet potatoes, peeled and roughly chopped
- ½ cup whole buttermilk
- 1 cup salted butter, softened
- 8 oz. crème fraîche
- 1½ tsp. kosher salt
- ½ tsp. ground white pepper

1. Place potatoes in a large Dutch oven with cold water to cover by 2 inches. Bring to a boil over medium-high. Boil until tender, 25 minutes. Drain; return potatoes to Dutch oven over medium. Cook, stirring once, until potatoes dry out slightly, 50 seconds.

2. Place buttermilk and softened butter in a microwavable glass bowl; microwave on HIGH until warm, 30 to 60 seconds. Add warm buttermilk mixture, crème fraîche, salt, and white pepper to potatoes; mash with a potato masher.

Mashed Potatoes with Bacon and Crispy Scallions:
Prepare recipe as directed; keep potatoes warm. Cook 4 bacon slices in a medium skillet over medium-high until crisp. Drain on paper towels, reserving drippings in skillet. Crumble bacon. Cook 1 cup sliced scallions in hot drippings until lightly browned and crispy, 3 to 4 minutes. Transfer to paper towels to drain. Top warm potatoes with scallions and bacon.

Rustic Mashed Red Potatoes with Parmesan: Omit crème fraîche. Substitute 3 pounds small unpeeled red potatoes, roughly chopped, for russet potatoes. Prepare recipe as directed, adding 4 ounces herbed cream cheese (about ½ cup) and 4 ounces Parmesan cheese, shredded (about 1 cup), to potatoes before coarsely mashing. Top with ¼ cup chopped fresh chives.

CARAMELIZED ONION MASHED POTATO BAKE

Caramelizing onions adds umami flavor to this mashed potato bake. To caramelize them, cut into ⅛-inch slices, and cook in a mix of oil and butter over medium-low until golden brown, about 45 minutes.

ACTIVE 25 MIN. · TOTAL 50 MIN.
SERVES 6 TO 8

- 4 lb. russet potatoes
- 3 tsp. table salt, divided
- 1¼ cups warm buttermilk
- ½ cup warm milk
- ¼ cup melted butter
- ½ tsp. freshly ground black pepper
- 5½ oz. freshly grated Gruyère cheese (1¼ cups)
- 1 cup chopped caramelized onions (see above)
- 2 Tbsp. chopped fresh flat-leaf parsley
- 1 (4-oz.) pkg. prosciutto

1. Preheat oven to 350°F. Peel potatoes; cut into 2-inch pieces. Bring potatoes, 2 teaspoons salt, and water to cover to a boil in a large Dutch oven over medium-high; boil 20 minutes or until tender. Drain. Return potatoes to Dutch oven, reduce heat to low, and cook, stirring occasionally, 3 to 5 minutes or until potatoes are dry.

2. Mash potatoes with a potato masher to desired consistency. Stir in warm buttermilk, warm milk, melted butter, pepper, and remaining 1 teaspoon salt, stirring just until blended.

3. Stir in Gruyère cheese, caramelized onions, and parsley. Spoon mixture into a lightly greased 2½-quart baking dish or 8 (10-ounce) ramekins. Bake in preheated oven until heated through, about 35 minutes.

4. Meanwhile, arrange half the prosciutto on a paper-towel-lined microwave-safe plate; cover with a paper towel. Microwave on HIGH 2 minutes or until crisp. Repeat procedure with remaining prosciutto. When cool enough to handle, break into large pieces.

5. Crumble prosciutto pieces on mashed potato bake.

CARAMELIZED ONION
MASHED POTATO BAKE

ZUCCHINI-POTATO
CASSEROLE

ZUCCHINI-POTATO CASSEROLE

The beauty of this casserole is in the layering. The potatoes, tomatoes, and zucchini are in the style of a tian, a French dish of layered vegetables. The dish makes an elegant presentation. Play with colors—try a variety of heirloom tomatoes, yellow squash, and purple potatoes!

ACTIVE 35 MIN. - TOTAL 1 HOUR, 50 MIN.
SERVES 6 TO 8

- 2 Tbsp. butter
- 2 medium sweet onions, chopped
- 1 medium Yukon gold potato, sliced
- 1 medium zucchini, sliced
- 4 plum tomatoes, sliced
- 1½ tsp. kosher salt
- ¾ tsp. freshly ground black pepper
- 2 Tbsp. butter, melted
- ⅓ cup freshly grated Parmesan cheese

1. Preheat oven to 375°F. Melt 2 tablespoons butter in a medium skillet over medium; add onions, and sauté 10 to 12 minutes or until tender and onions begin to caramelize.

2. Spoon onions into a 10-inch pie plate coated with cooking spray. Toss together potatoes slices and next 4 ingredients. Arrange potatoes, zucchini, and tomatoes in a single layer over onions, alternating and overlapping slightly. Drizzle with 2 tablespoons melted butter. Cover with aluminum foil.

3. Bake in preheated oven 30 minutes. Remove foil, and sprinkle with cheese. Bake until golden brown, 35 to 40 minutes. Let stand 10 minutes before serving.

SWEET POTATO-CARROT CASSEROLE

ACTIVE 40 MIN. - TOTAL 3 HOURS, 40 MIN., INCLUDING PECANS
SERVES 8 TO 10

- 6 large sweet potatoes (about 5 lb.)
- 1½ lb. carrots, sliced
- ¼ cup butter
- 1 cup sour cream
- 2 Tbsp. granulated sugar
- 1 tsp. firmly packed lemon zest
- ½ tsp. table salt
- ½ tsp. ground nutmeg
- ½ tsp. freshly ground black pepper
- 1½ cups miniature marshmallows
- 1 cup Sugar-and-Spice Pecans (recipe follows)

1. Preheat oven to 400°F. Bake sweet potatoes on a baking sheet 1 hour or until tender. Reduce oven temperature to 350°F. Let potatoes stand until cool to touch (about 20 minutes). Meanwhile, cook carrots in boiling water to cover 20 to 25 minutes or until very tender; drain.

2. Process carrots and butter in a food processor until smooth, stopping to scrape down sides as needed. Transfer carrot mixture to a large bowl.

3. Peel and cube sweet potatoes. Process, in batches, in until smooth, stopping to scrape down sides as needed. Add sweet potatoes to carrot mixture. Stir in sour cream and next 5 ingredients, stirring until blended. Spoon into a lightly greased 13- x 9-inch baking dish.

4. Bake at 350°F until thoroughly heated, about 30 minutes. Sprinkle with marshmallows. Bake until marshmallows are golden brown, about 10 minutes. Sprinkle with Sugar-and-Spice Pecans.

SUGAR-AND-SPICE PECANS

ACTIVE 10 MIN. - TOTAL 35 MIN.
MAKES 4 CUPS

Preheat oven to 350°F. Whisk 1 **egg white** in a large bowl until foamy. Add 4 cups **pecan halves and pieces**, and stir until evenly coated. Stir together ½ cup **granulated sugar**, 1 Tbsp. **orange zest**, 1 tsp. **ground cinnamon**, and 1 tsp. **ground ginger** in a small bowl until blended. Sprinkle sugar mixture over pecans; stir until pecans are coated. Spread pecans in a single layer in a lightly greased aluminum foil-lined 15- x 10-inch pan. Bake until pecans are toasted and dry, about 25 minutes, stirring once after 10 minutes. Let cool completely.

CREAMY BAKED MACARONI AND CHEESE WITH BACON

ACTIVE 30 MIN. - TOTAL 1 HOUR, 10 MIN.
SERVES 10

- 1 lb. uncooked large elbow macaroni
- 1 Tbsp. plus 1½ tsp. kosher salt, divided
- ¾ cup fresh breadcrumbs
- 2 oz. Parmesan cheese, shredded or grated (about ½ cup)
- 6 thick-cut bacon slices, cooked and crumbled, divided
- ⅓ cup all-purpose flour
- 1 tsp. black pepper
- 1 tsp. dry mustard
- 3 cups whole milk
- 1 cup buttermilk
- ⅓ cup unsalted butter, plus more for greasing dish
- 12 oz. extra-sharp cheddar cheese, shredded (3 cups)
- 4 oz. Monterey Jack, provolone, or mozzarella cheese, shredded (1 cup)
- 2 large eggs, well beaten

1. Preheat oven to 350°F. Bring 3 quarts water to a boil over high in a large stockpot. Stir in pasta and 1 tablespoon of the salt, and return to a boil. Cook, stirring occasionally, until pasta is tender but still firm, about 6 minutes. Reserve and set aside 2 cups cooking water, and then drain the pasta. Return pasta to pot, and remove from heat. Cover to keep warm.

2. Generously butter a 13- x 9-inch baking dish, and set aside. Toss together breadcrumbs, Parmesan cheese, and half the bacon in a bowl; set aside. Stir together flour, pepper, mustard, and remaining 1½ teaspoons salt in a small bowl. Heat milk and buttermilk in a medium saucepan over medium, undisturbed, until barely steaming but not boiling, 4 to 5 minutes. Set aside.

3. Melt butter in a large heavy saucepan over medium-high. Add flour mixture. Cook, whisking often, until mixture is smooth and thick and has a delicate golden color and toasted aroma, about 2 minutes. Slowly whisk in warm milk mixture. Bring to a boil over high. Cook, stirring often, until thickened to the texture of cream, about 3 minutes.

4. Stir shredded cheddar and Monterey Jack cheeses into milk mixture; remove from heat. Stir in beaten eggs until mixture forms a smooth sauce.

5. Uncover cooked pasta, and stir. (If pasta sticks together, stir in reserved warm cooking water, and drain again.) Stir cheese mixture and remaining bacon into drained pasta in stockpot.

6. Transfer pasta mixture to prepared baking dish, and sprinkle evenly with breadcrumb mixture. Bake in preheated oven until firm, puffed up, and lightly browned, 35 to 40 minutes.

FOUR-CHEESE MACARONI

ACTIVE 40 MIN. - TOTAL 1 HOUR, 15 MIN.
SERVES 8

- 12 oz. cavatappi pasta or macaroni
- ½ cup butter
- ½ cup all-purpose flour
- ½ tsp. cayenne pepper
- 3 cups milk
- 8 oz. white cheddar cheese, freshly shredded (2 cups)
- 4 oz. Monterey Jack cheese, freshly shredded (1 cup)
- 4 oz. fontina cheese, freshly shredded (1 cup)
- 4 oz. Asiago cheese, freshly shredded (1 cup)
- 1½ cups soft, fresh breadcrumbs
- ½ cup chopped cooked bacon
- ½ cup chopped pecans
- 2 Tbsp. butter, melted

1. Preheat oven to 350°F. Prepare pasta according to package directions; drain.

2. Meanwhile, melt ½ cup butter in a Dutch oven over low; whisk in flour and cayenne pepper until smooth. Cook, whisking constantly, 1 minute. Gradually whisk in milk; cook over medium, whisking constantly, 6 to 7 minutes or until milk mixture is thickened and bubbly. Remove from heat.

3. Toss together cheddar cheese and next 3 ingredients in a medium bowl; reserve 1½ cups cheese mixture. Add remaining cheese mixture and hot cooked pasta to sauce, tossing to coat. Spoon into a lightly greased 13- x 9-inch baking dish. Top with reserved 1½ cups cheese mixture.

4. Toss together breadcrumbs and remaining ingredients; sprinkle over cheese mixture.

5. Bake in preheated oven until bubbly and golden brown, 35 to 40 minutes.

CREAMY BAKED
MACARONI AND
CHEESE WITH BACON

SPICY CORNBREAD
DRESSING
WITH CHORIZO

SPICY CORNBREAD DRESSING WITH CHORIZO

ACTIVE 15 MIN. - TOTAL 40 MIN.
SERVES 8

- 2 Tbsp. vegetable oil, divided, plus more for greasing pan
- 1 cup chopped yellow onion
- 1 lb. fresh Mexican chorizo
- 1 cup chopped green bell pepper
- ¾ cup chopped celery
- 1 Tbsp. chopped garlic
- 3 scallions, chopped, white and green parts separated
- 8 cups coarsely crumbled cornbread
- ½ cup chopped fresh cilantro
- ⅓ cup chopped, seeded jalapeño chile
- 1 tsp. kosher salt
- 1 tsp. black pepper
- 2 large eggs, well beaten
- 4 cups chicken stock

1. Generously grease a 13- x 9-inch baking dish with vegetable oil. Preheat oven to 375°F. Heat a large cast-iron or nonstick skillet over medium-high. Add 1 tablespoon of the oil to skillet, and heat until a piece of onion sizzles when added. Add chorizo, and cook, tossing often and breaking up meat with a spoon, until fragrant and nicely browned, 3 to 5 minutes. Transfer chorizo to a bowl, and set aside. Reserve drippings in skillet.

2. Add remaining 1 tablespoon vegetable oil to drippings in skillet. Once oil is hot, add chopped yellow onion, green bell pepper, and celery. Cook over medium-high, tossing often, until mixture is fragrant and softened, 3 to 4 minutes. Add chopped garlic and white parts of scallions; cook, stirring constantly, until fragrant, about 1 minute. Remove pan from heat.

3. Transfer onion mixture to a large bowl. Add crumbled cornbread and cooked reserved chorizo to skillet. Stir mixture to combine well. Add cilantro, jalapeño, salt, and black pepper, and stir to combine well. Add beaten eggs and chicken stock; stir to combine well, making sure mixture is evenly moistened.

4. Transfer cornbread mixture to prepared baking dish. Bake in preheated oven until dressing is cooked through and browned, 25 to 35 minutes. Serve hot or warm. Sprinkle dressing with reserved green parts of scallions before serving.

BAKED HUSH PUPPIES

These hush puppies bake in miniature muffin pans for a significant fat and calorie reduction compared to traditional deep-fried versions.

ACTIVE 15 MIN. - TOTAL 30 MIN.
SERVES 18

- 1 cup yellow cornmeal
- 1 cup all-purpose flour
- 1 Tbsp. baking powder
- 1 tsp. granulated sugar
- 1 tsp. table salt
- ¼ tsp. cayenne pepper
- 2 large eggs, lightly beaten
- ¾ cup milk
- ¼ cup vegetable oil
- ½ cup finely chopped onion

1. Preheat oven to 425°F.

2. Combine first 6 ingredients in a large bowl; make a well in center of mixture. Set aside. Combine eggs and remaining ingredients, stirring well; add to dry mixture, stirring just until dry ingredients are moistened.

3. Coat miniature (1¾-inch) muffin pans with cooking spray. Spoon about 1 tablespoon batter into each muffin cup (cups will be about three-fourths full).

4. Bake in preheated oven until firm to the touch and golden brown around the edges, about 15 minutes. Remove from pans immediately.

FRESH CORN SPOONBREAD

Although they're called "breads," spoonbreads are moist and should have the consistency of a savory pudding. Most, such as this corn spoonbread, include cornmeal, and are so soft and creamy. They must be eaten with a fork or spoon—hence the name.

ACTIVE 10 MIN. - TOTAL 1 HOUR, 10 MIN.
SERVES 12

- 1 cup self-rising white cornmeal mix
- ½ cup all-purpose flour
- 2 Tbsp. granulated sugar
- 1 tsp. table salt
- 4 cups fresh corn kernels (about 8 ears)
- 2 cups plain yogurt
- ¼ cup butter, melted
- ¼ cup chopped fresh chives
- 2 Tbsp. chopped fresh flat-leaf parsley
- 1 tsp. minced fresh thyme
- 3 large eggs, lightly beaten
  Chopped fresh chives, for garnish

1. Preheat oven to 350°F. Stir together first 4 ingredients in a large bowl; make a well in center of mixture. Stir together corn and next 6 ingredients; add to cornmeal mixture, stirring just until dry ingredients are moistened. Divide mixture among 12 (6-ounce) greased ramekins.

2. Bake in preheated oven until golden brown and set, 35 to 40 minutes. Garnish with additional chives. Serve immediately.

CORN PUDDING

Creamed corn baked in custard is a traditional Southern dish worth preserving.

ACTIVE 15 MIN. - TOTAL 1 HOUR, 10 MIN.
SERVES 6 TO 8

- 9 ears fresh corn
- 4 large eggs, beaten
- ½ cup half-and-half
- 1½ tsp. baking powder
- ⅓ cup butter
- 2 Tbsp. granulated sugar
- 2 Tbsp. all-purpose flour
- 1 Tbsp. butter, melted
- ⅛ tsp. freshly ground black pepper

1. Remove and discard husks and silks from corn. Cut off tips of corn kernels into a bowl, and scrape milk and remaining pulp from cob with a paring knife to measure 3 to 4 cups total. Set corn aside.

2. Combine eggs, half-and-half, and baking powder, stirring well with a wire whisk.

3. Preheat oven to 350°F. Melt ⅓ cup butter in a large saucepan over low; add sugar and flour, stirring until smooth. Remove from heat; gradually add egg mixture, whisking constantly until smooth. Stir in corn.

4. Pour corn mixture into a greased 1- or 1½-quart baking dish.

5. Bake, uncovered, in preheated oven until pudding is set, 40 to 45 minutes. Drizzle pudding with 1 tablespoon butter; sprinkle with black pepper.

6. Broil 5½ inches from heat until golden, about 2 minutes. Let stand 5 minutes before serving.

CORN
PUDDING

CLASSIC GRILLED
CORN

HONEY-
CHIPOTLE
GLAZE

BACON WITH
RANCH DRIZZLE

BASIL BUTTER
WITH PARMESAN

SMOKY
BARBECUE
RUB

CLASSIC GRILLED CORN

ACTIVE 40 MIN. - TOTAL 40 MIN.
SERVES 6

- 6 large ears yellow or white corn with husks (about 5 lb.)
- ¼ cup butter, cut evenly into 12 pieces
- ¾ tsp. kosher salt
- ¼ tsp. black pepper

1. Preheat a gas grill to medium-high (400°F to 450°F) on one side, or push hot coals to one side of a charcoal grill.

2. Working with 1 ear at a time, grab silks at top of corn with half the silks in each hand. Slowly peel silks down, one side at a time, peeling back all silks and husks in one motion. Discard silks; pull husks together to form a ponytail-like handle. Tear off one small husk piece; use it to tie a knot around husks to secure.

3. Coat corn with cooking spray; place on unoiled grates on lit side of grill. Hang husks over edge of grill to prevent burning. Grill, uncovered, turning occasionally, until charred in spots, 15 to 18 minutes.

4. Remove corn from grill. Wrap individually in aluminum foil, excluding husks, placing 2 butter pieces on each ear. Put wrapped corn on unlit side of grill. Cover grill to keep warm until ready to serve, at least 5 minutes or up to 30 minutes. Unwrap corn; sprinkle with salt and pepper.

BASIL BUTTER WITH PARMESAN

ACTIVE 10 MIN. - TOTAL 10 MIN.
SERVES 6

Process ½ cup packed fresh **basil leaves**, ½ cup softened **butter**, 2 tsp. fresh **lemon juice**, and ¼ tsp. **kosher salt** in a food processor until smooth, 1 minute. Arrange Classic Grilled Corn on a platter. Rub corn with butter mixture; sprinkle evenly with ½ cup finely grated **Parmigiano-Reggiano**.

BACON WITH RANCH DRIZZLE

ACTIVE 20 MIN. - TOTAL 20 MIN.
SERVES 6

Cook 6 **bacon slices** in a large skillet over medium-high, turning occasionally, until very crisp, about 8 minutes. Transfer to a plate lined with paper towels, and let stand 5 minutes. Meanwhile, measure 2 Tbsp. drippings from skillet into a heatproof bowl. Add 3 Tbsp. each of **mayonnaise**, **sour cream**, and **whole-milk buttermilk** to bowl, whisking until combined. Add 2 tsp. each finely chopped **fresh flat-leaf parsley**, **fresh dill**, and **fresh chives**; 1 tsp. fresh **lemon juice**; ½ tsp. **kosher salt**; and ¼ tsp. **onion powder**, stirring to combine. Finely chop bacon. Arrange Classic Grilled Corn on a platter, and drizzle with ranch mixture. Sprinkle evenly with chopped bacon.

HONEY-CHIPOTLE GLAZE

ACTIVE 15 MIN. - TOTAL 15 MIN.
SERVES 6

Process 3 Tbsp. **honey**, 2 Tbsp. chopped **scallion** (white and light green parts only), 1½ Tbsp. **apple cider vinegar**, 1 Tbsp. **chipotle chile in adobo sauce** (from one 7-oz. can), 1 minced large **garlic clove**, and ½ tsp. **kosher salt** in a food processor until smooth, 1 minute. Brush mixture evenly over Classic Grilled Corn. Return corn to lit side of grill. Grill, uncovered, until glaze is warmed through and adheres to corn, 4 to 5 minutes. Arrange grilled corn on a platter, and sprinkle evenly with ¼ cup finely chopped **fresh chives**.

SMOKY BARBECUE RUB

ACTIVE 10 MIN. - TOTAL 15 MIN.
SERVES 6

Stir together 2 Tbsp. **dark brown sugar**; 1 Tbsp. **smoked paprika**; 1 tsp. fresh **lime zest**; and ½ tsp. each **ancho chile powder**, **kosher salt**, **black pepper**, and **garlic powder** in a small bowl. Sprinkle mixture evenly over Classic Grilled Corn. Return corn to lit side of grill. Grill, uncovered, turning occasionally, until sugar is melted, 4 to 5 minutes. Arrange grilled corn on a platter, and serve with **lime wedges**.

QUICK DOUBLE–CHEESE GRITS

ACTIVE 10 MIN. - TOTAL 15 MIN.
SERVES 8

- ½ tsp. table salt
- 1½ cups quick-cooking grits
- 4 oz. extra-sharp cheddar cheese, shredded (1 cup)
- 4 oz. Monterey Jack cheese, shredded (1 cup)
- 2 Tbsp. butter or margarine
- ½ tsp. black pepper

Bring 6 cups water and the salt to a boil in a large saucepan. Gradually stir in grits. Cook 4 to 5 minutes, stirring often, until thickened. Remove from heat. Add shredded cheeses, butter, and pepper, stirring until blended. Serve immediately.

Note: Grits may be chilled and reheated. Whisk ¼ cup warm water into grits over medium heat, adding more water as necessary.

SHRIMP AND GRITS DRESSING

In the South we serve dressing—mostly varieties of cornbread dressing. And this twist on another Southern staple proves we aren't afraid to re-imagine any dish as a form of this traditional holiday side.

ACTIVE 35 MIN. - TOTAL 1 HOUR, 50 MIN.
SERVES 6 TO 8

- 1 lb. medium peeled raw shrimp
- 3 cups chicken broth
- ½ tsp. table salt
- ¼ tsp. cayenne pepper
- 1 cup uncooked regular grits
- ½ cup butter
- 3 large eggs, lightly beaten
- 1 red bell pepper, diced
- 1 cup fine, dry breadcrumbs
- 1 cup chopped scallions
- ½ cup grated Parmesan cheese

1. Preheat oven to 325°F. Devein shrimp, if desired.

2. Bring broth, salt, and cayenne pepper to a boil in a large saucepan over medium-high. Whisk in grits, and return to a boil; reduce heat to low, and stir in butter. Cover and simmer, stirring occasionally, 10 minutes or until liquid is absorbed. Remove from heat.

3. Stir together eggs and next 4 ingredients in a large bowl. Gradually stir about one-fourth of hot grits mixture into egg mixture; add egg mixture to remaining hot grits mixture, stirring constantly. Stir in shrimp until blended. Pour dressing into a lightly greased 11- x 7-inch baking dish.

4. Bake in preheated oven until dressing is set, 55 minutes to 1 hour. Let stand 10 minutes.

SAUTÉED RADISHES WITH BACON AND CILANTRO

ACTIVE 20 MIN. - TOTAL 20 MIN.
SERVES 4

- 4 thick-cut bacon slices, chopped
- 1 lb. radishes, cut in half lengthwise (quartered if large)
- 1 Tbsp. apple cider vinegar
- ½ tsp. honey
- ½ tsp. kosher salt
- ¼ tsp. black pepper
- ⅓ cup packed fresh cilantro leaves

1. Place bacon in a large nonstick skillet; cook over medium, stirring occasionally, just until starting to brown, about 4 minutes.

2. Add radishes to skillet; cook, stirring occasionally, until radishes are tender and bacon is crispy, about 12 minutes.

3. Push radishes and bacon to one side of skillet using a spatula. Carefully tilt skillet to drain drippings. Discard bacon drippings, reserving 1 tablespoon drippings in skillet. Add vinegar, honey, salt, and pepper to skillet; stir until well incorporated. Stir in cilantro. Serve immediately.

SAUTÉED
RADISHES WITH
BACON AND
CILANTRO

ROASTED CARROTS WITH SPICED PECANS AND SORGHUM

ACTIVE 15 MIN. · TOTAL 1 HOUR, 10 MIN.
SERVES 6

- ½ cup pecan halves
- 1 Tbsp. unsalted butter, melted
- ¼ tsp. smoked paprika
- ⅛ tsp. cayenne pepper
- 3 lb. small carrots with tops
- 2 Tbsp. olive oil
- 1 tsp. kosher salt
- ¼ tsp. black pepper
- 1 Tbsp. apple cider vinegar
- 2 Tbsp. sorghum syrup
- 1 Tbsp. thinly sliced fresh chives

1. Preheat oven to 350°F. Toss together pecans, butter, paprika, and cayenne on a rimmed baking sheet. Bake until lightly browned and toasted, about 8 minutes. Remove from oven; cool completely on pan, about 15 minutes. Coarsely chop pecans; set aside.

2. Increase oven to 450°F. Peel carrots; trim carrot tops to 1 inch. (Discard the trimmed greens, or reserve for another use.) Toss together trimmed carrots, oil, salt, and black pepper in a bowl; spread in a single layer on a rimmed baking sheet. Roast, stirring once, until browned and tender, 30 to 35 minutes. Remove from oven; immediately drizzle hot carrots with vinegar, and toss to coat.

3. Arrange carrots on a serving platter. Drizzle with sorghum syrup; sprinkle with pecans and chives.

ROASTED BABY TURNIPS WITH TURNIP GREEN PESTO

ACTIVE 20 MIN. · TOTAL 40 MIN.
SERVES 4

- 4 (9-oz.) bunches baby turnips
- ¼ cup plus 2 Tbsp. olive oil, divided
- 1¼ tsp. kosher salt, divided
- ¾ tsp. black pepper, divided
- 2 Tbsp. chopped toasted pecans
- 1 small garlic clove
- 1 Tbsp. fresh lemon juice
- 2 Tbsp. plus 2 tsp. grated Parmesan cheese
- 1½ tsp. honey

1. Preheat oven to 425°F; place a rimmed baking sheet in oven 5 minutes while preheating. Trim turnip stems to 1 inch. Cut trimmed turnips in half lengthwise to measure 6 cups. Chop turnip greens to measure 4 cups. (Reserve remaining turnips and greens for another use.)

2. Toss together halved turnips, 2 tablespoons of the oil, ¾ teaspoon of the salt, and ½ teaspoon of the pepper in a bowl; spread in one even layer on warmed baking sheet. Roast in preheated oven until tender and golden brown, about 18 minutes.

3. While turnips roast, place 2 quarts water in a large saucepan, and bring to a boil over high. Add chopped greens; cook about 30 seconds. Fill a large bowl with ice water. Drain boiled greens, submerge in ice water, and stir once. Let stand until cold, about 1 minute. Remove greens, and squeeze out excess water. Transfer to a food processor.

4. Add pecans and garlic to the greens in the food processor, and process until a paste forms, stopping to scrape down sides as needed, about 1 minute. With processor running, pour lemon juice and remaining ¼ cup oil through food chute in a steady stream, processing until smooth, about 1 minute. Add Parmesan, honey, and remaining ½ teaspoon salt and ¼ teaspoon pepper, and process until blended, about 10 seconds. Set pesto aside until ready to serve.

5. Transfer roasted turnips to a serving platter; drizzle with pesto.

ROASTED BABY
TURNIPS WITH
TURNIP GREEN PESTO

TANGY POTATO-GREEN
BEAN SALAD

TANGY POTATO-GREEN BEAN SALAD

Party bound? Chill cooked potatoes and green beans in the dressing for 30 minutes. Then assemble the salad (with the radishes, dill, chives, and remaining dressing) on a platter just before serving.

ACTIVE 20 MIN. - TOTAL 1 HOUR, 20 MIN.
SERVES 8

- 3 lb. baby red potatoes (quartered or halved, depending on size)
- ¼ cup plus 1 tsp. kosher salt, divided
- 8 oz. haricots verts (French green beans), trimmed and cut into 1½-inch pieces
- 1 tsp. lemon zest plus ¼ cup fresh juice (from 2 lemons)
- 1 Tbsp. minced shallot
- 1 Tbsp. white wine vinegar
- 1 Tbsp. Dijon mustard
- ¼ tsp. black pepper
- 1 cup loosely packed fresh dill, chopped and divided
- ⅔ cup olive oil
- ½ cup thinly sliced radishes
- 2 Tbsp. thinly sliced chives

1. Bring potatoes, water to cover, and ¼ cup of the salt to a boil in a large Dutch oven over medium-high. Reduce heat to medium-low, and cook just until fork-tender but not falling apart, about 8 minutes. Add haricots verts, and cook until beans are tender-crisp, about 1 minute. Drain well; cool completely, about 30 minutes. Transfer to a large bowl and cover with plastic wrap; chill until ready to use.

2. Whisk together lemon zest and lemon juice, shallot, vinegar, mustard, pepper, remaining 1 teaspoon salt, and 1 tablespoon of the chopped dill in a medium bowl; gradually add olive oil in a slow, steady stream, whisking until smooth.

3. Gently toss together potato-green bean mixture and ½ cup of the dressing, and let stand 30 minutes. Before serving, gently stir in radishes, remaining fresh dill, and remaining dressing. Sprinkle with chives.

NEW POTATO AND FENNEL SALAD

This bright and tangy potato salad pairs wonderfully with ham. We prefer buttery Castelvetrano olives, if you can find them.

ACTIVE 35 MIN. - TOTAL 55 MIN.
SERVES 8

- 3 lb. baby red potatoes, halved
- 1 Tbsp. plus 1 tsp. kosher salt, divided
- 1 fennel bulb
- ¾ cup roughly chopped green olives
- ⅓ cup extra-virgin olive oil
- 3 Tbsp. fresh lemon juice (from 2 lemons)
- 2 scallions, finely chopped
- ⅛ tsp. black pepper

1. Combine potatoes, 8 cups water, and 1 tablespoon of the salt in a large saucepan. Bring to a boil over medium-high. Reduce heat to medium-low, and simmer until tender, 8 to 12 minutes. Drain; spread potatoes on a baking sheet in a single layer, and let stand until cool, about 20 minutes.

2. Chop fennel fronds to equal ½ cup. Thinly slice fennel bulb. Toss together chopped fronds, sliced fennel, green olives, oil, lemon juice, and scallions in a large bowl. Add cooled potatoes, pepper, and remaining 1 teaspoon salt; gently stir to combine. Serve at room temperature, or cover and chill up to 1 day.

BLT POTATO SALAD

Potato salad—pure and simple—remains one of the tastiest icons of a Southern picnic. Merging it with the flavors of a BLT is a real treat.

ACTIVE 20 MIN. · TOTAL 3 HOURS, 40 MIN., INCLUDING CHILLING
SERVES 8 TO 10

- 3 large baking potatoes (about 3½ lb.), peeled and chopped
- 1 cup mayonnaise
- 3 Tbsp. sweet pickle relish
- 2 Tbsp. Dijon mustard
- ¼ cup chopped fresh flat-leaf parsley
- 1 tsp. table salt
- 1 tsp. freshly ground black pepper
- 4 scallions, sliced
- 2 hard-cooked eggs, coarsely chopped
- 1 cup grape tomatoes, halved
- 8 bacon slices, cooked and crumbled
  Curly leaf lettuce leaves

1. Bring potatoes and salted water to cover to a boil in a Dutch oven. Boil 15 to 20 minutes or until tender (do not overcook). Drain and cool.

2. Stir together mayonnaise and next 5 ingredients in a large bowl; add cooked potatoes, scallions, and eggs, tossing gently until well blended. Gently stir in tomatoes. Cover and chill at least 3 hours. Stir in bacon just before serving. Serve on lettuce leaves.

- -

DILLED POTATO SALAD WITH FETA

Invite the flavor of Greece to your next cookout by serving a potato salad tossed with crumbled feta cheese. The rich, smooth cheese highlights the tart red wine vinegar and the crunchy fresh veggies.

ACTIVE 15 MIN. · TOTAL 2 HOURS, 50 MIN.
SERVES 6 TO 8

- 2 lb. small red potatoes, unpeeled
- ⅓ cup red wine vinegar
- ⅓ cup vegetable oil
- 3 Tbsp. chopped fresh or 1 Tbsp. dried dill
- ½ to 1 tsp. table salt
- ½ tsp. black pepper

- 1 large red bell pepper, chopped
- 1 cucumber, cut in half lengthwise and sliced
- ½ cup sliced scallions
- 1 (4-oz.) pkg. crumbled feta cheese

1. Bring potatoes and water to cover to a boil. Cook 25 to 30 minutes or just until tender; drain and cool. Cut potatoes into quarters.

2. Whisk together vinegar, oil, dill, salt, and black pepper. Pour over warm potatoes.

3. Stir in chopped bell pepper, cucumber, and scallions; add cheese, and toss to combine. Cover and chill at least 2 hours.

- -

BROCCOLI-CARROT SALAD

Variations of this old-fashioned, slightly sweet broccoli salad have made many appearances at church suppers across the South.

ACTIVE 20 MIN. · TOTAL 20 MIN.
SERVES 8

- 1½ lb. fresh broccoli
- 1 cup scraped, sliced, or shredded carrots
- 4 oz. cheddar cheese, shredded (1 cup)
- 1 cup raisins (optional)
- ½ cup mayonnaise
- 2 to 3 Tbsp. granulated sugar
- 2 tsp. red wine vinegar
  Lettuce leaves (optional)
- 8 bacon slices, cooked and crumbled

1. Remove broccoli leaves, and cut off tough ends of stalks; discard. Wash broccoli thoroughly, and cut into florets. Blanch broccoli in boiling water 10 seconds. Plunge into ice water to stop the cooking process; drain well.

2. Combine broccoli, carrots, cheese, and, if desired, raisins, tossing gently. Combine mayonnaise, sugar, and vinegar; stir well. Add mayonnaise dressing to broccoli mixture; toss gently.

3. Spoon broccoli salad onto lettuce-lined salad plates, if desired, using a slotted spoon. Sprinkle with bacon, and serve immediately.

BLT POTATO SALAD

CRISPY SWEET POTATO-GREEN ONION CAKES

CRISPY SWEET POTATO-GREEN ONION CAKES

ACTIVE 1 HOUR · TOTAL 1 HOUR, 5 MIN.
SERVES 6 TO 8

- 4 medium sweet potatoes (about 2¼ lb.)
- 2 eggs, lightly beaten
- ½ cup flour
- 2 red jalapeño peppers, chopped
- 1½ tsp. kosher salt
- ½ cup thinly sliced scallions, divided
- ¼ cup canola oil
- Lime wedges, sour cream, for serving

1. Pierce 1 sweet potato several times with a fork. Place on a microwave-safe plate; cover with damp paper towels. Microwave on HIGH 8 to 10 minutes or until tender. Let stand 5 minutes. Peel potato and place in a medium bowl; mash with a fork. Peel remaining sweet potatoes, and grate, using the large holes of a box grater. Stir grated potatoes into mashed potato. Gently stir in eggs, next 3 ingredients, and ¼ cup scallions just until combined.

2. Pour oil into a 12-inch cast-iron skillet; heat over medium to 350°F. Carefully drop mixture by tablespoonfuls, in batches, into hot oil, pressing lightly to flatten. Cook 5 to 6 minutes on each side or until golden brown. Drain on paper towels.

3. Place drained sweet potato cakes on a wire rack set over a baking sheet lined with aluminum foil. Keep warm in a 200°F oven up to 30 minutes. Sprinkle with remaining ¼ cup scallions just before serving. Serve with lime wedges and sour cream.

BLACK-EYED PEA CAKES

ACTIVE 20 MIN. · TOTAL 1 HOUR, 30 MIN., INCLUDING CHILLING
MAKES 30 CAKES

- 1 small onion, chopped
- 1 Tbsp. olive oil
- 2 (15.5-oz.) cans black-eyed peas, rinsed, drained, and divided
- 1 (8-oz.) container chive-and-onion-flavor cream cheese, softened
- 1 large egg
- ½ tsp. table salt
- 1 tsp. hot sauce
- 1 (8-oz.) pkg. hush puppy mix with onion
- Olive oil
- Sour cream, green tomato relish, for topping

1. Cook onion in 1 tablespoon hot oil in a large skillet over medium-high until tender, stirring often, about 5 minutes.

2. Process onion, 1 can of peas, and next 4 ingredients in a blender or food processor until mixture is smooth, stopping to scrape down sides. Stir in hush puppy mix, and gently fold in remaining can of peas.

3. Shape mixture by 2 tablespoonfuls into 3-inch patties. Place patties on a waxed paper-lined baking sheet. Cover and chill 1 hour.

4. Cook patties, in batches, in 3 tablespoons hot oil, adding oil as needed, in a large skillet over medium until patties are golden brown, about 1½ minutes on each side. Drain patties on paper towels, and keep them warm. Serve with desired toppings.

SWEET POTATO-AND-COLLARD GREEN GRATIN

ACTIVE 30 MIN. · TOTAL 1 HOUR, 45 MIN.
SERVES 8 TO 10

- ½ tsp. freshly grated nutmeg
  Pinch of ground allspice
- 2 tsp. coarse sea salt, divided
- 2 tsp. black pepper, divided
- 1 Tbsp. olive oil, plus more for greasing dish
- 8 oz. collard greens, stems trimmed, large ribs removed, and roughly chopped
- 2 garlic cloves, minced
- 2 Tbsp. unsalted butter
- 2 Tbsp. all-purpose flour
- 1½ cups 2% reduced-fat milk, warmed (about 120°F)
- 4 oz. Parmigiano-Reggiano cheese, grated (about ½ cup), divided
- 3 Tbsp. panko (Japanese breadcrumbs), divided
- 3 lb. sweet potatoes, peeled and cut into ¼-inch slices
- 2 Tbsp. melted unsalted butter

1. Preheat oven to 400°F. Combine nutmeg, allspice, and 1 teaspoon each of the salt and pepper in a bowl; set aside.

2. Heat 1 tablespoon of the oil in a large skillet over medium-high. Add collard greens; cook, stirring often, until bright green, about 2 minutes. Add garlic; cook, stirring constantly, until fragrant, about 1 minute. Season with ¼ teaspoon each of the salt and pepper.

3. Melt 2 tablespoons butter in a small heavy-bottomed saucepan over medium. Whisk in flour; cook, whisking constantly, until mixture bubbles and flour is cooked but not browned, about 2 minutes. Whisk in warm milk; bring to a boil, whisking occasionally. Reduce heat to low, and cook, whisking occasionally, until sauce thickens, about 2 minutes. Add ¼ cup of the cheese, stirring until melted. Season with ½ teaspoon each of the salt and pepper. Remove white sauce from heat.

4. Sprinkle 1 tablespoon of the panko on bottom of a 2-quart baking dish lightly greased with olive oil. Layer half the sweet potatoes evenly over breadcrumbs; season with remaining ¼ teaspoon each salt and pepper. Spoon collard green mixture over sweet potatoes; sprinkle with half the nutmeg mixture. Top with remaining sweet potatoes; sprinkle with remaining nutmeg mixture.

5. Pour white sauce over sweet potatoes, and cover dish with a piece of parchment paper. Bake in preheated oven until sweet potatoes are soft when pierced with the tip of a knife, about 40 minutes. Meanwhile, combine 2 tablespoons melted butter and remaining 2 tablespoons panko and ¼ cup cheese. Reduce oven temperature to 375°F. Remove dish from oven, discard parchment, and sprinkle panko mixture evenly over potatoes. Bake, uncovered, until golden brown, about 25 minutes. Transfer to a wire rack; let stand 10 minutes before serving.

- -

CANDIED YAMS

ACTIVE 20 MIN. · TOTAL 1 HOUR, 25 MIN.
SERVES 12

- 4 lb. sweet potatoes, peeled and cut into ½-inch-thick rounds
- ½ cup salted butter
- ¾ cup granulated sugar
- ¾ cup packed light brown sugar
- ¼ cup heavy cream
- 1 Tbsp. vanilla extract
- 1 tsp. ground cinnamon
- 1 tsp. kosher salt
- ¼ tsp. ground nutmeg

1. Preheat oven to 350°F. Layer sweet potato slices in a lightly greased 13- x 9-inch baking dish.

2. Melt butter in a small saucepan over medium. Add sugars, stirring until well combined. Stir in cream; cook, stirring often, just until mixture comes to a simmer, 5 to 7 minutes. Remove from heat; stir in vanilla extract, cinnamon, salt, and nutmeg.

3. Pour sugar mixture evenly over sweet potatoes. Cover with lightly greased aluminum foil. Bake, covered, in preheated oven, about 40 minutes. Uncover and gently stir potato mixture. Bake, uncovered, until potatoes are tender, 25 to 30 minutes more. Transfer potatoes to a serving bowl with a slotted spoon; pour syrup over potatoes. Serve immediately.

SWEET POTATO-AND-
COLLARD GREEN
GRATIN

BLISTERED
BRUSSELS SPROUTS

BLISTERED BRUSSELS SPROUTS

This is the absolute best way to cook Brussels sprouts. High-heat searing caramelizes the outside and yields perfect crisp-tender texture inside. Use a 12-inch cast-iron pan, or work in two batches.

ACTIVE 15 MIN. - TOTAL 15 MIN.
SERVES 4

- 3 Tbsp. canola oil
- 1 lb. fresh Brussels sprouts, trimmed and cut in half lengthwise
- ¾ tsp. kosher salt
- 1 Tbsp. honey
- 1 Tbsp. hot water
- 1 Tbsp. minced garlic
- 1 Tbsp. soy sauce
- ¼ tsp. crushed red pepper
- ½ cup torn fresh mint leaves

1. Heat a 12-inch cast-iron skillet over medium-high 5 minutes. Add oil to skillet, and tilt skillet to evenly coat bottom. Place Brussels sprouts, cut-side down, in a single layer in skillet. Cook, without stirring, 4 minutes or until browned. Sprinkle with salt; cook and stir 2 minutes.

2. Stir together honey and hot water in a small bowl. Stir garlic, soy sauce, crushed red pepper, and honey mixture into Brussels sprouts. Stir in mint.

SLOW-COOKER COLLARD GREENS WITH HAM HOCKS

ACTIVE 15 MIN. - TOTAL 9 HOURS, 15 MIN.
SERVES 12

- 2 smoked ham hocks (1¼ lb. total)
- 2 (14-oz.) cans chicken broth
- 2 (1-lb.) pkg. prewashed chopped fresh collard greens
- ½ cup chopped sweet onion
- 2 Tbsp. light brown sugar
- 2 Tbsp. apple cider vinegar
- 2 tsp. kosher salt
- 1 tsp. crushed red pepper
- ½ tsp. black pepper

Combine all ingredients in a 6-quart oval slow cooker. Cover and cook on LOW 9 hours. Carefully remove ham hocks and all bits of bone before stirring greens after cooking. Cool ham hocks, and thoroughly remove all fat and bone; return meat to slow cooker. Stir into greens, and serve.

Make Ahead: Make this recipe up to 2 days in advance. Refrigerate the cooked ingredients in the slow-cooker insert. Allow the insert to stand at room temperature for 30 minutes before returning it to the slow cooker to reheat the greens. (Immediately heating a chilled insert could cause it to crack.)

Vegetarian Slow-Cooker Collard Greens: Omit ham hocks and substitute vegetable broth for the chicken broth. Prepare recipe as directed, stirring 1 tablespoon smoked paprika and one 14.5-ounce can fire-roasted diced tomatoes, drained, into collard greens mixture in slow cooker before cooking.

CHARRED PEPPERS WITH FETA DIPPING SAUCE

Look for a colorful assortment of baby sweet peppers in the produce section of your local grocer. Hold them by the stems while dipping.

ACTIVE 20 MIN. - TOTAL 25 MIN.
SERVES 4

- ¼ cup crumbled feta cheese
- ¼ cup Greek yogurt
- 1 scallion, minced
- 2 tsp. chopped fresh mint
- 4 Tbsp. fresh lemon juice, divided
- 3 Tbsp. extra-virgin olive oil, divided
  Table salt and black pepper, to taste
- 1 (8-oz.) pkg. assorted mini sweet peppers

1. Heat a 12-inch cast-iron skillet over medium-high 5 minutes.

2. Whisk together feta cheese, yogurt, scallion, mint, 2 tablespoons lemon juice, and 2 tablespoons oil in a small bowl. Stir in salt and black pepper to taste. Let stand at room temperature until ready to use.

3. Toss sweet peppers with 1 tablespoon oil; sprinkle with desired amount of salt. Cook peppers in hot skillet over medium-high, turning occasionally, until charred and slightly wilted, about 8 minutes.

4. Transfer peppers to a plate; drizzle with remaining 2 tablespoons lemon juice. Serve with feta dipping sauce.

CRUMB-TOPPED SPINACH CASSEROLE

This quick, cheesy side, with its crunchy browned topping, can be ready to bake in about the time it takes to preheat the oven. This recipe is the one to introduce kids to spinach.

ACTIVE 20 MIN. - TOTAL 55 MIN.
SERVES 8 TO 10

- 2 Tbsp. butter
- 1 medium onion, chopped
- 2 garlic cloves, minced
- 4 (10-oz.) pkg. frozen chopped spinach, thawed
- 1 (8-oz.) pkg. cream cheese, softened
- 2 Tbsp. all-purpose flour
- 2 large eggs
- ½ tsp. table salt
- ¼ tsp. black pepper
- 1 cup milk
- 1 (8-oz.) pkg. shredded cheddar cheese
- 1 cup Italian-seasoned Panko (Japanese breadcrumbs)
- 3 to 4 Tbsp. butter, melted

1. Preheat oven to 350°F. Melt 2 tablespoons butter in a large nonstick skillet over medium. Add onion and garlic; cook, stirring often, until tender, about 8 minutes.

2. Meanwhile, drain spinach well, pressing between paper towels to remove excess moisture.

3. Stir together cream cheese and flour in a large bowl until smooth. Whisk in eggs, salt, and pepper. Gradually whisk in milk until blended. Add cooked onion, spinach, and cheddar cheese, stirring until blended. Spoon into a lightly greased 11- x 7-inch baking dish.

4. Combine breadcrumbs and 3 to 4 tablespoons butter in a small bowl; toss well. Sprinkle over casserole.

5. Bake, uncovered, in preheated oven until thoroughly heated and breadcrumbs are browned, 30 to 35 minutes.

Note: To make individual spinach casseroles, spoon spinach mixture into 8 (8-ounce) lightly greased ramekins; top each with buttered breadcrumbs. Bake, uncovered, at 375°F for 25 to 30 minutes or until browned.

CRUMB-TOPPED
SPINACH CASSEROLE

CRUNCHY FRIED
OKRA

CRUNCHY FRIED OKRA

Whole okra, halved lengthwise, gives a fun twist to this fried favorite.

ACTIVE 20 MIN. - TOTAL 30 MIN.
SERVES 4 TO 6

- 1½ cups buttermilk
- 1 large egg
- 2 cups saltine cracker crumbs (2 sleeves)
- 1½ cups all-purpose flour
- 1 tsp. table salt
- 1 lb. fresh okra, cut in half lengthwise
  Peanut oil
  Table salt (optional)

1. Stir together buttermilk and egg. Combine cracker crumbs, flour, and salt. Dip okra pieces in buttermilk mixture; dredge in cracker crumb mixture.

2. Pour oil to a depth of 2 inches into a Dutch oven or cast-iron skillet; heat to 375°F. Fry okra, in 3 batches, for 2 minutes or until golden, turning once. Drain on paper towels. Sprinkle lightly with salt, if desired.

- -

PAN-FRIED OKRA WITH CORNMEAL

(Photo, page 226)

Using two medium skillets gives the okra plenty of room to cook up extra crispy. If you prefer, make all the okra in a single large skillet.

ACTIVE 10 MIN. - TOTAL 30 MIN.
SERVES 4

- 6 Tbsp. canola oil, divided
- 2 lb. fresh okra, stems trimmed, cut into ½-inch pieces
- 1½ tsp. coarse sea salt
- 1 tsp. black pepper
- ⅔ cup fine yellow cornmeal
- ⅛ tsp. cayenne pepper

Place 1½ tablespoons of the canola oil in each of two medium-size nonstick skillets; heat over medium-high. Divide okra between skillets, and stir to coat. Cover and cook, stirring occasionally, until bright green, about 10 minutes. Sprinkle okra in each skillet with ¾ teaspoon

salt and ½ teaspoon black pepper. Divide yellow cornmeal and cayenne pepper evenly between skillets; stir to coat. Drizzle 1½ tablespoons oil over mixture in each skillet, and cook, uncovered, stirring occasionally, until okra is tender and browned, about 6 minutes.

- -

GRILLED OKRA AND TOMATOES

ACTIVE 10 MIN. - TOTAL 15 MIN.
SERVES 4

- 1 lb. fresh okra, trimmed
- 1 pt. cherry tomatoes
- 2 Tbsp. olive oil
- ½ tsp. table salt
- ½ tsp. black pepper
- 2 Tbsp. chopped fresh basil

1. Combine first 5 ingredients in a large bowl.

2. Preheat grill to medium-high (350°F to 400°F). Place okra and tomatoes on a grill rack, and grill with lid closed, just until they begin to pop, 3 minutes. Turn okra, and grill, with lid closed, until tender, 2 to 3 minutes more.

3. Transfer okra and tomatoes to a serving dish and sprinkle with basil. Serve immediately.

GREEN BEAN CASSEROLE WITH FRIED LEEKS

Remember the old green bean casserole made with convenience products: frozen or canned green beans, cream of mushroom soup, and French-fried onions? Here it is again, better than ever with some scrumptious flavor twists.

ACTIVE 10 MIN. · TOTAL 35 MIN.
SERVES 6

- 2 Tbsp. butter
- 2 (8-oz.) pkg. sliced fresh mushrooms
- 1 tsp. dried thyme
- 2 shallots, finely chopped
- ½ cup Madeira
- 1 cup whipping cream
- 1¼ lb. fresh green beans, trimmed
  Vegetable or peanut oil
- 2 large leeks, cleaned and thinly sliced crosswise
  Table salt, to taste

1. Preheat oven to 400°F. Melt butter in a large heavy skillet over medium-high. Add mushrooms and thyme; cook, stirring often, 5 minutes. Add shallots; cook, stirring often, until tender, about 3 minutes. Add Madeira, and cook over medium-high 3 minutes or until liquid evaporates. Add cream, and cook, stirring often, until slightly thickened, 2 to 5 minutes. Remove from heat.

2. Meanwhile, cook beans in a small amount of boiling water 5 minutes or just until crisp-tender; drain. Add beans to mushroom mixture; toss gently. Spoon into a greased 2-quart gratin dish or shallow baking dish. Cover and keep warm.

3. Pour oil to a depth of 2 inches into a 3-quart saucepan; heat to 350°F. Fry leeks, in 3 batches, 1 to 1½ minutes per batch or until golden. Remove leeks with a small metal strainer; drain on paper towels. Immediately sprinkle with salt. Sprinkle fried leeks over warm bean mixture.

4. Bake, uncovered, in preheated oven, until casserole is thoroughly heated, about 5 minutes.

GREEN BEAN–GOAT CHEESE GRATIN

Breadcrumbs and toasted pecans tossed with Parmesan and olive oil are sprinkled over these individual gratins, giving them the crunch factor we all crave on green bean casserole.

ACTIVE 20 MIN. · TOTAL 50 MIN.
SERVES 4

- 2 white bread slices
- 1 Tbsp. olive oil
- 3 oz. Parmesan cheese, freshly shredded (1 cup), divided
- ⅓ cup finely chopped pecans
- 1 lb. fresh haricots verts (French green beans), trimmed
- 2 oz. goat cheese, crumbled
- ½ cup whipping cream
- ¼ tsp. kosher salt
- ¼ tsp. freshly ground black pepper

1. Preheat oven to 400°F. Tear bread into large pieces; pulse in a food processor 2 or 3 times or until coarse crumbs form. Drizzle oil over crumbs; add ¼ cup Parmesan cheese. Pulse 5 or 6 times or until coated with oil. Stir in pecans.

2. Cut green beans crosswise into thirds. Cook in boiling water to cover 3 to 4 minutes or until crisp-tender; drain. Plunge into ice water to stop the cooking process; drain and pat dry with paper towels.

3. Toss together beans, next 4 ingredients, and remaining ½ cup Parmesan cheese. Firmly pack mixture into 4 (6-ounce) shallow ramekins. Cover each with aluminum foil and place on a baking sheet.

4. Bake in preheated oven 20 minutes. Uncover and sprinkle with crumb mixture. Bake until golden, about 8 minutes more. Let stand 5 minutes.

GREEN BEAN-GOAT
CHEESE GRATIN

KETTLE-CHIP-
CRUSTED FRIED GREEN
TOMATOES WITH TASSO
TARTAR SAUCE

KETTLE-CHIP-CRUSTED FRIED GREEN TOMATOES WITH TASSO TARTAR SAUCE

ACTIVE 30 MIN. - TOTAL 30 MIN.
SERVES 8

TASSO TARTAR SAUCE
- 3 oz. pork tasso, chopped (about ¾ cup)
- ½ cup chopped shallots
- ¼ cup chopped red onion
- 2 Tbsp. chopped celery
- 2 Tbsp. fresh lemon juice
- 1 garlic clove, crushed
- 1 cup mayonnaise
- 1 tsp. Creole mustard
- ⅛ tsp. cayenne pepper
- ⅛ tsp. granulated sugar
- ⅛ tsp. kosher salt

FRIED GREEN TOMATOES
- Canola oil, for frying
- 4 green tomatoes (about 1¾ lb.), cut into ⅓-inch slices
- 1 tsp. kosher salt
- ½ tsp. black pepper
- ¼ cup all-purpose flour
- 2 large eggs, lightly beaten
- 3 cups finely crushed spicy kettle-cooked potato chips (such as Zapp's Spicy Cajun Crawtators)

1. Prepare the Tasso Tartar Sauce: Place pork tasso, shallots, red onion, celery, fresh lemon juice, and garlic in bowl of a food processor; pulse until finely chopped, 6 to 8 times. Scrape mixture into a small bowl, and fold in mayonnaise, mustard, cayenne, sugar, and salt. Cover and refrigerate until ready to serve.

2. Prepare the Fried Green Tomatoes: Heat 1 inch of oil in a large heavy-bottomed skillet over medium to 350°F. Sprinkle tomato slices with salt and pepper. Place flour, beaten eggs, and crushed chips in three separate shallow bowls. Dredge tomato slices in flour; dip in egg, shaking off excess. Dredge in crushed chips until coated. Fry tomatoes, in batches, in hot oil until golden brown and crunchy, about 2 minutes per side. Serve immediately with Tasso Tartar Sauce.

FRIED GREEN TOMATOES

Dipped first in buttermilk then in a flour-and-cornmeal coating before frying, these tomatoes come out hot, crisp, and juicy.

ACTIVE 15 MIN. - TOTAL 35 MIN.
SERVES 6 TO 8

- 4 large green tomatoes
- 1½ cups buttermilk
- 1 Tbsp. table salt
- 1 tsp. black pepper
- 1 cup all-purpose flour
- 1 cup self-rising cornmeal
- 3 cups vegetable oil
- Table salt, to taste

1. Cut tomatoes into ¼- to ⅓-inch slices; place in a shallow dish. Pour buttermilk over tomatoes. Sprinkle with salt and pepper.

2. Combine flour and cornmeal in a shallow dish or pie plate. Dredge tomato slices in flour mixture.

3. Fry tomatoes, in batches, in hot oil in a large cast-iron skillet over medium heat 3 minutes on each side or until golden. Drain tomatoes on paper towels. Sprinkle with salt to taste.

OYSTER DRESSING

The key to this oyster dressing is the cornbread. It's prepared in a hot skillet coated with bacon drippings.

ACTIVE 30 MIN. - TOTAL 2 HOURS, 5 MIN., INCLUDING CORNBREAD
SERVES 8

- 2 medium onions, diced
- 4 celery ribs, diced
- 2 red bell peppers, diced
- 2 green bell peppers, diced
- 4 garlic cloves, minced
- ¼ cup olive oil
- 2 (8-oz.) containers fresh oysters, drained and coarsely chopped
- ⅔ cup dry white wine
- ½ cup chicken broth
- ¼ cup butter
- 3 bay leaves
- 2 Tbsp. fresh thyme leaves
- 2 tsp. freshly ground black pepper
- 1 tsp. table salt
- 1 tsp. crushed dried red pepper
- 1 tsp. hot pepper sauce
- 2 large eggs
- ½ cup grated Parmesan cheese
  Sizzlin' Skillet Cornbread, crumbled (recipe follows)

1. Preheat oven to 375°F. Cook first 5 ingredients in hot oil in a large skillet over medium, stirring often, until tender and lightly browned, 15 to 20 minutes. Stir in oysters and next 9 ingredients; cook until edges of oysters begin to curl, 3 to 4 minutes. Remove from heat; let stand 10 minutes. Remove and discard bay leaves.

2. Place mixture in a large bowl; stir in eggs and cheese. Fold in cornbread. Place mixture in a lightly greased 13- x 9-inch baking dish.

3. Bake in preheated oven until lightly browned, 40 to 45 minutes.

SIZZLIN' SKILLET CORNBREAD

ACTIVE 15 MIN. - TOTAL 50 MIN.
SERVES 6

- 2 Tbsp. bacon drippings
- 2 cups buttermilk
- 1 large egg
- 1¾ cups self-rising cornmeal mix

1. Preheat oven to 450°F. Coat bottom and sides of a 10-inch cast-iron skillet with bacon drippings; heat in oven 10 minutes.

2. Whisk together remaining ingredients; pour batter into hot skillet.

3. Bake in preheated oven until lightly browned, about 15 minutes. Invert onto a wire rack. Cool completely (about 30 minutes).

- -

OKRA AND CHICKPEAS IN FRESH TOMATO SAUCE

Serve this colorful medley as a side or boldly flavored vegetarian main dish.

ACTIVE 15 MIN. - TOTAL 30 MIN.
SERVES 6

- 2 Tbsp. extra-virgin olive oil, plus more for serving
- 1 medium-size yellow onion, chopped (about 1¾ cups)
- 2 garlic cloves, very finely chopped
- 5 garden-ripe tomatoes, cored and chopped (about 4 cups)
- 1 Tbsp. ground cumin
- 1 Tbsp. harissa or Sriracha chili sauce
- 1 tsp. lemon zest plus 1 Tbsp. fresh lemon juice
- 1 lb. fresh okra, stems trimmed, cut into ½-inch slices
- 1½ tsp. kosher salt, divided
- ¾ tsp. black pepper, divided
- 1 (15.5-oz.) can chickpeas, drained and rinsed
- ¼ cup chopped fresh flat-leaf parsley

1. Heat oil in a large skillet over medium-low. Add yellow onion; cook, stirring often, until soft and translucent, about 6 minutes. Add garlic; cook, stirring often, until fragrant, 45 to 60 seconds. Add tomatoes, cumin, harissa, lemon zest, and lemon juice, and cook, stirring once or twice, until tomatoes start to break down, about 5 minutes.

2. Add okra, 1 teaspoon of the salt, and ½ teaspoon of the black pepper. Reduce heat to low, and cover skillet. Cook, stirring occasionally, just until okra is just tender, about 10 minutes.

3. Add chickpeas and stir to combine. Cover and cook just until chickpeas are heated through, about 3 minutes. Stir in chopped parsley and remaining ½ teaspoon salt and ¼ teaspoon pepper. Serve immediately.

OKRA AND CHICKPEAS IN
FRESH TOMATO SAUCE

PIMIENTO CHEESE
CREAMED SPINACH

PIMIENTO CHEESE CREAMED SPINACH

Creamed spinach takes a trip to the South when mixed with pimientos and sharp cheddar cheese.

ACTIVE 30 MIN. - TOTAL 1 HOUR, 20 MIN.
SERVES 8

- 3 (10-oz.) pkg. frozen chopped spinach, thawed
- 2 Tbsp. unsalted butter
- ½ medium yellow onion, finely chopped
- 3 garlic cloves, minced
- 4 oz. cream cheese, cut into small pieces and softened
- 1 cup milk
- 1 (8-oz.) container sour cream
- ¼ cup mayonnaise
- 1 Tbsp. Dijon mustard
- 1 large egg, lightly beaten
- 1 (4-oz.) jar diced pimiento, drained and rinsed
- 8 oz. sharp cheddar cheese, shredded (2 cups), divided
- 1½ tsp. kosher salt
- ½ tsp. freshly ground black pepper
- ½ cup panko (Japanese breadcrumbs)
- 2 Tbsp. unsalted butter, melted

1. Preheat oven to 350°F. Drain spinach well, pressing between paper towels. Melt 2 tablespoons butter in a large Dutch oven over medium. Add onion, and cook until tender, about 5 minutes. Add garlic, and cook 1 minute; remove from heat.

2. Stir cream cheese into onion mixture until melted and well blended. Stir in spinach, milk, and next 3 ingredients. Stir together egg, pimiento, and 1½ cups cheese; stir egg mixture into spinach mixture. Spoon mixture into a 2-quart baking dish coated with cooking spray; sprinkle with salt and pepper.

3. Toss together panko, 2 tablespoons melted butter, and remaining ½ cup cheddar cheese; sprinkle over spinach mixture.

4. Bake in preheated oven until bubbly and golden, about 50 minutes.

CHICKEN-AND-FRUIT SALAD

ACTIVE 40 MIN. - TOTAL 8 HOURS, 50 MIN.
SERVES 6

- ¾ cup orange marmalade
- 3 Tbsp. soy sauce
- 3 Tbsp. lemon juice
- 1½ Tbsp. chopped fresh ginger
- 6 boneless, skinless chicken breast halves
- 1 cored fresh pineapple
- 1 large jicama
- 2 cups fresh strawberry halves
- 1 cup fresh raspberries
  Orange-Raspberry Vinaigrette (recipe follows)
  Lettuce leaves

1. Combine first 4 ingredients; remove and chill ¼ cup marmalade mixture.

2. Place chicken in a shallow dish or heavy-duty zip-top plastic bag; pour remaining marmalade mixture over chicken. Cover or seal; chill 8 hours, turning occasionally.

3. Cut pineapple into spears. Peel jicama, if desired, and cut into ½-inch slices.

4. Place pineapple and jicama in a shallow dish or heavy-duty zip-top plastic bag; pour ¼ cup reserved marmalade mixture over pineapple mixture. Cover or seal; chill 8 hours.

5. Remove chicken from marinade, discarding marinade; drain pineapple mixture. Coat chicken and pineapple mixture with cooking spray.

6. Grill chicken, covered with grill lid, over medium-high (350°F to 400°F) 5 to 6 minutes on each side or until done. Grill pineapple and jicama 2 to 3 minutes on each side.

7. Cut chicken and jicama into thin strips; cut pineapple into bite-size pieces. Combine chicken, jicama, pineapple, strawberry halves, and raspberries; toss gently with Orange-Raspberry Vinaigrette. Serve on lettuce leaves.

ORANGE-RASPBERRY VINAIGRETTE

ACTIVE 5 MIN. - TOTAL 5 MIN.
MAKES 1 CUP

Whisk together ½ cup **orange marmalade**, ¼ cup **raspberry vinegar**, 1 medium **jalapeño**, seeded and minced, 2 Tbsp. finely chopped fresh **cilantro**, and 2 Tbsp. **olive oil** in a small bowl.

HEARTY BAKED BEANS

ACTIVE 20 MIN. · TOTAL 3 HOURS, 20 MIN.
SERVES 6 TO 8

- 3 bacon slices, chopped
- 1 large onion, chopped
- 2 garlic cloves, minced
- 3 (16-oz.) cans pinto beans, drained
- 1/3 cup firmly packed brown sugar
- 1/3 cup molasses
- 1/3 cup ketchup
- 2½ Tbsp. prepared mustard
- ½ medium green bell pepper, chopped

1. Cook bacon in a large skillet over medium until crisp, 8 to 10 minutes; drain bacon on paper towels, reserving drippings in pan.

2. Cook onion and garlic in reserved drippings, stirring often, until tender, 6 to 8 minutes.

3. Combine bacon, onion mixture, beans, and remaining ingredients in a 3½- or 4-quart slow cooker.

4. Cover and cook on HIGH for 2½ to 3 hours or on LOW for 5 to 6 hours.

- -

BING CHERRY SALAD

ACTIVE 15 MIN. · TOTAL 10 HOURS, INCLUDING CHILLING
SERVES 8

- 1 (15-oz.) can Bing cherries (dark sweet pitted cherries)
- 2 (8-oz.) cans crushed pineapple in juice
- 1 (6-oz.) pkg. cherry-flavor gelatin
- 1 cup cold water
  Mayonnaise (optional)
  Poppy seeds, arugula leaves, for garnish

1. Drain cherries and pineapple, reserving 1½ cups juice in a saucepan. (If necessary, add water to equal 1½ cups.) Bring juice mixture to a boil over medium; stir in gelatin; cook, stirring constantly, 2 minutes or until gelatin dissolves. Remove from heat and stir in 1 cup cold water. Chill until consistency of unbeaten egg whites (about 1½ hours).

2. Gently stir in drained cherries and pineapple. Pour mixture into an 8-inch square baking dish or 8 (2/3-cup) molds. Cover and chill 8 hours or until firm. Dollop with mayonnaise, and garnish, if desired.

WILD RICE WITH BACON AND FENNEL

ACTIVE 40 MIN. · TOTAL 1 HOUR, 5 MIN.
SERVES 8

- 1 1/3 cups uncooked wild rice
- 4 bacon slices
- 1 large fennel bulb, thinly sliced
- 1 large onion, cut into thin wedges
- 2 garlic cloves, minced
- ½ cup reduced-sodium fat-free chicken broth
- 1/3 cup golden raisins
- ¼ tsp. table salt
- 1/8 tsp. freshly ground black pepper
- ¼ cup chopped fresh fennel fronds or flat-leaf parsley
- 1 Tbsp. white wine vinegar
- ½ cup chopped toasted walnuts

1. Cook wild rice according to package directions; drain.

2. Meanwhile, cook bacon in a large nonstick skillet over medium until crisp, 8 to 10 minutes; drain on paper towels, reserving 1 tablespoon drippings in skillet. Chop bacon.

3. Cook fennel and onion in hot drippings over medium-high, stirring often, until softened, about 5 minutes. Add garlic; cook 1 minute. Add broth and next 3 ingredients; bring to a boil. Reduce heat to medium-low; cover and simmer until tender, about 8 minutes. Stir in rice and bacon; cook, stirring often, 3 minutes.

4. Transfer to a large serving bowl. Stir in fennel fronds and vinegar. Stir in walnuts just before serving.

WILD RICE WITH
BACON AND FENNEL

ROASTED PUMPKIN
AND BABY KALE
SALAD

ROASTED PUMPKIN-AND-BABY KALE SALAD

ACTIVE 15 MIN. - TOTAL 40 MIN.
SERVES 4

- 1 (3-lb.) sugar pumpkin, cut into 12 (1-inch) wedges
- 1 small red onion, cut into 8 wedges
- 4 fresh thyme sprigs
- 2 fresh rosemary sprigs
- 6 Tbsp. extra-virgin olive oil, divided
- 2 Tbsp. honey, divided
- 1¾ tsp. kosher salt, divided
- 1 tsp. black pepper, divided
- 1 Tbsp. whole-grain Dijon mustard
- 1 Tbsp. apple cider vinegar
- 4 oz. baby kale greens (about 4 cups)
- ⅓ cup pomegranate arils
- ⅓ cup coarsely chopped toasted pecans
- 3 oz. goat cheese, crumbled (about ¾ cup)

1. Preheat oven to 450°F. Combine pumpkin, red onion, thyme, rosemary, 2 tablespoons of the olive oil, and 1 tablespoon of the honey in a large bowl; toss to coat. Divide vegetables evenly between two rimmed baking sheets coated with cooking spray, and sprinkle with 1 teaspoon of the salt and ¾ teaspoon of the pepper. Roast in preheated oven until browned and tender, about 20 minutes (do not stir). Cool 10 minutes.

2. Whisk together Dijon, vinegar, and remaining 4 tablespoons oil, 1 tablespoon honey, ¾ teaspoon salt, and ¼ teaspoon pepper in a small bowl. Toss kale with 1 tablespoon of the dressing, and arrange on a serving platter with pumpkin mixture. Sprinkle with pomegranate arils, pecans, and goat cheese; drizzle with remaining dressing.

Note: Change things up by using butternut squash for the pumpkin and spicy arugula leaves for the kale.

BABY BLUE SALAD

This recipe is from chef Franklin Biggs, and it is served at his restaurant in Homewood, Alabama.

ACTIVE 10 MIN. - TOTAL 10 MIN.
SERVES 6

- ¾ lb. mixed salad greens
  Balsamic Vinaigrette (recipe follows)
- 4 oz. blue cheese, crumbled
- 2 oranges, peeled and cut into thin slices
- 1 pint strawberries, quartered
  Sweet-and-Spicy Pecans (recipe follows)

Toss greens with Balsamic Vinaigrette and crumbled blue cheese. Place on six individual plates. Arrange orange slices over greens; sprinkle with strawberries and top with Sweet-and-Spicy Pecans.

BALSAMIC VINAIGRETTE

ACTIVE 5 MIN. - TOTAL 5 MIN.
MAKES 1⅔ CUPS

- ½ cup balsamic vinegar
- 3 Tbsp. Dijon mustard
- 3 Tbsp. honey
- 2 large garlic cloves, minced
- 2 small shallots, minced
- ¼ tsp. table salt
- ¼ tsp. black pepper
- 1 cup olive oil

Whisk together first 7 ingredients until blended. Gradually whisk in olive oil.

SWEET-AND-SPICY PECANS

ACTIVE 10 MIN. - TOTAL 30 MIN.
MAKES 1 CUP

- ¼ cup plus 2 Tbsp. granulated sugar, divided
- 1 cup warm water
- 1 cup pecan halves
- 1 Tbsp. chili powder
- ¼ tsp. cayenne pepper

Preheat oven to 350°F. Stir together ¼ cup sugar and the warm water in a bowl until sugar dissolves. Add pecans; soak 10 minutes. Drain; discard liquid. Combine 2 Tbsp. sugar, chili powder, and cayenne pepper. Add pecans; toss to coat. Arrange pecans in a single layer on a lightly greased baking sheet. Bake 10 minutes or until golden brown, stirring once.

273

HARVEST SALAD

ACTIVE 20 MIN. - TOTAL 50 MIN.
SERVES 6 TO 8

- 1 large butternut squash
- 2 Tbsp. olive oil
- 2 Tbsp. honey
- 1 tsp. kosher salt
- ½ tsp. freshly ground black pepper
- 1 (8-oz.) bottle poppy-seed dressing
- ¼ cup fresh or frozen cranberries
- 2 (4-oz.) pkg. mixed salad greens
- 4 oz. goat cheese, crumbled
- ¾ cup lightly salted roasted pecan halves
- 6 bacon slices, cooked and crumbled

1. Preheat oven to 400°F. Peel and seed butternut squash; cut into ¾-inch cubes. Toss together squash, olive oil, and next 3 ingredients in a large bowl; place in a single layer in a 15- x 10-inch pan lined with aluminum foil and lightly greased. Bake 20 to 25 minutes or until squash is tender and begins to brown, stirring once after 10 minutes. Remove from oven; cool in pan 10 minutes.

2. Meanwhile, pulse poppy-seed dressing and cranberries in a blender 3 to 4 times or until cranberries are coarsely chopped.

3. Toss together squash, salad greens, and next 3 ingredients on a large platter. Serve with dressing mixture.

LETTUCE WEDGE SALAD

What's old is new again—and with a certain tasty charm. Who can resist a simple iceberg wedge, especially when it's icy cold?

ACTIVE 30 MIN. - TOTAL 45 MIN.
SERVES 4

- 4 to 6 bacon slices
- 1 medium onion, sliced
- 1 cup buttermilk
- ½ cup sour cream
- 1 (1-oz.) envelope Ranch-style dressing mix
- ¼ cup chopped fresh basil
- 2 garlic cloves
- 1 large head iceberg lettuce, cut into 4 wedges
  Shredded fresh basil (optional)

1. Cook bacon in a large skillet over medium until crisp, 8 to 10 minutes; remove bacon, and drain on paper towels, reserving 1 tablespoon drippings in skillet. Crumble bacon, and set aside.

2. Cook onion in hot drippings in skillet over medium until tender and lightly browned, 10 minutes. Remove from heat; cool.

3. Process onion, buttermilk, and next 4 ingredients in a blender or food processor until smooth, stopping to scrape down sides.

4. Top each lettuce wedge with dressing; sprinkle with bacon, and top with shredded basil, if desired.

Note: Make the dressing ahead, if desired, and store in the refrigerator. Chilled dressing will have a thicker consistency.

BUTTERY CHIVE-
AND-MUSTARD DROP
BISCUITS

BUTTERY CHIVE-AND-MUSTARD DROP BISCUITS

ACTIVE 15 MIN. - TOTAL 35 MIN.
MAKES 24 BISCUITS

- 3 cups all-purpose flour
- 2 oz. Parmesan cheese, grated on smallest holes of box grater (about ½ cup)
- ¼ cup sliced fresh chives, plus more for garnish
- 1 Tbsp. baking powder
- 1 tsp. black pepper
- ¾ tsp. kosher salt
- ¾ tsp. garlic powder
- ¾ tsp. baking soda
- 1¾ cups whole buttermilk
- 3 Tbsp. whole-grain mustard
- ¾ cup unsalted butter, frozen, plus melted butter for serving

1. Preheat oven to 475°F. Stir together first 8 ingredients in a large bowl. Whisk together buttermilk and mustard in a small bowl. Grate frozen butter into flour mixture using the large holes of a box grater; stir until well coated. Add buttermilk mixture; stir until just combined.

2. Drop batter in 2½- to 3-tablespoonful rounds onto two baking sheets lined with parchment paper, leaving 3 inches between rounds.

3. Bake in preheated oven until biscuits are golden brown, 14 to 18 minutes, rotating baking sheets between top and bottom racks halfway through baking time. Brush biscuits with melted butter; garnish with sliced chives. Serve warm.

BEST EVER BUTTERMILK BISCUITS

ACTIVE 15 MIN. - TOTAL 30 MIN.
MAKES 16 BISCUITS

- 2 cups all-purpose flour
- 2 tsp. baking powder
- ¼ tsp. baking soda
- ¼ tsp. table salt
- ¼ cup butter or margarine
- 1 cup nonfat buttermilk

1. Preheat oven to 400°F. Combine first 4 ingredients in a large bowl.

2. Cut butter into flour mixture with a fork or pastry blender until crumbly; add buttermilk, stirring just until dry ingredients are moistened.

3. Turn dough out onto a lightly floured surface; knead 2 or 3 times.

4. Pat or roll to ½-inch thickness; cut with a 1½-inch round cutter, and place on a baking sheet.

5. Bake in preheated oven until biscuits are golden, about 15 minutes.

BUTTERY GARLIC BREAD

ACTIVE 10 MIN. - TOTAL 15 MIN.
MAKES 8 SLICES

- ½ cup butter or margarine
- 4 garlic cloves, pressed
- ½ tsp. table salt
- 1 (16-oz.) Italian bread loaf
- 1½ tsp. Italian seasoning
- ¼ cup freshly grated Parmesan cheese

1. Melt butter in a skillet over medium-high; add garlic and salt; cook, stirring, 2 minutes.

2. Cut bread into 1½-inch slices, and dip into butter mixture, coating both sides. Place on a baking sheet.

3. Stir together Italian seasoning and Parmesan cheese; sprinkle on one side of each bread slice.

4. Broil 5 inches from heat until cheese melts, about 4 minutes.

CHEDDAR-CARAMELIZED ONION BREAD

ACTIVE 35 MIN. · TOTAL 1 HOUR, 30 MIN.
SERVES 8

½ cup plus 2 Tbsp. unsalted butter, divided
2 tsp. caraway seeds
1 Tbsp. extra-virgin olive oil
1 large red onion, thinly sliced
1 tsp. kosher salt, divided
1 cup almond flour
1 cup all-purpose flour
1 tsp. baking powder
¼ tsp. baking soda
½ cup heavy cream
1 large egg
2 tsp. honey
4 oz. cheddar cheese, shredded (1 cup)
Whipped Sweet Potato Butter (recipe follows)
Chopped fresh thyme (optional)

1. Place ½ cup of the butter in freezer until solid, at least 30 minutes.

2. Preheat oven to 350°F. Heat a medium skillet over medium. Add caraway seeds, and cook, stirring constantly, until lightly toasted, about 1 minute. Remove seeds from skillet and set aside.

3. Add oil to skillet. Heat over medium-high. Add onion, and cook, stirring often, until starting to soften, about 3 minutes. Reduce heat to medium-low; cook, stirring occasionally, until tender and browned, about 15 minutes. Season with ¼ teaspoon of the salt. Remove onion from skillet, and let cool 10 minutes.

4. Place a 9-inch cast-iron skillet in preheated oven. Stir together flours, baking powder, baking soda, ½ teaspoon of the salt, and toasted caraway seeds in a medium bowl. Whisk together cream, egg, and honey in a separate bowl.

5. Remove butter from freezer. Using the large holes on a box grater, grate frozen butter into coarse shreds. Add shredded butter to flour mixture, stirring to combine. Add cream mixture, cheese, and caramelized onions to flour mixture; stir just until dough comes together. Turn dough out onto a lightly floured surface; pat into an 8-inch circle. Add remaining 2 tablespoons butter to hot cast-iron skillet, swirling to melt. Gently place dough in skillet; sprinkle with remaining ¼ teaspoon salt.

6. Bake in preheated oven until sides and top are golden brown, 20 to 25 minutes. Remove from oven and let cool in skillet 5 minutes. Remove bread from skillet and place on a wire rack to cool to room temperature, about 30 minutes. Sprinkle with thyme, if desired; serve with Whipped Sweet Potato Butter.

WHIPPED SWEET POTATO BUTTER

ACTIVE 15 MIN. · TOTAL 1 HOUR, 5 MIN.
SERVES 20

1 lb. sweet potatoes, peeled and cut into 2-inch chunks
2 tsp. white vinegar
2½ tsp. kosher salt, divided
1 cup unsalted butter, softened
¼ cup honey
¾ tsp. ground cinnamon
¼ tsp. black pepper

1. Place potatoes in a medium saucepan and cover with cold water by 1 inch. Add vinegar and 2 teaspoons of the salt. Bring to a boil over high. Reduce heat to medium and cook until tender, about 20 minutes.

2. Drain potatoes, transfer to a large bowl, and let cool, about 20 minutes. Add butter, honey, cinnamon, pepper, and remaining ½ teaspoon salt; beat with an electric mixer until smooth, about 45 seconds. Chill Whipped Sweet Potato Butter until ready to serve.

CORNBREAD FOCACCIA

A sprinkling of yeast is stirred into the batter—but there's no rise time or kneading.

ACTIVE 15 MIN. · TOTAL 45 MIN.
SERVES 8 TO 10

- 2 cups self-rising white cornmeal mix
- 2 cups buttermilk
- ½ cup all-purpose flour
- 1 (¼-oz.) envelope rapid-rise yeast
- 2 large eggs, lightly beaten
- ¼ cup butter, melted
- 2 Tbsp. granulated sugar
- 1 cup crumbled feta cheese
- 1 cup coarsely chopped black olives
- ¾ cup grape tomatoes, cut in half
- 1 Tbsp. coarsely chopped fresh rosemary

Preheat oven to 375°F. Heat a 12-inch cast-iron skillet coated with cooking spray in oven 5 minutes. Stir together cornmeal mix and next 6 ingredients just until moistened; pour into hot skillet. Sprinkle with feta cheese, olives, tomatoes, and rosemary. Bake until golden brown, about 30 minutes.

- -

CHEESE BREADSTICKS

ACTIVE 20 MIN. · TOTAL 1 HOUR, 25 MIN.
SERVES 12

- 1 pkg. dry active yeast (about 2¼ tsp.)
- ¾ cup warm fat-free milk (100°F to 110°F)
- 2 cups all-purpose flour, divided
- 3 oz. 2% reduced-fat sharp cheddar cheese, finely shredded (¾ cup)
- 2 Tbsp. olive oil
- 1 tsp. table salt
- 1 Tbsp. grated Parmesan cheese

1. Combine yeast and milk in a large bowl. Let stand 5 minutes.

2. Lightly spoon flour into dry measuring cups; level with a knife. Gradually stir 1¾ cups flour and next 3 ingredients into yeast mixture, using a wooden spoon. Turn dough out onto work surface and knead dough 5 minutes or until smooth and elastic, adding enough remaining flour to prevent dough from sticking to hands.

3. Coat a medium bowl with cooking spray. Place dough in bowl, turning to coat top. Cover and let rise in a warm place (85°F), free from drafts, until doubled in size, about 35 minutes. (Press two fingers into dough. If indentation remains, the dough has risen enough.)

4. Preheat oven to 400°F.

5. Punch dough down; divide into 12 equal portions. Roll each portion into a 10-inch rope about ½ inch in diameter. Place ropes on a large baking sheet coated with cooking spray. Coat ropes with cooking spray; sprinkle with Parmesan cheese.

6. Bake in preheated oven until golden, about 15 minutes.

- -

OLD-FASHIONED SKILLET CORNBREAD

ACTIVE 10 MIN. · TOTAL 35 MIN.
SERVES 25 TO 30

- 6 cups cornmeal
- 3 cups all-purpose flour
- 1 Tbsp. baking powder
- 1½ tsp. table salt
- 6 cups buttermilk
- ¼ cup plus 2 Tbsp. mayonnaise
- 3 eggs, beaten

1. Preheat oven to 425°F. Combine first 4 ingredients in a large bowl; mix well. Add remaining ingredients, mixing well.

2. Heat three well-greased 9-inch cast-iron skillets in a preheated oven until very hot, about 3 minutes. Divide batter among three skillets. Bake until golden brown, about 25 minutes.

CORNBREAD
FOCACCIA

CORNBREAD WITH
LEMON-THYME
BUTTER

CORNBREAD WITH LEMON-THYME BUTTER

Classic Southern cornbread is even better slathered with a bright citrus-herb compound butter.

ACTIVE 15 MIN. - TOTAL 1 HOUR
SERVES 8

- 3 Tbsp. canola oil
- 1 cup stone-ground cornmeal
- 1 cup all-purpose flour
- 2 Tbsp. granulated sugar
- 2 Tbsp. baking powder
- 1 tsp. kosher salt
- 2 large eggs
- 1¼ cups whole milk
- 2 Tbsp. unsalted butter, melted
  Lemon-Thyme Butter (recipe follows)

1. Preheat oven to 425°F. Grease a 10-inch cast-iron skillet with oil. Place skillet in preheated oven until hot, about 5 minutes.

2. Combine next 5 ingredients in a large bowl. Whisk together eggs, milk, and butter in a separate bowl; add to cornmeal mixture, stirring just until combined. Carefully pour batter into hot skillet.

3. Bake in preheated oven until golden brown, 15 to 20 minutes. Cool to room temperature in skillet, about 30 minutes. Serve with Lemon-Thyme Butter.

LEMON-THYME BUTTER

ACTIVE 5 MIN. - TOTAL 5 MIN.
MAKES ABOUT 1 CUP

- 1 cup unsalted butter, softened
- 1½ tsp. lemon zest plus 1 Tbsp. lemon juice
- 1 tsp. fresh thyme leaves
- 1 tsp. kosher salt

Stir together all ingredients in a small bowl.

SOUR CREAM BISCUITS

ACTIVE 10 MIN. - TOTAL 20 MIN.
MAKES 14 BISCUITS

- ¼ cup shortening
- 2 cups self-rising flour
- 1 (8-oz.) container sour cream

1. Preheat oven to 475°F. Cut shortening into flour with a pastry blender or fork until crumbly. Add sour cream, stirring just until dry ingredients are moistened.

2. Turn dough out onto a lightly floured surface, and knead lightly 3 or 4 times. Pat or roll dough to ½-inch thickness; cut with a 2-inch round cutter, and place biscuits on a lightly greased baking sheet.

3. Bake in preheated oven until golden brown, 10 to 12 minutes.

CHEESE GARLIC BISCUITS

ACTIVE 10 MIN. - TOTAL 20 MIN.
MAKES 10 TO 12 BISCUITS

- 2 cups all-purpose baking mix
- ⅔ cup milk
- ½ cup (2 oz.) shredded cheddar cheese
- ¼ cup butter, melted
- ¼ tsp. garlic powder

1. Preheat oven to 450°F. Stir together first 3 ingredients until soft dough forms. Stir vigorously 30 seconds. Drop by tablespoonfuls onto an ungreased baking sheet.

2. Bake in preheated oven until golden, 8 to 10 minutes.

3. Stir together butter and garlic powder in a small bowl; brush over warm biscuits.

PARMESAN BREADSTICKS

ACTIVE 15 MIN. · TOTAL 1 HOUR, 40 MIN.

MAKES 1 DOZEN BREADSTICKS

1	pkg. active dry yeast
1⅓	cups warm water (105°F to 115°F)
¼	cup extra-virgin olive oil
1	Tbsp. honey
1	tsp. table salt
4¼	cups all-purpose flour, divided
1½	oz. Parmesan cheese, freshly grated (½ cup)
2	tsp. freshly ground black pepper
2	Tbsp. all-purpose flour
1	egg white, lightly beaten
2	tsp. kosher salt

1. Combine yeast and warm water in a 2-cup liquid measuring cup; let stand 5 minutes. Combine yeast mixture, olive oil, honey, and 1 teaspoon salt in a large mixing bowl; beat at medium speed with an electric mixer until well blended. Add 2 cups flour; beat 2 minutes at medium speed. Stir in Parmesan cheese and pepper. Gradually stir in enough of the remaining 2¼ cups flour to make a soft dough.

2. Turn dough out onto lightly floured surface and knead until smooth and elastic (about 8 to 10 minutes). Place dough in a large well-greased bowl, turning to grease' top. Cover and let rise in a warm place (85°F), free from drafts, 1 hour or until doubled in bulk.

3. Preheat oven to 425°F. Punch dough down and divide into 12 equal portions; roll each portion into a 10-inch rope. Place ropes 1 inch apart on a large greased baking sheet. Brush breadsticks with egg white, and sprinkle evenly with kosher salt.

4. Bake in preheated oven until golden brown, 10 to 12 minutes. Remove from baking sheet, and let cool on a wire rack.

PIMIENTO CHEESE BISCUITS

Any Southerner would be proud to have a bowl of these piping-hot cheese biscuits on the breakfast table.

ACTIVE 20 MIN. · TOTAL 45 MIN.

MAKES 30 BISCUITS

4	oz. sharp cheddar cheese, shredded (1 cup)
2¼	cups self-rising soft-wheat flour
½	cup cold butter, cut into ¼-inch-thick slices
1	cup buttermilk
1	(4-oz.) jar diced pimiento, drained
	Self-rising soft-wheat flour
2	Tbsp. melted butter

1. Combine shredded cheese and 2¼ cups flour in a large bowl.

2. Sprinkle butter slices over flour-cheese mixture; toss gently. Cut butter into flour with a pastry blender until crumbly and mixture resembles small peas. Cover and chill 10 minutes.

3. Combine buttermilk and diced pimiento; add buttermilk mixture to flour mixture, stirring just until dry ingredients are moistened.

4. Turn dough out onto a lightly floured surface, and knead 3 or 4 times, gradually adding additional flour as needed. With floured hands, press or pat dough into a ¾-inch-thick rectangle (about 9 x 5 inches). Sprinkle top of dough with additional flour. Fold dough over onto itself in three sections, starting with one short end. (Fold dough rectangle as if folding a letter-size piece of paper.) Repeat twice, beginning with pressing into a ¾-inch-thick dough rectangle (about 9 x 5 inches).

5. Preheat oven to 450°F. Press or pat dough to ½-inch thickness on a lightly floured surface. Cut dough with a 2-inch round cutter and place, side by side, on a parchment paper-lined or lightly greased 15- x 10-inch pan. (Dough rounds should touch.)

6. Bake in preheated oven until lightly browned, 13 to 15 minutes. Remove from oven. Brush with 2 tablespoons melted butter.

LEMON-COCONUT CHESS
BARS, PAGE 292

COOKIES, BARS & CANDY

DEEP-DISH SKILLET COOKIE

ACTIVE 15 MIN. · TOTAL 1 HOUR, 20 MIN.
SERVES 8 TO 10

- 1 cup packed light brown sugar
- ½ cup granulated sugar
- ½ cup (4 oz.) salted butter, softened
- 1 large egg
- 3 Tbsp. whole milk
- 1½ tsp. vanilla extract
- 2 cups all-purpose flour
- 1 tsp. baking soda
- ¼ tsp. table salt
- 1½ cups semisweet chocolate chips, divided

1. Preheat oven to 325°F. Lightly coat a 10-inch cast-iron skillet with cooking spray. Beat brown sugar, granulated sugar, and butter with a heavy-duty electric stand mixer on medium speed until light and fluffy. Add egg, milk, and vanilla, beating until blended.

2. Whisk together flour, baking soda, and salt in a bowl. Add to butter mixture gradually, beating on low speed until combined.

3. Add 1 cup of the chocolate chips; beat until combined.

4. Spread mixture evenly in prepared skillet. Top with remaining ½ cup chocolate chips.

5. Bake in preheated oven until golden and set, about 50 minutes. Let stand 15 minutes; cut into wedges. Serve with vanilla ice cream.

Pecan Praline: Omit chocolate chips. Prepare recipe as directed, stirring in ½ cup chopped pecans and ½ cup toffee bits in Step 3, and topping mixture with ¾ cup pecan halves and 3 tablespoons jarred caramel sauce in Step 4. Sprinkle with sea salt just before serving.

Mississippi Mud: Increase milk to 5 tablespoons. Prepare recipe as directed, whisking 3 tablespoons unsweetened cocoa into flour mixture in Step 2, and topping cookie with ¼ cup miniature marshmallows during the last 30 minutes of baking in Step 5.

Strawberry Shortcake: Increase milk to ¼ cup. Substitute white chocolate chips for semisweet chocolate chips. Prepare recipe as directed, beating ¾ cup chopped frozen pound cake into mixture with white chocolate chips in Step 3. Top mixture with ¼ cup chopped frozen pound cake in Step 4. Serve cookie wedges with whipped cream and sliced strawberries.

Grasshopper: Omit milk and chocolate chips. Prepare recipe as directed, beating 3 tablespoons bourbon into mixture with egg and vanilla in Step 1 and stirring in 1 cup halved thin crème de menthe chocolate mints in Step 3. Top mixture with ¼ cup halved thin crème de menthe chocolate mints in Step 4.

Hummingbird: Omit milk and vanilla extract. Substitute white chocolate chips for semisweet chocolate chips. Prepare recipe as directed, adding ¼ cup mashed banana and 1½ teaspoons coconut extract to butter mixture in Step 1, and ½ cup sweetened flaked coconut and ½ cup chopped dried pineapple in Step 3.

- -

CHOCOLATE CHIP COOKIES

Extra stir-ins are what make a classic chocolate chip cookie unique. Here, chunks of milk chocolate candy bar and oats enhance the dough.

ACTIVE 20 MIN. · TOTAL 40 MIN.
MAKES 84 COOKIES

- 1 cup butter, softened
- 1 cup granulated sugar
- 1 cup firmly packed brown sugar
- 2 large eggs
- 2 tsp. vanilla extract
- 2½ cups uncooked regular oats
- 2 cups all-purpose flour
- 1 tsp. baking powder
- ½ tsp. baking soda
- ½ tsp. table salt
- 1 (12-oz.) pkg. semisweet chocolate morsels
- 3 (1.55-oz.) milk chocolate candy bars, coarsely chopped
- 1½ cups coarsely chopped pecans

1. Preheat oven to 375°F. Beat butter with an electric mixer on medium speed until creamy; add sugars, beating well. Add eggs and vanilla, beating until blended.

2. Process oats in a blender or food processor until finely ground. Combine oats, flour, and next 3 ingredients. Gradually add to butter mixture, beating well after each addition.

3. Stir in chocolate morsels, chopped candy bars, and pecans.

4. Shape dough into 1½-inch balls, and place 2 inches apart on ungreased baking sheets.

5. Bake in preheated oven until lightly browned, 8 to 10 minutes or. Transfer to wire racks to cool.

PECAN
PRALINE

GRASSHOPPER

STRAWBERRY
SHORTCAKE

MISSISSIPPI
MUD

HUMMINGBIRD

FUDGY FLOURLESS
CHOCOLATE PECAN
COOKIES

FUDGY FLOURLESS CHOCOLATE–PECAN COOKIES

Believe it or not, these chewy, brownie-like cookies are gluten-free.

ACTIVE 15 MIN. - TOTAL 45 MIN.
MAKES 20 COOKIES

- 3 cups powdered sugar
- 2/3 cup unsweetened cocoa
- 1/4 tsp. table salt
- 3 large egg whites, at room temperature
- 2 tsp. vanilla extract
- 1 (4-oz.) semisweet chocolate bar, chopped
- 1 cup chopped toasted pecans

1. Preheat oven to 350°F. Sift together powdered sugar, cocoa, and salt in a large bowl.

2. Whisk egg whites until frothy. Stir egg whites and vanilla into powdered sugar mixture. (Batter will be very thick.) Stir in chopped chocolate and pecans until well combined.

3. Drop cookies 3 inches apart using a 1 1/2-inch cookie scoop (about 2 tablespoons) on a parchment paper-lined baking sheet lightly greased with cooking spray.

4. Bake in preheated oven until tops are shiny and cracked, 8 to 10 minutes. Cool on baking sheet 5 minutes; transfer to wire racks, to cool completely, about 15 minutes.

GIANT OATMEAL COOKIES

A big, soft oatmeal cookie with raisins plus a cold glass of milk make the ideal afternoon snack at any age.

ACTIVE 20 MIN. - TOTAL 50 MIN.
MAKES 20 COOKIES

- 1 cup butter, softened
- 1 cup granulated sugar
- 1 cup firmly packed brown sugar
- 2 large eggs
- 1 Tbsp. vanilla extract
- 2 cups all-purpose flour
- 1 tsp. baking soda
- 1/2 tsp. baking powder
- 1/2 tsp. table salt
- 1 1/2 cups uncooked quick-cooking oats
- 1 1/2 cups chopped pecans
- 1 cup raisins

1. Preheat oven to 350°F. Beat butter with an electric mixer on medium speed until creamy; gradually add sugars, beating well. Add eggs and vanilla; beat well.

2. Combine flour and next 3 ingredients; gradually add to butter mixture, beating well after each addition. Stir in oats, pecans, and raisins.

3. Drop dough by 1/3 cupfuls 3 inches apart onto parchment paper-lined baking sheets.

4. Bake in preheated oven just until set and lightly browned, 15 to 18 minutes. Cool slightly on baking sheets; transfer to wire racks to cool completely.

Note: To make 7 dozen regular-size oatmeal cookies, drop dough by heaping teaspoonfuls onto lightly greased baking sheets. Bake at 375°F until lightly browned, about 8 minutes.

HELLO DOLLY BARS

ACTIVE 15 MIN. · TOTAL 1 HOUR, 45 MIN.
MAKES 36 BARS

- 2 cups graham cracker crumbs
- ⅓ cup melted butter
- 3 Tbsp. granulated sugar
- 1 cup chopped pecans
- 1 cup semisweet chocolate morsels
- ⅔ cup sweetened flaked coconut
- 1 (14-oz.) can sweetened condensed milk

1. Preheat oven to 350°. Combine first 3 ingredients in a medium bowl. Press mixture onto bottom of a lightly greased 13- x 9-inch pan. Bake 8 minutes. Sprinkle next 3 ingredients over hot crust. Pour condensed milk over top. (Do not stir.)

2. Bake at 350° for 20 minutes or until lightly browned and edges are bubbly. Let cool 1 hour on a wire rack. Cut into bars.

PEACH MELBA SHORTBREAD BARS

ACTIVE 20 MIN. · TOTAL 2 HOURS, 20 MIN.
MAKES 24 BARS

- 2 cups all-purpose flour
- ½ cup granulated sugar
- ¼ tsp. table salt
- 1 cup cold butter
- 1 cup peach preserves
- 6 tsp. raspberry preserves
- ½ cup sliced almonds
  Sweetened whipped cream, for garnish

1. Preheat oven to 350°F. Combine flour, sugar, and salt in a medium bowl. Cut butter into flour mixture with a pastry blender or fork until crumbly. Reserve 1 cup flour mixture. Press remaining flour mixture onto bottom of a lightly greased (with cooking spray) 9-inch square pan.

2. Bake in preheated oven until lightly browned, 25 to 30 minutes.

3. Spread peach preserves over crust in pan. Dollop ¼ teaspoon raspberry preserves over peach preserves. Sprinkle reserved 1 cup flour mixture over preserves. Sprinkle with sliced almonds.

4. Bake in preheated oven until golden brown, 35 to 40 minutes. Cool in pan 1 hour on a wire rack. Cut into bars. Garnish with sweetened whipped cream.

LEMON-COCONUT CHESS BARS

Coconut milk adds a hint of tropical flavor to these delightfully tangy bars. For the smoothest filling, whisk together the dry ingredients, and then stir in the wet ingredients until smooth. This will prevent tiny lumps of flour from forming.

ACTIVE 15 MIN. · TOTAL 3 HOURS, 45 MIN.
MAKES 32 BARS

CRUST
- Baking spray with flour
- 2½ cups all-purpose flour
- ¾ cup unsifted powdered sugar
- ½ cup sweetened flaked coconut
- 1½ tsp. kosher salt
- 1 cup cold unsalted butter, cubed

FILLING
- 2 cups granulated sugar
- 2 Tbsp. plain yellow cornmeal
- 2 Tbsp. all-purpose flour
- ½ tsp. kosher salt
- 5 large eggs
- 1 large egg yolk
- 1¼ cups well-shaken and stirred coconut milk (from 1 [13½-oz.] can)
- ½ cup unsalted butter, melted
- 1 Tbsp. lemon zest plus ½ cup fresh juice (from 3 lemons)
- 1 tsp. vanilla extract

GARNISH
- Toasted shaved coconut

1. Prepare the Crust: Preheat oven to 350°F. Coat a 13- x 9-inch baking pan with baking spray with flour. Pulse next 4 ingredients in a food processor until combined, 5 or 6 times. Add cold butter; pulse until coarse crumbs form, 6 or 7 times. Firmly press into bottom of prepared pan. Bake until light golden brown, about 25 minutes. Cool slightly, about 10 minutes.

2. Prepare the Filling: Whisk together first 4 ingredients in a bowl. Add next 6 ingredients; stir until smooth. Pour over Crust.

3. Bake in preheated oven until set, about 25 minutes. Remove from oven; cool completely in pan, about 1½ hours. Chill 1 hour. Slice into 32 bars. Garnish with shaved coconut.

MISSISSIPPI MUD

The origin of this luscious dessert can be found both as a pie and as a cake. Either way, it is Southern decadence at its best and is featured here as a gooey brownie hunk.

ACTIVE 15 MIN. - TOTAL 45 MIN.
MAKES 24 BARS

- 1½ cups all-purpose flour
- 2 cups granulated sugar
- ½ cup unsweetened cocoa
- 2 tsp. baking powder
- ½ tsp. table salt
- 1 cup butter, melted
- 4 large eggs, lightly beaten
- 1 Tbsp. vanilla extract
- 1 cup chopped pecans
- 3 cups miniature marshmallows
- Chocolate Frosting (recipe follows)

1. Preheat oven to 350°. Combine first 5 ingredients in a large mixing bowl. Add butter, eggs, and vanilla, stirring until smooth. Stir in pecans. Pour batter into a greased and floured 13- x 9-inch pan.

2. Bake at 350° for 25 to 30 minutes or until a wooden pick inserted in center comes out clean. Immediately sprinkle marshmallows over top; return to oven, and bake 1 to 2 minutes. Remove from oven. Carefully spread Chocolate Frosting over marshmallows. Cool completely, and cut into squares.

Note: For a hint of coffee, stir 1 tablespoon instant coffee powder into brownie batter along with dry ingredients.

CHOCOLATE FROSTING

ACTIVE 5 MIN. - TOTAL 5 MIN.
MAKES 2½ CUPS

- ½ cup butter, melted
- ⅓ cup cocoa
- ⅓ cup evaporated milk
- 1 tsp. vanilla extract
- 1 (16-oz.) pkg. powdered sugar, sifted

Beat all ingredients with an electric mixer on medium speed until dry ingredients are moistened. Beat at high speed until frosting reaches spreading consistency.

PRALINE BARS

ACTIVE 20 MIN. - TOTAL 1 HOUR
MAKES 60 BARS

- 15 graham cracker sheets
- ¾ cup chopped pecans
- 1¾ cups firmly packed brown sugar
- 1 cup butter
- Parchment paper
- ½ cup semisweet chocolate morsels
- ½ cup white chocolate morsels

1. Preheat oven to 350°F. Separate each graham cracker sheet into 4 crackers; place in a lightly greased (with cooking spray) 15- x 10-inch pan. Sprinkle chopped pecans over graham crackers.

2. Bring brown sugar and butter to a boil in a saucepan over medium-high. Boil 2 minutes. Pour brown sugar mixture evenly over graham crackers in pan.

3. Bake in preheated oven 10 minutes. Immediately transfer graham crackers to parchment paper, and cool completely (about 30 minutes).

4. Microwave semisweet chocolate morsels in a microwave-safe bowl on HIGH 1 minute or until melted and smooth, stirring on 30-second intervals. Drizzle chocolate evenly over cooled bars. Repeat procedure with white chocolate morsels.

PUMPKIN-CHOCOLATE BROWNIES

ACTIVE 40 MIN. - TOTAL 4 HOURS, 5 MIN.
MAKES 24 BROWNIES

- 1¼ cups semisweet chocolate morsels
- 1 cup unsalted butter, cut into pieces, plus more for greasing pan
- 3 (1-oz.) unsweetened chocolate baking squares, chopped
- 3 large eggs
- 1 cup plus 2 Tbsp. granulated sugar
- 2 Tbsp. cold brewed coffee
- 1 Tbsp. vanilla extract
- ⅔ cup all-purpose flour
- 1½ tsp. baking powder
- 1 tsp. kosher salt, divided
- 1 (15-oz.) can pumpkin
- 3 large eggs
- ½ cup heavy cream
- ⅓ cup firmly packed light brown sugar
- 1½ tsp. pumpkin pie spice

1. Preheat oven to 350°F. Pour water to a depth of 1 inch in the bottom of a double boiler over medium; bring to a boil. Reduce heat, and simmer. Place first 3 ingredients in top of double boiler over simmering water. Cook, stirring occasionally, 5 to 6 minutes or until melted. Remove from heat; cool 10 minutes.

2. Whisk together 3 eggs, granulated sugar, and next 2 ingredients in a large bowl. Gradually whisk warm chocolate mixture into egg mixture; cool 10 minutes.

3. Grease a 13- x 9-inch baking pan with butter. Line bottom and sides of pan with parchment paper, allowing 2 to 3 inches to extend over sides. Grease (with butter) and flour parchment paper.

4. Sift flour, baking powder, and ½ teaspoon salt in a bowl. Whisk into chocolate mixture. Pour batter into prepared pan, reserving ⅔ cup.

5. Whisk together pumpkin, next 4 ingredients, and remaining ½ teaspoon salt; pour over brownie batter in pan. Top with reserved brownie batter, and swirl batter gently 3 times in one direction and 3 times in the opposite direction with a knife or the end of a wooden spoon.

6. Bake in preheated oven until a wooden pick inserted in center comes out with a few moist crumbs, 45 to 50 minutes. Cool completely on a wire rack (about 2 hours). Lift brownies from pan, using parchment paper sides as handles. Gently remove parchment paper, and cut brownies into 24 squares.

Note: To make ahead, refrigerate cooled uncut brownies, uncovered, overnight; cut into squares while cold.

- -

BROWN BUTTER-MAPLE-PECAN BLONDIES

ACTIVE 40 MIN. - TOTAL 2 HOURS, 15 MIN.
MAKES 24 BARS

- 1½ cups unsalted butter
- 4 large eggs
- 1¾ cups granulated sugar
- 3 cups all-purpose flour
- 1 tsp. baking powder
- 1 tsp. kosher salt
- ½ cup pure maple syrup
- 1 tsp. vanilla extract
- 1¼ cups chopped toasted pecans, divided

1. Preheat oven to 350°F. Melt butter in a medium saucepan over medium. Cook, whisking constantly, until butter browns and smells nutty, 5 to 7 minutes. Immediately pour into a bowl. Place in freezer to cool, whisking every 5 minutes until thickened and creamy, about 20 minutes. (Butter should look like melted peanut butter.)

2. Beat eggs and sugar with an electric mixer on medium speed until thickened and pale yellow, about 3 minutes. Whisk together flour, baking powder, and salt in a bowl. Add to egg mixture in thirds, alternately with cooled butter, beginning and ending with flour mixture, beating on low after each addition. Slowly beat in maple syrup; add vanilla, and beat just until combined. Fold in 1 cup of the pecans with a spoon.

3. Pour batter into a greased and floured 13- x 9-inch baking pan, and spread into an even layer. Sprinkle with remaining ¼ cup pecans.

4. Bake in preheated oven until golden and a wooden pick inserted in middle comes out clean, about 35 minutes. Transfer pan to a wire rack to cool completely, about 1 hour. Cut into 24 bars.

PUMPKIN-
CHOCOLATE
BROWNIES

SWOON PIES

SWOON PIES

ACTIVE 45 MIN. · TOTAL 2 HOURS, 40 MIN.
MAKES 1 DOZEN

- 1 cup all-purpose flour
- ½ tsp. baking powder
- ½ tsp. baking soda
- ½ tsp. table salt
- 1 cup graham cracker crumbs
- ½ cup butter, softened
- ½ cup granulated sugar
- ½ cup firmly packed light brown sugar
- 1 large egg
- 1 tsp. vanilla extract
- 1 (8-oz.) container sour cream
- Parchment paper
- Marshmallow Filling (recipe follows)
- 1 (12-oz.) pkg. semisweet chocolate morsels
- 2 tsp. shortening
- Chopped roasted salted pecans, chopped crystallized ginger, sea salt, for topping

1. Preheat oven to 350°F. Sift together flour and next 3 ingredients in a medium bowl; stir in graham cracker crumbs.

2. Beat butter and sugars with a heavy-duty electric stand mixer on medium speed until fluffy. Add egg and vanilla, beating until blended.

3. Add flour mixture to butter mixture alternately with sour cream, beginning and ending with flour mixture. Beat on low speed until blended after each addition, stopping to scrape bowl as needed.

4. Drop batter by rounded tablespoonfuls 2 inches apart onto 2 parchment paper-lined baking sheets. Bake in preheated oven, in batches, until set and bottoms are golden brown, 13 to 15 minutes. Transfer cookies (on parchment paper) to wire racks, and cool completely (about 30 minutes).

5. Turn 12 cookies over, bottom sides up. Spread each with 1 heaping tablespoonful Marshmallow Filling. Top with remaining 12 cookies, bottom sides down, and press gently to spread filling to edges. Freeze on a parchment paper-lined baking sheet 30 minutes or until filling is set.

6. Pour water to depth of 1 inch in a medium saucepan over medium; bring to a boil. Reduce heat, and simmer; place chocolate and shortening in a medium-size heatproof bowl over simmering water. Cook, stirring occasionally, 5 to 6 minutes or until melted. Remove from heat, and let cool 10 minutes.

7. Meanwhile, remove cookies from freezer, and let stand 10 minutes.

8. Dip half of each cookie sandwich into melted chocolate mixture. Place on parchment paper-lined baking sheet.

MARSHMALLOW FILLING

ACTIVE 5 MIN. · TOTAL 5 MIN.
MAKES 1½ CUPS

- ½ cup butter, softened
- 1 cup sifted powdered sugar
- 1 cup marshmallow creme
- ½ tsp. vanilla extract

Beat butter with an electric mixer on medium speed until creamy; gradually add sugar, beating well. Add remaining ingredients, beating until well blended.

- -

PECAN BARS

ACTIVE 20 MIN. · TOTAL 50 MIN.
MAKES 28 BARS

- 2 cups all-purpose flour
- ⅔ cup powdered sugar
- ¾ cup butter, softened
- ½ cup firmly packed brown sugar
- ½ cup honey
- ⅔ cup butter
- 3 Tbsp. whipping cream
- 3½ cups coarsely chopped pecans

1. Preheat oven to 350°F. Sift together 2 cups flour and ⅔ cup powdered sugar. Cut in ¾ cup softened butter using a pastry blender or fork just until mixture resembles coarse meal. Pat mixture on bottom and 1½ inches up sides of a lightly greased 13- x 9-inch baking dish.

2. Bake in preheated oven until edges are lightly browned, about 20 minutes. Cool.

3. Bring brown sugar, honey, ⅔ cup butter, and whipping cream to a boil in a saucepan over medium-high. Stir in pecans, and pour hot filling into prepared crust.

4. Bake in preheated oven until golden and bubbly, 25 to 30 minutes. Cool completely before cutting into bars.

CARAMEL APPLES

Caramel apples are the stuff of fall festivals and Halloween carnivals. No doubt, with each messy bite, they bring out the child in us all.

ACTIVE 20 MIN. - TOTAL 35 MIN.
MAKES 6 APPLES

- 6 large Granny Smith apples
- 6 wooden craft sticks
- 1 (14-oz.) bag caramels, unwrapped*
- 1 Tbsp. vanilla extract
- 2 cups chopped pecans or peanuts, toasted
- 1 (12-oz.) bag semisweet chocolate morsels (optional)
  Pecan halves (optional)

1. Wash and dry apples; remove stems. Insert a craft stick into stem end of each apple; set aside.

2. Combine caramels, vanilla, and 1 tablespoon water in a microwave-safe glass bowl. Microwave on HIGH 90 seconds or until melted, stirring twice.

3. Dip each apple into the caramel mixture quickly, allowing excess caramel to drip off. Roll in chopped nuts; place apples on lightly greased wax paper. Chill at least 15 minutes.

4. If desired, to make chocolate-dipped caramel apples, microwave chocolate morsels on HIGH 90 seconds or until melted, stirring twice; cool 5 minutes. Pour chocolate where craft sticks and apples meet, allowing chocolate to drip down sides of caramel apples. Press pecan halves onto chocolate, if desired. Chill 15 minutes or until set.

SHORTCUT PRALINES

ACTIVE 20 MIN. - TOTAL 20 MIN.
MAKES 30 PRALINES

- 3 cups firmly packed light brown sugar
- 1 cup whipping cream
- 2 Tbsp. light corn syrup
- ¼ tsp. table salt
- ¼ cup butter or margarine
- 2 cups chopped pecans
- 1 tsp. vanilla extract

1. Bring first 4 ingredients to a boil in a 3-quart saucepan over medium, stirring mixture constantly. Cook, stirring occasionally, 6 to 8 minutes, or until a candy thermometer registers 236°F (soft ball stage).

2. Remove mixture from heat, and add butter (do not stir). Let stand until candy thermometer reaches 150°F. Stir in pecans and vanilla, using a wooden spoon; stir constantly until candy begins to thicken.

3. Drop by heaping teaspoonfuls, working rapidly, onto wax paper. Let stand until firm.

PECAN-ESPRESSO TOFFEE

Take a crack at this intensely rich and buttery holiday treat.

ACTIVE 35 MIN. - TOTAL 1 HOUR, 40 MIN.
SERVES 10 TO 12

- Parchment paper
- 1¼ cups butter
- 1 cup granulated sugar
- ⅓ cup firmly packed light brown sugar
- 1 Tbsp. instant espresso
- 1 Tbsp. dark unsulphured molasses
- ½ tsp. table salt
- 2 cups chopped toasted pecans
- 1 cup bittersweet chocolate morsels
- 1 cup semisweet chocolate morsels

1. Line a 15- x 10-inch pan with parchment paper, and lightly coat with cooking spray.

2. Melt butter in a large heavy saucepan over medium; stir in granulated sugar, next 4 ingredients, and ⅓ cup water. Cook, stirring constantly, until a candy thermometer registers 290°F (soft crack stage), about 17 to 20 minutes. Remove pan from heat, and stir in pecans.

3. Immediately pour mixture into prepared pan. Spread in an even layer, and sprinkle bittersweet and semisweet chocolate morsels over top. Let stand 5 minutes. Spread and swirl chocolate using an offset spatula. Chill 1 hour or until firm.

4. Break toffee into pieces. Store in an airtight container in refrigerator up to 7 days. Serve cold or at room temperature.

CARAMEL APPLE CAKE,
PAGE 311

DESSERTS

LEMON-ORANGE POUND CAKE

ACTIVE 25 MIN. · TOTAL 2 HOURS, 20 MIN.

SERVES 10 TO 12

CAKE

- 2 cups granulated sugar
- ½ cup unsalted butter, softened, plus more for greasing pan
- ½ cup vegetable shortening
- 6 large eggs
- 3 cups all-purpose flour, plus more for pan
- 1½ tsp. baking powder
- ½ tsp. table salt
- ½ tsp. baking soda
- 1 cup whole buttermilk
- 1 tsp. vanilla extract
- 1 tsp. lemon extract

VANILLA ICING

- 2 cups powdered sugar
- 3 Tbsp. whole milk
- ¼ tsp. vanilla extract

LEMON-ORANGE ICING

- 2 cups powdered sugar
- 1 Tbsp. fresh lemon juice
- 1 Tbsp. fresh orange juice
- 1 drop of yellow food coloring gel

ADDITIONAL INGREDIENTS

Thin lemon or orange slices (optional)

1. Prepare the Cake: Preheat oven to 350°F. Grease and flour a 12-cup Bundt pan.

2. Beat sugar, butter, and shortening in a large bowl with an electric mixer on medium speed until light and fluffy, 5 to 6 minutes. Add eggs, 1 at a time, beating well after each addition.

3. Whisk together flour, baking powder, salt, and baking soda in a bowl. Alternately add flour mixture and buttermilk to butter mixture in 5 additions, beginning and ending with flour mixture, beating until blended after each addition. Beat in vanilla and lemon extracts. Transfer batter to prepared pan; smooth top. Bake in preheated oven until a wooden pick inserted in center comes out clean, 45 to 50 minutes. Cool in pan on a wire rack 10 minutes; remove from pan. Cool completely on rack, 30 to 40 minutes.

4. Prepare the Vanilla Icing: Whisk together powdered sugar, milk, and vanilla in a bowl until smooth. Drizzle icing over cake, letting it drip down sides. Refrigerate 10 minutes to allow icing to set.

5. Prepare the Lemon-Orange Icing: Whisk together powdered sugar, fresh lemon and orange juices, and yellow food coloring gel in a bowl until smooth. Drizzle Lemon-Orange Icing over Vanilla Icing, letting it drip down sides. Let stand until set, about 20 minutes. Garnish with thin lemon or orange slices, if desired.

MILLION-DOLLAR POUND CAKE

ACTIVE 20 MIN. · TOTAL 2 HOURS, 55 MIN.

SERVES 10 TO 12

- 1 lb. butter, softened
- 3 cups granulated sugar
- 6 large eggs
- 4 cups all-purpose flour
- ¾ cup milk
- 1 tsp. almond extract
- 1 tsp. vanilla extract
  Sweetened whipped cream, blueberries, sliced peaches, for garnish

1. Preheat oven to 300°F. Generously grease and lightly flour a 10-inch (14-cup) tube pan. (Use shortening to grease the pan, covering every nook and cranny. Sprinkle a light coating of flour over the greased surface. Tap out any excess flour.)

2. Beat butter with an electric mixer on medium speed until light yellow in color and creamy. (This will take up to 7 minutes, depending on the power of your mixer.) Gradually add sugar, beating on medium speed until light and fluffy. Add eggs, 1 at a time, beating just until yellow disappears after each addition.

3. Add flour to butter mixture alternately with milk, beginning and ending with flour. Beat on low speed just until blended after each addition. (Batter should be smooth.) Stir in extracts. Pour batter into prepared pan.

4. Bake in preheated oven until a long wooden pick inserted in center comes out clean, about 1 hour and 40 minutes. Cool in pan on a wire rack 10 to 15 minutes. Remove from pan; cool completely on wire rack. Garnish each serving, if desired.

LEMON-ORANGE
POUND CAKE

PECAN POUND CAKE

PECAN POUND CAKE

ACTIVE 25 MIN. - TOTAL 3 HOURS, 25 MIN., INCLUDING GLAZE
SERVES 10 TO 12

2 cups butter, softened
1¼ cups granulated sugar
1¼ cups firmly packed light brown sugar
6 large eggs
1 Tbsp. vanilla extract
1½ tsp. baking powder
¼ tsp. table salt
4 cups all-purpose flour, divided
1 cup milk
4 cups chopped toasted pecans
 Citrus Glaze (recipe follows)

1. Preheat oven to 325°F. Beat butter with a heavy-duty electric stand mixer on medium speed until creamy. Gradually add sugars, beating 3 to 5 minutes or until light and fluffy. Add eggs, 1 at a time, beating just until blended after each addition. Stir in vanilla extract.

2. Stir together baking powder, salt, and 3¾ cups flour in a medium bowl. Add flour mixture to butter mixture alternately with milk, beginning and ending with flour mixture. Beat on low speed just until blended after each addition. Stir together pecans and remaining ¼ cup flour in a small bowl; add to batter, and stir just until combined. Pour batter into a greased (with shortening) and floured 10-inch tube pan.

3. Bake in preheated oven until a long wooden pick inserted in center comes out clean, 1 hour and 15 minutes to 1 hour and 30 minutes, shielding with foil after 55 minutes to prevent excessive browning. Cool in pan on a wire rack 15 minutes; transfer cake from pan to wire rack. Cool 20 minutes. Spoon Citrus Glaze over cake. Cool.

CITRUS GLAZE

ACTIVE 10 MIN. - TOTAL 10 MIN.
MAKES ABOUT ¾ CUP

2½ cups powdered sugar
2 Tbsp. butter, melted
1 tsp. orange zest plus 2 Tbsp. orange juice
1 tsp. lemon zest plus 1 Tbsp. lemon juice, plus
 1 Tbsp. more if needed

Whisk together powdered sugar, melted butter, orange zest and juice, and lemon zest and juice until smooth. Whisk in up to 1 tablespoon more lemon juice, 1 teaspoon at a time, until glaze consistency is reached.

COFFEE CAKE POUND CAKE

ACTIVE 30 MIN. - TOTAL 3 HOURS, 25 MIN.
SERVES 12

PECAN STREUSEL
½ cup firmly packed brown sugar
½ cup all-purpose flour
1 tsp. ground cinnamon
¼ cup butter
¾ cup chopped pecans

POUND CAKE BATTER
1 cup finely chopped pecans
1 cup butter, softened
2½ cups granulated sugar
6 large eggs
3 cups all-purpose flour
¼ tsp. baking soda
1 (8-oz.) container sour cream
2 tsp. vanilla extract
¼ cup firmly packed brown sugar
1½ tsp. ground cinnamon

1. Prepare Pecan Streusel: Combine first 3 ingredients in a bowl. Cut in butter with a pastry blender or fork until mixture resembles small peas. Stir in ¾ cup pecans.

2. Prepare Pound Cake Batter: Preheat oven to 350°F. Bake 1 cup pecans in a single layer in a shallow pan 5 to 7 minutes or until lightly toasted and fragrant, stirring halfway through. Cool 20 minutes. Reduce oven temperature to 325°F.

3. Beat butter with a heavy-duty electric stand mixer on medium speed until creamy. Gradually add granulated sugar, beating until light and fluffy. Add eggs, 1 at a time, beating just until blended after each addition.

4. Stir together flour and baking soda; add to butter mixture alternately with sour cream, beginning and ending with flour mixture. Beat on low speed just until blended after each addition. Stir in vanilla.

5. Pour half the batter into a greased and floured 10-inch (12-cup) tube pan. Stir together toasted pecans, brown sugar, and cinnamon; sprinkle over batter. Spoon remaining batter over pecan mixture; sprinkle with Pecan Streusel.

6. Bake at 325°F until a long wooden pick inserted in center comes out clean, 1 hour and 20 minutes to 1 hour and 30 minutes. Cool in pan on a wire rack 10 to 15 minutes; transfer from pan to wire rack, and cool completely (about 1 hour).

BLACKBERRY JAM CAKE

ACTIVE 35 MIN. - TOTAL 2 HOURS, 35 MIN.
SERVES 12

CAKE LAYERS
- 2¾ cups all-purpose flour
- 2 tsp. ground cinnamon
- 1½ tsp. baking soda
- 1½ tsp. baking powder
- 1½ tsp. ground cloves
- 1½ tsp. ground allspice
- 1 tsp. table salt
- 2 cups granulated sugar
- 5 large eggs
- 1½ cups vegetable oil
- 1¼ cups seedless blackberry jam or preserves
- 2 tsp. vanilla extract
- 1½ cups whole buttermilk
- 1 cup finely chopped pecans or black walnuts
- 1 cup golden raisins

FROSTING
- 3 (8-oz.) pkg. cream cheese, softened
- ¼ cup granulated sugar
- ½ cup jarred caramel topping
- ½ cup heavy cream
- ¼ tsp. table salt

GARNISHES
- 1 tsp. finely chopped pecans or black walnuts
- Fresh blackberries

1. Preheat oven to 350°F. Spray 3 (9-inch) round cake pans with cooking spray; line bottoms with parchment paper.

2. Prepare the Cake Layers: Whisk together first 7 ingredients in a large bowl; set aside.

3. Place sugar and eggs in bowl of a heavy-duty stand mixer fitted with whisk attachment; beat on medium speed until thick and smooth, 3 minutes. Change to paddle attachment. Add oil, jam, and vanilla extract; beat until combined, 1 minute.

4. Add half of the flour mixture to jam mixture; beat on low speed just until combined, 20 to 45 seconds. Add buttermilk; beat on low speed just until combined. Add remaining flour mixture; beat on low speed until smooth and combined, about 30 seconds. Fold in nuts and raisins; divide evenly among prepared pans.

5. Bake in preheated oven until edges of cake layers just start to pull from sides of pans and a wooden pick inserted in center comes out clean, 35 to 40 minutes, rotating pans between top and bottom racks halfway through baking. Press gently on top of layers to flatten any doming; cool in pans 10 minutes. Transfer from pans to wire racks; cool completely, about 1 hour.

6. Prepare the Frosting: Place cream cheese and sugar in bowl of a heavy-duty stand mixer fitted with whisk attachment; beat on medium-low speed until combined. Add caramel topping; beat until smooth, 1 to 2 minutes. With mixer running, slowly pour in cream and add salt. Beat on medium speed until thick and smooth, 3 to 4 minutes. (Mixture will be thin at first but will thicken as the cream is whipped.)

7. Transfer about two-thirds of the frosting to a piping bag. Place one cake layer on a serving plate. Pipe frosting on top of layer, using a circular motion and starting from edges and gradually moving toward center. Repeat process with remaining layers. Cover sides with remaining frosting. (Drag the back of a spoon in a side-to-side motion across the Frosting to textured frosting.) Garnish cake with nuts and blackberries.

MAMA DIP'S
CARROT CAKE

MAMA DIP'S CARROT CAKE

This recipe from Chapel Hill, North Carolina, restaurateur Mildred "Mama Dip" Council makes one of the best carrot cakes we've tasted.

ACTIVE 30 MIN. · TOTAL 2 HOURS
SERVES 12

2 cups chopped walnuts
2½ cups self-rising flour
1½ tsp. ground cinnamon
1 tsp. baking soda
2 cups granulated sugar
1 cup vegetable oil
4 large eggs
3 cups grated carrots
5-Cup Cream Cheese Frosting (recipe, page 316)

1. Preheat oven to 350°F. Arrange walnuts in a single layer in a shallow pan. Bake 12 minutes or until toasted and fragrant.

2. Sift together flour, cinnamon, and baking soda. Line bottoms of 3 lightly greased 9-inch round cake pans with parchment paper; lightly grease parchment paper.

3. Beat sugar and oil with an electric mixer on medium speed until smooth. Add eggs, 1 at a time, beating until blended after each addition. Gradually add flour mixture, beating on low speed just until blended after each addition. Fold in carrots and 1 cup toasted walnuts. Spoon batter into prepared pans.

4. Bake in preheated oven until a wooden pick inserted in center comes out clean, 35 to 40 minutes. Cool in pans on wire racks 10 minutes; transfer from pans to wire racks. Peel off parchment paper; let cakes cool 1 hour or until completely cool.

5. Spread frosting between layers and on top and sides of cake; sprinkle remaining 1 cup toasted walnuts onto cake.

- -

CARAMEL APPLE CAKE

(Photo, page 302)

ACTIVE 20 MIN. · TOTAL 2 HOURS, 20 MIN.
SERVES 8 TO 10

CAKE
1⅓ cups firmly packed light brown sugar
¾ cup butter, softened
3 large eggs
1 tsp. vanilla extract

2 cups all-purpose flour
1 tsp. baking powder
1 tsp. table salt
1 tsp. ground cinnamon
½ tsp. baking soda
¾ cup buttermilk
Shortening, for greasing pan

APPLES
2 lb. McIntosh apples (about 6 apples)
½ cup firmly packed light brown sugar
1 tsp. cornstarch
¼ tsp. ground cinnamon
Pinch of table salt
2 Tbsp. butter
Apple Brandy-Caramel Sauce (recipe follows)

1. Prepare Cake: Preheat oven to 350°F. Beat first 2 ingredients with a heavy-duty electric stand mixer on medium speed until light and fluffy. Add eggs, 1 at a time, beating just until blended after each addition; stir in vanilla.

2. Whisk together flour and next 4 ingredients in a medium bowl. Add flour mixture to sugar mixture alternately with buttermilk, beginning and ending with flour mixture. Beat just until blended after each addition. Spread batter in a greased (with shortening) and floured 9- x 2-inch round cake pan.

3. Bake in preheated oven until a wooden pick inserted in center comes out clean, about 50 minutes, shielding with aluminum foil after 35 minutes to prevent excessive browning. Cool in pan on a wire rack 10 minutes. Remove from pan; cool completely.

4. Meanwhile, prepare Apples: Cut apples into ½-inch-thick wedges. Toss together apples, brown sugar, and next 3 ingredients. Melt 2 tablespoons butter in a large skillet over medium-high; add apple mixture, and cook, stirring often, until golden, about 5 minutes. Cool.

5. Arrange apples over cooled cake. Drizzle with warm Apple Brandy-Caramel Sauce; serve with remaining sauce.

APPLE BRANDY–CARAMEL SAUCE

ACTIVE 10 MIN. · TOTAL 25 MIN.
MAKES ABOUT ⅔ CUP

Bring ½ cup firmly packed **light brown sugar**, ¼ cup **butter**, ¼ cup **heavy cream**, and a pinch of **table salt** to a boil in a small saucepan over medium, stirring constantly. Boil, stirring constantly, 1 minute. Remove from heat, and stir in 1 Tbsp. **apple brandy**. Whisk in 1 Tbsp. **powdered sugar**; cool 15 minutes before serving.

BUTTER TOFFEE–PECAN LAYER CAKE

This buttery vanilla layer cake is swathed in creamy toffee frosting made extra luscious with the addition of browned butter and lots of toasted pecans.

ACTIVE 1 HOUR · TOTAL 2 HOURS, 40 MIN.
SERVES 8

BROWN BUTTER TOFFEE FROSTING
- 1 cup unsalted butter, divided
- 2 cups packed dark brown sugar
- 1¼ cups heavy cream
- 2 Tbsp. golden cane syrup or light corn syrup
- ¼ tsp. kosher salt
- 1 Tbsp. bourbon, dark rum, or cognac (optional)
- 3 cups powdered sugar
- 1 tsp. vanilla extract

CAKE
- 2 cups all-purpose flour
- 2 tsp. baking powder
- ¾ tsp. kosher salt
- 2 cups granulated sugar
- 1 cup unsalted butter, softened
- 3 large eggs
- 1 tsp. vanilla extract
- 1 cup whole buttermilk
- 1 cup finely chopped toasted pecans
- ½ cup toffee bits (such as Heath Bits 'O Brickle Toffee Bits)

ADDITIONAL INGREDIENTS
- ½ cup toasted pecan halves
- ¼ tsp. flaky sea salt (such as Maldon), optional

1. Prepare the Frosting: Melt ¾ cup of the butter in a deep, heavy-duty saucepan over low. Increase heat to medium-high, and bring butter to a boil, stirring constantly. Cook, stirring constantly, until butter is fragrant and milk solids start to brown, about 5 minutes.

2. Remove pan from heat. Stir in brown sugar, cream, syrup, salt, and, if desired, bourbon. Return pan to medium heat; cook, stirring occasionally, until sugar dissolves. Increase heat to medium-high, and bring to a boil. Boil, stirring constantly, exactly 2 minutes. Remove mixture from heat, and pour into bowl of a heavy-duty electric stand mixer fitted with paddle attachment. Beat on low speed until mixture is lukewarm, 8 to 10 minutes. Gradually add powdered sugar and vanilla, and beat on low speed until combined after each addition. Beat until frosting is completely cool and consistency is thick, creamy, and spreadable, 6 to 10 minutes. Add remaining 4 tablespoons butter, 1 tablespoon at a time, and beat on medium speed until fully incorporated after each addition. Cover frosting, and let stand at room temperature until ready to use.

3. Prepare the Cake: Preheat oven to 350°F. Lightly coat two (9-inch-round x 2-inch-deep) cake pans with cooking spray, and line bottoms with parchment paper. Sift together flour, baking powder, and salt in a medium bowl. Set aside.

4. Beat sugar and butter in a large bowl with an electric mixer on medium-high speed until thick and creamy, 4 to 5 minutes. Add eggs, 1 at a time, and beat on medium speed until well blended after each addition. Beat in vanilla. Add flour mixture, one-third at a time, to butter mixture alternately with buttermilk, beginning and ending with flour mixture. Beat on low just until smooth after each addition. (Do not overbeat or the cake will be tough.) Fold in chopped pecans and toffee bits. Divide batter evenly between cake pans, smoothing surfaces.

5. Bake in preheated oven until a wooden pick or cake tester inserted into center of cake comes out clean, 30 to 35 minutes. Cool in pans on a wire rack 10 minutes. Invert layers onto wire rack. Peel off parchment paper. Cool completely, about 1 hour.

6. Place 1 cake layer on a serving plate; spread evenly with 1 heaping cup of frosting. Chill 15 minutes. Top with remaining cake layer. Frost top and sides of cake with remaining frosting. Sprinkle pecan halves in a ring around top edge of cake. If desired, crush sea salt with your fingers and sprinkle over pecans. Serve immediately, or store, covered, at room temperature for up to 5 days.

CRANBERRY-APPLE-PUMPKIN BUNDT

ACTIVE 30 MIN. - TOTAL 4 HOURS, 30 MIN.

SERVES 12

- ¾ cup finely chopped pecans
- 1½ cups peeled and diced Granny Smith apples
- 2 Tbsp. butter, melted
- ½ cup finely chopped sweetened dried cranberries
- ½ cup firmly packed light brown sugar
- 3 Tbsp. all-purpose flour
- 2 cups granulated sugar
- 1 cup butter, softened
- 4 large eggs
- 1 (15-oz.) can pumpkin
- 1 Tbsp. vanilla extract
- 3 cups all-purpose flour
- 2 tsp. baking powder
- 2 tsp. pumpkin pie spice
- ½ tsp. baking soda
  Sugared Pecans and Pepitas (recipe follows)
  Maple Glaze (recipe follows)

1. Preheat oven to 350°F. Bake pecans in a single layer in a shallow pan 6 to 8 minutes or until toasted, stirring halfway through. Cool 15 minutes. Reduce oven temperature to 325°F.

2. Toss diced apples in 2 Tbsp. melted butter to coat in a medium bowl; add cranberries, next 2 ingredients, and toasted pecans; toss until well blended.

3. Beat granulated sugar and 1 cup butter with an electric mixer on medium speed until light and fluffy. Add eggs, 1 at a time, beating just until blended after each addition. Add pumpkin and vanilla; beat just until blended.

4. Stir together 3 cups flour and next 3 ingredients. Gradually add flour mixture to butter mixture, beating at low speed just until blended after each addition. Spoon half the batter into a greased and floured 10-inch (12-cup) Bundt pan. Spoon apple mixture over batter, leaving a ½-inch border around edge. Spoon remaining batter over apple mixture.

5. Bake at 325°F for 1 hour and 10 minutes or until a long wooden pick inserted in center of cake comes out clean. Cool in pan on a wire rack 15 minutes. Transfer from pan to wire rack; cool completely (about 2 hours).

6. Meanwhile, prepare Sugared Pecans and Pepitas.

7. Prepare Maple Glaze, then immediately spoon the glaze onto cooled cake. Arrange pecans and pepitas on cake.

SUGARED PECANS AND PEPITAS

ACTIVE 5 MIN. - TOTAL 20 MIN.

MAKES 1½ CUPS

- 1 cup pecan halves and pieces
- ¼ cup roasted, salted shelled pepitas (pumpkin seeds)
- 2 Tbsp. butter, melted
- 2 cups granulated sugar

Preheat oven to 350°F. Stir together pecan halves and pieces, pepitas, and melted butter. Spread in a single layer in a 13- x 9-inch pan. Bake 12 to 15 minutes or until toasted and fragrant, stirring halfway through. Remove from oven; toss with sugar. Cool completely in pan on a wire rack.

MAPLE GLAZE

ACTIVE 10 MIN. - TOTAL 10 MIN.

MAKES 1 CUP

- ½ cup maple syrup
- 2 Tbsp. butter
- 1 Tbsp. milk
- 1 tsp. vanilla extract
- 1 cup powdered sugar

Bring maple syrup, butter, and milk to a boil in a small saucepan over medium-high, stirring constantly; boil, stirring constantly, 2 minutes. Remove from heat; whisk in vanilla. Gradually whisk in powdered sugar until smooth; stir gently 3 to 5 minutes or until mixture begins to thicken and cool slightly. Use immediately.

BANANAS FOSTER UPSIDE-DOWN CAKE

A cast-iron skillet is essential to this cake—it helps create the golden crust that slips right out of the skillet and onto your plate.

ACTIVE 20 MIN. · TOTAL 1 HOUR, 15 MIN.
SERVES 8

- ½ cup chopped pecans
- ½ cup butter, softened and divided
- 1 cup firmly packed light brown sugar
- 2 Tbsp. rum
- 2 ripe bananas
- ¾ cup granulated sugar
- 2 large eggs
- ¾ cup milk
- ½ cup sour cream
- 1 tsp. vanilla extract
- 2 cups all-purpose baking mix
- ¼ tsp. ground cinnamon

1. Preheat oven to 350°F.

2. Place pecans in a single layer on a baking pan. Bake in preheated oven until toasted and fragrant, stirring once, 8 to 10 minutes.

3. Melt ¼ cup butter in a lightly greased 10-inch cast-iron skillet over low heat. Remove from heat; stir in brown sugar and rum.

4. Cut bananas diagonally into ¼-inch slices. Arrange banana slices in concentric circles over brown sugar mixture. Sprinkle pecans over bananas.

5. Beat granulated sugar and remaining ¼ cup butter with an electric mixer on medium speed until blended. Add eggs, 1 at a time, beating just until blended after each addition. Add milk and next 2 ingredients; beat just until blended. Beat in baking mix and cinnamon until blended. (Batter will be slightly lumpy.) Pour batter over mixture in skillet, and spread to cover. Place skillet on an aluminum foil-lined jelly-roll pan.

6. Bake in preheated oven until a wooden pick inserted in center comes out clean, 40 to 45 minutes. Cool in skillet on a wire rack 10 minutes. Run a knife around edge to loosen. Invert onto a serving plate, spooning any topping in skillet over cake.

PATRIOTIC CUPCAKES

ACTIVE 40 MIN. · TOTAL 2 HOURS, INCLUDING COOLING
MAKES 2 DOZEN

- 2 cups granulated sugar
- 1 cup butter, softened
- 2 large eggs
- 2 tsp. fresh lemon juice
- 1 tsp. vanilla extract
- 2½ cups cake flour
- ½ tsp. baking soda
- 1 cup buttermilk
  5-Cup Cream Cheese Frosting (recipe follows)
  24 miniature American flags

1. Preheat oven to 350°F. Beat sugar and butter with an electric mixer on medium speed until creamy. Add eggs, 1 at a time, beating until yellow disappears after each addition. Beat in lemon juice and vanilla.

2. Combine flour and baking soda in a small bowl; add to sugar mixture alternately with buttermilk, beginning and ending with flour mixture. Beat on medium speed just until blended after each addition.

3. Place 24 paper baking cups in muffin pans. Spoon batter into baking cups, filling each two-thirds full.

4. Bake in preheated oven until a wooden pick inserted in center comes out clean, 18 to 22 minutes. Cool in pans on a wire rack 10 minutes. Transfer cupcakes from pans to wire rack; cool 45 minutes or until completely cool.

5. Spoon 5-Cup Cream Cheese Frosting into a zip-top plastic freezer bag (do not seal). Snip one corner of bag to make a hole (about 1 inch in diameter). Pipe frosting in little loops onto tops of cupcakes as desired. Insert 1 flag into top of each cupcake.

5-CUP CREAM CHEESE FROSTING

ACTIVE 10 MIN. · TOTAL 10 MIN.
MAKES ABOUT 5 CUPS

- 2 (8-oz.) pkg. cream cheese, softened
- ½ cup butter, softened
- 2 (16-oz.) pkg. powdered sugar
- 2 tsp. vanilla extract

Beat cream cheese and butter with an electric mixer on medium speed until creamy. Gradually add powdered sugar, beating until fluffy. Stir in vanilla.

BANANAS FOSTER
UPSIDE-DOWN
CAKE

MOCHA JAVA
CAKES

MOCHA JAVA CAKES

These chocolate soufflés are as sinful as you'd think— but much easier to prepare than you'd expect.

ACTIVE 15 MIN. · TOTAL 30 MIN.
SERVES 6

 1 cup butter plus 1 Tbsp. butter, divided
 8 oz. bittersweet chocolate morsels
 4 large egg yolks
 4 large eggs
 2 cups powdered sugar
 ¾ cup all-purpose flour
 1 tsp. instant espresso or instant coffee granules
   Pinch of table salt
   Powdered sugar, for garnish

1. Preheat oven to 425°F.

2. Grease 6 (6-oz.) ramekins or individual soufflé dishes with 1 tablespoon butter.

3. Microwave remaining 1 cup butter and chocolate morsels in a large microwave-safe bowl on HIGH 1½ to 2 minutes or until melted and smooth, stirring at 30-second intervals.

4. Beat egg yolks and eggs with an electric mixer on medium speed 1 minute. Gradually add chocolate mixture, beating at low speed until well blended.

5. Sift together sugar and next 3 ingredients. Gradually whisk sugar mixture into chocolate mixture until well blended. Divide batter among prepared ramekins. Place ramekins in a 15- x 10-inch jelly-roll pan.

6. Bake in preheated oven until a thermometer inserted into cakes registers 165°F, about 16 minutes. Remove from oven, and let stand 10 minutes. Run a knife around outer edge of each cake to loosen. Carefully invert cakes onto dessert plates. Garnish with powdered sugar.

Minty-Mocha Java Cakes: Prepare recipe as directed through Step 5. Chop 12 thin crème de menthe chocolate mints. Sprinkle center of batter in ramekins with chopped mints. Press mints into batter gently just until submerged. Proceed with recipe as directed in Step 6.

Orange-Mocha Java Cakes: Prepare recipe as directed through Step 4. Sift together sugar and next 3 ingredients. Gradually whisk sugar mixture into chocolate mixture until well blended. Whisk in ¼ cup orange liqueur and 1 teaspoon orange zest. Divide batter among prepared ramekins. Place ramekins in a 15- x 10-inch pan. Proceed with recipe as directed in Step 6, baking cakes until a thermometer inserted into cakes registers 165°F, 14 to 16 minutes.

MEXICAN CHOCOLATE PUDDING CAKE

Red pepper, chipotle chile pepper, and cinnamon combine to give this decadent chocolate pudding cake a subtle touch of heat. The molten center and crispy almonds create the ultimate texture combination—you'll have a hard time putting your spoon down.

ACTIVE 30 MIN. · TOTAL 1 HOUR, 10 MIN.
SERVES 6

 1½ cups semisweet chocolate morsels
 ½ cup butter
 ¾ cup granulated sugar
 4 large eggs
 1 cup all-purpose flour
 ½ tsp. ground cinnamon
 ¼ tsp. baking powder
 ¼ tsp. cayenne pepper
 ¼ tsp. ground chipotle chile pepper
 ½ tsp. kosher salt, divided
 ½ cup sliced almonds
 2 tsp. olive oil
 1 tsp. light brown sugar

1. Preheat oven to 350°F. Microwave chocolate and butter in a large microwave-safe bowl on HIGH 1 to 1½ minutes or until melted, stirring at 30-second intervals. Whisk in granulated sugar. Add eggs, 1 at a time, whisking just until blended after each addition. Whisk in flour, next 4 ingredients, and ¼ teaspoon salt.

2. Pour batter into a greased (with butter) 2-quart baking dish. Stir together sliced almonds, next 2 ingredients, and remaining ¼ teaspoon salt. Sprinkle almond mixture over cake batter. Bake in preheated oven 30 minutes. (Center will be soft.) Cool on a wire rack 5 minutes. Serve warm.

BLACKBERRY COBBLER

ACTIVE 15 MIN. - TOTAL 45 MIN.
SERVES 9

- 1 cup granulated sugar
- ¼ cup all-purpose flour
- 5 cups fresh blackberries or 2 (14-oz.) pkg. frozen blackberries, thawed and drained
- 1 Tbsp. lemon juice
  Crust (recipe follows)
- 2 Tbsp. butter, melted
- 1 tsp. granulated sugar

1. Preheat oven to 425°F. Combine 1 cup sugar and the flour; add berries, and toss well. (If using frozen berries, increase flour to ⅓ cup.) Sprinkle with lemon juice. Spoon into a greased 8- or 9-inch square baking dish.

2. Prepare Crust, and spoon 9 mounds over blackberries. Brush with butter, and sprinkle with 1 teaspoon sugar.

3. Bake, uncovered, in preheated oven until browned and bubbly, about 30 minutes. Serve warm.

CRUST

ACTIVE 10 MIN. - TOTAL 10 MIN.
MAKES ENOUGH TOPPING FOR 1 COBBLER

- 1¾ cups all-purpose flour
- 3 Tbsp. granulated sugar
- 1½ tsp. baking powder
- ¾ tsp. table salt
- ¼ cup shortening
- ½ cup whipping cream
- ½ cup buttermilk

Combine first 4 ingredients; cut in shortening with a pastry blender until mixture is crumbly. Stir in cream and buttermilk just until blended.

- -

RED VELVET–BERRY COBBLER

ACTIVE 20 MIN. - TOTAL 1 HOUR, 15 MIN.
SERVES 6 TO 8

- 1 Tbsp. cornstarch
- 1¼ cups granulated sugar, divided
- 6 cups assorted fresh berries (such as 2 cups each blackberries, raspberries, and blueberries.)
- ½ cup butter, softened
- 2 large eggs
- 2 Tbsp. red liquid food coloring
- 1 tsp. vanilla extract
- 1¼ cups all-purpose flour
- 1½ Tbsp. unsweetened cocoa
- ¼ tsp. table salt
- ½ cup buttermilk
- 1½ tsp. white vinegar
- ½ tsp. baking soda
  Cream Cheese Ice Cream (recipe follows)
  Fresh mint sprigs, for garnish

1. Preheat oven to 350°F. Stir together cornstarch and ½ cup sugar. Toss berries with cornstarch mixture; spoon into a lightly greased 11- x 7-inch baking dish.

3. Beat butter with an electric mixer on medium speed until fluffy; gradually add remaining ¾ cup sugar, beating well. Add eggs, 1 at a time, beating just until blended after each addition. Stir in food coloring and vanilla.

4. Combine flour, cocoa, and salt. Stir together buttermilk, vinegar, and baking soda in a 2-cup liquid measuring cup. Add flour mixture to butter mixture alternately with buttermilk mixture, beginning and ending with flour mixture. Beat at low speed until blended after each addition. Spoon batter over berry mixture.

5. Bake in preheated oven until a wooden pick inserted in center of cake topping comes out clean, 45 to 50 minutes. Cool on a wire rack 10 minutes. Serve with Cream Cheese Ice Cream on the side or layered in trifle glasses.

CREAM CHEESE ICE CREAM

ACTIVE 20 MIN. - TOTAL 1 HOUR, 15 MIN.
MAKES ABOUT 1 QT.

- 3 cups half-and-half
- 1¼ cups powdered sugar
- 2 egg yolks
- 1 (8-oz.) pkg. cream cheese
- 1 tsp. vanilla extract

Whisk together the first 3 ingredients in a large heavy saucepan. Cook over medium, whisking constantly, 8 to 10 minutes or until mixture thickens slightly. Remove from heat; whisk in cream cheese and vanilla until cheese is melted. Cool completely (about 1 hour), stirring occasionally. Place plastic wrap on mixture; chill 8 to 24 hours. Pour mixture into freezer container of a 1½-quart electric ice cream maker. Freeze according to manufacturer's instructions. Transfer ice cream to an airtight container. Freeze 4 hours before serving.

RED VELVET-BERRY
COBBLER

STRAWBERRY-RHUBARB CRISPS WITH SWEET-AND-SAVORY GRANOLA

The crunchy, lightly spiced granola topping takes a bit of time to make, but it's the star of this dish and can be made in advance in stages. Store the prepared, cooled quinoa and almonds in airtight containers at room temperature up to three days.

ACTIVE 25 MIN. - TOTAL 1 HOUR, 15 MIN.
SERVES 12

- 1½ lb. fresh rhubarb stalks, cut into ¾-inch pieces
- 1 lb. fresh strawberries, hulled and quartered
- 1 cup plus 3 Tbsp. granulated sugar
- 2 Tbsp. tapioca flour or starch
- ¾ tsp. kosher salt, divided
- 10 Tbsp. unsalted butter
- ¾ cup packed dark brown sugar
- 1 cup uncooked old-fashioned rolled oats
- ¾ cup all-purpose flour
- 1 tsp. ground cinnamon
- 1 cup Five-Spice Almonds (recipe follows), crushed
- ½ cup Fried Red Quinoa (recipe follows)
- ¼ cup roasted salted sunflower seeds

1. Preheat oven to 350°F. Combine rhubarb, strawberries, granulated sugar, tapioca flour, and ½ teaspoon salt in a saucepan. Cook over medium-low, stirring occasionally, until juices begin to thicken, 10 minutes.

2. Meanwhile, combine butter, brown sugar, oats, all-purpose flour, cinnamon, crushed Five-Spice Almonds, Fried Red Quinoa, sunflower seeds, and remaining ¼ teaspoon salt in the bowl of a heavy-duty stand mixer fitted with paddle attachment. Beat on medium-low speed until combined, about 1 minute.

3. Coat 12 (3-inch) 6- to 8-ounce ramekins with cooking spray. Spoon warm fruit mixture into ramekins, filling each halfway full (about ⅓ cup per ramekin). Top evenly with oat mixture (about ⅓ cup per ramekin), making sure fruit is covered. Place on a rimmed baking sheet. Bake in preheated oven until fruit is bubbling and topping is golden brown, about 20 minutes. Cool at least 30 minutes before serving.

FIVE-SPICE ALMONDS

ACTIVE 15 MIN. - TOTAL 2 HOURS
MAKES 1½ CUPS

- ¾ cup granulated sugar, divided
- 1½ cups raw almonds with skins
- ¼ tsp. Chinese five-spice powder, plus more to taste
- ¼ tsp. kosher salt
  Pinch of cayenne pepper

1. Preheat oven to 300°F. Bring 1½ quarts water and ½ cup sugar to a boil in a saucepan over high. Reduce heat to medium; add almonds. Cook until skins begin to soften, about 5 minutes. Drain almonds; transfer to a large bowl. Toss with Chinese five-spice powder, salt, cayenne pepper, and remaining ¼ cup granulated sugar. Add more five-spice powder to taste. Spread in an even layer on a rimmed baking sheet.

2. Bake until sugar crystallizes, about 1 hour and 15 minutes, stirring occasionally. Remove from oven. Cool completely, about 30 minutes.

FRIED RED QUINOA

ACTIVE 15 MIN. - TOTAL 1 HOUR, 30 MIN.
MAKES 1½ CUPS

- ½ cup uncooked red quinoa
- 1 qt. neutral cooking oil, such as canola or vegetable
  Pinch kosher salt

1. Cook quinoa according to package directions; drain. Spread in an even layer on a rimmed baking sheet lined with 2 layers of paper towels. Let stand until completely cool and dry, about 1 hour.

2. Pour oil into a large skillet; heat over medium-high to 350°F. Fry quinoa, in batches, until big bubbles stop forming (there will still be some small bubbles), about 1 minute. Drain on a second baking sheet lined with paper towels; sprinkle with a pinch of salt.

COUNTRY PEACH COBBLER

This cobbler not only has its share of fresh peaches, but also two crisp layers of pastry. If your peaches are really juicy, slide a foil-lined baking sheet underneath the baking dish in the oven to catch any drips.

ACTIVE 35 MIN. - TOTAL 1 HOUR, 45 MIN.
SERVES 8 TO 10

- 12 medium to large fresh peaches, peeled and sliced (about 12 cups)
- 3 cups granulated sugar
- ⅓ cup all-purpose flour
- ⅔ cup butter
- 1 Tbsp. vanilla extract
- 2 (15-oz.) pkg. refrigerated piecrusts
- 2 Tbsp. granulated sugar
  Vanilla ice cream

1. Combine first 3 ingredients in a Dutch oven; let stand 10 minutes or until sugar dissolves. Bring peach mixture to a boil; reduce heat to low and simmer 10 minutes or until tender. Remove pan from heat; add butter and vanilla, stirring until butter melts.

2. Preheat oven to 475°F. Unroll piecrusts. Cut 1½ crusts into 1½-inch-wide strips for the lattice top. Place strips in refrigerator. Trim another 1½ crusts to fit a 13- x 9-inch baking dish.

3. Spoon half the peach mixture into a lightly greased 13- x 9-inch baking dish. Arrange trimmed crusts over peach filling, overlapping slightly, if necessary. Cut several slits in pastry.

4. Bake in preheated oven until pastry is well browned, 20 to 22 minutes. Remove from oven; cool slightly. Spoon remaining peach mixture over baked pastry. Carefully arrange pastry strips in a lattice design over hot filling. Sprinkle with 2 tablespoons sugar. Bake 20 minutes more or until top pastry is well browned. Serve warm or cold with vanilla ice cream.

Note: If peaches aren't in season, substitute 2 (20-ounce) packages frozen peaches. Reduce sugar to 2 cups and flour to 3 tablespoons. Proceed as directed.

BANANA BREAD COBBLER

Once you've made this simple streusel-topped cobbler, you'll never go back to traditional banana bread again. Drizzle servings with heavy cream for even more indulgence and richness.

ACTIVE 15 MIN. - TOTAL 55 MIN.
SERVES 8

- 1 cup self-rising flour
- 1 cup granulated sugar
- 1 cup milk
- ½ cup butter, melted
- 4 medium ripe bananas, sliced
  Streusel Topping (recipe follows)

1. Preheat oven to 375°F.

2. Whisk together flour, sugar, and milk just until blended; whisk in melted butter. Pour batter into a lightly greased 11- x 7-inch baking dish. Top with banana slices and sprinkle with Streusel Topping.

3. Bake in preheated oven until golden brown and bubbly, 40 to 45 minutes.

STREUSEL TOPPING

ACTIVE 10 MIN. - TOTAL 10 MIN.
MAKES 3½ CUPS

- ¾ cup firmly packed light brown sugar
- ½ cup self-rising flour
- ½ cup butter, softened
- 1 cup uncooked regular oats
- ½ cup chopped pecans

Stir together brown sugar, flour, and butter until crumbly. Stir in oats and pecans.

BANANA BREAD
COBBLER

BREAD PUDDING
WITH RUM SAUCE

BREAD PUDDING WITH RUM SAUCE

Day-old bread is best for soaking up the liquid in this comforting dessert. The easy Rum Sauce makes each serving luscious.

ACTIVE 15 MIN. - TOTAL 1 HOUR, 5 MIN.
SERVES 12

- 4 large eggs
- 1½ cups granulated sugar
- 3 (12-oz.) cans evaporated milk
- ½ cup butter, melted
- 1 Tbsp. vanilla extract
- 2 tsp. ground cinnamon
- 6 cups torn, packed French bread
- 1 large Granny Smith apple, peeled and chopped
- 1½ cups coarsely chopped walnuts, toasted
- 1 cup golden raisins
  Rum Sauce (recipe follows)

1. Preheat oven to 350°F. Whisk eggs in a large bowl. Whisk in sugar and next 4 ingredients. Fold in bread and next 3 ingredients, stirring until bread is moistened. Pour into a greased 13- x 9-inch baking dish.

2. Bake, uncovered, in preheated oven until set, about 50 minutes. Cut into squares. Serve warm with Rum Sauce.

RUM SAUCE

ACTIVE 5 MIN. - TOTAL 5 MIN.
MAKES 2½ CUPS

- 2 (14-oz.) cans sweetened condensed milk
- 2 Tbsp. dark rum
- 1 Tbsp. vanilla extract

Pour condensed milk into a small saucepan; cook over medium until hot, stirring often. Remove from heat, and stir in rum and vanilla. Serve warm.

APPLE BROWN BETTY

This classic dessert is almost as American as apple pie. It's layered and garnished with a sweetened breadcrumb topping instead of piecrust.

ACTIVE 15 MIN. - TOTAL 1 HOUR
SERVES 6

- 4 cups soft, fresh breadcrumbs
- ⅓ cup butter, melted
- 1 cup firmly packed brown sugar
- 1 Tbsp. ground cinnamon
- 4 large Granny Smith apples, peeled and cut into ¼-inch-thick slices
- 1 cup apple cider

1. Preheat oven to 350°F.

2. Stir together breadcrumbs and butter. Stir together brown sugar and cinnamon. Place half the apple slices in a lightly greased 8-inch square baking dish; sprinkle apples with half the brown sugar mixture and half the breadcrumb mixture. Repeat procedure with remaining apples, brown sugar mixture, and breadcrumb mixture. Pour apple cider over top.

3. Bake in preheated oven until browned, 45 to 55 minutes.

- -

CARAMEL PIE

ACTIVE 5 MIN. - TOTAL 4 HOURS, 5 MIN.
SERVES 6 TO 8

- 2 (14-oz.) cans sweetened condensed milk
- 1 9-inch graham cracker crust
  Whipped topping, mini semisweet chocolate chips, for garnish

Pour condensed milk into a lightly greased (with cooking spray) 1-quart slow cooker. Cover and cook on LOW heat setting 4 hours, stirring every 30 minutes. Pour into crust and chill. Garnish, if desired.

OLD-FASHIONED APPLE PIE

ACTIVE 30 MIN. · TOTAL 1 HOUR, 40 MIN., PLUS 2 HOURS CHILLING
AND 1 HOUR COOLING

SERVES 8

CRUST

- 2 cups all-purpose flour, plus more for work surface
- 1 cup cold unsalted butter or cold vegetable shortening, cut into small pieces
- 1 tsp. kosher salt
- 2 to 4 Tbsp. very cold water

FILLING

- 9 or 10 tart apples such as Granny Smith or McIntosh (about 4 lb. total), peeled and thinly sliced
- ½ cup granulated sugar
- ¼ cup all-purpose flour
- 1 tsp. ground cinnamon
  Dash of kosher salt
- 2 Tbsp. unsalted butter, cut into small pieces

1. Prepare the Crust: Using your fingers, mix together flour, butter, and salt in a large bowl until butter is well incorporated. Gradually sprinkle very cold water into mixture, kneading as you add water, until dough just comes together. (You may not need to add all the water.) Turn dough out onto a lightly floured work surface; knead until it forms a smooth ball, 2 to 3 times. Divide dough in half and shape into 2 disks. Wrap each disk in plastic wrap; chill at least 2 hours or up to overnight.

2. Unwrap 1 chilled dough disk and place on a lightly floured work surface. Let stand at room temperature until slightly softened, about 5 minutes. Sprinkle with flour; roll into a 12-inch circle. Carefully fit dough round into a 9-inch deep-dish glass pie plate, leaving 1½-inch overhang around edges. Refrigerate until ready to use.

3. Prepare the Filling: Preheat oven to 425°F with oven rack in lowest position. Stir together apples, sugar, flour, cinnamon, and salt in a large bowl until apples are evenly coated. Spoon mixture into prepared piecrust; sprinkle mixture with butter.

4. Unwrap remaining chilled pie dough disk and place on a lightly floured work surface. Let stand at room temperature until slightly softened, about 5 minutes. Sprinkle with flour; roll into a 12-inch circle. Cut into 12 (¾-inch-wide) strips. (Discard remaining dough scraps, or use for another purpose.) Arrange strips in a lattice design over filling; trim strips as needed to meet the bottom crust overhang. Fold dough edges under and crimp using your fingers or a fork.

5. Place assembled pie on a rimmed baking sheet. Bake in preheated oven 15 minutes. Reduce oven temperature to 350°F (leaving pie in oven); continue baking 45 minutes. Cover loosely with aluminum foil to prevent excessive browning; continue baking until juices are thick and bubbly, crust is golden brown, and apples are tender when pierced with a long wooden pick, about 30 minutes. Transfer pie to a wire rack; cool at least 1 hour.

SKILLET APPLE PIE

The Granny Smith apples in this skillet apple pie are known as the go-to apple for baking because they hold up to heat, and they have a wonderful balance of sweet and tart flavors.

ACTIVE 20 MIN. · TOTAL 1 HOUR, 50 MIN.

SERVES 8 TO 10

- 2 lb. Granny Smith apples
- 2 lb. Braeburn apples
- 1 tsp. ground cinnamon
- ¾ cup plus 2 Tbsp. granulated sugar, divided
- ½ cup butter
- 1 cup firmly packed light brown sugar
- 1 (14.1-oz.) pkg. refrigerated piecrusts
- 1 large egg white

1. Preheat oven to 350°F.

2. Peel apples, then cut into ½-inch-thick wedges. Toss apples with cinnamon and ¾ cup granulated sugar.

3. Melt butter in a 10-inch cast-iron skillet over medium; add brown sugar, and cook, stirring constantly, 1 to 2 minutes or until sugar dissolves. Remove from heat. Place 1 piecrust in skillet over brown sugar mixture. Spoon apple mixture over piecrust, then top with remaining piecrust. Whisk egg white until foamy. Brush top of piecrust with egg white; sprinkle with 2 tablespoons granulated sugar. Cut 4 or 5 slits in top for steam to escape.

4. Bake in preheated oven until golden brown and bubbly, 1 hour to 1 hour and 10 minutes, shielding with aluminum foil during last 10 minutes to prevent excessive browning, if necessary. Cool on a wire rack 30 minutes before serving.

SKILLET
APPLE PIE

LEMON-LIME
MERINGUE PIE

LEMON–LIME MERINGUE PIE

ACTIVE 30 MIN. - TOTAL 3 HOURS, 15 MIN.

SERVES 8

CRUST
- 1½ cups crushed graham crackers (about 11 rectangles)
- 6 Tbsp. unsalted butter, melted
- ¼ cup granulated sugar
- 1 large egg white, beaten until foamy

FILLING
- 1 cup granulated sugar
- 6 Tbsp. cornstarch
- ¼ tsp. table salt
- 5 large egg yolks
- 1 Tbsp. lemon zest plus ¼ cup fresh juice (from 1 large lemon), divided
- 1 Tbsp. lime zest plus ¼ cup fresh juice (from 2 limes), divided
- 2 Tbsp. unsalted butter

MERINGUE
- 6 large egg whites
- ½ tsp. cream of tartar
- ¾ cup granulated sugar

1. Prepare the Crust: Preheat oven to 350°F. Stir together crushed graham crackers, butter, and sugar in a medium bowl until combined.

2. Transfer crust mixture to a 9-inch tart pan or pie plate. (If using a tart pan with removable bottom, surround bottom of pan with aluminum foil to prevent Filling from leaking.) Press mixture evenly in bottom and up sides of pan. Freeze until set, 5 to 10 minutes. Brush bottom and sides of crust with egg white. Bake in preheated oven 10 minutes. Cool on a rack while preparing filling.

3. Prepare the Filling: Whisk together sugar, cornstarch, and salt in a medium saucepan. In a medium bowl, whisk together 1 cup water, egg yolks, lemon juice, and lime juice. Gradually whisk yolk mixture into sugar mixture until combined. Cook over medium-high, whisking often, until filling thickens and just begins to bubble, 6 to 8 minutes. Cook, whisking constantly, 1 minute more.

4. Remove from heat. Whisk in butter, lemon zest, and lime zest. Allow to cool 30 minutes before pouring into crust.

5. Prepare the Meringue: Beat together egg whites and cream of tartar with an electric mixer on medium speed until soft peaks form. Gradually add sugar, 1 tablespoon at a time, beating until stiff peaks form.

6. Spread meringue over filling, being sure to spread to outside of Crust to seal in Filling and prevent shrinkage. Bake in preheated oven until Meringue is golden brown, 14 to 15 minutes. Cool before serving.

- -

OUR EASIEST PUMPKIN PIE EVER

ACTIVE 15 MIN. - TOTAL 2 HOURS, 15 MIN.

SERVES 8

- 1 (14.1-oz.) pkg. refrigerated piecrusts
- 1½ cups plus 2 Tbsp. buttermilk, divided
- 1 (15-oz.) can pumpkin
- ¾ cup granulated sugar
- 2 tsp. ground cinnamon
- ½ tsp. kosher salt
- 1 tsp. vanilla extract
- 2 large eggs
- 1 large egg yolk

1. Preheat oven to 425°F. Fit 1 piecrust into a 9-inch metal pie pan according to package directions, pressing excess dough onto rim of pie pan. Cut shapes from remaining piecrust to use around pie edge. (We used a ½-inch round cutter.) Brush 1 tablespoon buttermilk around pie edge; arrange shapes around pie edge, pressing to adhere. Brush shapes with 1 tablespoon buttermilk. Prick bottom and sides of piecrust 8 to 10 times with a fork. Line piecrust with parchment paper, and fill with pie weights. Bake 15 minutes.

2. Whisk together pumpkin, next 6 ingredients, and remaining 1½ cups buttermilk in a large bowl. Pour mixture into piecrust.

3. Bake in preheated oven 10 minutes. Reduce heat to 325°F; bake 35 minutes more or until edge of filling is slightly puffed and center is slightly jiggly. Cool on a wire rack 1 hour.

STRAWBERRY-RHUBARB PRETZEL PIE

We turned the strawberry-pretzel salad into a rich and creamy pie. Rhubarb is a vegetable that needs sugar to temper its tangy flavor. Enter the strawberry for rounding out this sweet-and-salty dessert.

ACTIVE 30 MIN. · TOTAL 4 HOURS, 20 MIN.
SERVES 8

CRUST
- 1½ cups finely crushed pretzel sticks
- ¼ cup packed light brown sugar
- 6 Tbsp. butter, melted

FILLING
- 1 (8-oz.) pkg. cream cheese, softened
- 1 tsp. vanilla extract
- ½ cup granulated sugar
- 1 cup heavy cream

TOPPING
- 6 Tbsp. granulated sugar
- 8 oz. fresh or frozen rhubarb, cut into ½-inch-thick slices (about 1 cup)
- 3 Tbsp. strawberry jam
- 2 cups sliced strawberries

1. Prepare the Crust: Preheat oven to 350°F. Stir together all 3 ingredients in a small bowl. Firmly press crumb mixture on bottom, up sides, and onto lip of a lightly greased 9-inch pie pan. Bake until lightly browned, about 14 minutes. Transfer pan to a wire rack; cool completely, about 1 hour.

2. Prepare the Filling: Beat first 3 ingredients with an electric mixer on low speed until sugar dissolves and mixture is completely smooth; set aside. Beat cream at high speed using whisk attachment until medium-soft peaks form, about 2 minutes. Stir whipped cream into cream cheese mixture until fully incorporated. Spread into crust. Cover and chill 2 hours or overnight.

3. Prepare the Topping: Combine 2 cups water and 6 tablespoons granulated sugar in a small saucepan; bring to a boil over high. Remove pan from heat. Add rhubarb slices; cover and let stand 5 minutes. Drain rhubarb; cool completely, about 30 minutes.

4. Microwave jam in a microwave-safe bowl on HIGH until hot, about 20 seconds. Add strawberries and gently stir to coat. Add rhubarb slices and gently stir to coat. Top pie with fruit, and serve.

- -

CLASSIC CHESS PIE

ACTIVE 20 MIN. · TOTAL 1 HOUR, 20 MIN.
SERVES 8

- ½ (15-oz.) pkg. refrigerated piecrusts
- 2 cups granulated sugar
- 2 Tbsp. cornmeal
- 1 Tbsp. all-purpose flour
- ¼ tsp. table salt
- ½ cup butter, melted
- ¼ cup milk
- 1 Tbsp. white vinegar
- ½ tsp. vanilla extract
- 4 large eggs, lightly beaten

1. Preheat oven to 425°F. Fit piecrust into a 9-inch pie plate according to package directions; fold edges under and crimp.

2. Line piecrust with aluminum foil; fill with pie weights or dried beans.

3. Bake in preheated oven 4 to 5 minutes. Remove weights and foil; bake 2 minutes more or until golden. Cool completely.

4. Reduce oven temperature to 350°F. Stir together sugar and next 7 ingredients until blended. Add eggs, stirring well. Pour filling into prebaked crust.

5. Bake at 350°F until edges are puffy and set but center just wiggles slightly, 45 to 55 minutes, shielding edges with aluminum foil after 10 minutes to prevent excessive browning. Cool completely on a wire rack.

STRAWBERRY RHUBARB
PRETZEL PIE

BANANA
PUDDING PIE

BANANA PUDDING PIE

Pie just doesn't get any better than this tasty twist on banana pudding. Hang onto the egg yolks—you'll be using them in the Vanilla Cream Filling.

ACTIVE 20 MIN. - TOTAL 6 HOURS, 25 MIN., INCLUDING COOLING AND CHILLING
SERVES 8

- 1 (12-oz.) box vanilla wafers, divided
- ½ cup butter, melted
- 2 large bananas, sliced
  Vanilla Cream Filling (recipe follows)
- 4 egg whites
- ½ cup granulated sugar

1. Preheat oven to 350°F. Set aside 30 vanilla wafers; pulse remaining vanilla wafers in a food processor 8 to 10 times or until coarsely crushed. (Yield should be about 2½ cups.) Stir together crushed vanilla wafers and butter until blended. Firmly press on bottom, up sides, and onto lip of a 9-inch pie plate.

2. Bake in preheated oven until lightly browned, 10 to 12 minutes. Transfer to a wire rack; let cool 30 minutes or until completely cool.

3. Arrange banana slices over bottom of crust. Prepare Vanilla Cream Filling. Spread half the hot filling over bananas; top with 20 vanilla wafers. Spread remaining hot filling over vanilla wafers. (Filling will be about ¼ inch higher than top edge of crust.)

4. Beat egg whites at high speed with an electric mixer until foamy. Add sugar, 1 tablespoon at a time, beating until stiff peaks form and sugar dissolves. Spread meringue over hot filling, sealing edges.

5. Bake in preheated oven until golden brown, 10 to 12 minutes. Remove from oven; let cool 1 hour on a wire rack or until completely cool. Coarsely crush remaining 10 vanilla wafers and sprinkle over top of pie. Chill 4 hours. Store leftovers in refrigerator.

VANILLA CREAM FILLING

ACTIVE 5 MIN. - TOTAL 15 MIN.
MAKES 2½ CUPS

- ¾ cup granulated sugar
- ⅓ cup all-purpose flour
- 2 large eggs
- 4 egg yolks
- 2 cups milk
- 2 tsp. vanilla extract

Whisk together first 5 ingredients in a heavy saucepan. Cook over medium-low, whisking constantly, 8 to 10 minutes or until mixture reaches the thickness of chilled pudding. (Mixture will just begin to bubble and will be thick enough to hold soft peaks when whisk is lifted.) Remove from heat, and stir in vanilla. Use immediately.

- -

PEANUT BUTTER PIE

ACTIVE 15 MIN. - TOTAL 3 HOURS, 40 MIN.
SERVES 8

- 1¼ cups graham cracker crumbs
- ⅓ cup dry-roasted peanuts, coarsely ground
- 2 Tbsp. granulated sugar
- ¼ cup plus 2 Tbsp. butter, melted
- ⅔ cup granulated sugar
- 3 Tbsp. cornstarch
- ¼ tsp. table salt
- 2½ cups evaporated milk
- 2 egg yolks, lightly beaten
- ½ cup peanut butter
- ½ cup peanut butter morsels
- 1 tsp. vanilla extract
- ½ cup whipping cream
- 1 Tbsp. powdered sugar
- ¼ tsp. vanilla extract
  Chopped dry-roasted peanuts

1. Preheat oven to 350°F. Combine first 3 ingredients; stir in melted butter. Firmly press crumb mixture into a lightly greased 9-inch pie plate.

2. Bake in preheated oven until browned, about 10 minutes. Set aside to cool.

3. Combine ⅔ cup sugar, cornstarch, and salt in a heavy saucepan. Gradually stir in evaporated milk. Cook over medium heat, stirring constantly, until mixture is thickened and bubbly. Gradually stir about one-fourth of the hot mixture into beaten egg yolks; add to remaining hot mixture, stirring constantly. Cook, stirring constantly with a wire whisk, 3 minutes or until thickened. Remove from heat. Stir in peanut butter, morsels, and 1 teaspoon vanilla. Stir until morsels melt.

4. Pour filling into prebaked crust. Cover and chill pie 3 hours or until firm.

5. Beat whipping cream with an electric mixer on medium speed until foamy; add powdered sugar and ¼ teaspoon vanilla; beat until soft peaks form. Top each serving with whipped cream and sprinkle with chopped peanuts.

DOUBLE-DECKER PECAN CHEESECAKE PIE

ACTIVE 20 MIN. · TOTAL 4 HOURS, 20 MIN, INCLUDING COOLING
SERVES 8

CRUST
> **Single-Crust Pie Pastry (recipe follows)**

CREAM CHEESE FILLING
- 1 (8-oz.) pkg. cream cheese, at room temperature
- 1 large egg
- 1 tsp. vanilla bean paste
- ½ tsp. kosher salt
- ⅓ cup granulated sugar

BROWN SUGAR FILLING
- 2 large eggs
- ½ cup packed light brown sugar
- ½ cup dark or light corn syrup
- 1 to 2 Tbsp. (½ to 1 oz.) Tennessee whiskey
- 1 tsp. vanilla bean paste or vanilla extract

ADDITIONAL INGREDIENTS
- ½ cup chopped pecans
- 1¼ cups pecan halves

1. Prepare the Crust: Preheat oven to 375°F. Unwrap chilled pie dough disk from Single-Crust Pie Pastry and place on a lightly floured surface. Let stand at room temperature until slightly softened, about 5 minutes. Sprinkle dough with flour, then roll into a 12-inch circle. Carefully fit dough circle into a 9-inch deep-dish glass pie plate; fold edges under and crimp. Line pastry with parchment paper, and fill with pie weights or dried beans.

2. Bake in preheated oven 15 minutes. Transfer piecrust to a wire rack. Remove pie weights and parchment. Let crust cool 30 minutes.

3. Prepare the Cream Cheese Filling: Beat cream cheese, egg, vanilla bean paste, and salt in a medium bowl with an electric mixer on medium speed until light and fluffy, 1 to 2 minutes. Add sugar and beat until filling is smooth and fluffy, about 2 minutes. Spoon filling into prepared piecrust.

4. Prepare the Brown Sugar Filling: Whisk eggs until bright yellow and well combined. Add brown sugar, corn syrup, Tennessee whiskey, and vanilla bean paste; whisk together until thickened and smooth.

5. Sprinkle chopped pecans over Cream Cheese Filling in piecrust. Gently spoon Brown Sugar Filling over chopped pecans. Arrange pecan halves over Brown Sugar Filling. Place pie on a baking sheet.

6. Bake in preheated oven 10 minutes. Reduce oven temperature to 350°F; bake until filling is puffed and set and crust is golden brown, 40 to 45 minutes. Transfer pie to a wire rack and cool completely, 2 to 3 hours.

SINGLE-CRUST PIE PASTRY

ACTIVE 10 MIN. · TOTAL 2 HOURS, 10 MIN.
MAKES 1 CHILLED DOUGH DISK

- 1½ cups all-purpose flour
- ½ tsp. table salt
- 6 Tbsp. cold unsalted butter, cubed
- 2 Tbsp. cold shortening, cubed
- 3 to 4 Tbsp. ice water

1. Pulse flour and salt in a food processor until combined, 3 or 4 times. Add cubed butter and shortening; pulse until mixture resembles small peas, 4 or 5 times. Sprinkle 3 tablespoons ice water over top of mixture. Pulse 4 times. Add up to 1 tablespoon more water, 1 teaspoon at a time, pulsing after each addition until dough just begins to clump together.

2. Turn dough out onto a lightly floured work surface; knead until dough comes together, 2 or 3 times. Shape and flatten dough into a disk. Wrap in plastic wrap and chill 2 hours or up to 2 days.

GERMAN CHOCOLATE CHEESECAKE

With a nod to the traditional three-layer cake, this luscious cheesecake takeoff comes pretty close to perfection.

ACTIVE 30 MIN. - TOTAL 9 HOURS, 15 MIN., INCLUDING CHILLING.
SERVES 12

- 1 cup chocolate wafer crumbs
- 2 Tbsp. granulated sugar
- 3 Tbsp. butter, melted
- 3 (8-oz.) pkg. cream cheese, softened
- ¾ cup granulated sugar
- ¼ cup unsweetened cocoa
- 2 tsp. vanilla extract
- 3 large eggs
- ⅓ cup evaporated milk
- ⅓ cup granulated sugar
- ¼ cup butter
- 1 large egg, lightly beaten
- ½ tsp. vanilla extract
- ½ cup coarsely chopped pecans, toasted
- ½ cup organic coconut chips or flaked coconut

1. Preheat oven to 325°F. Stir together the first 3 ingredients; press into bottom of an ungreased 9-inch springform pan. Bake 10 minutes. Cool crust.

2. Increase oven temperature to 350°F. Beat cream cheese and next 3 ingredients with an electric mixer on medium speed until blended. Add eggs, 1 at a time, beating just until blended after each addition. Pour into prepared crust.

3. Bake at 350°F for 35 minutes. Remove from oven; run a knife around edge of pan. Cool completely in pan on a wire rack. Cover and chill 8 hours.

4. Stir together evaporated milk and next 4 ingredients in a saucepan. Cook over medium, stirring constantly, 7 minutes. Stir in pecans and coconut. Remove sides of pan; spread topping over cheesecake.

WHITE CHOCOLATE–RASPBERRY CHEESECAKE

ACTIVE 20 MIN. - TOTAL 9 HOURS, 20 MIN. INCLUDING CHILLING
SERVES 12

CRUST
- 2 cups graham cracker crumbs
- 3 Tbsp. granulated sugar
- ½ cup butter, melted

FILLING
- 5 (8-oz.) pkg. cream cheese, softened
- 1 cup granulated sugar
- 2 large eggs
- 1 Tbsp. vanilla extract
- 12 oz. white chocolate, melted and cooled slightly
- ¾ cup raspberry preserves*
  Fresh raspberries, for garnish

1. Prepare the Crust: Preheat oven to 350°F. Combine all ingredients; press crumb mixture into bottom of a lightly greased 9-inch springform pan. Bake 8 minutes; cool slightly.

2. Prepare the Filling: Beat cream cheese with a mixer on medium speed until creamy; gradually add 1 cup sugar, beating well. Add eggs, 1 at a time, beating after each addition. Stir in vanilla. Add melted white chocolate, beating well.

3. Microwave raspberry preserves in a small microwave-safe bowl on HIGH 30 seconds to 1 minute or until melted; stir well.

4. Spoon half the filling into prepared crust; spread a little more than half of melted preserves over filling, leaving a ¾-inch border. Spoon remaining filling around edges of pan, spreading toward the center. Cover and chill remaining raspberry preserves.

5. Bake in preheated oven until cheesecake is just set and slightly browned, about 50 minutes. Remove from oven; cool completely on a wire rack. Cover and chill at least 8 hours.

6. Gently run a knife around outer edge of cheesecake to loosen from sides of pan. Reheat remaining preserves briefly in microwave to melt. Pour preserves over top of cheesecake, leaving a 1-inch border. Remove sides of pan. Store in refrigerator. Garnish, if desired.

***Note:** To remove seeds from raspberry preserves, press preserves through a fine-mesh strainer using the back of a spoon.

SWEET TEA TIRAMISÙ

How does the South do Italian tiramisù? By replacing espresso with sweet tea, of course!

ACTIVE 20 MIN. - TOTAL 13 HOURS, 30 MIN., INCLUDING CHILLING
SERVES 10 TO 12

- 2 family-size tea bags
- 1½ cups granulated sugar, divided
- 2 (8-oz.) containers mascarpone cheese
- 1 Tbsp. vanilla bean paste or vanilla extract
- 2 cups whipping cream
- 2 (3-oz.) pkg. ladyfingers
- 1 to 2 tsp. unsweetened cocoa

1. Bring 4 cups water to a boil in a 3-quart heavy saucepan; add tea bags. Remove from heat; cover and steep 10 minutes.

2. Discard tea bags. Add 1 cup sugar, stirring until dissolved. Bring tea mixture to a boil over medium-high; cook, stirring occasionally, 20 to 22 minutes or until mixture is reduced to 1 cup. Remove mixture from heat; cool to room temperature (about 30 minutes).

3. Stir together mascarpone cheese, vanilla, and remaining ½ cup sugar.

4. Beat whipping cream with an electric mixer on medium speed until soft peaks form; fold into cheese mixture.

5. Separate ladyfingers in half. Arrange 24 ladyfinger halves, flat sides up, in the bottom of an 11- x 7-inch baking dish. Drizzle with half the tea mixture. Top with half the cheese mixture. Repeat layers once. Cover and chill 12 hours. Sift cocoa over top just before serving.

Tip: Add fresh fruit and chocolate to round out the rich flavors. Toss sliced strawberries and pitted fresh cherries with a little sugar and almond liqueur; add shaved chocolate. Spoon onto Sweet Tea Tiramisù.

PUMPKIN TART WITH WHIPPED CREAM AND ALMOND TOFFEE

ACTIVE 45 MIN. - TOTAL 13 HOURS, INCLUDING CHILLING
SERVES 8 TO 10

TART
- ½ (14.1-oz.) pkg. refrigerated piecrusts
- ¾ cup granulated sugar
- 1½ Tbsp. all-purpose flour
- 2 tsp. pumpkin pie spice
- ¼ tsp. ground cloves
- 3 cups canned pumpkin
- ½ cup blackstrap molasses
- 6 Tbsp. butter, melted
- 4 large eggs
- 1 (12-oz.) can evaporated milk

ALMOND TOFFEE
- ½ cup firmly packed light brown sugar
- 4 Tbsp. butter
- 1 cup slivered almonds

WHIPPED CREAM
- 2½ cups whipping cream
- ¼ tsp. pumpkin pie spice
- ½ cup plus 2 Tbsp. powdered sugar

1. Prepare Tart: Preheat oven to 350°F. Fit piecrust into a 9-inch deep-dish tart pan with removable bottom; press into fluted edges. Whisk together granulated sugar and next 3 ingredients in a large bowl. Whisk together pumpkin and next 2 ingredients in a separate bowl. Whisk pumpkin mixture into sugar mixture. Add eggs, 1 at a time, whisking until blended after each addition. Whisk in evaporated milk, and pour into crust.

2. Bake in preheated oven until a knife inserted in center comes out clean, about 1 hour and 30 minutes. Cool completely on a wire rack. Cover and chill 8 to 24 hours.

3. Prepare Almond Toffee: Cook light brown sugar and 4 tablespoons butter in a small skillet over medium, stirring constantly, until bubbly. Add slivered almonds and cook, stirring constantly, 2 minutes or until golden. Pour mixture onto lightly greased (with cooking spray) parchment paper; cool completely. Break into pieces.

4. Prepare Whipped Cream: Beat cream and ¼ teaspoon pumpkin pie spice with an electric mixer on medium-high speed until foamy; gradually add powdered sugar, beating until soft peaks form. Top tart with whipped cream; sprinkle with toffee.

PUMPKIN TART WITH
WHIPPED CREAM AND
ALMOND TOFFEE

BLACK-AND-BLUE
BUTTERMILK TART

BLACK-AND-BLUE BUTTERMILK TART

ACTIVE 25 MIN. - TOTAL 55 MIN., PLUS 8 HOURS CHILLING
SERVES 8 TO 10

56	round buttery crackers (such as Ritz; from 2 sleeves)
1	large egg white
¼	cup unsalted butter, melted
½	cup plus 3 Tbsp. granulated sugar, divided
¾	cup heavy cream
1	large vanilla bean pod
1¼	tsp. unflavored gelatin (from 1 [¼-oz.] envelope)
1½	(8-oz.) pkg. cream cheese, softened
¾	cup whole buttermilk
¼	tsp. kosher salt
1½	cups fresh blackberries
1½	cups fresh blueberries
	Small fresh basil leaves

1. Preheat oven to 350°F. Pulse crackers in a food processor until finely ground, 6 to 8 times. Add egg white, butter, and 3 tablespoons of the sugar. Pulse until well combined, about 4 times.

2. Scatter crumb mixture evenly on bottom of a 9- or 10-inch tart pan with removable bottom. Using a straight-sided glass or dry measuring cup, firmly press crumbs on bottom and against sides of pan.

3. Bake crust in preheated oven until golden brown around the edges, 12 to 14 minutes. Cool completely on a wire rack, about 30 minutes.

4. Meanwhile, pour cream into a small saucepan. Using a small knife, split the vanilla bean lengthwise. Using back of knife, scrape seeds from bean into cream; discard pod. Sprinkle gelatin evenly over cream. Let stand 5 minutes. Stir in remaining ½ cup sugar. Cook over medium-low, stirring constantly, until gelatin and sugar are dissolved, 4 to 5 minutes.

5. Transfer cream mixture to food processor. Pinch cream cheese into 1- to 2-inch pieces and place in food processor. Add buttermilk and salt. Process mixture until smooth, 20 to 30 seconds; pour into cooled tart crust. Chill until set, 8 hours or up to 1 day. Before serving, scatter berries over top; garnish with basil leaves.

Note: If you don't have a tart pan, use a 9-inch pie plate. The crust will be a bit shallower but will still look and taste great.

QUICK APPLE DUMPLING BUNDLES

Guests will love getting their own little apple goodies topped with luscious, warm caramel.

ACTIVE 20 MIN. - TOTAL 40 MIN.
SERVES 4

½	cup chopped pecans
½	(14.1-oz.) pkg. refrigerated piecrusts
1	(12-oz.) pkg. frozen spiced apples, thawed
1	large egg white, lightly beaten
	Granulated sugar
1	(12-oz.) jar caramel topping, warmed

1. Preheat oven to 350°F. Bake pecans in a single layer in a shallow pan 5 to 6 minutes or until toasted and fragrant. Remove from oven; increase oven temperature to 425°F.

2. Unroll piecrust on a lightly floured surface. Cut piecrust into fourths. Divide apples among each fourth, placing in center. Pull corners together over apples, pinching edges to seal. Place on a lightly greased-aluminum foil-lined baking sheet; brush with egg white, and sprinkle with sugar.

3. Bake at 425°F until golden, about 20 minutes. Serve apple bundles with warm caramel topping. Sprinkle with pecans.

APPLE CINNAMON DUTCH BABY

This puffy, light pancake will fall as soon as it leaves the oven, but don't worry, it's still tasty. Be sure to use low-fat or fat-free milk—it will puff higher.

ACTIVE 25 MIN. - TOTAL 45 MIN.
SERVES 6

- 1 large Gala apple, peeled and sliced
- 1 Tbsp. granulated sugar
- 3 Tbsp. butter, divided
- 2 large eggs
- ½ cup fat-free or low-fat milk
- ½ cup all-purpose flour, sifted
- ½ tsp. ground cinnamon
- ¼ tsp. table salt
- ¼ tsp. ground nutmeg
- 1 cup sour cream
- ½ cup firmly packed light brown sugar
- 1 to 4 Tbsp. apple cider or orange juice
  Powdered sugar, for garnish

1. Preheat oven to 450°F. Heat a 10-inch cast-iron skillet over medium-high 5 minutes. Toss together apple slices and sugar in a small bowl. Melt 1 tablespoon butter in skillet. Add apples, and cook, stirring often, 5 minutes or until tender. Remove apples from skillet, and wipe skillet clean.

2. Whisk together eggs and milk in a medium bowl. Whisk in flour and next 3 ingredients. Melt remaining 2 tablespoons butter in skillet over medium-high. Immediately pour egg mixture into hot skillet, and top with cooked apples.

3. Bake in preheated oven until pancake is golden and puffed, 20 minutes.

4. Meanwhile, stir together sour cream and brown sugar in a small microwave-safe bowl. Microwave at HIGH 45 seconds. Whisk until sugar dissolves. Stir in apple cider. Serve sauce with pancake; garnish with powdered sugar.

DECADENT CREAM PUFFS WITH PRALINE SAUCE

ACTIVE 30 MIN. - TOTAL 1 HOUR, 25 MIN., INCLUDING SAUCE
SERVES 8

- ½ cup butter
- 1 cup all-purpose flour
- ⅛ tsp. table salt
- 4 large eggs
- 4 cups butter-pecan ice cream
  Praline Sauce (recipe follows)
- 1 cup coarsely chopped toasted pecans

1. Preheat oven to 400°F. Bring 1 cup water to a boil in a large saucepan over medium-high. Reduce heat to low, and add butter, stirring until melted.

2. Stir in flour and salt, beating vigorously with a wooden spoon 1 minute or until mixture leaves sides of saucepan. Remove from heat, and cool 5 minutes. Add eggs, 1 at a time, beating with wooden spoon until smooth. Drop by rounded ¼ cupfuls, 2 inches apart, onto a lightly greased (with cooking spray) parchment-paper-lined baking sheet.

3. Bake in preheated oven until puffed and golden brown, 30 to 35 minutes. Remove from oven, and, using a wooden pick, poke a small hole into side of each cream puff to allow steam to escape. Cool completely on baking sheet on a wire rack (about 30 minutes).

4. Cut each cream puff in half horizontally; remove and discard any soft dough inside. Spoon ½ cup ice cream onto each bottom half; top cream puffs with remaining halves. Spoon 3 tablespoons Praline Sauce over each puff; sprinkle with toasted pecans. Serve immediately with remaining sauce.

PRALINE SAUCE

ACTIVE 10 MIN. - TOTAL 20 MIN.
MAKES ABOUT 1½ CUPS

- 1 cup firmly packed light brown sugar
- ½ cup half-and-half
- ½ cup butter
  Pinch of table salt
- 1 tsp. vanilla extract

Bring first 4 ingredients to a boil in a small saucepan over medium, stirring constantly. Cook, stirring constantly, 1 minute. Remove from heat, and stir in vanilla. Let stand 10 minutes.

—

DECADENT CREAM
PUFFS WITH
PRALINE SAUCE

GINGER BREAD
SOUFFLÉS

COLD LEMON SOUFFLÉS WITH WINE SAUCE

ACTIVE 55 MIN. · TOTAL 3 HOURS, 15 MIN.
SERVES 8

SOUFFLÉS

- 1 (¼-oz.) envelope unflavored gelatin
- ¼ cup cold water
- 5 large eggs, separated
- 2 tsp. lemon zest plus ¾ cup fresh juice (from about 5 lemons)
- 1½ cups granulated sugar
- 1 cup heavy cream

WINE SAUCE

- ½ cup granulated sugar
- 1 Tbsp. cornstarch
- 1 tsp. lemon zest plus 3 Tbsp. fresh juice (from 1 lemon), plus more zest for topping (optional)
- 2 Tbsp. salted butter
- ½ cup dry white wine

1. Prepare the Soufflés: Sprinkle gelatin over cold water in a small bowl. Let stand 5 minutes.

2. Combine egg yolks, lemon zest, lemon juice, and ¾ cup of the sugar in top of a double boiler over boiling water. Cook, stirring constantly, until lemon mixture is slightly thickened, 8 to 10 minutes. Remove pan from heat, and stir in gelatin until completely combined and smooth. Transfer mixture to a large bowl. Place bowl in an ice bath and let stand, stirring occasionally until mixture has cooled, about 15 minutes. Thoroughly clean top of double boiler.

3. Combine egg whites and remaining ¾ cup granulated sugar in top of double boiler over simmering water; cook, stirring constantly, until sugar dissolves and mixture is hot, 4 to 5 minutes. Transfer to a medium bowl, and beat with an electric mixer on high speed until medium peaks form, 7 to 8 minutes.

4. Beat cream with electric mixer on high speed until medium peaks form, 3 to 4 minutes.

5. Gently fold egg white mixture into yolk mixture. Gently fold whipped cream into egg mixture. Divide soufflé mixture evenly among 8 (8-ounce) ramekins or dessert glasses. Cover and chill 2 hours or overnight.

6. Prepare the Wine Sauce: Whisk together sugar and cornstarch in a small saucepan. Stir in ½ cup water, lemon zest, and lemon juice until smooth. Bring to a boil over medium-high; reduce heat to medium and cook until thickened, about 3 minutes. Remove from heat, and stir in butter until melted and combined; stir in wine. Cover and chill until ready to serve. Drizzle wine sauce over soufflés, and sprinkle with lemon zest, if desired.

- -

GINGER BREAD SOUFFLÉS

Even gingerbread men have to admit these soufflés are superior. Pop them in the oven just before dinner, and they'll be done by the time you finish eating.

ACTIVE 20 MIN. · TOTAL 1 HOUR, 30 MIN.
SERVES 10

- 1 cup milk
- ½ cup granulated sugar, plus more for ramekins
- ¼ cup all-purpose flour
- ¼ tsp. table salt
- ⅓ cup molasses
- 2 Tbsp. butter, softened
- 2 tsp. pumpkin pie spice
- 1 tsp. ground ginger
- 2 tsp. vanilla extract
- 6 large eggs, separated
- ⅛ tsp. cream of tartar
- Sweetened whipped cream, crushed gingersnaps, for garnish

1. Preheat oven to 350°F.

2. Whisk together first 4 ingredients in a medium saucepan until smooth. Bring to a boil over medium, whisking constantly. Transfer mixture to a large bowl; whisk in molasses and next 4 ingredients. Cool 15 minutes. Whisk in egg yolks.

3. Grease 10 (7-oz.) ramekins; sprinkle with sugar to coat and shake out excess.

4. Beat egg whites and cream of tartar with an electric mixer on high speed until stiff peaks form. Fold one-third of egg white mixture into milk mixture until well blended. Repeat twice with remaining egg white mixture. Spoon batter into prepared ramekins, leaving ¾-inch space at top of each.

5. Bake in preheated oven until puffy and set, 25 minutes. Serve immediately.

Note: Or bake soufflés in a 2½-quart soufflé dish. Bake at 350°F until puffy and set, 55 to 60 minutes.

EASY MOCHA CHIP ICE CREAM CAKE

ACTIVE 20 MIN.- TOTAL 5 HOURS, 15 MIN., INCLUDING GANACHE
SERVES 8 TO 10

- 1 pt. premium dark chocolate chunk-coffee ice cream, softened
- 3 sugar cones, crushed
- ⅓ cup chocolate fudge shell topping
- 1 (14-oz.) container premium chocolate-chocolate chip ice cream, softened
- 6 cream-filled chocolate sandwich cookies, finely crushed
  Mocha Ganache (recipe follows)
  Chocolate-covered coffee beans, for garnish

1. Line an 8- x 5-inch loaf pan with plastic wrap, allowing 3 inches to extend over sides. Spread chocolate chunk-coffee ice cream in pan. Sprinkle with crushed cones, and drizzle with shell topping. Freeze 30 minutes.

2. Spread chocolate-chocolate chip ice cream over topping. Top with crushed cookies, pressing into ice cream. Freeze 4 hours or until firm.

3. Lift ice cream loaf from pan, using plastic wrap as handles; invert onto a serving plate. Discard plastic wrap. Prepare Mocha Ganache, and slowly pour over ice cream loaf, allowing ganache to drip down sides. Freeze 10 minutes. Let stand at room temperature 10 minutes before serving. Garnish with chocolate-covered coffee beans.

MOCHA GANACHE

ACTIVE 2 MIN. - TOTAL 5 MIN.
MAKES ABOUT ½ CUP

- 1 (4-oz.) semisweet chocolate baking bar, chopped
- 1 tsp. instant espresso
- 4 Tbsp. whipping cream, divided

Microwave chocolate, espresso, and 3 tablespoons cream in a microwave-safe bowl on HIGH 1 minute or until melted and smooth, stirring at 30-second intervals. Whisk in an additional 1 tablespoon cream until smooth. Use immediately.

STRAWBERRY-MANGO SEMIFREDDO

The tangy golden mango sorbet is a delicious contrast to the rich, milky sweetness of the strawberry ice cream. Make the semifreddo up to five days ahead, and pile on the fresh fruit just before serving.

ACTIVE 30 MIN. - TOTAL 5 HOURS, 30 MIN., INCLUDING FREEZING
SERVES 8

- 1 cup heavy cream
- 2 tsp. fresh lemon juice
- 1 (16-oz.) container strawberry ice cream, softened
- 1 (16-oz.) container mango sorbet, softened
- ½ cup crushed shortbread cookies
  Diced mango and sliced strawberries

1. Line bottom and sides of an 8½- x 4-inch loaf pan with plastic wrap, allowing 4 to 5 inches to extend over all sides.

2. Beat ½ cup of the heavy cream with an electric mixer on high speed until soft peaks form. Gently stir lemon juice into softened strawberry ice cream, and gently fold in whipped cream. Spread mixture into prepared pan, smoothing with a small offset spatula. Freeze 1 hour.

3. Beat remaining ½ cup heavy cream on high speed until soft peaks form. Gently fold whipped cream into softened mango sorbet. Spread mixture over strawberry mixture in loaf pan, smoothing with a small offset spatula, and sprinkle with cookie crumbs.

4. Pull excess plastic wrap at sides tightly over cake, gently pressing down on cookie crumbs. Freeze 4 to 24 hours.

5. Lift semifreddo from pan, using plastic wrap as handles, and transfer, crumb-side down, to a serving plate. Garnish with diced mango and sliced strawberries. Cut semifreddo into 8 slices, using a serrated knife dipped in hot water and wiped dry.

STRAWBERRY-MANGO
SEMIFREDDO

POUND CAKE
BANANA
PUDDING

POUND CAKE BANANA PUDDING

This recipe was inspired by the pudding served at the famous Mrs. Wilkes' Dining Room in Savannah, Georgia—a family-style comfort-food restaurant to write home about.

ACTIVE 20 MIN. - TOTAL 6 HOURS, 50 MIN., INCLUDING CHILLING

SERVES 10 TO 12

- 4 cups half-and-half
- 4 egg yolks
- 1½ cups granulated sugar
- ¼ cup cornstarch
- ¼ tsp. table salt
- 3 Tbsp. butter
- 2 tsp. vanilla extract
- 1 (1-lb.) pound cake, cubed
- 4 large ripe bananas, sliced
  Meringue (recipe follows)

1. Whisk together first 5 ingredients in a saucepan over medium-low; cook, whisking constantly, 13 to 15 minutes or until thickened. Remove from heat; add butter and vanilla, stirring until butter melts.

2. Layer half of pound cake cubes, half of bananas, and half of pudding mixture in a lightly greased 3-quart round baking dish. Repeat layers. Cover pudding and chill 6 hours.

3. Preheat oven to 375°F. Prepare Meringue, and spread over pudding.

4. Bake in preheated oven until golden brown, about 15 minutes. Spoon into glasses, if desired.

MERINGUE

ACTIVE 10 MIN. - TOTAL 10 MIN.

MAKES 3½ CUPS

- ¼ cup granulated sugar
- ⅛ tsp. table salt
- 4 egg whites
- ¼ tsp. vanilla extract

Combine sugar and salt in a medium bowl. Beat egg whites and vanilla with an electric mixer on high speed until foamy. Add sugar mixture, 1 tablespoon at a time, and beat 2 to 3 minutes or until stiff peaks form and sugar dissolves.

CHOCOLATE PUDDING

ACTIVE 15 MIN. - TOTAL 2 HOURS, 15 MIN.

SERVES 5

- 2 cups fat-free milk
- ⅔ cup granulated sugar
- ⅓ cup unsweetened cocoa
- 3 Tbsp. cornstarch
- ⅛ tsp. table salt
- 1 large egg, lightly beaten
- ½ (4-oz.) semisweet chocolate baking bar, chopped
- 1 tsp. vanilla extract
- ⅓ cup thawed reduced-fat frozen whipped topping
  Toasted sliced almonds, chocolate shavings, for garnish

1. Whisk together first 5 ingredients in a medium-size heavy saucepan over medium-high. Cook, whisking constantly, 5 minutes or until mixture is hot. Gradually whisk ⅓ cup hot milk mixture into egg. Whisk egg mixture into remaining hot milk mixture.

2. Cook, whisking constantly, 3 minutes or until mixture thickens. Remove from heat and add chopped chocolate, stirring until chocolate melts and mixture is smooth. Stir in vanilla. Pour mixture into a glass bowl. Place heavy-duty plastic wrap directly on warm mixture (to prevent a film from forming), and chill 2 hours or until pudding is completely cool.

3. Spoon ½ cup pudding into each of 5 individual serving dishes. Top each with 1 tablespoon whipped topping. Garnish, if desired.

Chocolate-Espresso Pudding: Whisk first 5 ingredients, adding 1 tablespoon instant espresso to milk mixture. Proceed with recipe as directed.

Raspberry-Chocolate Pudding: Prepare pudding as directed through Step 2. Microwave ⅓ cup raspberry jam in a small microwave-safe bowl on HIGH 30 seconds or until melted. Spoon 1 tablespoon melted jam into bottom of each individual serving dish, and top each with ½ cup pudding and 1 tablespoon whipped topping. Stir 1 teaspoon water into remaining melted jam, and drizzle ½ teaspoon jam mixture on whipped topping on each pudding. Garnish with fresh raspberries, if desired.

OLD-FASHIONED VANILLA ICE CREAM

ACTIVE 10 MIN. - TOTAL 1 HOUR, 10 MIN.
MAKES 3½ QUARTS

  6 large eggs, lightly beaten
2⅓ cups granulated sugar
  4 cups milk
  2 cups half-and-half
  ¼ tsp. table salt
2½ Tbsp. vanilla extract
  3 cups whipping cream

1. Combine first 3 ingredients in a large saucepan; cook over low heat, stirring constantly, 25 to 30 minutes or until mixture thickens and coats a spoon; chill.

2. Stir in half-and-half and remaining ingredients; pour into freezer container of a 5- or 6-quart hand-turned or electric ice cream freezer. Freeze according to manufacturer's instructions.

3. Serve immediately, or spoon into an airtight container; freeze until firm.

HOT FUDGE SUNDAE SHAKE

A good hot fudge sundae brings out the child in us all. This version takes the sundae to a crazy-good level with brownie chunks and caramel topping. Microwave the caramel and fudge toppings according to package directions. Pick up brownies from your favorite bakery.

ACTIVE 10 MIN. - TOTAL 10 MIN.
SERVES 4

  1 pint vanilla bean ice cream
  ½ cup milk
  8 Tbsp. hot fudge topping, warmed
  8 Tbsp. caramel topping, warmed
  1 (8.5-oz.) can refrigerated instant whipped cream
  ¼ cup crumbled brownies, divided
  4 maraschino cherries (with stems)

1. Process ice cream and milk in a blender until smooth, stopping to scrape down sides.

2. Divide half of ice cream mixture among 4 (8-ounce) glasses. Top each with 1 tablespoon fudge topping and 1 tablespoon caramel topping. Repeat layers with remaining ice cream mixture and fudge and caramel toppings.

3. Top each with instant whipped cream; sprinkle each with 1 tablespoon crumbled brownies, and top with a cherry. Serve immediately.

ROOT BEER FLOAT

Use premium root beer and a high-quality vanilla ice cream to make the best dessert drink.

ACTIVE 5 MIN - TOTAL 5 MIN.
SERVES 1

     Vanilla ice cream
  1 (12-oz.) can root beer

Scoop ice cream into a tall glass, filling half full. Top with root beer, and gently stir. Serve immediately.

CLASSIC COLA FLOAT

Add cherry syrup or flavored soda to this kid-friendly quencher. It's even better topped with a maraschino cherry with a stem.

ACTIVE 5 MIN - TOTAL 5 MIN.
SERVES 1

     Vanilla ice cream
  1 (12-oz.) can cola soft drink
  ¼ tsp. vanilla extract

Scoop ice cream into a tall glass, filling half full. Top with cola, and gently stir in vanilla. Serve immediately.

CLASSIC
COLA FLOAT

RECIPE INDEX

A

Almond French Toast, 41
Almonds, Five-Spice, 323
Aloha Punch, 30
"Any-Berry" Muffins with Cornmeal Streusel, 59
Appetizers. *See also* **Dips; Salsa**
  Balsamic Marinated Olives, 22
  Barbecue Deviled Eggs, 21
  Best-Ever Crab Cakes with Green Tomato Slaw, 10
  Blue Cheese Crisps, 25
  Butternut-Goat Cheese-Stuffed Mushrooms, 10
  Chicken Wontons with Hoisin-Peanut Dipping Sauce, 13
  Classic Pimiento Cheese, 25
  Cocktail Meatballs, 18
  Fig Flatbread, 18
  Grilled Salt-and-Pepper Chicken Wings, 13
  Muffuletta Deviled Eggs, 14
  Party-Perfect Meatballs, 21
  Pepperoni Pizza Pinwheels, 17
  Queso-Filled Mini Peppers, 14
  Santa Fe Chicken Quesadillas, 17
  Sheet Pan Nachos with Chorizo and Refried Beans, 17
  Spiced Pecans, 30
  Sweet 'n' Savory Snack Mix, 29
  Tomato Crostini, 25
Apple Brandy-Caramel Sauce, 311
Apples
  Apple Brown Betty, 327
  Apple Cinnamon Dutch Baby, 344
  Caramel Apple Cake, 311
  Caramel Apples, 300
  Cranberry-Apple-Pumpkin Bundt, 315
  Fennel-Apple Slaw, 228
  Homemade Applesauce, 228
  Old-Fashioned Apple Pie, 328
  Pork Chops, Cabbage, and Apples, 94
  Pork Chops with Roasted Apples and Brussels Sprouts, 97
  Quick Apple Dumpling Bundles, 343
  Skillet Apple Pie, 328
  Spiced Applesauce, 228
  Turkey, Brie, and Apple Panini with Bacon Marmalade, 195
Artichoke-Spinach Dip, Hot, 26
Avocados
  Avocado-Corn Salsa, 159
  Avocado-Mango Salsa, 212
  Spicy Pumpkin Soup with Avocado Cream, 223

B

Baby Blue Salad, 273
Bacon
  Bacon and Eggs Bread Pudding, 46
  Bacon-and-Sweet Onion Jam, 188
  Bacon-Blue Cheese Dip, 26
  Bacon Marmalade, 195
  Bacon with Ranch Drizzle, 243
  BLT Potato Salad, 250
  BLTS with a Twist, 192
  Creamy Baked Macaroni and Cheese with Bacon, 236
  Creamy Chicken and Bacon with Herbed Puff Pastry, 123
  Grilled Bacon, Cheese, and Tomato Sandwiches, 192
  Loaded Chicken-Bacon Pot Pie, 176
  Mashed Potatoes with Bacon and Crispy Scallions, 232
  Sautéed Radishes with Bacon and Cilantro, 244
  Smoky Brown Sugar Bacon, 58
  Wild Rice with Bacon and Fennel, 270
Baked Eggs with Spinach and Tomatoes, 46
Baked Hush Puppies, 239
Baked Linguine with Meat Sauce, 167
Baked Penne with Turkey, 130
Balsamic Marinated Olives, 22
Balsamic Vinaigrette, 273
Bananas
  Banana Bread Cobbler, 324
  Banana Bread with variations, 68
  Banana Pudding Pie, 335
  Bananas Foster Upside-Down Cake, 316
  Easy Banana Pancakes, 45
  Gluten-Free Banana Bread, 68
  Pound Cake Banana Pudding, 351
Barbecue Deviled Eggs, 21
Basil Butter with Parmesan, 243
Beans. *See also* **Green beans**
  Bean-and-Cheese Chimichangas, 159
  Black Bean Cakes and Avocado-Corn Salsa, 159
  Black Bean 'n' Spinach Enchiladas, 156
  Black Bean Soup, 220
  Chicken-and-Black Bean Chimichangas, 192
  Easy Skillet Tacos, 86
  Enchilada Casserole, 155
  Hearty Baked Beans, 270
  Layered Nacho Dip, 29
  Okra and Chickpeas in Fresh Tomato Sauce, 266
  Picnic in a Glass, 201
  Sheet Pan Nachos with Chorizo and Refried Beans, 17
  Shrimp-and-Black Bean Stir-Fry, 136

Spicy Steak and Black Bean Chili, 223
Spicy-Sweet Ribs and Beans, 98
Taco Casserole, 165
Tex-Mex Chicken Chili with Lime, 219
White Lightning Chicken Chili, 212

Beef
Baked Linguine with Meat Sauce, 167
Beef Burgundy, 74
Beef Lombardi, 167
Beef Stew with Buttery Garlic Bread, 206
Beef Stroganoff, 77
Cast-Iron Cowboy Steak, 77
Chicken-Fried Steak, 82
Chunky Beef Chili, 208
Cocktail Meatballs, 18
Cola Pot Roast, 74
Easy Skillet Tacos, 86
Easy Sloppy Joes, 89
Fiesta Burgers, 90
Garlic-Herb Steaks, 81
Golden-Baked Mini Reubens, 191
Gonzales Meat Loaf, 85
Grilled Asian Flank Steak, 78
Grilled Steak with Blistered Beans and Peppers, 82
Herb-and-Potato-Chip-Crusted Beef Tenderloin, 73
Homestyle Ground Beef Casserole, 165
Meatball Pasta Bake, 164
Mexican Lasagna, 86
One-Skillet Spaghetti, 86
Open-Faced Philly Sandwiches, 195
Pan-Seared Steaks with Roasted Red Pepper Sauce, 78
Party-Perfect Meatballs, 21
Peppered Filet Mignon with Horseradish Cream, 81
Perfect Burgers, The, 90
Prime Rib with Herbes de Provence Crust and Red Wine Sauce, 73
Shepherd's Pie, 162
Skillet Steak and Wilted Kale, 78
Southwestern Meat Loaf, 85
Speedy Shepherd's Pie, 164
Spicy Steak and Black Bean Chili, 223
Swiss Burgers in Tomato Gravy with Roasted Potatoes, 89
Taco Casserole, 165
Teriyaki Burgers, 90
Tyler's Country-Fried Steak with Uncle Ellis's Cornmeal Gravy, 81
Beer-Cheese Fondue, 29
Beer-Cheese Soup, 220
Berry-Colada Punch, 30
Best Ever Buttermilk Biscuits, 277
Best-Ever Crab Cakes with Green Tomato Slaw, 10

Beverages
Aloha Punch, 30
Berry-Colada Punch, 30
Big-Batch Arnold Palmers, 33
Blackberry Lemonade, 33
Bourbon-Peach Iced Tea, 33
Cherry Sparkler, 34
Classic Cola Float, 352
Cranberry Sangría Punch, 30
Frosted Bellinis, 34
Hot Fudge Sundae Shake, 352
Mango Margarita, 34
Praline Coffee, 37
Root Beer Float, 352
Southern Eggnog, 37
Southern Sunrise, 34
Strawberry-Mint Tea, 33
Watermelon-Ginger Mojitos, 37
Big-Batch Arnold Palmers, 33
Bing Cherry Salad, 270
Black-and-Blue Buttermilk Tart, 343
Black Bean Cakes and Avocado-Corn Salsa, 159
Black Bean 'n' Spinach Enchiladas, 156
Black Bean Soup, 220

Blackberries
"Any-Berry" Muffins with Cornmeal Streusel, 59
Black-and-Blue Buttermilk Tart, 343
Blackberry Cobbler, 320
Blackberry-Honey Mustard Sauce, 188
Blackberry Jam Cake, 308
Blackberry Lemonade, 33
Red Velvet-Berry Cobbler, 320

Black-eyed peas
Black-Eyed Pea Cakes, 253
Black-Eyed Pea Ranchero Sauce, 135
Classic Hoppin' John, 105
Louisiana Gumbo, 212
Southern Italian Chicken Soup, 215
Blistered Brussels Sprouts, 257

Blueberries
"Any-Berry" Muffins with Cornmeal Streusel, 59
Black-and-Blue Buttermilk Tart, 343
Blueberry Coffee Cake, 62
Blueberry-Streusel Muffins, 61
Brunch Popover Pancake, 45
Blue Cheese Crisps, 25
Bourbon-Peach Iced Tea, 33
Bratwurst with Peppers and Onions, 102
Bread Pudding with Rum Sauce, 327

Breads

"Any-Berry" Muffins with Cornmeal Streusel, 59

Baked Hush Puppies, 239

Banana Bread with variations, 68

Best Ever Buttermilk Biscuits, 277

Blueberry-Streusel Muffins, 61

Buttery Chive-and-Mustard Drop Biscuits, 277

Buttery Garlic Bread, 277

Caramel-Nut Pull-Apart Bread, 66

Caramel-Pecan Rolls, 65

Cheddar-Caramelized Onion Bread, 279

Cheese Breadsticks, 280

Cheese Garlic Biscuits, 283

Chocolate-Pear Muffins, 61

Cinnamon-Pecan Rolls, 66

Cinnamon-Raisin Rolls, 65

Cornbread Focaccia, 280

Cornbread with Lemon-Thyme Butter, 283

Family Cornbread, 178

Gluten-Free Banana Bread, 68

Ham-and-Dijon Biscuits with Caramelized Onion Butter, 101

Lemon-Poppy Seed Zucchini Bread, 66

Old-Fashioned Skillet Cornbread, 280

Parmesan Breadsticks, 284

Pimiento Cheese Biscuits, 284

Sizzlin' Skillet Cornbread, 266

Sour Cream Biscuits, 283

Breakfast Burritos, 46

Breakfast Enchiladas, 49

Broccoli

Broccoli-Carrot Salad, 250

Crispy Oven-Fried Chicken Cutlets with Roasted Broccoli, 115

Dixie Chicken Salad with Grapes, Honey, Almonds, and Broccoli, 201

Lemon-Garlic Butter Shrimp and Broccoli, 140

Pasta-Chicken-Broccoli Bake, 176

Ziti with Sausage and Broccoli, 102

Brown Butter-Maple-Pecan Blondies, 296

Brunch Popover Pancake, 45

Brunswick Stew, 219

Brussels Sprouts, Blistered, 257

Brussels Sprouts, Pork Chops with Roasted Apples and, 97

Buttermilk Mashed Potatoes, 232

Butternut-Goat Cheese-Stuffed Mushrooms, 10

Butternut Squash Soup, 221

Butter Toffee-Pecan Layer Cake, 312

Buttery Chive-and-Mustard Drop Biscuits, 277

Buttery Garlic Bread, 277

C

Cakes

Bananas Foster Upside-Down Cake, 316

Blackberry Jam Cake, 308

Blueberry Coffee Cake, 62

Butter Toffee-Pecan Layer Cake, 312

Caramel Apple Cake, 311

Coffee Cake Pound Cake, 307

Cranberry-Apple-Pumpkin Bundt, 315

Cranberry-Pecan Coffee Cake, 62

Lemon-Orange Pound Cake, 304

Mama Dip's Carrot Cake, 311

Million-Dollar Pound Cake, 304

Mocha Java Cakes with variations, 319

Patriotic Cupcakes, 316

Pecan Pound Cake, 307

Candied Yams, 254

Candies

Caramel Apples, 300

Pecan-Espresso Toffee, 300

Shortcut Pralines, 300

Caramel Apple Cake, 311

Caramel Apples, 300

Caramelized Onion Butter, 101

Caramelized Onion Mashed Potato Bake, 232

Caramel-Nut Pull-Apart Bread, 66

Caramel-Pecan Rolls, 65

Caramel Pie, 327

Carrots

Broccoli-Carrot Salad, 250

Cheese-and-Carrot Mashed Potatoes, 162

Couscous Pilaf with Roasted Carrots, Chicken, and Feta, 124

Mama Dip's Carrot Cake, 311

Roasted Carrots with Spiced Pecans and Sorghum, 246

Sweet Potato-Carrot Casserole, 235

Cast-Iron Cowboy Steak, 77

Cast-Iron Salsa, 22

Charred Peppers with Feta Dipping Sauce, 258

Cheddar-Caramelized Onion Bread, 279

Cheddar Cheese Grits Casserole, 50

Cheese. *See also* **Cream cheese**

Baby Blue Salad, 273

Bacon-Blue Cheese Dip, 26

Basil Butter with Parmesan, 243

Bean-and-Cheese Chimichangas, 159

Beer-Cheese Fondue, 29

Beer-Cheese Soup, 220

Blue Cheese Crisps, 25

Butternut-Goat Cheese-Stuffed Mushrooms, 10

Charred Peppers with Feta Dipping Sauce, 258

Cheddar-Caramelized Onion Bread, 279

Cheddar Cheese Grits Casserole, 50
Cheese-and-Carrot Mashed Potatoes, 162
Cheese Breadsticks, 280
Cheese Garlic Biscuits, 283
Cheese Sauce, 49
Cheesy Chicken Penne, 119
Chicken Parmesan, 111
Classic Pimiento Cheese, 25
Couscous Pilaf with Roasted Carrots, Chicken, and Feta, 124
Creamy Baked Macaroni and Cheese with Bacon, 236
Dilled Potato Salad with Feta, 250
Four-Cheese Macaroni, 236
Gouda Grits, 54
Green Bean-Goat Cheese Gratin, 262
Green Chile Cheese Toast, 219
Grilled Bacon, Cheese, and Tomato Sandwiches, 192
Ham and Cheese Strata, 53
Ham 'n' Swiss Omelets, 54
Macaroni and Cheese, 148
Parmesan Breadsticks, 284
Parmesan Cream Sauce, 115
Pimiento Cheese Biscuits, 284
Pimiento Cheese Creamed Spinach, 269
Queso-Filled Mini Peppers, 14
Quick Double-Cheese Grits, 244
Roasted Pumpkin-and-Baby Kale Salad, 273
Roasted Vegetable Orzo Salad, 206
Rustic Mashed Red Potatoes with Parmesan, 232
Savory Ham-and-Swiss Breakfast Pie, 59
Skillet Vegetable Pie with Goat Cheese, 147
Smoky Pimiento Cheese Finger Sandwiches, 199
Sweet Tea Tiramisù, 340
Swiss Burgers in Tomato Gravy with Roasted Potatoes, 89
Three-Cheese Pasta Bake, 148
Tomato Crostini, 25
Turkey, Brie, and Apple Panini with Bacon Marmalade, 195
White Calzones with Marinara Sauce, 196
Cherry Salad, Bing, 270
Cherry Sparkler, 34

Chicken
Brunswick Stew, 219
Cheesy Chicken Penne, 119
Chicken-and-Biscuit Cobbler, 172
Chicken-and-Black Bean Chimichangas, 192
Chicken and Dressing, 178
Chicken-and-Fruit Salad, 269
Chicken and Gnocchi, 216
Chicken-Andouille Gumbo with Roasted Potatoes, 211
Chicken and Sausage Jambalaya, 211
Chicken and Snow Pea Stir-Fry, 119

Chicken and Wild Rice with Pecans, 181
Chicken Caesar Salad Sandwiches, 196
Chicken Caprese Pasta, 120
Chicken Lasagna with Roasted Red Bell Pepper Sauce, 119
Chicken-Mushroom-Sage Casserole, 181
Chicken Noodle Soup, 216
Chicken Parmesan, 111
Chicken Piccata, 112
Chicken Pot Pie, 124
Chicken-Quinoa Salad with Green Goddess Dressing, 202
Chicken Tetrazzini, 172
Chicken Wontons with Hoisin-Peanut Dipping Sauce, 13
Citrus-Braised Chicken Thighs, 112
Classic Chicken Tetrazzini, 171
Classic Double Roast Chickens, 105
Couscous Pilaf with Roasted Carrots, Chicken, and Feta, 124
Creamy Chicken and Bacon with Herbed Puff Pastry, 123
Crispy Oven-Fried Chicken Cutlets with Roasted Broccoli, 115
Crunchy Chicken Casserole, 179
Dixie Chicken Salad with Grapes, Honey, Almonds, and Broccoli, 201
Double-Crust Chicken Pot Pie, 175
Easy Chicken Pot Pie, 123
Greek Chicken with Roasted Potatoes, 115
Grilled Chicken Kebabs with Arugula Pesto, 116
Grilled Chicken Tacos, 116
Grilled Salt-and-Pepper Chicken Wings, 13
Kale and Sweet Potato Salad with Chicken, 202
King Ranch Breakfast Strata, 57
Lemon Chicken Stir-Fry, 120
Lemon-Garlic Roast Chicken with Sautéed Green Beans, 107
Lemon-Rosemary-Garlic Chicken and Potatoes, 111
Lighter Pan-Fried Chicken with Green Beans and Tomatoes, 108
Loaded Chicken-Bacon Pot Pie, 176
Louisiana Gumbo, 212
Mama's Fried Chicken, 108
Pasta-Chicken-Broccoli Bake, 176
Pecan Chicken, 111
Picnic in a Glass, 201
Poppy Seed-Chicken Casserole, 179
Quick-and-Easy King Ranch Chicken Casserole, 178
Santa Fe Chicken Quesadillas, 17
Skillet Chicken Pot Pie, 175
Smoked Chicken Tortilla Soup, 215
Southern Italian Chicken Soup, 215
Southwestern Chicken Salad, 198
Southwestern Chopped Chicken Salad, 205
Spicy Tortilla Soup, 224

Summer Tortellini Salad, 205
Tex-Mex Chicken Chili with Lime, 219
Top-Shelf Chicken Under a Brick, 107
White Lightning Chicken Chili, 212
Chicken-Fried Steak, 82
Chili-Lemon Honey Drizzle, 13
Chipotle Scalloped Potatoes, 231

Chocolate
Chocolate Chip-Banana Bread, 68
Chocolate Chip Cookies, 288
Chocolate Frosting, 295
Chocolate-Pear Muffins, 61
Chocolate Pudding with variations, 351
Deep-Dish Skillet Cookie, 288
Easy Mocha Chip Ice-Cream Cake, 348
Fudgy Flourless Chocolate-Pecan Cookies, 291
German Chocolate Cheesecake, 339
Grasshopper Skillet Cookie, 288
Hello Dolly Bars, 292
Hummingbird Skillet Cookie, 288
Mexican Chocolate Pudding Cake, 319
Mississippi Mud, 295
Mississippi Mud Skillet Cookie, 288
Mocha Ganache, 348
Mocha Java Cakes with variations, 319
Pecan-Espresso Toffee, 300
Praline Bars, 295
Pumpkin-Chocolate Brownies, 296
Red Velvet-Berry Cobbler, 320
Strawberry Shortcake Skillet Cookie, 288
Swoon Pies, 299
White Chocolate-Raspberry Cheesecake, 339
Chunky Beef Chili, 208
Cider Vinegar-Brown Butter Honey Drizzle, 13
Cilantro Pesto, 49
Cinnamon-Pecan Rolls, 66
Cinnamon-Raisin Rolls, 65
Citrus-Braised Chicken Thighs, 112
Citrus Glaze, 307
Classic Chess Pie, 332
Classic Chicken Tetrazzini, 171
Classic Cola Float, 352
Classic Double Roast Chickens, 105
Classic Grilled Corn, 243
Classic Hoppin' John, 105
Classic Pimiento Cheese, 25
Cobb Clubs, 191
Cocktail Meatballs, 18
Coffee Cake Pound Cake, 307
Cola Pot Roast, 74
Cold Lemon Soufflés with Wine Sauce, 347

Collard greens
Slow-Cooker Collard Greens with Ham Hocks, 257
Sweet Potato-and-Collard Green Gratin, 254
Vegetarian Slow-Cooker Collard Greens, 257
Cookies and bars
Brown Butter-Maple-Pecan Blondies, 296
Chocolate Chip Cookies, 288
Deep-Dish Skillet Cookie with variations, 288
Fudgy Flourless Chocolate-Pecan Cookies, 291
Giant Oatmeal Cookies, 291
Hello Dolly Bars, 292
Lemon-Coconut Chess Bars, 292
Mississippi Mud, 295
Peach Melba Shortbread Bars, 292
Pecan Bars, 299
Praline Bars, 295
Pumpkin-Chocolate Brownies, 296
Swoon Pies, 299
Corn
Avocado-Corn Salsa, 159
Classic Grilled Corn, 243
Corn Pudding, 240
Fresh Corn Spoonbread, 240
Grilled Clambake Foil Packets with Herb Butter, 143
Cornbread Focaccia, 280
Cornbread with Lemon-Thyme Butter, 283
Country Breakfast Casserole, 50
Country Grits-and-Sausage Casserole, 53
Country Ham-and-Peach Panini, 191
Country Ham with Red-Eye Gravy, 102
Country Peach Cobbler, 324
Couscous Pilaf with Roasted Carrots, Chicken, and Feta, 124
Cracked Pepper-Rosemary Honey Drizzle, 13
Cranberry-Apple-Pumpkin Bundt, 315
Cranberry-Pecan Coffee Cake, 62
Cranberry-Pecan Crusts, 182
Cranberry Sangría Punch, 30
Cream cheese
Black-and-Blue Buttermilk Tart, 343
Blackberry Jam Cake, 308
Black-Eyed Pea Cakes, 253
Cream Cheese Ice Cream, 320
Crumb-Topped Spinach Casserole, 258
Cucumber Sandwiches, 199
Double-Decker Pecan Cheesecake Pie, 336
Five-Cup Cream Cheese Frosting, 316
German Chocolate Cheesecake, 339
Pizza Dip, 26
Strawberry-Rhubarb Pretzel Pie, 332
White Chocolate-Raspberry Cheesecake, 339
Creamy Baked Macaroni and Cheese with Bacon, 236

Creamy Chicken and Bacon with Herbed Puff Pastry, 123
Creole Deep-Fried Turkey, 126
Crispy Oven-Fried Chicken Cutlets with Roasted Broccoli, 115
Crispy Pan-Fried Catfish, 136
Crispy Sweet Potato-Green Onion Cakes, 253
Crumb-Topped Spinach Casserole, 258
Crunchy Chicken Casserole, 179
Crunchy Fried Okra, 261
Crust, 320
Cucumber Sandwiches, 199

D

Decadent Cream Puffs with Praline Sauce, 344
Deep-Dish Skillet Cookie, 288
Desserts. *See also* **Cakes; Candies; Cookies and bars; Pies and tarts**
    Apple Brown Betty, 327
    Apple Cinnamon Dutch Baby, 344
    Banana Bread Cobbler, 324
    Blackberry Cobbler, 320
    Bread Pudding with Rum Sauce, 327
    Chocolate Pudding with variations, 351
    Cold Lemon Soufflés with Wine Sauce, 347
    Country Peach Cobbler, 324
    Cream Cheese Ice Cream, 320
    Decadent Cream Puffs with Praline Sauce, 344
    Double-Decker Pecan Cheesecake Pie, 336
    Easy Mocha Chip Ice-Cream Cake, 348
    German Chocolate Cheesecake, 339
    Ginger Bread Soufflés, 347
    Mexican Chocolate Pudding Cake, 319
    Old-Fashioned Vanilla Ice Cream, 352
    Pound Cake Banana Pudding, 351
    Quick Apple Dumpling Bundles, 343
    Red Velvet-Berry Cobbler, 320
    Strawberry-Mango Semifreddo, 348
    Strawberry-Rhubarb Crisps with Sweet-and-Savory Granola, 323
    Strawberry-Rhubarb Pretzel Pie, 332
    Sweet Tea Tiramisù, 340
    White Chocolate-Raspberry Cheesecake, 339
Dilled Potato Salad with Feta, 250
Dips
    Bacon-Blue Cheese Dip, 26
    Beer-Cheese Fondue, 29
    Hot Spinach-Artichoke Dip, 26
    Layered Nacho Dip, 29
    Pizza Dip, 26
    Quick Creamy Vegetable Dip, 29
Dixie Chicken Salad with Grapes, Honey, Almonds, and Broccoli, 201

Double-Crust Chicken Pot Pie, 175
Double-Decker Egg Salad Sandwiches, 198
Double-Decker Pecan Cheesecake Pie, 336

E

Easy Banana Pancakes, 45
Easy Chicken Pot Pie, 123
Easy French Toast Casserole, 41
Easy Mocha Chip Ice Cream Cake, 348
Easy Skillet Tacos, 86
Easy Sloppy Joes, 89
Eggplant Parmesan Lasagna, 151
Eggplant Pizzas, 152
Eggs
    Bacon and Eggs Bread Pudding, 46
    Baked Eggs with Spinach and Tomatoes, 46
    Barbecue Deviled Eggs, 21
    Breakfast Burritos, 46
    Breakfast Enchiladas, 49
    Country Breakfast Casserole, 50
    Double-Decker Egg Salad Sandwiches with variations, 198
    Egg Salad Sandwiches, 198
    Ham 'n' Swiss Omelets, 54
    Individual Country Grits-and-Sausage Casseroles with variations, 53
    King Ranch Breakfast Strata, 57
    Muffuletta Deviled Eggs, 14
    Sunny Skillet Breakfast, 57
    Veggie Confetti Frittata, 57
Enchilada Casserole, 155

F

Fabulous Tuna-Noodle Casserole, 182
Family Cornbread, 178
Fennel-Apple Slaw, 228
Fettuccine Primavera, 147
Field Pea Cakes with Tomato-Ginger Jam, 144
Fiesta Burgers, 90
Fig Flatbread, 18
Fish. *See also* **Shellfish; Shrimp**
    Crispy Pan-Fried Catfish, 136
    Fabulous Tuna-Noodle Casserole, 182
    Fried Delacata Catfish, 135
    Grilled Tuna Steaks with Horseradish Sauce, 136
    Honey-Soy-Glazed Salmon with Veggies and Oranges, 132
    New Tuna Casserole, 185
Five-Cup Cream Cheese Frosting, 316
Five-Spice Almonds, 323
Four-Cheese Macaroni, 236
French Fries, 228
French Onion Sandwiches, 199

Fresh Corn Spoonbread, 240
Fresh Herb Pesto, 120
Fresh Vegetable Lasagna, 151
Fried Delacata Catfish, 135
Fried Green Tomatoes, 265
Fried Red Quinoa, 323
Frosted Bellinis, 34
Fudgy Flourless Chocolate-Pecan Cookies, 291

G
Garlic-Herb Steaks, 81
German Chocolate Cheesecake, 339
Giant Oatmeal Cookies, 291
Gingerbread Soufflés, 347
Gluten-Free Banana Bread, 68
Golden-Baked Mini Reubens, 191
Golden Potato-and-Smoked Sausage Hash, 50
Gonzales Meat Loaf, 85
Gouda Grits, 54
Grasshopper Skillet Cookie, 288
Greek Chicken with Roasted Potatoes, 115
Green beans
   Green Bean Casserole with Fried Leeks, 262
   Green Bean-Goat Cheese Gratin, 262
   Grilled Steak with Blistered Beans and Peppers, 82
   Honey-Soy-Glazed Salmon with Veggies and Oranges, 132
   Lemon-Garlic Roast Chicken with Sautéed Green Beans, 107
   Lighter Pan-Fried Chicken with Green Beans and Tomatoes, 108
   Mini Turkey Pot Pies with Dressing Tops, 129
   New Tuna Casserole, 185
   Tangy Potato-Green Bean Salad, 249
Green Chile Cheese Toast, 219
Grilled Asian Flank Steak, 78
Grilled Bacon, Cheese, and Tomato Sandwiches, 192
Grilled Chicken Kebabs with Arugula Pesto, 116
Grilled Chicken Tacos, 116
Grilled Clambake Foil Packets with Herb Butter, 143
Grilled Okra and Tomatoes, 261
Grilled Oysters, 143
Grilled Salt-and-Pepper Chicken Wings, 13
Grilled Steak with Blistered Beans and Peppers, 82
Grilled Tuna Steaks with Horseradish Sauce, 136
Grits
   Cheddar Cheese Grits Casserole, 50
   Country Breakfast Casserole, 50
   Gouda Grits, 54
   Individual Country Grits-and-Sausage Casseroles with variations, 53
   Quick Double-Cheese Grits, 244
   Sausage, Pepper, and Grits Casserole, 58

Savory Ham-and-Swiss Breakfast Pie, 59
Shrimp and Grits Dressing, 244

H
Ham
   Country Ham-and-Peach Panini, 191
   Country Ham with Red-Eye Gravy, 102
   Ham and Cheese Strata, 53
   Ham-and-Dijon Biscuits with Caramelized Onion Butter, 101
   Ham-and-Vegetable Cobbler, 171
   Ham 'n' Swiss Omelets, 54
   Holiday Ham, 101
   Savory Ham-and-Swiss Breakfast Pie, 59
   Seafood Gumbo, 208
   Slow-Cooker Collard Greens with Ham Hocks, 257
Harvest Salad, 274
Hash Brown Casserole, 231
Hearty Baked Beans, 270
Hello Dolly Bars, 292
Herb-and-Potato-Chip-Crusted Beef Tenderloin, 73
Herb-Roasted Pork Loin, 93
Holiday Ham, 101
Homemade Applesauce, 228
Homestyle Ground Beef Casserole, 165
Honey-and-Soy-Lacquered Ribs, 98
Honey-Chipotle Glaze, 243
Honey-Soy-Glazed Salmon with Veggies and Oranges, 132
Horseradish-Honey Mustard Drizzle, 13
Hot Fudge Sundae Shake, 352
Hot 'n' Spicy Grits-and-Sausage Casseroles, 53
Hot Pepper Vinegar, 143
Hot Spinach-Artichoke Dip, 26
Hot Spinach-Artichoke Dip with Crab, 26
Hummingbird Skillet Cookie, 288

I
Individual Country Grits-and-Sausage Casseroles, 53
Italian Sausage and Peppers Skillet, 102
Italian-Style Salsa Verde, 188

J
Jambalaya Kebabs, 139

K
Kale
   Kale and Sweet Potato Salad with Chicken, 202
   Roasted Pumpkin-and-Baby Kale Salad, 273
   Skillet Steak and Wilted Kale, 78
Kettle-Chip-Crusted Fried Green Tomatoes with Tasso Tartar Sauce, 265
King Ranch Breakfast Strata, 57

L

Layered Nacho Dip, 29
Lemon(s)
    Blackberry Lemonade, 33
    Citrus Glaze, 307
    Cold Lemon Soufflés with Wine Sauce, 347
    Lemon Chicken Stir-Fry, 120
    Lemon-Coconut Chess Bars, 292
    Lemon-Garlic Butter Shrimp and Broccoli, 140
    Lemon-Garlic Roast Chicken with Sautéed Green Beans, 107
    Lemon-Lime Meringue Pie, 331
    Lemon-Orange Pound Cake, 304
    Lemon-Poppy Seed Zucchini Bread, 66
    Lemon-Rosemary-Garlic Chicken and Potatoes, 111
    Lemon-Thyme Butter, 283
    Meyer Lemon-Ginger Mignonette, 143
Lentils and Rice, Spanish-Style, 156
Lettuce Wedge Salad, 274
Lighter Pan-Fried Chicken with Green Beans and Tomatoes, 108
Lime(s)
    Lemon-Lime Meringue Pie, 331
    Lime Cream, 219
    Tex-Mex Chicken Chili with Lime, 219
Loaded Chicken-Bacon Pot Pie, 176
Louisiana Gumbo, 212

M

Macaroni and Cheese, 148
Mama Dip's Carrot Cake, 311
Mama's Fried Chicken, 108
Mangoes
    Avocado-Mango Salsa, 212
    Mango Margarita, 34
    Shrimp-and-Black Bean Stir-Fry, 136
    Strawberry-Mango Semifreddo, 348
Maple Glaze, 315
Marshmallow Filling, 299
Mashed Potatoes with Bacon and Crispy Scallions, 232
Meatball Pasta Bake, 164
Meringue, 351
Mexican Chocolate Pudding Cake, 319
Mexican Lasagna, 86
Meyer Lemon-Ginger Mignonette, 143
Million-Dollar Pound Cake, 304
Mini Turkey Pot Pies with Dressing Tops, 129
Minty-Mocha Java Cakes, 319
Mississippi Mud, 295
Mississippi Mud Skillet Cookie, 288
Mocha Ganache, 348

Mocha Java Cakes, 319
Molasses-Grilled Pork Tenderloin, 93
Muffuletta Deviled Eggs, 14
Mushrooms
    Butternut-Goat Cheese-Stuffed Mushrooms, 10
    Chicken-Mushroom-Sage Casserole, 181
    Portobello 'n' Shiitake Mushroom Pot Pies, 152

N

New Potato and Fennel Salad, 249
New Tuna Casserole, 185
Noodles
    Beef Burgundy, 74
    Beef Lombardi, 167
    Beef Stroganoff, 77
    Chicken Noodle Soup, 216
    Chicken Piccata, 112
    Fabulous Tuna-Noodle Casserole, 182
    Homestyle Ground Beef Casserole, 165

O

Okra
    Crunchy Fried Okra, 261
    Grilled Okra and Tomatoes, 261
    Okra and Chickpeas in Fresh Tomato Sauce, 266
    Pan-Fried Okra with Cornmeal, 261
    Seafood Gumbo, 208
    Southern Italian Chicken Soup, 215
    Spicy Vegetable Soup, 220
Old-Fashioned Apple Pie, 328
Old-Fashioned Skillet Cornbread, 280
Old-Fashioned Vanilla Ice Cream, 352
Olive Salad, 14
One Minute Salsa, 22
One-Skillet Spaghetti, 86
Onions
    Bacon-and-Sweet Onion Jam, 188
    Bratwurst with Peppers and Onions, 102
    Caramelized Onion Butter, 101
    Caramelized Onion Mashed Potato Bake, 232
    Cheddar-Caramelized Onion Bread, 279
    Crispy Sweet Potato-Green Onion Cakes, 253
    French Onion Sandwiches, 199
    Pickled Red Onions, 205
    Spring Onion Pie, 155
Open-Faced Philly Sandwiches, 195
Orange(s)
    Baby Blue Salad, 273
    Citrus-Braised Chicken Thighs, 112
    Citrus Glaze, 307
    Honey-Soy-Glazed Salmon with Veggies and Oranges, 132

Lemon-Orange Pound Cake, 304
Orange-Mocha Java Cakes, 319
Orange-Raspberry Vinaigrette, 269
Southern Sunrise, 34
Sparkling Orange Wheels, 34
Our Easiest Pumpkin Pie Ever, 331
Oyster Dressing, 266

P

Pan-Fried Okra with Cornmeal, 261
Pan-Seared Steaks with Roasted Red Pepper Sauce, 78
Parmesan Breadsticks, 284
Parmesan Cream Sauce, 115
Party-Perfect Meatballs, 21
Pasta. *See also* **Noodles**
Baked Linguine with Meat Sauce, 167
Baked Penne with Turkey, 130
Cheesy Chicken Penne, 119
Chicken and Gnocchi, 216
Chicken Caprese Pasta, 120
Chicken Lasagna with Roasted Red Bell Peppers Sauce, 119
Chicken Tetrazzini, 172
Classic Chicken Tetrazzini, 171
Creamy Baked Macaroni and Cheese with Bacon, 236
Eggplant Parmesan Lasagna, 151
Fettuccine Primavera, 147
Four-Cheese Macaroni, 236
Macaroni and Cheese, 148
Meatball Pasta Bake, 164
New Tuna Casserole, 185
One-Skillet Spaghetti, 86
Pasta-Chicken-Broccoli Bake, 176
Pasta Primavera with Shrimp, 140
Pizza Casserole Deluxe, 168
Roasted Vegetable Orzo Salad, 206
Saucy Sausage Manicotti, 168
Southern Italian Chicken Soup, 215
Spinach-Ravioli Bake, 148
Summer Tortellini Salad, 205
Three-Cheese Pasta Bake, 148
Ziti with Sausage and Broccoli, 102
Patriotic Cupcakes, 316
Peaches
Bourbon-Peach Iced Tea, 33
Brunch Popover Pancake, 45
Country Ham-and-Peach Panini, 191
Country Peach Cobbler, 324
Peaches-and-Cream Pancakes, 42
Peach Melba Shortbread Bars, 292
Peanut Butter Pie, 335
Peanut Dipping Sauce, 13

Peas. *See also* **Black-eyed peas**
Chicken and Snow Pea Stir-Fry, 119
Field Pea Cakes with Tomato-Ginger Jam, 144
Lemon Chicken Stir-Fry, 120
Pasta Primavera with Shrimp, 140
Pecan Bars, 299
Pecan Chicken, 111
Pecan-Espresso Toffee, 300
Pecan Pound Cake, 307
Pecan Praline Skillet Cookie, 288
Pecans and Pepitas, Sugared, 315
Pecans, Spiced, 30
Peppered Filet Mignon with Horseradish Cream, 81
Pepperoni Pizza Pinwheels, 17
Peppers, bell
Bratwurst with Peppers and Onions, 102
Charred Peppers with Feta Dipping Sauce, 258
Grilled Steak with Blistered Beans and Peppers, 82
Italian Sausage and Peppers Skillet, 102
Pan-Seared Steaks with Roasted Red Pepper Sauce, 78
Queso-Filled Mini Peppers, 14
Roasted Red Bell Pepper Sauce, 119
Sausage, Pepper, and Grits Casserole, 58
Tomato-and-Red Pepper Soup, 224
Peppers, chile
Black Bean Soup, 220
Black-Eyed Pea Ranchero Sauce, 135
Chipotle Scalloped Potatoes, 231
Crispy Sweet Potato-Green Onion Cakes, 253
Green Chile Cheese Toast, 219
Honey-Chipotle Glaze, 243
Hot Pepper Vinegar, 143
Italian-Style Salsa Verde, 188
Southwestern Chicken Salad, 198
Spicy Cornbread Dressing with Chorizo, 239
Tex-Mex Chicken Chili with Lime, 219
Perfect Burgers, The, 90
Pickled Red Onions, 205
Picnic in a Glass, 201
Pies and tarts
Banana Pudding Pie, 335
Black-and-Blue Buttermilk Tart, 343
Caramel Pie, 327
Classic Chess Pie, 332
Double-Decker Pecan Cheesecake Pie, 336
Lemon-Lime Meringue Pie, 331
Old-Fashioned Apple Pie, 328
Our Easiest Pumpkin Pie Ever, 331
Peanut Butter Pie, 335
Pumpkin Tart with Whipped Cream and Almond Toffee, 340

Skillet Apple Pie, 328
Strawberry-Rhubarb Pretzel Pie, 332
Pimiento Cheese Biscuits, 284
Pimiento Cheese Creamed Spinach, 269

Pineapple
Bing Cherry Salad, 270
Chicken-and-Fruit Salad, 269
Grilled Chicken Tacos, 116
Hummingbird Skillet Cookie, 288
Pizza Casserole Deluxe, 168
Pizza Dip, 26
Poppy Seed-Chicken Casserole, 179

Pork. *See also* **Bacon; Ham; Prosciutto; Sausages**
Barbecue Deviled Eggs, 21
Herb-Roasted Pork Loin, 93
Honey-and-Soy-Lacquered Ribs, 98
Molasses-Grilled Pork Tenderloin, 93
Pork Chops and Gravy, 97
Pork Chops, Cabbage, and Apples, 94
Pork Chops with Roasted Apples and Brussels Sprouts, 97
Pork Tenderloin Sliders, 188
Slow-Cooker BBQ Pork, 93
Spicy-Sweet Ribs and Beans, 98
Stuffed Pork Chops, 94
Portobello 'n' Shiitake Mushroom Pot Pies, 152

Potatoes. *See also* **Sweet potatoes**
BLT Potato Salad, 250
Buttermilk Mashed Potatoes with variations, 232
Caramelized Onion Mashed Potato Bake, 232
Cheese-and-Carrot Mashed Potatoes, 162
Chipotle Scalloped Potatoes, 231
Dilled Potato Salad with Feta, 250
French Fries, 228
Golden Potato-and-Smoked Sausage Hash, 50
Greek Chicken with Roasted Potatoes, 115
Grilled Clambake Foil Packets with Herb Butter, 143
Hash Brown Casserole, 231
Lemon-Rosemary-Garlic Chicken and Potatoes, 111
New Potato and Fennel Salad, 249
Roasted Garlic-Potato Soup, 221
Roasted Potatoes, 211
Sausage-Hash Brown Breakfast Casserole, 54
Shrimp-and-New Potato Chowder, 224
Sunny Skillet Breakfast, 57
Swiss Burgers in Tomato Gravy with Roasted Potatoes, 89
Tangy Potato-Green Bean Salad, 249
Top-Shelf Chicken Under a Brick, 107
Walnut Mashed Potatoes, 164
Zucchini-Potato Casserole, 235
Pound Cake Banana Pudding, 351

Praline Bars, 295
Praline Coffee, 37
Praline-Pecan French Toast, 42
Praline Sauce, 344
Prime Rib with Herbes de Provence Crust and Red Wine Sauce, 73

Pumpkin
Cranberry-Apple-Pumpkin Bundt, 315
Our Easiest Pumpkin Pie Ever, 331
Pumpkin-Chocolate Brownies, 296
Pumpkin Tart with Whipped Cream and Almond Toffee, 340
Roasted Pumpkin-and-Baby Kale Salad, 273
Spicy Pumpkin Soup with Avocado Cream, 223

Q

Queso-Filled Mini Peppers, 14
Quick-and-Easy King Ranch Chicken Casserole, 178
Quick Apple Dumpling Bundles, 343
Quick Creamy Vegetable Dip, 29
Quick Double-Cheese Grits, 244
Quinoa-Chicken Salad with Green Goddess Dressing, 202
Quinoa, Fried Red, 323

R

Radishes with Bacon and Cilantro, Sautéed, 244
Ranch Turkey Burgers, 130

Raspberries
"Any-Berry" Muffins with Cornmeal Streusel, 59
Chicken-and-Fruit Salad, 269
Raspberry-Chocolate Pudding, 351
Red Velvet-Berry Cobbler, 320
White Chocolate-Raspberry Cheesecake, 339
Red Velvet-Berry Cobbler, 320

Rhubarb
Strawberry-Rhubarb Crisps with Sweet-and-Savory Granola, 323
Strawberry-Rhubarb Pretzel Pie, 332

Rice
Bean-and-Cheese Chimichangas, 159
Chicken and Sausage Jambalaya, 211
Chicken and Wild Rice with Pecans, 181
Chicken-Mushroom-Sage Casserole, 181
Classic Hoppin' John, 105
Crunchy Chicken Casserole, 179
Lemon Chicken Stir-Fry, 120
Lemon-Garlic Butter Shrimp and Broccoli, 140
Spanish-Style Lentils and Rice, 156
Roasted Baby Turnips with Turnip Green Pesto, 246
Roasted Carrots with Spiced Pecans and Sorghum, 246
Roasted Garlic-Potato Soup, 221

Roasted Potatoes, 211
Roasted Pumpkin-and-Baby Kale Salad, 273
Roasted Red Bell Pepper Sauce, 119
Roasted Vegetable Orzo Salad, 206
Roast Turkey and Gravy, 126
Root Beer Float, 352
Rum Sauce, 327
Rustic Mashed Red Potatoes with Parmesan, 232

S

Salads
Baby Blue Salad, 273
BLT Potato Salad, 250
Broccoli-Carrot Salad, 250
Chicken-and-Fruit Salad, 269
Chicken-Quinoa Salad with Green Goddess
    Dressing, 202
Dilled Potato Salad with Feta, 250
Dixie Chicken Salad with Grapes, Honey, Almonds, and
    Broccoli, 201
Fennel-Apple Slaw, 228
Harvest Salad, 274
Kale and Sweet Potato Salad with Chicken, 202
Lettuce Wedge Salad, 274
New Potato and Fennel Salad, 249
Picnic in a Glass, 201
Roasted Pumpkin-and-Baby Kale Salad, 273
Roasted Vegetable Orzo Salad, 206
Southwestern Chicken Salad, 198
Southwestern Chopped Chicken Salad, 205
Summer Tortellini Salad, 205
Tangy Potato-Green Bean Salad, 249
Salsa
Avocado-Corn Salsa, 159
Avocado-Mango Salsa, 212
Cast-Iron Salsa, 22
Italian-Style Salsa Verde, 188
One Minute Salsa, 22
Santa Fe Chicken Quesadillas, 17
Sauces
Apple Brandy-Caramel Sauce, 311
Bacon with Ranch Drizzle, 243
Basil Butter with Parmesan, 243
Blackberry-Honey Mustard Sauce, 188
Black-Eyed Pea Ranchero Sauce, 135
Cheese Sauce, 49
Chili-Lemon Honey Drizzle, 13
Cider Vinegar-Brown Butter Honey Drizzle, 13
Cilantro Pesto, 49
Cracked Pepper-Rosemary Honey Drizzle, 13
Fresh Herb Pesto, 120

Honey-Chipotle Glaze, 243
Horseradish-Honey Mustard Drizzle, 13
Mocha Ganache, 348
Parmesan Cream Sauce, 115
Peanut Dipping Sauce, 13
Praline Sauce, 344
Roasted Red Bell Pepper Sauce, 119
Rum Sauce, 327
Uncle Ellis's Cornmeal Gravy, 81
Saucy Sausage Manicotti, 168
Sausages
Bratwurst with Peppers and Onions, 102
Breakfast Burritos, 46
Breakfast Enchiladas, 49
Chicken-Andouille Gumbo with Roasted Potatoes, 211
Chicken and Sausage Jambalaya, 211
Country Breakfast Casserole, 50
Golden Potato-and-Smoked Sausage Hash, 50
Grilled Clambake Foil Packets with Herb Butter, 143
Individual Country Grits-and-Sausage Casseroles with
    variations, 53
Italian Sausage and Peppers Skillet, 102
Jambalaya Skewers, 139
Louisiana Gumbo, 212
Muffuletta Deviled Eggs, 14
Party-Perfect Meatballs, 21
Pepperoni Pizza Pinwheels, 17
Pizza Casserole Deluxe, 168
Saucy Sausage Manicotti, 168
Sausage-Hash Brown Breakfast Casserole, 54
Sausage, Pepper, and Grits Casserole, 58
Sheet Pan Nachos with Chorizo and Refried Beans, 17
Spicy Cornbread Dressing with Chorizo, 239
Spicy Pumpkin Soup with Avocado Cream, 223
Ziti with Sausage and Broccoli, 102
Sautéed Radishes with Bacon and Cilantro, 244
Savory Ham-and-Swiss Breakfast Pie, 59
Seafood Gumbo, 208
Sheet Pan Nachos with Chorizo and Refried Beans, 17
Shellfish. *See also* **Shrimp**
Best-Ever Crab Cakes with Green Tomato Slaw, 10
Grilled Clambake Foil Packets with Herb Butter, 143
Grilled Oysters, 143
Hot Spinach-Artichoke Dip with Crab, 26
Oyster Dressing, 266
Seafood Gumbo, 208
Shepherd's Pie, 162
Shortcut Pralines, 300
Shrimp
Jambalaya Kebabs, 139
Lemon-Garlic Butter Shrimp and Broccoli, 140

Louisiana Gumbo, 212
Pasta Primavera with Shrimp, 140
Shrimp-and-Black Bean Stir-Fry, 136
Shrimp and Grits Dressing, 244
Shrimp-and-New Potato Chowder, 224
Shrimp-Egg Salad Club, 198
Shrimp Kebabs, 139
Snappy Cajun Shrimp, 139
Simple Syrup, 34
Single-Crust Pie Pastry, 336
Sizzlin' Skillet Cornbread, 266
Skillet Apple Pie, 328
Skillet Chicken Pot Pie, 175
Skillet Steak and Wilted Kale, 78
Skillet Vegetable Pie with Goat Cheese, 147
Slow-Cooker BBQ Pork, 93
Slow-Cooker Collard Greens with Ham Hocks, 257
Smoked Chicken Tortilla Soup, 215
Smoky Barbecue Rub, 243
Smoky Brown Sugar Bacon, 58
Smoky Pimiento Cheese Finger Sandwiches, 199
Snappy Cajun Shrimp, 139
Soups and stews
Beef Burgundy, 74
Beef Stew with Buttery Garlic Bread, 206
Beer-Cheese Soup, 220
Black Bean Soup, 220
Brunswick Stew, 219
Butternut Squash Soup, 221
Chicken and Gnocchi, 216
Chicken-Andouille Gumbo with Roasted Potatoes, 211
Chicken and Sausage Jambalaya, 211
Chicken Noodle Soup, 216
Chunky Beef Chili, 208
Louisiana Gumbo, 212
Roasted Garlic-Potato Soup, 221
Seafood Gumbo, 208
Shrimp-and-New Potato Chowder, 224
Smoked Chicken Tortilla Soup, 215
Southern Italian Chicken Soup, 215
Spicy Pumpkin Soup with Avocado Cream, 223
Spicy Steak and Black Bean Chili, 223
Spicy Tortilla Soup, 224
Spicy Vegetable Soup, 220
Tex-Mex Chicken Chili with Lime, 219
Tomato-and-Red Pepper Soup, 224
White Lightning Chicken Chili, 212
Sour Cream Biscuits, 283
Southern Eggnog, 37
Southern Italian Chicken Soup, 215
Southern Sunrise, 34

Southwestern Chicken Salad, 198
Southwestern Chopped Chicken Salad, 205
Southwestern Meat Loaf, 85
Spanish-Style Lentils and Rice, 156
Sparkling Orange Wheels, 34
Speedy Shepherd's Pie, 164
Spiced Applesauce, 228
Spiced Pecans, 30
Spicy Cornbread Dressing with Chorizo, 239
Spicy Pumpkin Soup with Avocado Cream, 223
Spicy Steak and Black Bean Chili, 223
Spicy Tortilla Soup, 224
Spicy Vegetable Soup, 220
Spinach
Baked Eggs with Spinach and Tomatoes, 46
Black Bean 'n' Spinach Enchiladas, 156
Crumb-Topped Spinach Casserole, 258
Hot Spinach-Artichoke Dip, 26
Hot Spinach-Artichoke Dip with Crab, 26
Pasta Primavera with Shrimp, 140
Pimiento Cheese Creamed Spinach, 269
Spinach Madeleine, 156
Spinach-Ravioli Bake, 148
Turkey and Spinach Meatball Sandwiches, 132
Spring Onion Pie, 155
Squash. *See also* **Pumpkin; Zucchini**
Butternut-Goat Cheese-Stuffed Mushrooms, 10
Butternut Squash Soup, 221
Harvest Salad, 274
Skillet Vegetable Pie with Goat Cheese, 147
Strawberries
"Any-Berry" Muffins with Cornmeal Streusel, 59
Baby Blue Salad, 273
Chicken-and-Fruit Salad, 269
Red Velvet-Berry Cobbler, 320
Strawberry-Mango Semifreddo, 348
Strawberry-Mint Tea, 33
Strawberry-Rhubarb Crisps with Sweet-and-Savory Granola, 323
Strawberry-Rhubarb Pretzel Pie, 332
Strawberry Shortcake Skillet Cookie, 288
Streusel Topping, 324
Stuffed Pork Chops, 94
Sugar-and-Spice Pecans, 235
Sugared Pecans and Pepitas, 315
Summer Tortellini Salad, 205
Sunny Skillet Breakfast, 57
Sweet-and-Spicy Pecans, 273
Sweet 'n' Savory Snack Mix, 29
Sweet-Pickle Egg Salad Club, 198

Sweet potatoes

Candied Yams, 254

Crispy Sweet Potato–Green Onion Cakes, 253

Kale and Sweet Potato Salad with Chicken, 202

Sweet Potato-and-Collard Green Gratin, 254

Sweet Potato-Carrot Casserole, 235

Tex-Mex Chicken Chili with Lime, 219

Whipped Sweet Potato Butter, 279

Sweet Tea Tiramisù, 340

Swiss Burgers in Tomato Gravy with Roasted Potatoes, 89

Swoon Pies, 299

T

Taco Casserole, 165

Tangy Potato–Green Bean Salad, 249

Teriyaki Burgers, 90

Tex-Mex Chicken Chili with Lime, 219

Three-Cheese Pasta Bake, 148

Tomatoes

Baked Eggs with Spinach and Tomatoes, 46

Best-Ever Crab Cakes with Green Tomato Slaw, 10

BLT Potato Salad, 250

BLTS with a Twist, 192

Cast-Iron Salsa, 22

Fried Green Tomatoes, 265

Grilled Bacon, Cheese, and Tomato Sandwiches, 192

Grilled Okra and Tomatoes, 261

Kettle-Chip-Crusted Fried Green Tomatoes with Tasso Tartar Sauce, 265

Lighter Pan-Fried Chicken with Green Beans and Tomatoes, 108

Okra and Chickpeas in Fresh Tomato Sauce, 266

One-Minute Salsa, 22

Swiss Burgers in Tomato Gravy with Roasted Potatoes, 89

Tomato-and-Red Pepper Soup, 224

Tomato Crostini, 25

Tomato-Ginger Jam, 144

Top-Shelf Chicken Under a Brick, 107

Turkey

Baked Penne with Turkey, 130

Cobb Clubs, 191

Creole Deep-Fried Turkey, 126

Mini Turkey Pot Pies with Dressing Tops, 129

Ranch Turkey Burgers, 130

Roast Turkey and Gravy, 126

Turkey and Spinach Meatball Sandwiches, 132

Turkey, Brie, and Apple Panini with Bacon Marmalade, 195

Turkey Pot Pie with Cranberry-Pecan Crusts, 182

Turnips with Turnip Green Pesto, Roasted Baby, 246

Tyler's Country-Fried Steak with Uncle Ellis's Cornmeal Gravy, 81

U

Uncle Ellis's Cornmeal Gravy, 81

V

Vanilla Cream Filling, 335

Vegetarian Slow-Cooker Collard Greens, 257

Veggie Confetti Frittata, 57

W

Walnut Mashed Potatoes, 164

Watermelon–Ginger Mojitos, 37

Whipped Sweet Potato Butter, 279

White Calzones with Marinara Sauce, 196

White Chocolate–Raspberry Cheesecake, 339

White Lightning Chicken Chili, 212

Wild Rice with Bacon and Fennel, 270

Y

Yogurt Dressing, 201

Z

Ziti with Sausage and Broccoli, 102

Zucchini

Eggplant Pizzas, 152

Fresh Vegetable Lasagna, 151

Grilled Chicken Kebabs with Arugula Pesto, 116

Lemon-Poppy Seed Zucchini Bread, 66

Roasted Vegetable Orzo Salad, 206

Zucchini-Potato Casserole, 235

METRIC EQUIVALENTS

The information in the following charts is provided to help cooks outside the United States successfully use the recipes in this book. All equivalents are approximate.

Equivalents for Different Types of Ingredients

Standard Cup	Fine Powder (ex. flour)	Grain (ex. rice)	Granular (ex. sugar)	Liquid Solids (ex. butter)	Liquid (ex. milk)
1	140 g	150 g	190 g	200 g	240 ml
¾	105 g	113 g	143 g	150 g	180 ml
⅔	93 g	100 g	125 g	133 g	160 ml
½	70 g	75 g	95 g	100 g	120 ml
⅓	47 g	50 g	63 g	67 g	80 ml
¼	35 g	38 g	48 g	50 g	60 ml
⅛	18 g	19 g	24 g	25 g	30 ml

Liquid Ingredients by Volume

¼ tsp =				1 ml
½ tsp =				2 ml
1 tsp =				5 ml
3 tsp =	1 Tbsp =		½ fl oz =	15 ml
	2 Tbsp =	⅛ cup =	1 fl oz =	30 ml
	4 Tbsp =	¼ cup =	2 fl oz =	60 ml
	5⅓ Tbsp =	⅓ cup =	3 fl oz =	80 ml
	8 Tbsp =	½ cup =	4 fl oz =	120 ml
	10⅔ Tbsp =	⅔ cup =	5 fl oz =	160 ml
	12 Tbsp =	¾ cup =	6 fl oz =	180 ml
	16 Tbsp =	1 cup =	8 fl oz =	240 ml
	1 pt =	2 cups =	16 fl oz =	480 ml
	1 qt =	4 cups =	32 fl oz =	960 ml
			33 fl oz =	1000 ml = 1 l

Dry Ingredients by Weight

(To convert ounces to grams, multiply the number of ounces by 30.)

1 oz	=	¹⁄₁₆ lb	=	30 g
4 oz	=	¼ lb	=	120 g
8 oz	=	½ lb	=	240 g
12 oz	=	¾ lb	=	360 g
16 oz	=	1 lb	=	480 g

Length

(To convert inches to centimeters, multiply the number of inches by 2.5.)

1 in	=	2.5 cm				
6 in	=	½ ft	=	15 cm		
12 in	=	1 ft	=	30 cm		
36 in	=	3 ft	=	1 yd	=	90 cm
40 in	=	100 cm	=	1 m		

Cooking/Oven Temperatures

	Fahrenheit	Celsius	Gas Mark
Freeze Water	32° F	0° C	
Room Temperature	68° F	20° C	
Boil Water	212° F	100° C	
Bake	325° F	160° C	3
	350° F	180° C	4
	375° F	190° C	5
	400° F	200° C	6
	425° F	220° C	7
	450° F	230° C	8
Broil			Grill

MEREDITH CONSUMER MARKETING
Director, Direct Marketing-Books: Daniel Fagan
Marketing Operations Manager: Max Daily
Assistant Marketing Manager: Kylie Dazzo
Content Manager: Julie Doll
Senior Production Manager: Liza Ward

WATERBURY PUBLICATIONS, INC.
Editorial Director: Lisa Kingsley
Associate Editor: Tricia Bergman
Creative Director: Ken Carlson
Associate Design Director: Doug Samuelson
Production Assistant: Mindy Samuelson
Contributing Copy Editor: Peg Smith
Contributing Proofreader: Carrie Truesdell
Contributing Indexer: Mary Williams

Recipe Developers and Testers: Meredith Food Studios

MEREDITH CORPORATION
Executive Chairman: Stephen M. Lacy

In Memoriam: E. T. Meredith III (1933–2003)

ISBN-13: 978-0-8487-8432-4

Printed in the United States of America
10 9 8 7 6 5 4 3 2 1
Call 1-800-826-4707 for more information.

All of us at Meredith Consumer Marketing are dedicated to providing you with information and ideas to enhance your home. We welcome your comments and suggestions. Write to us at: Meredith Consumer Marketing, 1716 Locust St., Des Moines, IA 50309-3023.

Pictured on front cover:
Lemon-Orange Pound Cake, page 304